ZWINGLI AND BULLINGER

Richard B. Miller

THE LIBRARY OF CHRISTIAN CLASSICS

ICHTHUS EDITION

ZWINGLI AND BULLINGER

Selected Translations with
Introductions and Notes by

THE REV. G. W. BROMILEY, Ph.D., D.Litt.

Philadelphia

THE WESTMINSTER PRESS

Published simultaneously in Great Britain and the United States of America
by the S.C.M. Press, Ltd., London, and The Westminster Press, Philadelphia.

First published MCMLIII

Library of Congress Catalog Card No. 53-1533

9   8   7   6   5   4   3   2   1

Printed in the United States of America

GENERAL EDITORS' PREFACE

The Christian Church possesses in its literature an abundant and incomparable treasure. But it is an inheritance that must be reclaimed by each generation. THE LIBRARY OF CHRISTIAN CLASSICS is designed to present in the English language, and in twenty-six volumes of convenient size, a selection of the most indispensable Christian treatises written prior to the end of the sixteenth century.

The practice of giving circulation to writings selected for superior worth or special interest was adopted at the beginning of Christian history. The canonical Scriptures were themselves a selection from a much wider literature. In the Patristic era there began to appear a class of works of compilation (often designed for ready reference in controversy) of the opinions of well-reputed predecessors, and in the Middle Ages many such works were produced. These medieval anthologies actually preserve some noteworthy materials from works otherwise lost.

In modern times, with the increasing inability even of those trained in universities and theological colleges to read Latin and Greek texts with ease and familiarity, the translation of selected portions of earlier Christian literature into modern languages has become more necessary than ever; while the wide range of distinguished books written in vernaculars such as English makes selection there also needful. The efforts that have been made to meet this need are too numerous to be noted here, but none of these collections serves the purpose of the reader who desires a library of representative treatises spanning the Christian centuries as a whole. Most of them embrace only the age of the Church Fathers, and some of them have long been out of print. A fresh translation of a work already translated may shed much new light upon its meaning. This is true even of Bible translations despite the work of many experts through the centuries. In some instances old translations have been adopted in this series, but wherever necessary or desirable, new ones have been made. Notes have been supplied where these were needed to explain the author's meaning. The introductions provided for the several treatises and extracts will, we believe, furnish welcome guidance.

JOHN BAILLIE
JOHN T. McNEILL
HENRY P. VAN DUSEN

CONTENTS

GENERAL INTRODUCTION 13

ZWINGLI

OF THE CLARITY AND CERTAINTY OF THE WORD OF GOD
    Introduction 49
    The Text 59

OF THE EDUCATION OF YOUTH
    Introduction 96
    The Text 102

OF BAPTISM
    Introduction 119
    The Text 129

ON THE LORD'S SUPPER
    Introduction 176
    The Text 185

AN EXPOSITION OF THE FAITH
    Introduction 239
    The Text 245

BULLINGER

OF THE HOLY CATHOLIC CHURCH
    Introduction 283
    The Text 288

NOTES 327
BIBLIOGRAPHY 353
INDEXES 359

ABBREVIATIONS

A.S.   . E. Egli: *Actensammlung zur Geschichte der Zürcher Reformation in den Jahren* 1519–1523.

C.R.   . *Corpus Reformatorum* edition of Zwingli's works.

D.C.R.   . B. J. Kidd: *Documents illustrative of the Continental Reformation.*

Opera   . Schuler & Schultess edition of Zwingli's works.

R.G.   . H. Bullinger: *Reformationsgeschichte* (Ed. Hottinger & Vögelin).

General Introduction

1. THE LIFE OF ZWINGLI

Huldrych (or Ulrich) Zwingli was born in 1484, the same year as Luther. His birthplace was Wildhaus in the Toggenburg, some 40 miles from Zurich and over 3,000 feet above sea-level. He came of peasant stock, but his father was a man of means and ability, and both he and his father before him acted as chief magistrate for the district. The home in which the young Zwingli was nurtured was characterized by those qualities which marked Swiss life at its best, a sturdy independence, a strong patriotism, a zeal for religion and a real interest in scholarship. The later life and character of Zwingli bear ample evidence of the debt which he owed to this early environment.[1]

Zwingli's first teacher was his uncle Bartholomew,[2] who himself had formerly been priest of Wildhaus but was now dean of Weesen. Bartholomew Zwingli was a man of wide intellectual interests and he was able to give to his young nephew an early acquaintance with the New Learning and an appreciation of the value of academic studies. From the very first Zwingli's sympathies were with that movement of Renaissance which was to contribute so much to the loosening of the mediaeval structure.

In view of the promise which he showed, Zwingli was sent to the high school at Basel in the autumn term 1494. His teacher there was Gregor Bünzli, who came from Weesen district and had formerly been assisted by Bartholomew.[3] Zwingli's studies

---

[1] See O. Farner, *Huldrych Zwingli*, I, pp. 1–138, for interesting material on Zwingli's early background.

[2] Farner, *op. cit.*, pp. 152 f., suggests that Zwingli probably attended a regular school in Weesen, but there is no doubt that his uncle took charge of his education. [3] *Op. cit.*, p. 162.

13

at Basel included Latin, dialectic and music, and it was there that he first began to develop that talent and passion for music which was to remain with him throughout his life.[4] From Basel he came to Berne, probably in 1496 or 1497, and in Berne he came under the formative influence of Heinrich Wölflin, or Lupulus, a famous teacher and thorough-going exponent of the ideas and methods of the Renaissance.[5] While in Berne, Zwingli seems almost to have become a Dominican, apparently being attracted by the opportunity for serious musical training. He did in fact enter the Dominican house,[6] but his relatives intervened, and probably in 1498[7] he was removed to the University of Vienna.

With a possible short break[8] Zwingli continued in Vienna until 1502, but in the spring of that year he matriculated at the University of Basel, where he was finally to complete his student days. He enrolled for the Arts course, which included a certain amount of theology and enabled him to gain a first-hand acquaintance with scholastic method. He helped to support himself by taking a teaching post at the St. Martin's school. He graduated B.A. in 1504, but perhaps the crucial year was 1506, when he had already taken his M.A. and he attended a course of lectures given by Thomas Wyttenbach on the *Sentences* of Peter Lombard.[9] For it was under the influence of Wyttenbach that Zwingli was set on the path which was to lead to the two cardinal doctrines of the supremacy of Holy Scripture and justification by grace and faith.[10] The effect of Wyttenbach's teaching must not be exaggerated, for neither on the one side nor the other was there any question at that time of a break with the mediaeval system. But the seeds of evangelical teaching were undoubtedly sown, for not only did Wyttenbach himself later suffer great hardships for his doctrine, but Leo Jud, Capito and Pellican were all conscious of an indebtedness to him as well as Zwingli.

It was in the same year 1506 that Zwingli received a call to the parish of Glarus where he was to remain for the next ten years. His ordination probably took place at Constance, and

[4] *Ibid.*, p. 168 f.   [5] Farner, *op. cit.*, p. 164.
[6] C.R., III, p. 486. This seems to be the implication.
[7] The date usually given is 1500, but Farner argues convincingly for 1498, *op. cit.*, pp. 176 f.
[8] *Ibid.*, pp. 184 f. Farner thinks that he may have been temporarily expelled, probably for political reasons.
[9] *Ibid.*, pp. 226 f.
[10] Cf. Zwingli's famous statement, C.R., V, p. 718.

he celebrated his first Mass at Wildhaus. The parish of Glarus was a large and busy one, for it included three neighbouring villages in addition to the small town, but in spite of his many pastoral duties, which he seems to have fulfilled conscientiously enough, Zwingli was able to continue his humanistic and theological studies.[11]

During the period at Glarus Zwingli first became interested in that question of mercenary service which was to play a considerable part in the later work of reform.[12] By reason of their known hardihood and proved military prowess the Swiss were in great demand at this time as mercenary soldiers, and both the Confederacy as a whole and the individual recruit could command high prices from the various European Courts, not excluding the papacy. But the whole system of mercenary service and the riches which it brought were a source of serious moral deterioration in Switzerland, and as early as 1503 the Confederate Diet had made a futile effort to prohibit all foreign payments.[13]

Both as patriot and pastor Zwingli deplored the inherent and consequent evils of the system, and his first two literary productions were both aimed against it. But at first Zwingli made an exemption in the case of service on behalf of the papacy, and in 1512 he himself acted as chaplain to the Glarus contingent fighting with the papal armies. For his services in that year and again in 1513 and 1515 he earned the commendation of the papacy and a papal pension, and he was also made papal agent for the Glarus district. In point of fact the final period had disillusioned him even in respect of papal service,[14] but the favour which he enjoyed was to stand him in good stead in the early years at Zurich, for even as late as 1523 Adrian VI could write him in flattering terms,[15] and the first reforms were carried through without serious ecclesiastical intervention. A further indirect result of the mercenary service was that Zwingli had opportunity to survey something of the Church's life and activity in Italy. Not only was he not impressed by what he saw, but when he compared the modern Mass with that found in ancient Mass-books (especially at Milan)[16] he was led to question the authenticity of contemporary forms of

[11] For an account of the years at Glarus see Farner, *op. cit.*, II, pp. 7 f.
[12] *Ibid.*, pp. 88 f.   [13] D.C. 153.
[14] Cf. the poem *Das Labyrinth*, C.R., I, pp. 39 f.
[15] D.C.R. 187.
[16] *Ibid.*, 161.

Christianity and also, of course, the authority upon which they were grounded.

More important than the military service was Zwingli's continued interest in classical and theological learning. He seems to have used the papal pension for the purchase of books, and with this assistance he was able to acquire a considerable library, keeping abreast of all the latest productions.[17] His sympathies were still for the most part with the Renaissance scholars, and he started a highly prized correspondence with Erasmus.[18] The classes which he held for promising youngsters helped to keep him actively engaged in academic work, and in 1513 he planned to teach himself Greek, a language which he had not had any occasion to acquire during his days at school or university. It is no little credit to his industry and ability that in spite of the poverty of available text-books he gradually attained a considerable mastery of the language. As a good humanist Zwingli used his knowledge of Greek to make first-hand acquaintance with the ancient classics, but there can be no doubt that the primary purpose of the study was to enable him to read the New Testament in the original. For although Zwingli maintained his wider humanistic interest, it was the religious problem which emerged finally as his principal concern.

From the point of view of his inward development the final year at Glarus (1516) was probably the crucial one.[19] Zwingli himself constantly referred back to this period as the time when he won through to an evangelical understanding of Holy Scripture,[20] and at the same time the influence of Erasmus had been helping to undermine whatever confidence he still had in the traditional system. Zwingli himself was not unconscious of his indebtedness to Erasmus and he later acknowledged the debt in generous terms.[21] But the revolution was not entirely intellectual, for Farner has shown that the moral problem of sensuality was much exercising him at this time, and that he found relief and a new power against it in the evangelical faith.[22]

In the meantime Zwingli had continued his pastoral work at Glarus, and had acquired quite a reputation as an interesting and effective preacher. However, his increasing hostility to the whole mercenary system provoked the opposition of other

[17] Cf. Farner, *op. cit.*, II, pp. 107 f.   [18] *Ibid.*, p. 153.
[19] *Ibid.*, pp. 234 f.   [20] Cf. C.R., II, p. 145.
[21] D.C.R. 160.   [22] Farner, *op. cit.*, II, pp. 140 f.

pensionaries in Glarus, and although he still had a strong and sympathetic following, in 1516 he found it more congenial to accept a new appointment as people's priest at Einsiedeln. It is worth noting that the people of Glarus would not allow him officially to relinquish his office there, and for some time Zwingli was a pluralist, paying a "vicar" to fulfil his duties in the former parish.[23]

The work at Einsiedeln was very different from that at Glarus and it gave him ample opportunity for exploiting his gifts both as a preacher and as a scholar. Einsiedeln was only a small place, some 20 miles south-east of Zurich, but as the site of a famous shrine to the Virgin (with an alleged angelic dedication and a plenary indulgence) it attracted pilgrims from all parts of Switzerland. A sermon was preached every Sunday and Feast Day, and a fair audience could always be expected. In addition a special festival was held to mark the angelic dedication, and when the day (September 14) fell on a Sunday, a major celebration took place with services and sermons spread over a fortnight. There was a major celebration in the year of Zwingli's appointment, and the new priest took a prominent part in the proceedings. These wider opportunities not only helped to develop Zwingli's talents as a preacher, but also gave him much more than a local reputation and influence, thus preparing the way for the spread of evangelical teaching in other cantons.

But Einsiedeln had other advantages. Zwingli had rather more leisure than at Glarus, and he was able to pursue his patristic and New Testament studies. There was a reasonably good library at the local monastery where both abbot and administrator were kindly disposed to the New Learning.[24] In addition Zwingli's friends in larger centres kept him well posted with the latest publications.[25] The period of comparative withdrawal enabled him to work out his newly won apprehension of evangelical truth, and in his sermons he replaced the usual theological or topical discussions by expositions of the Gospels of the day, his main commentary being simply the Bible itself.[26]

At this time, of course, Zwingli had no thought of separation from the Church. Indeed, he was on the friendliest terms not only with the Bishop and his Vicar-General but also with the

[23] Cf. Opera, VII, p. 30, where in a letter dated Oct. 30, 1517, he styles himself Pastor of Glarus.

[24] Opera, VII, p. 59.   [25] Farner, op. cit., II, p. 257.

[26] C.R., II, p. 145.

Papal Legate, who to some extent sympathized with him and were conscious of the need for reform. A minor indulgence crisis arose in 1518 with the coming of the Franciscan preacher Samson, but Zwingli's superiors encouraged him in his rather amused castigation of the abuse.[27] In his attitude to this scandal Zwingli certainly displayed more of the spirit of Erasmus than of Luther, but the situation was not so serious as at Wittenberg, for there were no vested interests in Samson's work. Certainly, Zwingli's attitude did not cost him anything in ecclesiastical favour, for in the same year 1518 he was made acolyte chaplain to the Pope and released from certain censures which he had incurred.[28] In 1519 Leo X admonished Samson and gave the Diet liberty to dismiss him from the country.[29]

Zwingli made good use of his time at Einsiedeln, but it was obviously not a post which could satisfy him for long. In 1518 he almost accepted an invitation to Winterthur, but the people of Glarus would not release him. At the end of the same year, through the good offices of his friend Myconius, and in spite of considerable opposition, he was finally called to the office of people's priest at the Great Minster at Zurich.[30] The objections were on the score of his love of music and worldly pleasures and his unchaste life, of which there was still concrete evidence in spite of the great reform which he had effected.[31] He was succeeded at Einsiedeln by his one-time fellow-student Leo Jud, and one of his former pupils, Tschudi, was elected to the parish of Glarus.

The post which Zwingli accepted at the Great Minster was not a well paid one, and in the early period when he had no voice on the City Council he had only a restricted influence upon the conduct of affairs. But the office was important, for Zwingli had the opportunity to preach regularly in the Great Minster. From the very outset he began a course of direct biblical expositions[32] which helped to spread a knowledge of Scripture amongst the townspeople, thus preparing the ground for the eventual work of reform. By means of market-day sermons he was also able to reach the country people who came in from the surrounding districts. The attempted intervention of Samson led only to his virtual dismissal from the Confederacy, and the Papal Legate protected Zwingli from the attack of a

[27] Cf. the reply of Beatus Rhenanus, D.C.R. 163.
[28] C.R., VII, pp. 95 f. The honour was of course an empty one.
[29] D.C.R. 164.   [30] For a full account see Farner, *op. cit.*, II, pp. 285 f.
[31] *Ibid.*, pp. 298–301.   [32] Cf. Farner, *op. cit.*, II, p. 293.

hostile monk by prohibiting the publication of his work.[33] Unfortunately Zurich suffered badly from the plague in the autumn of 1519. Zwingli stayed faithfully at his post, but he himself caught the infection, and after a period of severe sickness he made only a slow recovery to normal health. The fact that he was spared when so many perished seems to have made a deep impression upon Zwingli, for he interpreted it as a divine seal set upon his reforming mission to the city.[34] The more serious turn given to his thinking was strengthened when his brother Andrew died in November, 1520.

During the period which followed Zwingli's main energies were devoted to the reforming work which will call for consideration in the next section. In the present context we may review certain more personal or external matters. In 1522 Zwingli entered into correspondence with Oecolampadius of Basel, who was to continue his warm friend and supporter in the dispute with the Lutherans.[35] This new friendship compensated to some extent for the loss of that with Erasmus in the summer of 1523.[36] Erasmus enjoyed the role of satirist and critic, but he had no taste for the actual work of reform, and he viewed with alarm the events now taking place at Zurich. Matters came to a head when Zwingli gave protection to Ulrich of Hutten, who had had the temerity to write against Erasmus and whose expulsion Erasmus requested from the City Council of Zurich. From the safety of Zurich Hutten unwisely made a fresh attack on Erasmus (August 15), but died a few days later (on the 31st). Erasmus made a reply which he dedicated to Zwingli, but he never wrote Zwingli again. Zwingli much regretted the turn which events had taken, for he had a warm regard not only for Erasmus but also for the Swiss humanist Glareanus whose friendship he also lost. But the break was perhaps inevitable in view of the decisive differences in policy and outlook, and it is fortunate that it did not involve the same dogmatic bitterness as the rift between Erasmus and Luther.

An important new step which Zwingli took in 1524 was to enter into an official marriage with Anna Reinhard, the widow of Hans Meyer, and mother of the Gerold to whom Zwingli had addressed his *Education of Christian Youth*. There is strong evidence to suggest that Zwingli had been "clerically" married

[33] Opera, VII, p. 96.   [34] Farner, *op. cit.*, II, pp. 347 f.
[35] Opera, VII, pp. 251–252, 261.
[36] *Ibid.*, p. 251, 302, 307–311.

to Anna at any rate since 1522,[37] but on April 2, 1524, the position was regularized, and the Council gave their formal recognition on July 26.

It was during this period that Zwingli began his extensive literary labours in defence of the Swiss Reformation. The *Archeteles* and the sermons on the Word of God and the Virgin had appeared in 1522, together with the *Exposition of the Articles* and the sermon on Divine and Human Righteousness. In 1523 Zwingli composed the tract *The Education of Youth* which was followed in 1524 by his sermon on the Pastor and various Addresses, Epistles and Replies. The *Commentarius* and the treatises on Baptism and the Lord's Supper appeared in 1525, initiating a lengthy series of controversial writings directed mainly against the Anabaptists and the Lutherans. To the final period (1530–1531) belonged *The Refutation of the Tricks of the Catabaptists*, the *Fidei Ratio*, and *The Exposition of the Christian Faith*. Of almost all these writings it must be said that they were controversial in design and far too hasty in composition. Zwingli himself seems to have been quite aware of the latter fault, but he was unable to remedy it. For one thing, he was far too occupied with practical matters to devote himself to more studied theological writing. For another he lacked the necessary patience. Once he had started on a work his whole aim was to see it in print at the earliest possible moment. The result is that while his writings do not lack acuteness or profundity, they lack that unity and balance which characterize the greater works of theology and in the German works especially the style is distinctive by reason of its forcefulness rather than its grace or compactness.

But the defects in Zwingli's work are not entirely the reflection of corresponding defects in his character. It is true that his reasoning is often more acute than convincing, and to that extent his work testifies faithfully to his more rational understanding of evangelical truth. But if sometimes his polemical writings suggest an almost supercilious sense of intellectual superiority, the impression is not at all borne out by his personal relationships. In fact, Zwingli seems to have been of a warm-hearted and friendly disposition, and much of his success was due to the appeal of his open and generous nature. He was roused to scorn only when it appeared that his opponents were wilfully refusing to accept what he himself saw as plain and self-evident truth, sheltering themselves either in the

[37] Opera, VII, pp. 210, 226, 253.

invincible obstinacy of ignorance, or in all too evident evasions and falsehoods.

By the year 1524 the reforming movement was not only firmly under way in Zurich but it had begun to have its effect in other cities and cantons. The result was that Zwingli was increasingly caught up in a mesh of wider activities in the defence and propagation of evangelical teaching. For the opponents of reform were also busy. Alarmed by the trend of events, the Catholic cantons accepted an offer made by Dr. Eck to maintain against Zwingli and his supporters the "scriptural nature of old true Christian beliefs and practices" (October, 1524).[38] Zwingli himself declined the invitation, but it was taken up by Oecolampadius of Basel and Berchthold Haller of Berne. For the moment the traditionalists maintained the day, but first in Berne and then in Basel the upper hand was gained by the party of reform.[39] A number of other cantons declared themselves for the evangelical cause, including Appenzell, Glarus and Schaffhausen and such allied or subject territories as the Toggenburg, St. Gall and Thurgau.[40]

Zwingli himself did not play a direct part in the extension of reform to these districts, but in a real sense Zurich was the centre or spearhead of the movement and Zwingli its recognized ecclesiastical and theological leader. Accordingly, although Zwingli did not make any attempt to force a unified order or liturgy upon the loosely interrelated communions, he did feel a sense of responsibility for their maintenance and welfare, especially in view of their dangerous isolation from the Lutheran states as a result of the bitter eucharistic controversy. In the final years of his life his main concentration was upon the securing of the ground already won by a system of doctrinal and political alliances. Naturally, he continued his incessant activities as a theologian and pastor, but more and more he had to concern himself with the less congruous affairs of the statesman and diplomat.

The political activity of Zwingli was directed into three main channels. First, he aimed to create a common evangelical front within Switzerland itself, and it was in pursuit of this aim that the Christian Civic Alliance was founded and extended.[41] The Alliance was modelled on the treaty by which the city of Basel had been received into the Confederacy, except that confessional agreement was made one of the necessary

38 Opera, II, 2, pp. 399 f.   39 D.C.R. 459.
40 Loc. cit.   41 D.C.R. 220.

preconditions.[42] The Alliance quickly gained strength, but it had the inevitable result of provoking the Catholic cantons to form a rival organization.[43] The existence of these powerful and hostile groups made a collision almost inevitable, but when it did come in June, 1529, it was the Reformed side which had the initiative.[44] The Catholic cantons were taken by surprise, and the war ended in an easy victory for the evangelical cause, with advantageous although hotly disputed terms at the First Peace of Cappel.[45] To that extent the Civic Alliance seemed to have justified itself as a safeguard against internal aggression.

In 1529, however, the more serious threat was from outside, for the Diet of Speier had proscribed all evangelical teaching and called for the extirpation of sacramentarian groups. The menace of the situation compelled Zwingli to consider the possibilities of some wider union with the Lutheran states, and he welcomed the invitation of Philip of Hesse to participate in preparatory theological discussions with the Lutheran leaders.[46] It is likely enough that Zwingli would have been content with a bare recognition of his teaching, and upon the basis of toleration a working agreement might well have been attained, for there was virtual unanimity in the majority of subjects discussed. But Luther went to Marburg with another mind. For one thing he felt that a doctrine of the real presence was demanded by the Word of God: hence there could be no possible toleration for those who denied it. For another, Luther had no real trust in alliances or military action, and he regarded it as quite wrong to barter theological principle for political advantage. The inflexibility of Luther destroyed from the outset all possibility of real union, although Zwingli himself felt that enough had been done at any rate to give the Emperor pause in his aggressive designs.[47] The evil results of the failure were seen at the Diet of Augsburg in 1530, when the Protestant groups were forced to present three separate confessions of faith, the Augustana, the Tetrapolitan and the Fidei Ratio, in place of the one united confession which might have made some impact upon the forces arrayed against them. The position was particularly difficult for the Civic Alliance, for on February 27, 1531, the four cities entered into the Schmalkaldic League, accepting a mediating eucharistic doctrine which Zwingli himself could not possibly approve.[48]

[42] *Ibid.*   [43] Bullinger, *Reformationsgeschichte*, II, p. 264.
[44] *Ibid.*, pp. 297–298.   [45] *Ibid.*, p. 314. Cf. Opera, VIII, p. 296.
[46] Opera, VIII, p. 287.   [47] *Ibid* , p. 370.   [48] *Ibid.*, p. 579.

It was in face of the growing threat of isolation that even after Marburg Zwingli had had recourse to the third and final policy of alliances with anti-imperial but not necessarily evangelical powers. His first ally in 1529 was of course Philip of Hesse,[49] and in the same year an approach was also made to Venice[50] and in 1530 to France.[51] Zwingli himself possibly believed that by means of these alliances the way might ultimately open up for a wider propagation and triumph of the Reformed faith. Certainly he had some such hopes in the case of France, but quite naturally they had no real foundation and were destined never to be realized. Negotiations with the French were tardy and in the long run futile, and in the meantime events supervened which led not merely to Zwingli's own death but to the halting of the reforming movement which he had initiated.

The loss of the four cities in February, 1531, deprived Zwingli of his most important allies both doctrinally and geographically. At the same time the hostility of the Lutherans and the suspicion of the French exposed Zurich and its immediate supporters to the perils of complete isolation. Zwingli himself evidently had fears of an overwhelming invasion by the Emperor[52] and it was in these circumstances that he pressed for a fresh effort to reduce the Five Forest cantons.[53] But Berne would not consent to this extreme step, preferring to weaken the cantons by economic sanctions.[54] As Zwingli foresaw, this policy not merely provoked the resentment of their opponents, but actually transferred to them the military initiative. The climax came in October, 1531, when the Foresters could stand the strain no longer and invaded the cantonal territory of Zurich. The Zurichers naturally rallied to defend themselves, but they were ill-prepared and half-hearted in the venture, and their ill-concerted efforts came to a tragic end on the fatal field of Cappel (October 11). Zwingli himself seems to have had a premonition of disaster,[55] but he accompanied the troops as field-chaplain, and was killed in the action. The death of Zwingli and the terms of the Second Peace of Cappel[56] combined to put a decisive stop to the progress of reform in the German-speaking cantons.

[49] *Ibid.*, p. 665.   [50] *Loc. cit.*   [51] *Ibid.*, p. 397
[52] *Ibid.*, p. 593.   [53] *Ibid.*, p. 586.
[54] Bullinger, *op. cit.*, II, p. 377. An embargo was placed upon sales to the Cantons of wheat, wine, salt, iron and steel.
[55] S. M. Jackson, *Ulrich Zwingli*, p. 352.   [56] D.C.R. 227.

2. THE WORK OF ZWINGLI

The wider schemes of Zwingli were destined never to be realized, but his work was not destroyed, for Zurich itself remained loyal to the reforms which he had initiated. Indeed, it is in the scope and effectiveness of these reforms that the main historical importance of Zwingli is to be found, for although only on a small scale he presented the first example and pattern of a church thoroughly reorganized according to the evangelical understanding of the New Testament.

The first and perhaps the decisive impact which Zwingli made on Zurich was as an evangelist and preacher. In this respect his aim and method did not materially differ from that of Luther, who believed that the true key to the situation was not ecclesiastical action but the proclamation of the Word of God. In his earlier days at Zurich Zwingli had no seat either on the Council or on the Chapter, but as people's priest he had the ear of the congregation, which on Friday included many people from the surrounding districts. His primary aim was to expound continuously successive books of the Bible, but he was not afraid to make a practical or topical application, attacking unbelief and moral abuses and taking up the cudgels against indulgences. His position in the city was strengthened by his loyal and devoted service during the plague, and his classes both at his own house and at the Minster school gave him an opportunity to influence the future leaders of the community.

The bold evangelical preaching of Zwingli naturally aroused opposition, especially from the monastic orders,[57] but as early as 1520 it was evident that he was carrying the day, for in spite of complaints the Council issued a mandate allowing freedom to preach 'the holy Gospels and Epistles of the Apostles conformably with the word of God, and the true divine Scriptures of the Old and New Testaments'.[58] Zwingli's attacks upon the mercenary system were also having their effect, especially after he freed his hands by renouncing his own pension from the Papacy in 1520.[59] It is significant that when Francis I was seeking mercenaries in May, 1521, he could make agreement only with the other twelve cantons.[60] Zurich and its Communes repudiated the whole mercenary system.[61]

[57] D.C.R. 165.   [58] Ibid., 166.   [59] Opera, I, p. 365.
[60] Oechsli, I, 116.   [61] Ibid., II, 160.

By this time, however, the way had opened up for Zwingli to play a wider part in affairs, for with his appointment to the Chapter on April 29, 1521, he automatically became a member of the Council.[62] Yet Zwingli never forgot that the true secret of reform is the preparation of the people by instruction. In all the activity which followed he never attempted to force his way upon the church by legislative enactment, but was content to wait the right moment when the demand for action came spontaneously from the congregation. It was because the future reforms were all carefully prepared by preaching and instruction that they were carried through with the minimum of opposition and on a solid and durable basis.

There were two fundamental principles underlying the whole reforming programme, first, that all doctrinal and ecclesiastical questions must be settled in accordance with the teaching or example of Scripture, and second, that a Christian government has both the right and the duty to see that the rulings of Scripture are observed.[63]

The first issues which arose were in relation to three practices all sanctioned and enforced only by the Church: fasting, the celibacy of the clergy, and the intercession of the saints; and all three were settled quite irrespective of either traditional usage or episcopal order. The question of fasting came up abruptly in 1522 when certain individuals independently violated the Lenten fast.[64] Zwingli defended their action in his sermon on the right use of meats. A commission was sent down by the Bishop, but in spite of appeals and admonitions the Council would not do more than require the observance of the fast until the matter was elucidated.[65] In relation to celibacy Zwingli himself felt the absurdity of the existing position, and in July, 1522, joined with other clergy in a direct petition to the Bishop and the Diet requesting permission for the clergy to marry.[66] The issue was not immediately debated by the Council, but during the months which followed celibacy was fairly generally abandoned in Zurich with at any rate the connivance of the authorities. The intercession of the saints was the subject of an early disputation in the summer of 1521, when Zwingli took the evangelical side and the traditional view was stated by a visiting Franciscan, Francis Lambert.[67] The result was a victory for Zwingli, for after a further disputation with the local friars the Burgomaster issued an order that

[62] Egli, *Analecta Reformatoria*, I, 22 f.   [63] Cf. Opera, III, p. 339.
[64] Egli, A.S., 233.   [65] *Ibid.*, 236.   [66] D.C.R. 178.   [67] *Ibid.*, 180.

preaching should be "from Holy Scripture, to the exclusion of Scotus and Thomas and suchlike."[68] A notable success was when the Chapter accepted the same principle in a resolution of August 19,[69] and the Council followed up their decision by opening the Oetenbach convent to the preaching of the secular clergy.[70] The authority of the Council was further emphasized on November 12 when Zwingli deliberately resigned his office as people's priest and accepted a new authorization to preach, not this time from the Bishop but from the City Council.[71] The implications of this action were not necessarily Erastian, for Zwingli accepted the authority of the Council in ecclesiastical matters only on the understanding that the Council itself was subject to the Word of God.

The year 1522 had seen the acceptance of Zwingli's fundamental contention, but the application had been in respect of only comparatively trivial matters which the papacy was prepared to overlook in view of Zwingli's past services and possible usefulness. The feebleness of the opposition and the obvious support of the majority of the people encouraged the reformer to undertake a rather more ambitious programme in the following year, and in January he published his Sixty-Seven Articles in preparation for the First Disputation which opened on the 29th.[72] Once again the Council gave judgment in Zwingli's favour and the tempo of reform now increased. Celibacy was being abandoned by many clergy and monks;[73] the Articles were enforced;[74] a first translation of the baptismal office was prepared;[75] the canon of the Mass came in for criticism;[76] and a plan was drawn up for the reform of the Great Minster.[77]

Swift and drastic as many of these changes were, Zwingli took good care not to outstrip public sympathy, and the constant propaganda of the pulpit prepared the people for every step. Indeed, in the autumn of 1522, certain sections of the population took the law into their own hands and began the destruction of images.[78] The Council punished the offenders, but conceded a Second Disputation on the subject of images and the Mass.[79] The Bishop made a futile attempt to have the matter deferred until the Diet, but this intervention

[68] Bullinger, op. cit., I, p. 78.
[70] D.C.R. 389.
[72] Opera, I, pp. 141–148.
[74] Ibid., p. 60.
[76] Ibid., III, p. 83 f.
[78] Ibid., 421.

[69] Egli, A.S., 490.
[71] Egli, A.S., 290.
[73] Bullinger, op. cit., I, p. 63.
[75] Opera, II, 2, p. 224.
[77] Egli, A.S., 426.
[79] Opera, VII, p. 311 f.

was ignored, and the disputation took place in October before the Council. Instructed by Zwingli and Leo Jud the Council decided against both images and the Mass, and in defiance of the authority of the Bishop they issued a mandate for the abolition of both.[80] The break with diocesan authority was now complete, and the Council recognized it by proposing to appoint their own preachers to take the evangelical message to the country districts.[81]

The decision to replace the Mass by a communion met with a good deal of opposition in the Chapter, and its enforcement had to be delayed for several months. Further disputations in December, 1523, and January, 1524, resulted in a confirmation of the previous judgment, but protests from the other cantons again prevented its immediate execution.[82] However, the work of reform still continued, for the Whitsuntide procession to Einsiedeln was prohibited on May 14,[83] organs and relics were suppressed in June,[84] images were officially removed in July,[85] and the religious houses were dissolved in December, their revenues being redirected to religious and charitable objects.[86] In the meantime the Mass temporarily remained, but in the first quarter of 1525 a new and concentrated attack was made upon it, first of all in writing, in Zwingli's *Commentarius*, and then in fresh representations to the City Council. The attack was successful, for on April 12 the Council finally decreed its abolition.[87] The last Mass was said in Zurich on the Wednesday of Holy Week, its place being taken by the new Communion Service on the days which followed.[88] A purified Baptismal Office was introduced in the same year,[89] so that it remained only to replace the Choir Office by Bible Readings or Prophesyings[90] and the liturgical reconstruction was more or less complete. In the reform of the Church Calendar which took place in 1527 only the major festivals like Christmas Day, Easter and All Saints' Day were retained, all work being prohibited on these days and Sundays except for the essential work of harvesting.[91] At the end of 1527 the disused organ in the Great Minster was broken up and the costly ornaments which had previously adorned the city churches were either sold or destroyed.

80 Egli, A.S., 436.   81 *Loc. cit.*   82 Bullinger, *op. cit.*, I, p. 85.
83 Egli, A.S., 527.   84 *Ibid.*, 547.   85 *Ibid.*, 552.
86 *Ibid.*, 598.   87 *Ibid.*, 684.   88 *Loc. cit.*
89 Opera, II, 2, p. 230.   90 Bullinger, *op. cit.*, I, p. 160.
91 Jackson, *op. cit.*, pp. 291–292.

The decisive break which came with the Mandate of 1523 had committed Zwingli and his party to the task both of ecclesiastical reorganization and also of the recruitment of an evangelical ministry. The latter task was the more immediately urgent, and it was tackled at once by instituting a theological seminary as part of the reform of the school attached to the Great Minster.[92] Lectures were provided in both Greek and Hebrew for the instruction of future pastors, and Leo Jud was responsible for German courses on the various Biblical books, courses which were attended by the city clergy and even by some of the laity. From the very first high standards were set, for from his own experience Zwingli appreciated the value of scholarship, and he saw that if the reformation was to take deep root in the parishes it must be on a sound intellectual as well as spiritual foundation.

The question of ecclesiastical organization emerged only with the wider spread of evangelical teaching. The breakdown of episcopal authority naturally involved the withdrawal of immediate spiritual oversight, and the rise of Anabaptism carried with it the danger of a lawless individualism both in teaching and practice. It was, no doubt, because of this danger that the Anabaptists were ruthlessly suppressed both by Zwingli himself and also by the city authorities.[93] Within the cantonal territories the pastors were of course officially responsible to the City Council, but apart from the ordinary processes of the law there was no real machinery to exercise spiritual or moral discipline. The need was met not by the creation of a new hierarchy but by the establishment of ecclesiastical synods charged with the task of enforcing a basic conformity in doctrine and reasonable standards of moral and pastoral life.[94] With the accession of other cantons and districts to the Reformed faith more general synods were convened, but the wider organization was of the Confederate type to which the Swiss were politically accustomed. A common confessional outlook was the main bond of union. In liturgical and ecclesiastical questions the individual cities or cantons retained the individual right to order their own affairs.[95]

The most striking feature of the reforming work actually accomplished by Zwingli is perhaps the thoroughness and consistency with which it was carried through. In this respect a comparison with Luther is particularly illuminating. Luther

[92] Ibid., p. 293.
[94] Jackson, op. cit., p. 286.
[93] Egli, A.S., 622, 624.
[95] Ibid., p. 294.

aimed to purify the Church by the proclamation of the Word of God, but he had little or no programme of practical reform, and his liturgical and ecclesiastical rearrangements were more in the nature of a concession to circumstances than the fulfilment of a consistent plan. Now Zwingli had the same basic aim as Luther, but for him the purification of the Church by the proclamation of the Word of God involved necessarily not merely the revivification of its faith and reconstruction of its doctrine, but the overhauling of every department of ecclesiastical life and practice. For Zwingli there were, strictly speaking, no *adiaphora*. Practice as well as doctrine must be tested at every point by the Word of God, and there could be no question of retaining traditional forms or ceremonies simply on the ground that they were not actually forbidden by Scripture. It would be far too much to say that Zwingli came to Zurich with a fully worked out programme of reform. But he certainly came with the principle which involved his whole programme of reform: the principle that the Word of God must be the supreme court of appeal not merely in matters of faith and ethics but in all the co-related questions of ecclesiastical practice. It was the inflexible application of that principle which gave to Zwingli's work its consistency and thoroughness.

Yet Zwingli was not primarily an ecclesiastical statesman but a preacher of evangelical truth. That is why fundamentally the reformation in Zurich was a doctrinal and spiritual matter rather than a political. It is true, of course, that Zwingli did exploit the instinctive desire of the Council to achieve autonomy in ecclesiastical affairs. It is also true that he made use of his influence on the Council to put the various reforms into practical effect. But it is no less true that the real secret of Zwingli's success was his ability to direct the religious thought of the city from the Minster pulpit. Zwingli himself had no doubts concerning the true basis of his work. Reform was possible only as the Word of God was taught and proclaimed. That is why Zwingli was so insistent that there should be an instructed and zealous clergy, for only as the people were taught from Holy Scripture could they see for themselves the falsity of traditional belief and practice and demand and maintain a faith and order conformable with that of the New Testament. Outwardly the reforming work at Zurich was severely practical, but at bottom the practical measures were simply an outworking of the inward revolution accomplished by the preaching of the divine Word.

The emphasis upon preaching involved ultimately an educated laity which could play a full part in the counsels of the Church. In this respect Zwingli built better perhaps than he himself knew, but he certainly must have realized some of the implications of his teaching. As we have already noticed, in many cases he allowed the demand for reform to well up spontaneously from the people. In addition, he expected the Council to be able to give judgment on disputed theological questions, and he conceded to it the right of government in ecclesiastical matters. For the most part, of course, this concession was the general concession to lawfully established authority which Zwingli shared with Luther and indeed all the Reformers. Yet he could make it with a good conscience, because the Council as he envisaged it would consist of Christians who all had a solid grounding in evangelical truth and were thus qualified to exercise their responsibilities in ecclesiastical questions. In this respect Zwingli always maintained an ultimate superiority of the true pastorate, for the magistracy had no authority either to break or to exceed the divine Word which it was the task of the pastorate to expound and proclaim. The final authority in Zurich was not to be the City Council, but Holy Scripture.

It was the stress upon Holy Scripture and its authority which determined the character of the liturgical reconstruction carried through at Zurich. It did so in two ways: first, the worship of the Church was to conform at all points to scriptural patterns; and second, it was to serve the over-riding end ot instruction in scriptural truth. In practice, the two ways were one and the same, for naturally it was the forms which were most agreeable to Scripture which best served the final end of instruction in Scripture. Thus Zwingli insisted that all the services should be in the vernacular. This was obviously a return to the normal practice of the New Testament but it was also an indispensable aid to the task of teaching. Again, extraneous and distracting ornaments and ceremonies were ruthlessly suppressed and all the liturgical forms which remained were plain and simple, conforming to the basic structure of New Testament worship and giving ample scope for the active propagation of the evangelical faith.

Perhaps the greatest testimony to the solidity of Zwingli's work is the fact that the radical changes which he made in so short a period not only survived the shock of his own death but also exercised a wider influence in and through the ever-extend-ing Reformed communities of the later part of the century. In a sense, of course, we must admit that the work which he did was limited, and to that extent incomplete. His programme was radical and thorough, but he was able to carry it through only on a comparatively small scale. His direct influence was restricted to Zurich and the neighbouring cities and cantons of the Swiss Confederacy. Had he lived, events might possibly have given him that wider range and opportunity which was reserved for his true successor in the leadership of the Reformed churches, John Calvin. As it was, Zwingli was never able to complete his ambitious designs. Yet what he did do, he did thoroughly and well. The church of Zurich never attained to the world-wide prominence and authority of Geneva, but it had good reason for pride and not a little importance as the first example of a church wholly reformed according to the Word of God. And it was to the pioneer of the Reformed tradition that it owed both the fact and the form of that reformation.

3. THE THEOLOGY OF ZWINGLI

In the strict sense it is wrong to separate the theology of Zwingli from his work. The two belong together, for the ecclesiastical activity was simply the practical application of his theological principles. Behind all the activity there stood the two great doctrines on which his whole thought finally centred: the supremacy of the divine revelation in Holy Scripture, and the sovereignty of God in his election and grace. Which of the two doctrines has the priority it is perhaps futile to ask and certainly impossible to decide. On the one hand the perception of the biblical revelation is dependent upon the inward operation of grace, and to that extent the knowledge of Holy Scripture is secondary to the divine sovereignty. But on the other hand the doctrines of grace are themselves revealed and known through Holy Scripture, and to that extent Holy Scripture emerges as the true source of religious life and thought. From the purely historical standpoint, it is likely enough that Zwingli moved towards an apprehension of the absolute sovereignty of God by way of his philosophical and general theological reading. But at the same time he was engaged on a systematic investigation of the Scriptures, and it was when the content of the scriptural revelation inwardly met and confirmed his earlier teaching that the theology of Zwingli took on its distinctive character.

At any rate, it is noticeable that in his dogmatic expositions Zwingli always gives pride of place to the doctrine of God rather than to that of Holy Scripture or of the fall and wretchedness of man. In this respect he conforms to the traditional order of the Creeds,[96] which more or less took the Bible for granted as the source and norm of truth. And he set an example which was followed by the majority of the Reformed Confessions. In faithful reflection of his own experience he usually prefaces his statement of Christian doctrine by a philosophical introduction in which he asserts on rational grounds the unity and uniqueness of God as the source and norm of all things.[97] In the *Commentarius* he begins with a more general discussion on the nature of religion, which he defines as a relationship between God and man, thus opening up the way for a consideration first of the being and nature of God.[98] He then follows his usual order, arguing that philosophy gives us the basic facts of God's existence and providence and thus demonstrates the rationality of faith.[99]

It must be noted, however, that although in these discussions reason plays roughly the same part as it does in the classical scholastic formulation, the doctrine of God advanced by Zwingli is to all intents and purposes strictly biblical. The starting-point and the external form are both rational, but the office and power of reason are closely delimited. Reason cannot even give to us a clearly monotheistic picture of God. It certainly cannot disclose anything consistent concerning the divine nature and attributes. And it is completely powerless to establish an inward relationship with God as opposed to the merely external apprehension of his existence. For a perception of who and what God is, and for an inward apprehension oɪ his person, it is necessary to turn to the divine self-revelation attested in the Old and New Testament Scriptures.

From the Bible Zwingli learned three main facts concerning God: his self-existence, his goodness, and his perfection. As the self-existent One God is unique and sole-sufficient. He is not in any way dependent upon any other creature nor is he limited by any other creature. He is eternal and infinite, and he is alone in his infinity and eternity. But the transcendent God is also the God of goodness. And the goodness of God is not a static attribute, but an active goodness which expresses

[96] Zwingli, *Hauptschriften*, XI, pp. 302 f.
[97] As, for example, in the *Exposition of the Faith*.
[98] *Ibid.*, IX, pp. 18 f.   [99] *Ibid.*, pp. 20 f.

itself outwards in the divine works of creation, providence and redemption. It comprises within itself all the divine attributes. And God is also a God of perfection, for all the excellencies reflected in man are seen in him in the highest possible form, as omniscience, omnipotence and love. The grace of God is the necessary concomitant of his goodness and perfection, for by the logic of their own nature the righteousness and love of God express themselves *ad extra* in works of gratuitous benevolence.[1]

It will be seen that Zwingli asserted strongly both the sole sovereignty of God and also his perfection as the sum of wisdom, power and goodness. But this twofold assertion posed in an acute form the problem of God's providential disposing of things in relation to the existence of evil and more particularly to the fall. Zwingli naturally perceived the problem, and he discussed it in detail and with considerable acumen in his *Treatise on Providence*. On the one hand he argued that the providence of God is absolute. God is the direct cause of every action or event. It was for that reason that Zwingli could attribute even the goodness of pagans to the causality of the same sovereign Spirit. But on the other hand, Zwingli tried to deny that God is in any sense morally responsible for the sinful acts of men. He had to admit that God is the direct cause of those acts. But he denied any moral responsibility: formally, because God himself is above the law imposed upon man, and substantially, because he always has higher and valid reasons for causing men to commit acts which from their standpoint are contrary to his moral will. Thus although God is the cause of sinful acts, the sin in those acts derives from man and not from God. And that means that the guilt attaches to man because he does them in direct contravention of the divine will. There is therefore no contradiction in God meting out eternal retribution upon acts of which he is in a very real sense the direct cause.

The sole causality of God necessarily involved for Zwingli a rigorous doctrine of the divine predestination and election, for all that is good in man derives from God, and faith itself is possible only where God himself has sovereignly decreed to give it. Zwingli could not possibly explain predestination as a mere foreknowledge of belief or unbelief: on the contrary, it is a free determination of the divine will concerning those who are to be saved. This determination is the true source of all the

[1] *Ibid.*, IX, pp. 20 f.; XI, pp. 302.

redemptive activity of God, for in fulfilment of it God provides
everything which is necessary for the salvation of his elect. On
the one hand, he makes atonement for the sin of men by means
of the incarnation and death and resurrection of Jesus Christ.
And on the other he provokes to faith and good works by the
secret operation of the Holy Spirit.[2]

It was because of this tremendous stress upon the divine
initiative and sovereignty that Zwingli was compelled to protest
violently against the existing theory and practice of Christianity. It was not merely that the mediaeval system was
contrary to the New Testament norm, although that in itself
was a valid point and one which Zwingli consistently made.
But at a deeper level the mediaeval system rested upon semi-
Pelagian presuppositions which were in direct contrast with
the evangelical doctrine of Holy Scripture. Zwingli could test
all the details of the system by the specific teaching of Scripture,
but in the last analysis it was because the basic doctrine was
unscriptural that the details were weighed and found wanting.
For if salvation is by election and grace, if even faith itself is a
direct work of God by the Holy Spirit, then there can be no
place for schemes of religious life or thought which allow
either for the merit of human works or for the *ex opere operato*
efficacy of sacramental observances.

Again in accordance with his basic teaching, Zwingli was
impelled as Luther was to a new and evangelical understanding
of the doctrine of justification.[3] Justification became the
sovereign and creative declaration of God by which those who
are elected to faith in Jesus Christ are accepted as righteous
on account of the merits of Christ. The true ground of justification is not the human act of faith, but the life and death of
Jesus Christ in which the justice and mercy of God are conjoined in a single act of divine goodness. As Zwingli put it
in *The Exposition of the Faith*, goodness as justice required
the sacrifice and goodness as mercy provided it.[4] The means
by which justification is applied to the individual is saving
faith, that faith which is not merely rational assent, but a
movement of the whole nature by the direct action of the Holy
Spirit. Good works still retained an honourable place in this
view of the matter, for it was stressed that they are the necessary
but spontaneous fruits of a true faith.[5] But of themselves good
works could have no power to justify, for it is God who reckons

[2] *Ibid.*, XI, pp. 266–268.   [3] *Ibid.*, IX, pp. 102 f.; XI, pp. 337 f.
[4] *Ibid.*, XI, pp. 307–308.   [5] *Ibid.*, pp. 339 f.

righteous and it is God who himself produces the acceptable fruits of righteousness. Again, the emphasis upon free justification by faith did not mean the negation of the Law, for as a permanent expression of the divine will for man the Law continues both as a guide to the believer and as a warning and restraint to the evil-doer.[6] What Zwingli did negate was legalism, and especially that mediaeval form of legalism which had given rise to such corrupt and fictional notions as purgatory, indulgences, the power of the keys, the treasury of merit, prayers for the dead and the merit of works of supererogation.[7]

It was the same doctrine of the divine sovereignty in election and grace which determined Zwingli's understanding of the Church.[8] The true Church which the New Testament describes as the body or bride of Christ is not at all co-terminous with that visible organization or complex of organizations which is its outward expression in the world. In its strictest and most proper sense the Church is the whole company of the elect or redeemed as called out from every age and country. And it is to this Church that the traditional notes apply. It is one by virtue of its union in faith with Jesus Christ. It is holy by virtue of the justification which it has in Christ. It is catholic in that it is not restricted to any particular epoch or locality. It is apostolic in that it is in the true succession of the faith and practice of the apostles. To this inward Church of the elect Zwingli applied the term "invisible." By this he did not mean that the Church finds no external expression in the world, but that membership of it cannot be known merely by the external tests which can be applied by man. The election of God remains always the secret of God and of those who know the inward work of the Spirit. In point of fact, the invisible Church always does express itself in external organization, for the people of God all belong to visible communities consisting of all those who make outward profession of the Christian faith. In so far as true believers belong both to the invisible Church and the visible, there is a real identity between the two, but in so far as the visible Church includes professors who are not true believers, there is a distinctness. The notes of the visible Church are the three external ones; the preaching of the Word of God, the due administration of the two dominical sacraments, and church discipline.

[6] Ibid., p. 345; IX, pp. 127–129.   [7] Ibid., XI, p. 288, pp. 314–315.
[8] Ibid., pp. 267–270; IX, pp. 184 f.

It is interesting that Zwingli developed his ecclesiology in strict accordance with his doctrine of the incarnation. The Church of God had both its divine-human side and also its human. And there was a certain fundamental unity, although not a complete identity, between the two aspects. If this fact is true in relation to his doctrine of the Church, it is even more true, and perhaps more consciously so, in relation to that of the Word and sacraments, which are the means by which the Holy Spirit applies the divine gifts of grace to the elect.[9] About both Word and sacraments there is the same duality as that which characterizes the Church. On the one hand there is the external form, which has its own meaning and value on the purely human level. And on the other hand there is the inward content, that divine message which is life and salvation to the soul as it comes in the power of the Holy Ghost. And here again there is a fundamental unity between the divine-human and human aspects, for it is the external word of the Bible which is also the internal Word of God when it comes with the enlightenment of the divine Spirit. But the identity is not absolute in the sense that everyone who receives the external Word or rite receives also the internal Word or grace. The external Word and rite are always "of God" or "divine" in the sense that they are appointed by God and are the sphere and the means of the divine calling or rejection. But they are not always "of God" in the sense that they infallibly bring conviction and faith to all who receive them. In this respect the decisive thing is that inward operation of the Holy Spirit which is the true source of individual repentance and assurance. It is in the heart of each believer or unbeliever that it is decided whether at this or that point the external Church is coextensive with the internal, the letter of Scripture is also the living Word of God, the sign is conjoined with the thing signified. But to say that is once again to suspend everything upon that divine sovereignty which is not controlled by the human choice, but ordains and directs it.

Of a piece with the rejection of any absolute identity between sign and thing signified was Zwingli's vehement denial of a literal presence of the body and blood of Christ either in place of or in, with and under the substances of the bread and wine.[10] The arguments which he used to support

[9] On this point see especially the sermon *On the Clarity and Certainty of the Word*, C.R., I, pp. 338 f.
[10] Zwingli, *Hauptschriften*, XI, pp. 275 f.

this denial were threefold: The assertion of a literal presence is contrary to the evidence of the New Testament, it destroys the true nature of the sacrament, and it is inconsistent with the historical doctrine of the incarnation. It is important to remember that what Zwingli was denying was not the spiritual presence of Christ to true believers, but a literal physical presence to all recipients. Certainly a conjunction of sign and thing signified could be expected where there was the internal operation of the Spirit. But there was no necessary conjunction by virtue of a magical change in the elements themselves.

The fact that all these doctrines were based upon the same simple pre-suppositions, the supremacy of Holy Scripture and the absolute divine sovereignty, certainly gave to Zwingli's theology a clarity and consistency which are not always apparent in the more diffuse if more profound writings of Luther. Indeed, the common impression made by Zwingli's dogmatic works is that he has brought to the task a more powerful intellectual understanding than spiritual inwardness and insight. In spite of his obvious stylistic weaknesses, he always presses home his arguments with great acuteness and dialectical skill, yet with all the logic of his presentation he often fails to carry complete conviction because even his constant appeals to Scripture suggest a lack of perception of the deeper bearing of the passages cited. It is not that Zwingli does not penetrate to the ultimate themes of Scripture. Nor is it that he is without a genuinely personal apprehension. But in his handling of individual passages he relies far too much upon logical subtlety rather than a basic spiritual appreciation. In fact, such power as his exposition has derives from the combination of that intellectual acuteness with the almost severe consistency of his essential message.

The unifying factor in Zwingli's theology was the overwhelming emphasis upon the divine sovereignty. It was undoubtedly his secure grasp of this basal truth which enabled him to reconstruct the mediaeval faith after a strictly evangelical form. But the same emphasis also exposed Zwingli's schemes to its greatest difficulties, for like Calvin after him he found it necessary both to include the fall of man in the providential ordering of the universe and also to assert a rigid predestination both to life and perdition. The devices by which Zwingli tried to harmonize the direct divine causality with a purely human responsibility for sin can hardly be described as successful, and the rigorous doctrine of election necessarily

destroyed any real freedom of man even to choose his own
eternal destiny.

Yet in defence of Zwingli two things must be said. First, he
had a fine sense of the fact that God's providence must in some
way include all events within the sphere of its operation. In
the last analysis, if God is God, it is true enough that no man
can either sin or believe without God. The error of Zwingli
was perhaps that he asserted the direct or sole causality of
God, not that he asserted his supreme or over-ruling
causality. And second, Zwingli did not apply his doctrine with
the harshness which has marred so many doctrines of the
divine sovereignty. His Augustinian theology was tempered
always by his humanistic training and impulses. In this connection it is significant that Zwingli had no very pronounced
doctrine of original sin, or at any rate original guilt. And he
certainly did not restrict the electing grace of God to sacramental agencies. Indeed, his sense of the divine causality above
all things enabled him quite easily to discern the divine working
even in pagan thought and life.[11] The body of the elect as
Zwingli envisaged it was not a small and exclusive company
but a wide assemblage from every age and race and culture,
probably including all children who died in infancy.[12] The
very sovereignty which pre-supposes election involves also the
divine independence in respect of the divine operation of grace.
And the fact that the election is known only to God forbids
any anticipation or attempted restriction of it according to
external human standards.

It was very likely the same consciousness of the divine
operation in all things which enabled Zwingli to appropriate
the arguments of pagan philosophers in defence of his primary
assertions. Naturally, he could see clearly the limitations of
even the best of classical thought. He knew that Holy Scripture
alone can give that clear knowledge of God and his work
which cannot possibly be attained by reason. But Zwingli
also believed that that which is true in philosophy is eternally
true because it derives from the one Spirit of truth. He did not
regard all rational effort as so perverted by the fall that it
not only cannot reveal God but necessarily obscures him. In
the relation between Scripture and philosophy as he saw it,
Scripture plays so overwhelmingly the greater part that
philosophy is of little account by comparison. Yet what it can
and does tell us may serve as a useful introduction to the fuller

[11] *Ibid.*, p. 349.   [12] *Ibid.*, pp. 265–266.

knowledge imparted by the divine Word. It is, in fact, an important point of departure.

A valuable feature of Zwingli's teaching is that by his sharp repudiation of all forms of belief in a literal presence of Christ in the Supper he prepared the ground for a far more satisfying doctrine of the sacramental presence and efficacy. His contribution in this respect was largely negative: his denials were more prominent than his assertions. But the mediaeval insistence upon one extreme almost inevitably demanded a more persistent emphasis upon the other, and it was left to Zwingli's successors to draw out more fully the positive implications of his teaching. Zwingli did not deny either the true presence of Christ after his deity, or the possible conjunction of sign and thing signified by the sovereign working of the Spirit. What he did deny was a corporal presence of Christ after his humanity and a necessary conjunction of sign and thing signified by virtue of the valid administration of the rite. And it was necessary that these denials should be made if superstitious notions were to be cleared away and a more scriptural doctrine constructed.

A further valuable feature is the presentation of the doctrine of the atonement. The forms of expression were sometimes unfortunate, but Zwingli did retain a firm conception of the unity of the divine action. This emerges clearly at two decisive points: first, he derived both judgment and redemption from that single goodness of God which comprises both justice and mercy; and second, he related the incarnation of Christ, as well as his death and resurrection, to the accomplishment of man's salvation.[13] On the one side, as we have seen already, it is the same goodness of God which both demands and provides the sacrifice. And on the other, it is Christ's identification with man which enables him both to enter into our death and also to take us up into his own resurrection. In this way Zwingli not only avoids any false separation between the divine Persons or attributes, but he can also relate every aspect of Christ and his work to the one redemptive mission.

The theology of Zwingli was a magnificent first attempt to restate Christian doctrine in a consistent evangelical and scriptural form. By virtue of its bold and radical character it must always lay claim to admiration even where it cannot command assent. Yet as a first attempt it was almost necessarily provisional and incomplete. On the one hand, it gave rise to questions to which it did not return any very adequate answer.

13 Cf. Zwingli, *Hauptschriften* XI, pp. 311–313.

And on the other, it left undeveloped many insights and lines of thought along which essential constructive work was demanded. The truth is, of course, that Zwingli himself had neither the opportunity nor perhaps the temperament or talent to engage in the larger task of comprehensive systematic construction. In his theology as in his practical work it was given to Zwingli to prepare and initiate rather than to expand and complete. Taken by itself, Zwingli's theology must always leave the impression of disjointedness and disproportion, but in the light of what it became its permanent value and importance most certainly cannot be denied.

4. HEINRICH BULLINGER

The twofold tragedy of the defeat at Cappel and the death of Zwingli threatened immediate catastrophe to the evangelical cause in Zurich. The Church had been deprived of its outstanding ecclesiastical leader and theological spokesman. The Romanist opponents of Zurich took advantage of the situation to overturn the work of reform in the immediate environs of the city. All hopes of a future propagation of evangelical teaching in the Catholic cantons were decisively frustrated. And on every hand the military disaster at Cappel was being hailed as a divine judgment upon the heretical movement and its most prominent champion.

The hour of danger called for high qualities of steadfastness and moderation if collapse was to be averted, and it was fortunate for Zurich that a leader was available who had the very qualities demanded. When Heinrich Bullinger was appointed to the post of people's priest previously occupied by Zwingli, he could not bring to that office the same genius or far-reaching vision as his predecessor, but he could and did bring the talents which enabled him if not to extend at any rate to continue and consolidate the more local work which Zwingli had so brilliantly and effectively initiated.

Bullinger was born some twenty years later than Zwingli, on July 18, 1504. His father, also Heinrich Bullinger, was parish priest and dean of the small town of Bremgarten, about 10 miles west of Zurich. The young Heinrich was the fifth child of a clerical marriage which his father had contracted with one Anna Widerkehr, a marriage which was not regularized until 1529. From a very early period Bullinger displayed a marked aptitude for scholarship, and after learning his first letters at Bremgarten[14] he was sent away to Emmerich-on-Rhine for more advanced instruction, especially in Latin.[15] His father was not without means, but Bullinger records in his diary that he made him only the most meagre of allowances in order to teach him the virtues of moderation and sympathy with the poor and needy. If this was at all a common method of instruction it may perhaps shed some light upon the well-known episode from Luther's student-days. In this case, at any rate, the treatment was effective, for Bullinger was attracted for a while to the monastic life.[16]

From Emmerich Bullinger proceeded to Cologne where he took up the study of theology at the college of Bursa Montis. Already his mind seems to have been moving in the direction of reform, for after completing his preliminary course he pressed back through Lombard and Gratian to the earlier fathers, especially Chrysostom, Ambrose, Origen and Augustine. He also commenced a direct study of the New Testament itself, a book which he describes as completely unknown to the majority of his fellow students. Events at home perhaps contributed to this questioning of accepted thought and practice, for in 1519, the very year that he moved to Cologne, his father took the initiative in opposing the indulgence-monger, Samson. The witness of Luther also had its effect, for Bullinger read carefully the earlier tracts of Luther, and he also consulted the *Loci communes* of Melanchthon as soon as it appeared.[17]

Having graduated Bachelor of Arts in 1520 and Master in 1522, Bullinger returned temporarily to Bremgarten, where he continued his biblical and patristic studies. In the following year he received an invitation to give lectures to the monks and other students at the neighbouring Cistercian monastery of Cappel.[18] The abbot there, Wolfgang Joner, was a man who saw clearly the need for spiritual and doctrinal reform, and he made the way easy for Bullinger both by supporting him against opponents and also by accepting his services without laying any constraint upon him to take the monastic vows.

For the most part the next years were spent in regular reading and lecturing, with a little early writing, but in 1527 Bullinger was granted leave of absence to pay a visit of some months to

14 Cf. K. Pestalozzi, *Heinrich Bullinger*, p. 9.
15 He probably went to Emmerich because his brother John was also there. Cf. Blanke, *Der junge Bullinger*, p. 24.
16 *Ibid.*, pp. 26 f.   17 *Ibid.*, pp. 50–52.   18 *Diarium* 7.

Zurich, where he attended the lectures given by Zwingli and also took the opportunity to improve his knowledge of Greek and Hebrew. The visit was an important one, for it brought Bullinger into closer and more intimate contact with Zwingli and Leo Jud,[19] and it gave to him a better understanding and appreciation of Zwingli's eucharistic teaching. But Bullinger's obvious learning and ability must also have made their mark, for later in the year 1527 he was appointed to accompany Zwingli to the disputation which opened at Berne on January 7, 1528.

Eventually, in 1528, Bullinger was persuaded to undertake the office of pastor,[20] and he preached his first sermon at Hausen, near Cappel, on June 21. The following year his father publicly announced his adherence to the evangelical teaching. He was forced to resign his office, but at the request of the people of Bremgarten and the persuasions of Joner and his relatives Bullinger himself returned to the town as its first pastor according to the reformed pattern.[21] This year was also the year of his marriage with Anne Adlischweiler, a former nun of the Oetenbach convent, with whom he had become engaged during his visit to Zurich.

The two years which followed were busy years in which Bullinger helped towards the spread of the reformed teaching both by an extensive preaching ministry and also by his literary work. It was at this period that he began his long series of commentaries on the books of the New Testament. But the events of 1531 brought a sudden end to this Bremgarten ministry and made necessary an unexpected return to Zurich. The defeat at neighbouring Cappel, in which Joner too was killed, exposed Bremgarten to the enemies of the reforming movement, and since the Five Cantons refused to include Bullinger in the armistice proposals the people forced him to take refuge in Zurich.[22] Perhaps it is worth noting that Bullinger himself had openly opposed the aggressive policy which culminated in the catastrophe. Once in Zurich Bullinger quickly received invitations to more responsible pastoral work. The Senate of Basel approached him as a possible successor

[19] Bullinger had already made their acquaintance during a shorter visit at the end of 1523. *Diarium* 8.
[20] *Diarium* 12.
[21] So important was his work at this juncture that he declined an invitation to accompany Zwingli to the Colloquy of Marburg. *Diarium* 18.
[22] *Diarium* 20. Bullinger would only go when actually ordered to do so.

to Oecolampadius and Berne too was anxious to secure his services. However, the Council of Zurich had other plans, and it was the office of people's priest at Zurich which Bullinger eventually accepted.[23]

The task as Bullinger saw it in 1531 was threefold: to maintain the work which had already been begun in Zurich; to give to the people a clearer and fuller understanding of their new faith, more particularly upon the basis of Holy Scripture; and to tighten the bonds of fellowship which already existed between Zurich and other like-minded communions. At the fulfilment of this threefold task Bullinger laboured steadily and faithfully for the remaining years of his life. As compared with the crowded and eventful period of Zwingli's pastorate these were not spectacular years, for Bullinger had little to add to Zwingli's work in the way of either practical or indeed theological reforms. Nor had he the same ambitions of an immediate extension of the reformation first to the neighbouring cantons and ultimately to the whole of Europe. But for all that they were years of hard and not unproductive work: the almost daily ministration of the Word of God; the steady composition of treatises and defences and commentaries; [24] the conducting of a fair-sized correspondence; the entertainment of refugees, especially from England and Italy; [25] and the establishment of a common evangelical front with all churches which accepted the Reformed position. The outstanding episodes were almost all on the ecumenical side. In 1536 Bullinger took a prominent part in the conference which resulted in the First Helvetic Confession. An even more important step was the negotiation of the Consensus Tigurinus with Calvin and Farel in 1549. And by his hospitable treatment of many of the Marian exiles Bullinger was able to establish the most cordial relationships with the future leaders of the Elizabethan church. He also contributed largely to the defence of the distinctive Reformed teaching against the renewed attacks of Westphalus and Brentius. The closing years of Bullinger were clouded by the deaths of his wife and three daughters in successive outbreaks of the plague in 1564 and

23 Simler and Lavater in their biographies state that Bullinger had been nominated by Zwingli himself. See E. Egli, *Zwingliana*, 1904, 2, pp. 443–444, also Blanke, *op. cit.*, p. 152.
24 Bullinger himself collected the chief of these into ten volumes, but his complete works would be much larger.
25 Cf. Pilkington's description of Bullinger as "that common father of the afflicted," *Zurich Letters*, I, p. 135.

1565. Bullinger himself was severely ill during the second outbreak, and his health remained poor until the last and fatal
illness in the autumn of 1574–1575.

The comparative stability of Bullinger's long ministry is
perhaps the best testimony to its success. In marked contrast
to that of Zwingli, the ecclesiastical leadership of Bullinger
was a period of steady and peaceful development. Certainly,
the decisive changes prior to 1531 could never have been
attained without the dynamic inspiration of Zwingli. Yet the
Zurich of those years was being launched upon a career of
evangelical conquest for which the city had not the resources
nor Zwingli himself perhaps the necessary qualities of states-
manship. When the crash came with the Second War of Cappel,
Bullinger brought to the situation the less brilliant but steadying
qualities of moderation and conciliatoriness not unmixed with
unwavering conviction and a quiet and effective persistence.
The result was that church life in Zurich settled down again
to a steady routine, and the changes effected so rapidly in the
previous decade were able to establish themselves as the norm
of Christian faith and piety.

Under Bullinger Zurich did undoubtedly lose that wider
leadership of the Reformed cause which in some sense it had
held under Zwingli. The reason for this was twofold. On the
one hand, although Zurich was still revered and visited as an
early centre of the tradition, although Bullinger himself
maintained a high standard both of scholarship and also of
ministerial life, yet Zurich ceased to be in any way an outstanding centre as compared with other cities like Berne or Basel.
And on the other hand, the rise of Calvin, and the growing
impact both of his theology and his practical work, contributed
inevitably to a shifting of attention away from the older communion in German-speaking Switzerland to its counterpart
in the French-speaking part of the country. Calvin's ministry
at Geneva was roughly contemporary with that of Bullinger
at Zurich, although some years shorter. And at the end of that
ministry it was primarily to Geneva and not to Zurich that the
more active propagators of the Reformed tradition made their
appeal. Bullinger succeeded Zwingli in the local leadership
at Zurich, but it was Calvin who succeeded him in the ever-
widening leadership of the Reformed fellowship of churches.

But to say that is again to emphasize the value of the peculiar
contribution which Bullinger made. For it was Bullinger who
by his charitable and conciliatory spirit enabled the transition

to be made without controversy or bitterness. Not only did he prepare the way by the creation of a common confessional bond between the earlier communions, but when the time came he did not hesitate to take that decisive step which meant a recognition of basic kinship with Geneva, and the emergence of Calvin as a virtual leader of the whole evangelical cause. We must not exaggerate, of course, for at the time it could hardly be recognized how decisive was the change in initiative which was taking place, or how far-reaching its consequences. Yet had Zwingli himself lived, it is difficult to believe that unity between Zurich and Geneva would have been achieved or maintained so peacefully, or the advantages of it exploited so swiftly and profitably. From the wider standpoint of ecclesiastical history in general, Bullinger's acceptance of that agreement may not inaccurately be described as the most momentous and indeed the culminating act of his career.

To a large extent the writings of Bullinger reveal the same qualities as those which marked his public ministry. The writings extend over the whole period from 1526 to his death in 1575. Amongst the most interesting we may note the following: the commentaries on the various books of the New Testament; the doctrinal treatises on the Eucharist, the primitive faith, the authority and certainty of Scripture, matrimony and the sacraments; the sermons on the true Christian sacrifice, the Lord's Supper and the Last Judgment: the five books of the *Decades*, which are series of sermons on the main points of Christian doctrine; the controversial works against the Anabaptists and Lutherans; and the history of the Reformation, which was completed but never published in Bullinger's lifetime. Nowhere in these extensive writings do we find any great originality of thought, or in fact the desire for it. But everywhere we see clear evidence of a judicious and scholarly mind which is able to give lucid and balanced expression to doctrines already commonly received and taught.

Superficially, the doctrinal discussions of Bullinger are more impressive than those of Zwingli. For one thing they are much better arranged, and the thought moves with a logic which is lacking in the more hurried compositions of Zwingli. Again, with the better arrangement there is also a fuller and more proportionate discussion. Where Zwingli had seized upon this or that point, Bullinger looks upon the whole, and he is able to treat of his theme not merely as controversial needs demand, but comprehensively and in all its various aspects. Again,

Bullinger brings to bear perhaps a greater weight of scholarship, for not only was he well-versed in the Fathers (the same could be said of Zwingli), but he was able to deploy his resources with more telling effect. Indeed, Bullinger's arguments as a whole present a much more solid appearance than the acute but not always convincing reasonings of Zwingli.

Yet when all that is said, the works of Bullinger are undoubtedly pedestrian as compared with the bold but hasty flights of his predecessor. They lack that freshness, that vitality of thought and expression which means genius and not mere scholarship. They reflect everywhere the able defender and expositor of an existing teaching, but not the original and creative thinker who initiates or wins through to that teaching. In a sense they are more closely akin to the writings of Calvin than to those of Zwingli, for they have the qualities of order and precision and high scholarship which are so conspicuous in the *Commentaries* and *Institutes*. But here again, they lack that impress of a masterful and constructive spirit which made Calvin and not Bullinger the true successor of Zwingli no less in the sphere of theology than in that of ecclesiastical organization. For a clear and effective but in no way outstanding statement of the evangelical position we can hardly do better than turn to Bullinger. But for a challenging and vital reconstruction of the Christian faith it is to Zwingli and Calvin that we must look as the true representatives of the Reformed tradition.

ZWINGLI

Of the Clarity and Certainty
of the Word of God

INTRODUCTION

AT ZURICH, AS AT WITTENBERG, THE READING AND proclamation of the Word formed the main weapon in the dissemination of Reformed teaching and the purification of the Church. And it was realized that the work of reform would be done more smoothly and effectively if scriptural truth could be introduced into the monastic houses, which were the natural centres of religious life under the old regime. It was in the pursuance of this end that in the summer of 1522 Zwingli succeeded in gaining access to the Oetenbach convent, and characteristically he took as his two themes the Word of God and the Virgin Mary.

For the details concerning this venture we are indebted to the two prefaces to successive edition of the sermon on the Word in 1522 and 1524.[1] The convent of the Oetenbach was an old-established house of Dominican nuns. It was a place of considerable wealth and influence, for all its members came from amongst the best families of Zurich, and even at the time of the Reformation it numbered some sixty professed nuns and twelve lay-sisters.[2] For over two hundred years the spiritual direction of the convent had been in the hands of the Dominicans of the Predigerkloster. The Dominicans were from the first opposed to religious change, and they took all possible steps to prevent the nuns from coming into contact with the evangelical teaching. Zwingli, however, worked through the City Council to open up the convent to the Reformed preachers, and in 1522 a decree was passed which forced the hands of the Dominican directors. According to this order the nuns were to accept the ministrations of a secular priest, and Zwingli himself

[1] C.R., I, pp. 338–341. [2] *Ibid.*, p. 328.

was appointed to undertake the work of instruction.[3] The Dominicans did succeed in persuading some of the nuns to avoid Zwingli's teaching, and later to remain true to their vocation, but in order that their effect might not be lost Zwingli proceeded to publish the sermons in a revised and expanded form.

It is of interest to note that although no evidence of this incident has been preserved apart from what Zwingli himself tells us in the prefaces—even the decree of the Council has not survived—the struggle for the Oetenbach was a result or even a part of that wider battle which Zwingli was now fighting against the friars in general.[4] The battle was joined in July, 1522, when two disputations were held in Zurich, the first on the 16th on the adoration of Mary and the Saints, and the second on the 21st on the wider topic of the authority of Holy Scripture. It is significant that these were the two topics upon which Zwingli preached to the nuns of Oetenbach. In the first disputation Zwingli was opposed by the visiting Franciscan, Francis Lambert of Avignon,[5] in the second by the lectors and preachers of the city orders, especially the Dominicans and Augustinians. As was customary, the disputations were held before the temporal as well as the spiritual authorities. They ended in a decisive victory for the Reformed party, and the Burgomaster gave judgment for the preaching of the Gospels, Epistles and Prophets rather than Thomas, Scotus and other schoolmen.[6]

The official sentence did not end the controversy, for although the Dominican lector left Zurich, the monks as a whole were prepared to disregard the judgment. Their obstinacy was expressed in the determined exclusion of evangelical preaching from the Oetenbach convent. But this opposition led at once to forceful action on the part of the Council, and it contributed ultimately to the complete dissolution of the monastic orders. As one of the first steps the Council passed the decree ordering the convent of Oetenbach to receive a non-regular minister. The exact date of this decree is not known, but it must have been late in July or early in August,

[3] Ibid., p. 338.
[4] On this conflict see Bernhard Wyss, Die Chronik, 1519–1530, pp. 13–20, also Bullinger, R.G., I, pp. 76–78.
[5] Cf. D.C.R. 180. Lambert confessed himself won over, and later worked for the Reformation in Hesse, being Professor of Theology at Marburg 1527–1530. (See Jackson, op. cit., p. 171 n.1.)
[6] C.R., I, p. 257.

for in his *Archeteles*, which appeared on August 23, Zwingli made a reference to the printed form of the sermon on the Word.[7] The sermon itself was published on September 6, so that it was probably in the press when the *Archeteles* came out. As a result of Zwingli's preaching quite a few of the nuns seem to have accepted the Reformed view, some of them desiring a secular as spiritual director, and others being prepared to leave the convent altogether.[8] But there was still a strong and resolute party which clung to the old faith.[9] On March 7, 1523, the Council ousted the Dominicans and appointed Leo Jud pastor of the convent,[10] and the house was eventually dissolved at the end of 1524.

Two other historical points may be briefly noted. The year 1522 was especially critical for Zwingli, for apart from the opposition of the friars he was the subject of complaints in the document *Articuli frivole dicti a Zwinglio*.[11] This statement accuses Zwingli of contempt for the schoolmen, attacks on the monastic orders and disrespect of the Saints. It is undated, but there is little doubt that it belongs to the summer of 1522, and it shows something of the struggle which preceded the decisive victory of that year. But in securing the verdict in favour of evangelical preaching Zwingli could apparently appeal to a prior decision of 1520 which had sanctioned preaching according to the Word of God.[12] The contents of this decree are known only from Bullinger's accounts,[13] but its existence is officially attested in an *Answer* to the Confederates dated March 21, 1524.[14]

The sermon itself is a clear and forcible statement of the all-important doctrine of the Word of God in two of its principal aspects, its power and its perspicuity. But before he takes up the two main points, Zwingli devotes a very interesting introductory section to what he evidently regards as the essential foundation of his teaching on Scripture, the concept of the *imago dei*. He takes as his starting-point the text in Gen. 1:25, drawing attention in passing to the implicit Trinitarian reference. In the light of this verse he first discusses the nature of the divine image, pointing out that it necessarily relates to the spiritual and not the physical part of man's nature. With Augustine, he allows that we may discern the image in the

[7] *Ibid.*, p. 312.   [8] D.C.R. 184.   [9] C.R., I, p. 340–341.
[10] Egli, A.S., 346, 348, 366.   [11] Egli, *Analecta*, III.
[12] D.C.R. 166.   [13] Bullinger, R.G., I, p. 32, 38.
[14] *Amtliche Sammlung der älteren Eidgenössischen Abschiede*, IV, p. 399 f.

properties of mind, will and memory, but after a short discussion he concludes that the *imago* is most clearly revealed in the universal longing for blessedness and the natural thirst for the revelation or Word of God. The true life of man does not consist in his formation of the dust of the earth but in the inbreathing of the Spirit, which means that man is created for an eternal destiny. And in spite of the hindrances of earthly and sinful desires, in the redemptive power of Christ man can still attain again to the reality of the divine likeness (the new man in Christ Jesus), and experience the power and enlightenment of the Word of God which is the answer to his innermost longing.

The dissertation on the *imago dei* is not strictly relevant to Zwingli's main theme, but it has an importance of its own, and it gives to the whole sermon an added interest and force. Two points call for more specific notice. First, Zwingli apparently does not envisage any general obliteration of the divine image as a result of the fall. True, the fall affects and to some extent obscures the image, and in some cases, where worldly interests have come to dominate the whole life of a man, the desire for the Word of God and the longing for eternity are completely submerged. But deep in the heart of every man the *imago dei* is there, ready to be raised up to new life by the regenerative power of the Holy Spirit, and manifesting itself already in the religious aspirations and attainments of the race. As Zwingli understands it, the Christian regeneration is not a completely new creation. It is a re-creation after the likeness of Christ of that spiritual nature which at the very first was created in the divine image and similitude.

Yet with all his insistence upon the persistence of the *imago* Zwingli guards himself against incipient Pelagian deductions. The fact that man enjoys the divine likeness does not enable him to achieve righteousness in his own strength. There are two reasons for this. First, apart from the redemptive work of Christ the *imago* is always obscured to some extent by the sinful desires of the flesh. And second, the image is the image of God, and therefore it is seen fully when we reflect not our own righteousness but the righteousness of God. Certainly, Zwingli avoids that severe doctrine of a complete forfeiture of the *imago* which some modern writers seem to regard as the necessary corollary of the Reformed doctrine of grace. His less rigorous understanding of original sin, or at any rate original guilt, may be recalled in the same connection. But at the same time Zwingli has no intention of opening the way to a purely humanistic understanding of man's nature and destiny.

Indeed, the discussion of the *imago* is designed simply to lead up to and to prove Zwingli's main point. And the main point is this, that there is in all men a secret longing for the Word of God, and that where the regenerative work of the Spirit is done, it will express itself naturally and necessarily in an open and intensified desire for the divine Word. There is a very good reason why that should be the case, for it is only in the Word of God that the divine nature in man can find its true life and nourishment and consolation. The Word of God inevitably meets that part of man which seeks eternal life and blessedness because it is a word of power and a word of enlightenment; it gives life and light. And it is of these two characteristics of the Word, its certainty and clarity, that Zwingli proceeds to speak.

By the certainty or power of the Word Zwingli means its capacity to bring to pass the things which it declares or signifies. Of that capacity he finds plain confirmation in many parts of Scripture. It appears at the very outset in the divine Word by which God created the heavens and the earth. God had simply to say the words, "Let there be light," and at once light sprang forth out of darkness. It appears again in the New Testament in the redemptive activity of Christ. The sick and the maimed and the devil-possessed and even the dead were brought to Christ, and he had only to utter the command, "Be ye healed," or "Depart," or "Come forth," and the miracle of restoration was accomplished. From these clear and convincing examples Zwingli deduces that all God's sayings or promises must inevitably be fulfilled at the appropriate time. Where God himself speaks, the whole of creation must give place. It is for us then to open our hearts to the redemptive power of the Word, so that we are not overtaken by its no less certain judgments.

By the clarity of the Word Zwingli does not mean so much the lucidity of that which is spoken or written (although like all the Reformers he did regard the divine message as essentially plain and straightforward), but the power of the Word to bring with it its own inward enlightenment and assurance in spite of all appearances to the contrary. To make his meaning clear and to confirm the truth of his teaching Zwingli gives several illustrations and texts from the Old and New Testaments. He instances the case of Noah, who received a message which his contemporaries might well have understood just as he himself did. But because they did not receive it in humility and faith, they did not perceive its truth, they were not granted the insight into the divine purposes which turned to the salvation of Noah. Noah received the Word humbly and in faith, and the Word brought with it its own enlightenment and conviction even though there was no external guarantee of its authenticity. Other instances which might be cited are those of Abraham and Moses, and the truth illustrated in the Old Testament is stated in such New Testament passages as John 3:27 and 6:44 and I Cor. 2:12, which make it plain that inward faith and understanding are not the product of human intelligence or scholarship but of the Spirit of God working directly through the Word itself. Zwingli's conclusion is that we must all open our hearts and minds to the Word, for in so doing we shall fulfil our true destiny as the sons of God and experience the power and the enlightenment which are proper only to the Word.

A noteworthy feature of the sermon is that Zwingli does not offer any precise definition of the Word of God, nor does he make any attempt to differentiate between the Word spoken and the Word written, or to fix the relationship between the two. In the section on the certainty of the Word it is noticeable that the examples quoted by Zwingli are illustrations of the power of the spoken word rather than the written word. The commands of God at creation and the redemptive utterances of Christ were primarily words spoken by the tongue rather than words inscribed in a record. There is no doubt, of course, that Zwingli does equate the record of Scripture with that direct and living utterance, but he does not show how or why that identification is to be made, and he clearly does not believe that the Bible exhausts the whole significance of the concept. Indeed, the impression is distinctly left that the power and effectiveness of the record depends upon that divine operation by which the external letter becomes the living spiritual message of God himself. In one sense it is perhaps a weakness in the discussion that Zwingli does not indicate how the transition may be made from the Word as utterance to the Word as record. But in another sense it is a gain, for it means that Zwingli is preserved from that static and theoretical conception of the Bible which is the evangelical counterpart of *ex opere operato* views of the sacraments. By refusing to make an exact equation of the Word and the Bible Zwingli holds fast to the truth that the Word in its full and true sense is living speech. The Word is mediated through written documents, but it has its character and effectiveness as Word only in so far as it is directed and applied by the Holy Spirit.

A second point which calls for emphasis is that the the clarity envisaged by Zwingli is something far more than an ordinary lucidity of thought and expression. Naturally, Zwingli had no wish to deny that the essential message of the Bible is within the grasp of any ordinary rational intelligence. For that reason the lay Christian may understand the Bible just as well as the learned exegete or theologian, although, of course, the work of the scholar is useful and necessary in order to elucidate more difficult passages and to fix the precise meaning of individual words or sentences. But because the Bible is essentially straightforward in its teaching, it does not at all follow that everyone will receive or comprehend it. To do that there is need of an inward illumination as well as the light of rational understanding. The truth of God must be perceived as well as seen. It must be comprehended as well as understood. And the clarity of which Zwingli speaks is the enlightenment which makes possible such inward comprehension or perception. It is the illumination which comes when the Holy Spirit applies the message to the penitent and faithful recipient.

In this respect Zwingli has a fine apprehension of that twofoldness of the Word of God which is obscured, or at any rate misunderstood, when the truth of the Bible is thought of in terms of abstract proposition rather than dynamic truth. He sees that the Word is a Word of life and light, but he sees too that the Word does not automatically give light and life to all who read and understand. It does so only where a true response is kindled. In other words, it calls for a decision of faith. And where there is that decision, as in the case of Noah or Abraham, there can be no doubt as to the inward meaning or truth of the Word. It carries with it its own enlightenment and assurance. But where there is no such decision, even if the Word is outwardly understood, it is not inwardly perceived, and that which is light and life to the believer is to the unbeliever darkness and destruction.

The appeal to the Word of God made by the Reformers was not merely an appeal to the outward text of the Bible correctly interpreted and understood. And the importance attached to the Word was not merely due to the desire to replace one external authority by another. The appeal of the Reformers was to a living and effective Word which verifies itself inwardly to all those who are prepared to hear it in penitence and faith. And that Word is authoritative not because its authority can be outwardly demonstrated but because it is inwardly apprehended. The Word is in fact the means by which God makes known his redemptive will and summons his hearers to decision. The clarity of the Word is the self-illumination and self-attestation by which the inward meaning and truth of the Word are guaranteed to those who accept it in faith.

A further point is that this conception of the clarity of the Word gave to Zwingli an assured knowledge of biblical truth which he could nowhere find in the confusion of academic theological discussion. All the Reformers had to face an acute problem of certainty in their presentation of truth. How could they know that their interpretation was the right one when the greatest scholars differed amongst themselves, and the majority of theologians past and present were arrayed decisively against them? In tackling this problem they saw that it was not enough to appeal simply to the external text of Scripture, for plain though the text might be, it could be interpreted and applied in many different ways. True, the Reformers did insist, and quite rightly from their own standpoint, that a true and straightforward exegesis would support their own particular interpretation. But they were keenly aware, first, that they could not base the correctness of their understanding upon the superiority of their scholarship, and second, that to attain to a true interpretation of the text there is need of something more than an ordinary linguistic equipment or exegetical acumen. The certainty which they enjoyed rested ultimately upon the immediacy of inward understanding, the internal testimony of the Spirit. And it was because Zwingli was conscious of this inward and spiritual enlightenment that he could point scornfully to the confusion which results when certainty is looked for in some external and merely human authority. The Papacy, the Fathers, the Friars: all these make claims to give certainty in spiritual knowledge and understanding. But Zwingli claims nothing for himself. The certainty to which he points does not derive from an alleged superiority of either intellectual endowment or religious attainment. He has a sure and inflexible knowledge of the truth, not merely because he understands the plain statements of Scripture, but because the Holy Spirit has given him an inward apprehension of the divine teaching which Scripture proclaims. And he argues that everyone who approaches the Bible in prayer and in faith must inevitably come to the same general apprehension of its truth as he himself enjoys.

As we have already seen, the nature of Zwingli's teaching upon the clarity of the Word makes it plain that he was not advocating an abstract biblicism such as that evolved in later Protestant orthodoxy. But we must not exaggerate. Zwingli had no reason to deny the particular inspiration of the written Word, and he saw no specific need to lay any pronounced emphasis upon it. Certainly, there is no evidence in the sermon that he favoured that decisive separation between form and content which some modern theologians have proclaimed as the true Reformed insight. Yet Zwingli does see clearly that the Word is more than the external letter of Scripture, and that it has its effect and carries with it inward conviction only in so far as the Holy Spirit applies it as the living Word. The sermon is in fact a plea for a dynamic conception of the Word and its operation. Naturally, the Word is expressed in the external forms of speech and writing. But its power and authority do not lie in the external expression. The speech and writing have necessarily a rational meaning, but the true significance is perceived and known only where it is brought home to the individual by divine power. There is power and clarity in the Word, but it is the power and clarity of the creative activity of God the Holy Spirit and not of some static relationship between the text of the Word and its true meaning and operation. And that means that in the last resort the Word is present in fulness only where it is the living and miraculous utterance of God himself.

Surveying the sermon as a whole, we must allow that it suffers from the faults which mar almost all Zwingli's writings. It is tendentious in purpose, and its formlessness betrays the customary overhastiness of composition. The scriptural examples are unnecessarily numerous, and there is too much exegesis of passages which are not directly related to the main theme. Yet in spite of these obvious defects there is a fine power and freedom in the statement, and the vitality of the thought and the originality and freshness of the treatment combine to make it one of the more impressive and important of the earlier theological writings. In style it belongs unmistakably to Zwingli's own age, but in thought it has a relevance which marks it as a work of more permanent value.

Editions

The sermon was first published on September 6, 1522, in Zurich. The name of the printer was not given, but it was undoubtedly the work of Christopher Froschauer. This first edition was careful and accurate. Another edition came out probably in the same year, and most likely in Augsburg, but it did not carry either the printer's name or the date or place of publication. For the most part it followed the first edition, but it corrected a few errors, introduced some new ones, and replaced many dialect forms by those more commonly used in the German-speaking world. Christopher Froschauer issued a new edition in 1524, this time giving his name. The edition was substantially the same as that of 1522, but a new and longer preface was introduced, leading to some rearrangement of the type, and a few errors were also corrected. A further edition by Froschauer was almost exactly identical with that of 1524.[15]

Translations

The sermon was translated into Latin by Gwalter under the title *De certitudine et claritate verbi dei liber* (G).[16] Christoffel gave a rendering in modern German in his *Zeitgemässige Auswahl*, I (Zurich, 1843). An early translation into English was that of John Veron, who published it under the rather misleading title, *A Short Pathway to the Right and True Understanding of the Holy and Sacred Scriptures* (Worcester, 1550).

The present translation is based on the original edition as reproduced in the *Corpus Reformatorum* (Zwingli, Volume I).

[15] For full details of these editions, with title-pages, see C.R., I, pp. 332–337.
[16] Opp. Zw., Tom I, fol. 160b–175a. It will be noted that Gwalter puts *certitudine* before *claritate*, thus bringing the order of the title into line with that of the treatment.

Of the Clarity and Certainty
or Power of the Word of God (1)

THE TEXT

When in the beginning of creation Almighty God purposed to create the wonderful creature man he deliberated[1] with himself as follows: "Let us make man in our image and likeness; let him have dominion over the fish of the sea, the fowl of the air, the cattle and all the earth, and everything that creepeth upon the earth! And God created man in his own image, in the image of God created he him" (Gen. 1). In this passage we see from the words "let us" that God is speaking of more than one person, although he is still speaking of himself. For if he had been speaking of only one person he would have said, "I will make." But when he says, "Let us make" he is undoubtedly speaking of the three Persons who are one God. This is revealed specifically by the next words, which are "after our likeness," and immediately afterwards "in the image of God," for he does not say "after our likenesses," which would have suggested a plurality of essences or gods. However, it is not our present task to speak of the unity of the one God and the trinity of Persons,(2) for we have before us another subject, namely that which follows in the self-deliberation of God, that man is created in the divine image and after the divine likeness. At this point we must enquire with what part of our nature we are made in the divine image, with the body or the soul. Now if we are made in the divine image in respect of the body, then that means that God has a body composed of different members and that our body is a copy of his. But if we grant that, then it follows that God is a being which has been constituted and may finally be dissolved.[2] But this is a negation of the constancy of the divine essence, and it is therefore non-Christian, heretical

[1] *erwag er sich, deliberare* (G).　　　[2] *entfügt (auseinandergenommen)*.

59

and blasphemous. For in John 1 it says: "No man hath seen God". But if no one has ever seen God, how can we say that he is formed in any particular way, as did the heretic Melitus and the Anthropomorphites,(3) who rashly[3] presumed to say that God has human form. These men were no doubt led astray by the fact that eyes, ears, a mouth, a face, hands and feet are all ascribed to God in Scripture. But in Scripture these members are used simply to indicate the works of God, which we understand most clearly when we speak of them in the form in which they appear amongst men. We see with our eyes, therefore Scripture ascribes eyes to God when it wishes to indicate his perfect knowledge and perception of all things. It ascribes ears to God because in his omnipresence he hears and takes knowledge of all our prayers or blasphemies or secret counsels. And a mouth, because he reveals his will by his Word. And a face, to signify the bestowal and withdrawal of his graces. And hands to signify his omnipotence, and feet the speed and swiftness with which he overtakes the wicked. To prove this from Scripture would take too long, as it is beside our present purpose. But it was because he did not understand this biblical usage that Melitus fell into the error of making God in the image of man, which is a heresy, for in Deuteronomy 4 Moses says to the children of Israel that God did not show them his face lest they should express or represent him after the similitude of any figure, the likeness of male or female or any creature, lest they should set up his image and similitude and worship it, which is idolatry. And Christ himself says in John 5: "Ye have not . . . seen his shape." We are not thinking here of the humanity of Jesus Christ, for he took to himself all the nature and frailty of man apart from the defect of sin.[4] But the human nature of Christ was a form of humanity and not of deity, and he did not have it from all eternity, but took it upon himself late in time when he was conceived and born of the pure virgin, Mary.(4)

It remains then that it is in respect of the mind or soul that we are made in the image of God. The exact form of that likeness it is not for us to know except that the soul is the substance upon which that likeness is particularly stamped. The opinion of Augustine (5) and the early doctors is that the three faculties of intellect, will and memory,[5] which are distinct and yet constitute the one soul, are a similitude of the one God in

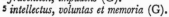

[3] frävenlich, impudens (G).   [4] den prästen der sünde, i.e., original sin.
[5] intellectus, voluntas et memoria (G).

respect of the existence and the trinity of the Persons. This I do not dispute, so long as we are not led astray by the three faculties and imagine that in God as in us there is a conflict of will. For we must remember that in God there is no duality or contradiction as there is in us; for the desire of the flesh which we also call our will strives against the will of the mind and spirit, as St. Paul teaches in Romans 7. Now we have never seen God as he is in himself. Therefore we can never know in what respect our soul is like him in its substance and essence. For the soul does not even know itself in its substance and essence. And in the last analysis we can only conclude that the activities and faculties of the soul, will, intellect and memory, are merely the signs of that essential likeness which we shall never see until we see God as he is in himself, and ourselves in him: I Cor. 13 "For now we see through a glass, darkly; but then face to face: now I know in part, but then shall I know even as also I am known"; I John 3 "We know that, when he shall appear, we shall be like him; for we shall see him as he is." Let everyone ponder well this saying of John. I know, of course, that in the symbol *Quicunque* Athanasius says that as the reasonable soul and flesh are one man, so God and man are one Christ.(6) But this is only a similitude and not the express image. We are here speaking of God at a time when he had not assumed human nature and yet formed man in his own likeness. Therefore it is right to conclude that man is not in the divine image in respect of the body, for it was only later that God assumed bodily form, but in respect of the soul.

Now there are many ways in which we experience the divine likeness within us more specifically than we do with the three faculties, intellect, will and memory. I do not reject the opinion of Augustine, but I think that there are many things which give us an awareness of the divine likeness apart from those which Augustine singled out as the chief. There is in particular that looking to God and to the words of God which is a sure sign of the divine relationship,[6] image and similitude within us.(7) We will explain this first by means of an illustration and then from Scripture. When we compare man with plants and trees, we find that the plants do not pay any heed to man or his words. This is because they are so far removed from man's nature that there is no relationship, communion or fellowship between them. But the irrational brutes do take note of man, however slightly, for they are much closer to man's nature in

[6] *früntschafft, cognatio* (G).

respect of their physical structure and life. So too it is in the case of man, for he has this in common with God, not merely that he is rational, but that he looks to God and to the words of God, thus signifying that by nature he is more closely related, more nearly akin to God, far more like God,[7] all of which undoubtedly derives from the fact that he is created in the divine image. St. Paul testifies to the truth of this in Acts 17: "We are his offspring," and again in the very next verse: "Forasmuch then as we are his offspring, etc." And the Spirit of God gives direct witness in Psalm 81 (A.V. 82), saying: "I have said, Ye are gods; and all of you are children of the most High." And in Isaiah 19: "My inheritance is Israel." We Christians are the true Israelites, his inheritance. And there are many other sayings to the same effect in the Psalms and the Prophets. Now if we are his inheritance, it is necessarily by descent. Additional testimonies are given by Christ and Paul and Peter, who all recognize clearly that we are the sons of God, but we will keep these until later. The three quoted, with the saying of God mentioned at the outset, will be quite sufficient to show us that the thirst after God which is a universal experience is native to us, inasmuch as we are all created in the divine image and partake of the divine nature and kindred, as it is written in Psalm 4: "Lord, the light of thy countenance is lifted up upon us." It is for this reason that we thirst after God and believe his word above all things. For everywhere we find the universal desire for eternal blessedness after this present distress, a desire which would never have concerned us, any more than it does the beasts or plants, had it not been native to us. The fact that there are writings, the utterances of Sardanapoli and Neros and Heliogabali (8) and suchlike filthy creatures,[8] in which there is neither the desire for eternal bliss nor the belief that there is a blessedness after this present life does not affect the argument. For if they do not see the need of eternal blessedness, at least they have the fear of eternal loss. For every human spirit looks forward to eternal joy and fears eternal loss, desiring like all else to return to its first beginning, as Solomon shows in Ecclesiastes 1: "The spirit or wind whirleth about continually and searcheth out all things and returneth again according to his circuits. All the rivers run into the sea; yet the sea is not full; and the rivers return again unto the place whence they come." If therefore there are those who

7 etwas zůzůgs zů im hat, i.e., mehr Ähnlichkeit mit ihm hat.
8 süw, lit. swine.

do not labour for blessedness, it is the result of despair and of the depths of the flesh and of bestial lusts into which they are sunk, so that they have no knowledge of themselves (Isaiah 51). For the carnal man is not capable of the things which are of the Spirit (I Cor. 2). And Judas—not the traitor, but the pious Judas surnamed Lebbaeus (9)—foresaw the coming of mockers in the last time, who should walk after their own lusts[9] and godlessness, and separate themselves, being sensual and having not the Spirit. And by their deeds we see clearly that they have at least the fear of damnation even if they have no hope of felicity, for they rage furiously and live shamelessly and desire inordinately and persecute arrogantly and seize and grasp everything that they can plunder or steal or gain or lay hands upon, and all these things are tokens of their godlessness and despair, or they have damnation in their hearts even though—like their father the devil—they are harsh towards all men and refuse the joy and consolation of salvation and despise every warning which might turn them from error and bring them to eternal comfort, as Solomon shows in Proverbs 18: "When the wicked cometh into the depth of sins, then cometh contempt—that is, of God and of every creature—but ignominy and reproach follow him." For if they will not retain God in their knowledge (Rom. 1), or nourish their hungry soul with a sweet hope in God, God the righteous Judge will undoubtedly fill their hearts with the foreboding, fear and anguish of eternal torment, so that not having the desire to enter now upon eternal life in quiet expectation, they begin to experience already that eternal perdition which in the world to come they will fulfil eternally. So then, though they have no concern for eternal blessedness, they have a concern about eternal loss. And for our present purpose it is enough that they do experience within themselves some concern for eternity, whether it be eternal torment or eternal felicity.

We are taught then that the desire for salvation is present within us by nature, not the nature of the flesh and its lusts, but the likeness which God the masterworkman has impressed upon us. For truly, that spirit of life which God blew or breathed into Adam's nostrils is no vain or powerless breath like the breath of man. In Genesis 2 it says: "And the Lord God formed man of the clay or dust[10] of the ground, and breathed

---

9 anfechtungen—a favourite word of Zwingli, signifying sinful desires or temptations.
10 uss dem lätt (lehm) oder stoub. . . .

into his nostrils the breath or the air of life." This breath of life which the eternal God breathed into Adam undoubtedly imparted and implanted within him the longing not for a material but for an eternal life, so that he has always a yearning for that which first gave him life and breath. For as Psalm 32 (A.V. 33) says, "all the host of heaven was made by the breath of his mouth." Much more did the inbreathing of that lifegiving breath inspire in Adam an imperishable longing for life. And when the word breath or air or wind is used, we must understand always the Spirit of God. For in Scripture the Spirit is called a breath, etc. For as we live physically by the inbreathing of air, so the Spirit of God is that true life in which all things live and from which they derive their life. For the Latin word *spiraculum*, in English "breath", is the equivalent of the Greek *pnoe*, in English "blast" or "air" or "wind." And in Genesis 2 the next words are: "And man became a living soul."(10) Which plainly show that man is created for eternal life, for if he died body and soul like the beasts it would not have been necessary to add the words "a living soul": for earlier, in the account of the creation of the beasts, it does not say: they became a living soul. Nor does it say that God gave them life with the breath of his lips. Nor does it say that God took the earth and formed the beasts out of it, as it does in the account of man's creation—in the Septuagint *choun labon tes ges*. What it does say is this: "And God said, Let the earth bring forth the living creature after his kind, cattle,[11] and creeping thing, and beast of the earth after his kind: and it was so." And first, we see here that God commanded the earth to bring forth the beasts. But in the creation of man he himself takes the earth and forms it into a man. Again, when he says "the living creature after his kind" he makes it clear that the soul of creature is its life, but only according to its kind or nature, which is transitory and perishable. Finally, he does not say of the beasts that they are made a living soul. But he does say that of man. And he does not add any weakening or qualifying clause[12] like "after his kind," which would be equivalent to saying: Man is made a living soul, but only according to his nature, just as the beasts are living according to their nature. No: without any addition he says "a living soul." We see then at once that by creation man belongs to that order of creatures whose nature it is to live essentially and physically and never to perish. But all our dili-

[11] *arbeitsame* (beasts of burden).
[12] *luter und alles mindern hindan gesetzt, sine omni diminutione aut exceptione* (G).

gent weighing of the Scriptures would be useless if we could
not sustain our interpretation of the divine likeness within us
by authentic Scriptures: that is, that inasmuch as we are made
in the divine image we have a particular longing after God.

In Colossians 3 Paul writes: "Lie not one to another. Put off
the old man with his deeds and put on the new, which is renewed in knowledge after the image of him that created him."
The old man is that which partakes of the weakness of the
nature of Adam and allows itself to be seduced and overcome
by temptations because of the power of the flesh. What the
new man is we learn from Paul's own words: it is that which is
freed from the inordinate desires of the flesh and increases more
and more in the knowledge of God, bringing out and clarifying
and making brighter the image of the creator, according to the
full meaning of the Greek. And on the basis of the fact that he
is the image of God this new man studies more and more to
come to knowledge—the knowledge of him that created him
and impressed this image upon him—in order that he may
be made new. For the old man obscures and darkens the new,
which is not called the new beause it is created later in time,
but because it is always fresh, because it is not defiled by the
shameful weaknesses[13] of the flesh, and because it is ordained
to possess eternity, in which there is neither age nor sin.(11)
Paul brings out the same point in Ephesians 4: "Put off concerning the former conversation the old man, which is corrupt
according to the deceitful lusts. Be renewed in the spirit of your
mind, and put on the new man, which after God is created in
righteousness and the holiness of truth.[14] Wherefore putting
away deceit or falsehood, speak every man truth with his
neighbour, for we are members one of another." Note that the
man who is created after God is called a new man because he
studies righteousness and truth, which can never age, for God
himself is righteousness and truth.

These passages will be sufficient, we feel, to prove our point,
that we are made in the image of God and that that image is
implanted within us in order that it may enjoy the closest
possible relationship with its maker and creator; and if it were
not that the old man, that which not merely ages but decays and
perishes, is so powerful in his assaults and temptations, the new
or inner man would seek more fully after God and live a more
godly life. But as it is, there are times when it can hardly give
us the power even to long or strive after him in whose image

13 *prästen.*   14 *heylige der warheit.*

we are created. And we have that power most of all when the body is weakest, as St. Paul says in II Corinthians 12: "When I am weak, then I am strong." It is when he is sick in the body that he is strong in the soul, which equips itself to follow after God by nature of the divine image, although it is never able to attain to him because of the hindrances of the flesh. For that reason Paul rejoices again when the old man is humiliated and destroyed and the new is able to win back its true form, II Cor. 4: "But though our outward man perish, yet the inward man is renewed day by day." Note that if it is renewed, that means that it had already been created and formed and set up, and having decayed and crumbled, it is now restored to its first estate,[15] in which we perceive the original creation of the divine image. Paul speaks similarly to the Romans in chapter 7: "For I know that in me—that is, in my flesh—dwelleth no good thing: for to will is present with me; but how to perform that which is good I find not. For the good that I would I do not; but the evil that I would not, that I do. If I do that which I would not, it is no more I that do it, but sin that dwelleth in me. I find then a law, that, when I would do good, evil is present with me, for I delight in the law of God after the inward man; but I see another law in my members, warring against the law of my mind, and bringing me into captivity to the law of sin which is in my members." These words are all Paul's, and of themselves they are almost enough to prove the correctness of our interpretation, for Paul says clearly that our inward man—which is created in the divine image—has a desire to live according to the law and will of God, but that it is opposed by the outward man—in the members of which—that is, in which—sin dwells, that is, a proneness to sin:[16] for by the word sin Paul here means the weakness which gives rise to sin.(12) Now from this passage of Paul we must not jump to the erroneous conclusion of the Sophists, who say: Note that there is something which we can do of our own nature. Not at all. For tell me, what is it that we have of our own nature? For if the image is our own, then we are an image of ourselves. And if it is of God, how can we call it our own? You see then that we ourselves are absolutely nothing and in the flesh we can do nothing. Therefore immediately after the complaint that he is brought into captivity to sin St. Paul cries out: "O wretched man that I am! who shall deliver me from the body of this death?"

15 zů seiner ursprünglichen erste, in pristinum statum (G).
16 der süntlich prästen, i.e., sinful weakness.

meaning that the imprisonment of the inward man is a death.
And at once he takes comfort again: "I thank God through
Jesus Christ," that is, that through the Lord Jesus Christ he is
saved from the curse of sin and it can no longer bring him into
condemnation. Therefore he adds: "So then with the mind I
myself serve the law of God; but with the flesh the law of sin."
Let it be noted that here Paul looks upon himself as a servant
of God and also a servant of sin. But how can he be both at the
same time? In this way: according to I John 1 we are never
without sin, indeed, as we have already seen, sin always dwells
within us, even though it has been overcome and led captive
by Christ, Heb. 9, Rom. 6 "Sin shall not have dominion over
you." Thus we are under an obligation to live according to the
law of God which we cannot fulfil. Like St. Paul, then, we can
only cry out:[17] "O wretched man that I am! who shall deliver
me from the body of this death?" And we must return the same
answer: The grace of God through the Lord Jesus Christ. The
outward man is always subject to the law—that is, to the
weakness—of sin, but we should see to it that the inward
man is not dominated by the outward in such a way as to
serve the flesh and its lusts, etc. In the present context there
is no space to develop this point further. But so much by
the way.

Now if we have found that the inward man is as stated, and
that it delights in the law of God because it is created in the
divine image in order to have fellowship with him, it follows
necessarily that there is no law or word which will give
greater delight to the inward man than the Word of God.
For according to the saying of Isaiah 28, "the bed is shorter
than that the adulterer can stretch himself on it, and the
covering narrower than that he can wrap himself in it." That
is, God is the bridegroom and husband of the soul. He wills that
it should remain inviolate, for he cannot allow any other to
be loved—that is, to be as highly esteemed and precious—as
he is. Nor does he will that the soul should seek comfort anywhere but in him, or allow any other word to minister comfort
but his Word. For in the same way it is the husband's will
that the wife should cleave only to him, lavishing all her care
upon him and seeking no other comfort but that which he
can give. As Isaiah says, "God is *zelotes*, a strong lover[18] of
souls." In proof of that we do not need to adduce the many
passages from the Old Testament. For Christ himself says in

[17] *streng schryen.*   [18] *yfrer*, i.e., one who is zealous for.

Matthew 22: "Thou shalt love the Lord thy God with all thy heart, with all thy soul, with all thy mind," and, Mark 12 adds, "with all thy strength." But if we love him in that way, there is no word which can give greater joy or comfort than his Word, for he is our Creator and Father. And there is no word which can give greater joy or comfort or fear to a man than that of the father whom he loves. It was with that Word that Christ answered the devil in Matthew 4: "Man shall not live by bread alone, but by every word that proceedeth out of the mouth of God." Such is the life and power of that Word, which sustains the soul of man as food sustains his body, but more so and in a different fashion. For he who keeps the Word or sayings of God will not see eternal death. So then we have come to the point where, from the fact that we are the image of God, we may see that there is nothing which can give greater joy or assurance or comfort to the soul than the Word of its creator and maker. We can now apply ourselves to understand the clarity and infallibility of the Word of God. And first:

The Certainty or Power of the Word of God

The Word of God is so sure and strong that if God wills all things are done the moment that he speaks his Word. For it is so living and powerful that even the things which are irrational immediately conform themselves to it, or to be more accurate, things both rational and irrational are fashioned and despatched and constrained in conformity with its purpose. The proof may be found in Genesis 1: "And God said, Let there be light; and there was light." Note how alive and strong the Word is, not merely ruling all things but creating out of nothing that which it wills. You may discover for yourselves many other proofs which for the sake of brevity we will here pass over.(13) The earth is commanded to bud and the waters to bring forth and bear fish, and it is done that very day. Such is the might of that eternally empowering Word. Again, in Genesis 3, God said to the woman Eve: "I will greatly multiply thy sorrow and thy conception; in sorrow thou shalt bring forth children; and thy desire shall be to thy husband,[19] and he shall rule over thee." And it all came to pass that very day, and will continue as long as life in the body. At the same time he said to Adam: "Cursed be the ground when thou tillest

[19] lit. thou shalt be under the authority of thy husband.

it; in labour shalt thou eat of it all the days of thy life; thorns also and thistles shall it bring forth to thee; in the sweat of thy face shalt thou eat bread, till thou return unto the ground out of which thou wast taken." Note here how toil and death were laid inescapably upon man by the all-powerful Word of God. Again, when the human race corrupted itself more and more, God shortened the span of life to 120 years (Gen. 6). And so it is to the world's end. Again, he told Adam and Eve that in the day that they ate the forbidden fruit they would die (Gen. 2). And this assuredly came to pass as God had said (Gen. 3). Again, God told Noah to make an ark, because it would rain forty days and forty nights and all living creatures would be destroyed (Gen. 7). And assuredly it came to pass, for even the heathen have written about the flood, although they give Noah the name of Deucaleon.(14) Again, by his angels God declared that he would destroy Sodom and Gomorrah and the other cities, and it did not fail to happen as he said (Gen. 19). Again, Lot and his family were commanded not to look behind, and Lot's wife was disobedient, therefore she was turned into a pillar of salt (Gen. 19). Again, God told Abraham: "I will certainly return unto thee according to the time of life; and Sarah thy wife shall have a son, etc." (Gen. 18). Sarah herself did not believe, for she was some eighty years old, but it came to pass as God had said (Gen. 21). The Scriptures of the Old Testament are full of illustrations of the *certainty* certainty of God's Word, for all the passages mentioned are taken from the one book Genesis, and indeed from only one part of that book. If I were to begin to tell of the great miracles which God promised Moses that he would work in Egypt and amongst the children of Israel, all of which he most certainly performed, or of what he accomplished through Joshua, Gideon and Jephtha, or through Samuel, Saul, David and Solomon, I should never come to an end. Read these things for yourselves or take note and ponder them when you hear them preached.

We will now turn to the New Testament and consider the strength and certainty and power of God's Word as we find it there.

The divine declaration to Zechariah by the angel Gabriel seemed at first sight completely incredible, for his wife Elisabeth had always been barren and both of them were now advanced in years. And because he did not believe, Zechariah was deprived of the power of speech. But that which he regarded as impossible assuredly came to pass—such is the strength and certainty and life of the Word of God—and John the Baptist, the righteous forerunner of the Messiah,[20] was born. The pure Virgin Mary was taken aback when the angel announced and declared the birth of Jesus Christ, for she knew not a man; but the Word of God was so alive and sure that without any detraction from her purity that holy thing was conceived and grew in her and was eventually born of her for the salvation of the world. Thus we see that the whole course of nature must be altered rather than that the Word of God should not remain and be fulfilled. In Luke 1 again the angel said to her: "And he shall be great," meaning Christ. And when has the world seen anyone greater than he? Alexander and Julius Caesar were great, yet their dominion hardly extended over half the world, but believers in Christ have come from the rising of the sun to the going down of the same, and indeed the whole world has believed in him and recognized and magnified in him the son of the Most High, and of his kingdom there is no end. For where shall we find a ruler with dominion and authority as ancient as that of the faith of Christ, a faith which will never be destroyed, even though it be preserved only amongst the few? Indeed, this divine prophecy is visibly fulfilled before us every day. And when Christ grew and began to teach and to work miracles, all things were subservient to him and fashioned themselves in accordance with his will. The leper said to him: "If thou wilt, thou canst make me clean." And he replied: "I will, be thou clean." And from that hour his leprosy was cleansed, for God willed it, and the words "Be thou clean," had the power to accomplish it (Matt. 8). To the centurion he said: "Go thy way, and as thou hast believed, so be it done unto thee." And his servant was healed in the self-same hour. Note that in this case the certainty of healing was made dependent upon the faith of the centurion, to teach us a sure trust in God and the work of God (Matt. 8). To the ruler he said: "Thy son liveth", and it was so (John 4), though he was not even present, to teach us that nothing is too hard or distant for the Word of God to accomplish. To the man who was blind and deaf and had an impediment he said: "Ephphatha, that is, be opened" (Mark 7), and all his bands were loosed. To the blind he said: "Receive thy sight: thy faith hath saved thee," and immediately he received his sight (Luke 18). To Matthew he said: "Follow me," and he

[20] lit. of God—*gottesvorgenger.*

followed him without delay (Matt. 9). To the man lying on
the bed [21] he said: "Thy sins be forgiven thee." And so that the
outward sign might give the assurance of inward cleansing
he said: "Arise, take up thy bed and go into thine house."
And he arose and departed to his house (Matt. 9). To the
woman bowed together he said: "Woman, thou art loosed
from thine infirmity"—by the laying on of hands he gave her
a sure sign, or perhaps testified to his good will (15)—and immediately she was made straight (Luke 13). Over the loaves and
fishes he pronounced a blessing and they were increased, so that
many thousands ate of them and there still remained far more
than there had been at the first, as we may see in all the Gospels.
He rebuked the unclean spirit, and immediately it left the man
possessed by it (Matt. 17). He commanded the disciples to
cast their nets on the right side and they would find, and
immediately they caught 153 great fishes (John 21). He commanded Peter to come to him on the water, and immediately
he bore him up (Matt. 14). From heaven he told Ananias
that Paul was a chosen vessel to him to bear his name before
kings and princes of the earth and the children of Israel (Acts
9), and so it came to pass. When Paul was journeying towards
Rome, and the shipwreck intervened, he told him that no one
would be lost, but only the ship, and that is how it turned out
(Acts 27). These passages from the New Testament will be quite
enough to show that the Word of God is so alive and strong
and powerful that all things have necessarily to obey it, and
that as often and at the time that God himself appoints. And
let us beware lest we murmur against God like the ungodly
in the days of Ezekiel, chapter 12, who said that the Word
spoken by the prophets was prolonged: for the forbearance of
God is not negligence, but a respect for the most convenient
time. Not that this respect is at all necessary to God, but beneficial to us, for with God there can be no time, seeing he is
not subject to anything, and that which is duration to us is to
him eternally present.(16) With God, in fact, there is no such
thing as past or future, but all things are naked and open to
his eyes. He does not learn with time or forget with time, but
with unerring knowledge and perception he sees all things
present in eternity. It is in time that we who are temporal find
the meaning and measure of longness or shortness. Yet what
seems long to us is not long to God, but eternally present. If
you think that God often fails to punish a wicked individual

21 *bettrisen, paralyticus* (G).

or nation, suffering their arrogance far too long, you are completely mistaken. For note that they can never escape him. The
whole world is before him, where then can they hide from his
presence? Most certainly he will find them (Ps. 138) (A.V. 139).
And if you think that he does not punish or save according to
his Word you are quite wrong. His Word can never be undone
or destroyed or resisted. For if it could, if God could not always
fulfil it, if some other were stronger than he and could resist it,
it would not be almighty. But it must always be fulfilled. If it
is not fulfilled at the time when you desire, that is not due to
any deficiency of power but to the freedom of his will. For if
he had to act according to your will, you would be stronger
than he and he would have to consult you. But what could be
more nonsensical? God will never leave his Word powerless,
as he says in Ezekiel 12: "O you that are rebellious, I will
say the word and will perform it." And just after: "The word
which I have spoken shall be done." The whole teaching of the
Gospel is a sure demonstration that what God has promised
will certainly be performed. For the Gospel is now an accomplished fact: the One who was promised to the patriarchs, and
to the whole race, has now been given to us, and in him we
have the assurance of all our hope, as Simeon said in Luke 2.
"For what can he withhold when he delivered up his own Son
for us, and how shall he not with him freely give us all things?"
(Rom. 8).

So much then concerning the power or certainty of the Word
of God. And now,

The Clarity of the Word of God

Before we begin to speak of the clarity of the Word we will
first forestall the objections of those who might resist it, saying:
Where is this clarity? If God wants his Word to be understood,
why does he speak in parables and riddles? Answer: first note
that I do not undertake to give you this reply because I think
that we are under an obligation to answer your insolent
questions, or that the counsels of God stand in need of vindication by us, or that any man may know the grounds of all God's
actions. But so far as the clear testimony of Scripture permits,
I will stop your mouths, that you may learn not to blaspheme
(I Tim. 1). The fact that in times past God taught by parables
but in these last days has revealed himself fully by the Lord
Jesus Christ indicates to us that God wished to give his message

to man in a gentle and attractive way; for it is of the nature of that which is presented in parables and proverbs and riddles that it appeals to the understanding of men and brings them to knowledge and indeed increases that knowledge: Eccles. 39 "The wise man will seek out the heavenly things of grave sayings, and be conversant in dark parables." (17) For when the parable or proverb has provoked us to search out its hidden meaning, once we have found it we value it more highly than if it had been presented to us plainly. So then, as it says in Psalm 48 (A.V. 49): "My mouth shall speak of wisdom, and the meditation of my heart shall be of understanding:[22] I will incline mine ear to a parable, I will open my dark saying upon the sweet harp"—the heavenly and divine wisdom reveals its will to men in the form of sweet parables, so that those who might otherwise be dull and unwilling are persuaded to listen, and the truth which is discovered is received the more firmly and valued the more highly, and the divine lesson is busy and active all the longer in the understanding, and its roots sink deeper into the heart. Illustration: Who could ever give us a better picture of the unequal fruits of the Word of God than Christ himself did in the parable of the sower and the seed (Matt. 13)? And this parable provoked the disciples to search out and to find the lesson concealed within it. But it repelled the ungodly, not that the parable itself did it, but their own unreceptive heart, (18) which would not allow itself to be taught or provoked to give heed to that which is required, as the prophet Isaiah foresaw in chapter 6: "Hear ye indeed, but understand not; and see ye indeed, but perceive not. Make the heart of this people fat, and make their ears heavy, and shut their eyes; lest they see with their eyes, and hear with their ears, and understand with their heart, and convert, and be healed. Then said I (that is, Isaiah), Lord, how long? And he answered, Until the cities be wasted without inhabitant, and the houses without man, and the land be utterly desolate, and the Lord hath removed men far away." In the passage already mentioned Christ used these words of Isaiah, showing that the greatness of their sins and iniquities had blinded them, so that they opposed God and angered him, with the result that that which was spoken to all men to salvation, and was intended to provoke them to knowledge, turned to their hurt because of their sins, although to believers it was profitable to salvation, as he himself says shortly afterwards in Matthew 13: "For whosoever

[22] or prudence—*fürsichtigkeit, prudentia* (G).

hath, to him shall be given, but whosoever hath not, from him shall be taken away even that he hath." The meaning is this: that he who desires the divine message, and has something of the Word of God, to him it shall be given, or better, he who comes to the Word of God, not bringing his own understanding but—as Hilary (19) says—having a mind to learn from the Word of God, that man already has something, that is, he is not looking to himself, but gives himself wholly to God and to the voice of God. Do you not think that he really has something? Therefore to that man it shall be given. But whosoever hath not, that is, he who comes to the Scriptures with his own opinion and interpretation and wrests the Scriptures into conformity with it, do you think that he has anything? No. From him will be taken away the opinion and interpretation which he thinks he has, and it will be with him according to the saying in Wisdom 2: "For their own wickedness hath blinded them, so that they did not receive the things of the spirit of God!" O good Christians, (20) how far do you suppose many of us are from the divine displeasure? We see the shamelessness of sin, we see everywhere covetousness and self-will, and even our righteousness is hypocrisy and men-pleasing. But when it is proposed to rebuke and expose and amend our evil deeds by that evangelical doctrine which is the Word of God, we refuse to listen, we stop our ears, and that which God has sent for our good we reject so long and so often that at the last judgment falls. In II Chronicles 36 you will find that time and time again God warned the children of Israel, and when they did not amend at last he let them be taken away captive out of their own land: "And the Lord God of their fathers sent to them by his messengers, rising up betimes, and sending; because he had compassion on his people, and on his dwelling-place: but they mocked the messengers of God, and despised his words, and misused his prophets, until the wrath of the Lord arose against his people, till there was no remedy. Therefore he brought upon them the king of the Chaldees, who slew their young men with the sword in the house of their sanctuary, and had no compassion upon young man or maiden, old man or him that stooped for age: he gave them all into the hand of the Chaldean king. And all the vessels of the house of God, and all the treasures he brought to Babylon. And they burnt the house of God, and brake down the wall of Jerusalem, and burnt all the palaces thereof with fire, and destroyed all the goodly vessels thereof." Note what calamities ensue when the

Word of God is despised and contemned. And note too that failure to believe the Word of God is a sure sign that the wrath of God will soon overtake us. The Word of God and the messenger of the Word are a sweet smell or savour (II Cor. 2); but a savour of life to some, and of death to others. Illustration. Consider a good strong wine. To the healthy it tastes excellent. It makes him merry and strengthens him and warms his blood. But if there is someone who is sick of a disease or fever, he cannot even taste it, let alone drink it, and he marvels that the healthy is able to do so. This is not due to any defect in the wine, but to that of the sickness. So too it is with the Word of God. It is right in itself and its proclamation is always for good. If there are those who cannot bear or understand or receive it, it is because they are sick. So much by way of answer to those who rashly maintain that God does not want us to understand his words, as though it were his will to bring us into danger.(21) If we fail to understand him, it is because we are out of favour. A son knows that he enjoys his father's favour even when his father speaks roughly to him or rebukes him. He is outside his grace only when he does not speak to him at all either to teach or admonish. So too it is the most bitter punishment and a sure sign of imminent calamities to be deprived of the consolation of the Word of God.

We will now turn to consider the clarity and light of the Word. May God be glorified, and may he put the right words in our mouth that we may give them clear utterance, Amen.

When the Word of God shines on the human understanding, it enlightens it in such a way that it understands and confesses the Word and knows the certainty of it. This was the inner experience of David, and he spoke of it in Psalm 118 (A.V. 119): "The entrance of thy words, O Lord, giveth light; it giveth understanding unto the simple," meaning, those who in themselves are nothing, resembling the child whom Jesus set in the midst of his disciples to teach them humility (Matt. 18), saying: "Except ye be converted, and become as little children, ye shall not enter into the kingdom of heaven." This concurrent or prevenient clarity of the word found outward representation at the birth of Christ when the glory of the Lord shone round about the shepherds, and then the angel began to speak with them (Luke 2), and the shepherds believed the words of the angel and found all things as he had said.

I. First then we will demonstrate the clarity of the word with some illustrations from the Old Testament, then from the New.

1. When Noah was commanded to build the ark he believed God, that he would indeed destroy the whole earth with the flood. That he did so was not due to any human enlightenment, otherwise the many who paid no heed but built houses and married and lived according to their desires would easily have sowed doubt in his mind, saying: Ah, but that which was told you is simply a delusion presented to your mind no doubt by an apparition. It may be seen, then, that the Word of God brought with it its own enlightenment, by which Noah knew that it was from God and not from any other (Gen. 6).

2. When Abraham was commanded to offer up his son Isaac he believed that the voice was the voice of God. That he did so was not by any human enlightenment or perception, for Abraham had been promised salvation in the seed of Isaac (Gen. 21). But now God commanded him to sacrifice his son Isaac whom he loved (Gen. 22). Looking at it from a human standpoint Abraham must inevitably have thought: The voice is wrong. It is not of God. For God gave you this son Isaac, by your beloved wife Sarah, as a special token of his friendship. And in so doing he promised that of his seed the Saviour of all men should be born. But if you slay him, the promise is nullified, and the gift is contradicted: for why did he wish to give him if now that you are beginning to take pleasure in him he wishes to take him away again? No, the voice cannot be of God. It is rather of the devil, to tempt you, and to destroy your best-loved son. But Abraham did not allow himself to be deflected by such acute questioning and extremity, nor did he follow his own counsel. And that was all of God, who so enlightened him with the Word that he knew it to be the Word of God, even though he was commanded to do something quite contrary to God's former promise. The nerves and bones and muscles of faith all braced themselves. His reason could not accept the command, but faith withstood reason (Rom. 4), saying: The one who promised and gave thy son at the first can raise him up again from the dead, or he can use some other means to give to the world the Saviour promised through him. He has the power and the resources to perform all that he has said. And faith gained the victory; note well that it did so by the light which the Word of God had itself brought with it.

3. When Moses had brought the children of Israel into sore straits,[23] that is, as Josephus says,(22) between the mountain,

[23] lit. between the horse and the wall, *zwüschen ross und wand.*

the sea and the enemy, he did not despair. And when the people began to murmur angrily[24] against him (Exod. 14): "Because there were no graves in Egypt, hast thou taken us away to die in the wilderness? Is not this the word that we did tell thee in Egypt?"—he gave them assurance and comfort: "Fear ye not, the Lord shall fight for you and ye shall hold your peace". And he cried secretly in his heart to God. And God answered him: "Lift up thy rod, and stretch out thine hand over the sea, and divide it, and the children of Israel shall go dryshod through the midst of the sea." And the fact that he did not give way to despair, thinking that if the voice of God was only a delusion then all was lost, but recognized with utter certainty the voice of God; that was due, not to the understanding of Moses himself, even though he was learned in all the skill and wisdom of the Egyptians (Acts 7), but to the light of the Word of God, which comes with such clarity and assurance that it is surely known and believed.

4. Jacob knew the voice of the One who stood at the top of the ladder and said: "I am the Lord God of thy father Abraham and Isaac, etc." And the fact that he did so, and did not dismiss the voice as an empty dream, was not due to his own understanding: for where had he seen God, or heard his voice so as to be able to recognize it? But the Word of God gave him such clear understanding that he had no doubt that it was the voice of God, and when he awoke he said: "Truly the Lord is in this place, and I knew it not." Tell me, you that are wise, on the authority of what council or arbiter did he accept God's Word as true or believe that it was really God's? You see, cavillers, that God's Word brought with it its own clarity and enlightenment, so that he perceived clearly that it was God's, and believed in it steadfastly, and in all the promises which it contained (Gen. 28).

5. Micaiah recognized as the Word of God the vision which God gave him and the message which accompanied it. And the fact that he did not dismiss it as a phantasy was not of man but of God (I Kings 22). For when 400 prophets stood up against him and contradicted Micaiah, especially Zedekiah who smote him on the cheek and said: "Which way went the Spirit of the Lord from me to speak unto thee?" the opposition of so many prophets of repute and the power of the two kings Ahab and Jehoshaphat ought naturally to have made him think: You cannot possibly be right, you either did not see or understand

24 *mit mülichen worten, verba molestissima* (G).

rightly. And if he had had no other light but that of the understanding there can be little doubt that that is what would have
happened. But the Word of God revealed itself to him and
brought with it its own clarity, holding and assuring the understanding in such a way that he held fast by that which he had
heard and seen. Tell me, you who are wise—in your own
understanding—what would have become of the truth of God
if the divine vision and word had been surrendered to the
multitude of prophets? (23) And where was the man who could
pronounce Micaiah to be right, as indeed he was? For the other
prophets all promised the two kings victory. Micaiah told them
that they lied: there would be no victory. And it came to pass
according to the saying of the man who was taught of God
without any intervention by man, and all the rest spoke falsely.

6. Jeremiah when he was commanded to do so proclaimed
the Word of God without fear, even though the people dared
to lay hands on him and destroy him because of it. And
the fact that he did so was because he had a firm trust in the
Word of God and had been taught by God to understand it
(Jer. 26).

7. Through the Word of God in I Kings 18: "Go, shew thyself unto Ahab; and I will send rain upon the earth," Elijah
perceived and accomplished the whole matter with the priests
of Baal. And the fact that he did so was not of his own understanding, but by divine enlightenment, which taught him how
to carry through the whole affair apart altogether from the
judgment of man—for Elijah believed that he was completely
alone (I Kings 19, Rom. 11).

These seven passages from the Old Testament will be enough
to show conclusively that God's Word can be understood by
a man without any human direction: not that this is due to
man's own understanding, but to the light and Spirit of God,
illuminating and inspiring the words in such a way that the
light of the divine content is seen in his own light, as it says in
Psalm 35 (A.V. 36): "For with thee, Lord, is the well of light,
and in thy light shall we see light". And similarly in John 1.

II. We will now turn to the New Testament passages.

In John 1 it says that the Word, or Son, of God was the true
light which lighteth every man that cometh into the world.
But if the light lighteth every man, undoubtedly it is clarity
itself: for however bright and clear a thing may be, it cannot
light every man unless it is clarity itself: and if it is to continue
lighting every man, it must necessarily be eternal. For all things

that are clear are necessarily clear by virtue of clarity. Note, you cavillers, who have no trust in the Scriptures, that it is the Word of God, which is God himself, that lighteth every man. Away then with that light of your own which you would give to the Word of God with your interpreters.[25] (24) In John 3, John the Baptist says: "A man can receive nothing except it be given him from above." If we are to receive and understand anything it must come from above. But if that is so, then no other man can attain it for us. The comprehension and understanding of divine doctrine comes then from above and not from interpreters, who are just as liable to be led into temptation as Balaam was. See II Peter 2.

The Samaritan woman was clever enough to say to Christ (John 4): "I know that Messias cometh, which is called Christ: when he cometh, he will tell us all things." And our theologians have not yet learned that lesson. Ask them if they understand the words: Christ is *caput ecclesiae*, that is, Christ is head of the congregation or church which is his body. They will answer: Yes, they understand them very well, but they may not do so apart from the official pronouncements of men.(25) What poor creatures! Rather than allow themselves to be vanquished by the truth, they deny that they are men, as if they had no ordinary intelligence and did not know the meaning of *caput*. And all that in order to subject the truth to the Caiaphas's and Annas's, its official interpreters.(26) It is not of the slightest account to them that Christ himself said (John 6): "They shall all be taught of God," in the words of Isaiah 54. But if all Christians are taught of God, why can you not leave them the certainty and freedom of that teaching according to the understanding which God himself has imparted? And that God himself is the teacher of the hearts of believers we learn from Christ in the words immediately following, when he says (John 6): "Every man that hath heard, and hath learned of the Father, cometh unto me." None can come to the Lord Jesus Christ except he has learned to know him of the Father. And note who the teacher is: not *doctores*, not *patres*, not pope, not *cathedra*, nor *concilia*, but the Father of Jesus Christ. And you cannot say, we are taught of men as well. No, for just before he says: "No man can come to me, except my heavenly Father draw him." Even if you hear the gospel of Jesus Christ from an apostle, you cannot act upon it unless the heavenly Father teach and draw you by the Spirit. The words are clear;

25 *mit üweren richteren.*

enlightenment, instruction and assurance are by divine teaching without any intervention on the part of that which is human. And if they are taught of God, they are well taught, with clarity and conviction: if they had first to be taught and assured by men, we should have to describe them as taught of men rather than of God.

But Christ says (John 6): "Therefore I said, that no man can come to me, except it be given him of my Father." But if the Father gives it, as the text says, then what need is there of any other teacher, or guide or interpreter? For just after, when Christ asked: "Will ye also go away?" Peter spoke on behalf of all the disciples and his answer was this: "Lord, to whom shall we go? Thou hast the words of eternal life. And we believe and are sure that thou art the Christ, the Son of the living God." Note that the disciples did not know of any other teacher who could minister comfort to them and teach them the words of life. And yet you try to convince me that I am not able to understand his words but must first learn them from some other man. And note, too, that the apostles have no doubts, but speak as those who are taught of God and not of man: "We believe and are sure." You say: If only God had taught me! Answer: I perceive that God has not taught you: for if he had taught you, then like the disciples you would know for certain that he had done so; indeed, the words themselves would show you. For "he that is of the earth is earthly: he that cometh from heaven is above all (John 3). If you ask further, How can I be taught of him so that I know with certainty that this or that doctrine is according to his will? there is just one answer: Ask of him, and he will give you all that is needed; for he knows what is needed far better than you do yourself; for he says: "He that asketh, receiveth, etc." (Matt. 7). At this point faith must stretch itself. It must be as strong as the mustard-seed (Matt. 17). But I am afraid that the words of Christ which follow in John 6 might well be applied to you too: "There are some of you that believe not." (27)

In Matthew 11 Christ gives thanks to God his heavenly Father, saying: "I thank thee, O Father, Lord of heaven and earth, because thou hast hid these things from the wise and prudent, and hast revealed them unto babes, for so it seemed good in thy sight." Note that Christ gives thanks because God has concealed the heavenly wisdom from the wise of this world. And yet you would re-direct the hearts that are taught of God to the selfsame wise of this world? He reveals that wisdom to babes, to the humble; the high and mighty [26] he cannot reach, for he will not cry, as Isaiah says: "His voice is lowly." With all the pomp and circumstance of their horses and servants and music and triumphs [27] they cannot hear.(28) But you say: Their wisdom is from God, and you prove it with the fine example of Caiaphas, saying that even though they are wicked, God still uses them to proclaim the truth. But tell me, what do they tell us about God? For myself, I never hear them speak about God at all. It is all voices, and holy fathers, and ancestors, and the throne of Peter, about which we do not read anything either in the Gospels or in the teaching of Peter himself. Oh what they would give if only that throne were mentioned in the Gospel. They speak of it everywhere but they still cannot find any solid support for it in the teaching of the Gospel. *Summa*: I do not see any indications that they are sent by God. In teaching I note that they are the friends of tyrants. By their fruits ye shall know them. God himself has revealed these things to the lowly.

Again, in John 6, he says: "I am the bread of life. He that cometh to me shall never hunger; and he that believeth on me shall never thirst." In this verse it is quite certain that Christ is speaking of the nourishment of teaching. And this is to be found in himself. He does not say: Go to those who are robed in hoods and purple.[28] For there is no certainty there. It is when God gives a man certainty that he is nourished and refreshed and will never hunger or thirst again. But if he has already been nourished by God, why tell him to turn away from this bread to the Fathers?

In the same way St. Paul applies the saying of Christ in John 6: "They shall all be taught of God," and in the same context (Heb. 8 and 10) the prophecy of Jeremiah 31 is also quoted, where God himself says: "I will put my laws into their hearts, and in their minds will I write them; and their sins and iniquities will I remember no more." Note that he will write the law itself in our hearts, for he continues: "And they shall not teach every man his neighbour, and every man his brother, saying, Know the Lord: for all shall know me, from the least to the greatest." Note that God instructs with such certainty that there is no need to ask of man; for God himself

26 lit. to high horses—*uff die hohen ross.*
27 *jo triumphe*—the well-known cry at Roman triumphs.
28 *zu den gehübten, purperten.* In this context *haube* may perhaps be used for mitre.
z.b.—6

instructs the heart of man, and there is no need of anyone
else.

Again, in I Corinthians 2 Paul says: "Now we have received,
not the spirit of the world, but the spirit which is of God;
that we might know the things which are freely given to us of
God. Which things also we speak, not in the words which man's
wisdom teacheth, but with those which are taught in the Holy
Ghost." Note that the gifts which God gives are known by
the Spirit of God, not by the clever display of the words and
wisdom of man, which is the spirit of this world. But you say: I
consider that a council of bishops also has the Spirit of God.
But do you not see that they are too lofty and distant for him?
He does not allow himself to be known by the spirit of this world;
he reveals himself to babes. How should the poor carpenter
entrust himself to such princes (or beggar-princes, as the
common man [29] would call them)? If we are to incline to his
grace, there is no room for princely graces, for titles are of
this world and not of God. God reveals himself by his own
Spirit, and we cannot learn of him without his Spirit. He gives
himself truly to all those who surrender self and come to him.
Indeed, he himself invites us to come (John 7): "If any man
thirst, let him come unto me and drink, etc.". And you may be
no less certain that God will enlighten them as he does others
if only they will seek it with humility.

In Acts 9 Paul was thrown to the ground and rebuked:
"Saul, Saul, why persecutest thou me?" And when he asked:
"Who art thou, Lord?" he received the answer: "I am Jesus
whom thou persecutest." And the fact that he knew that it was
Jesus was not due to his own understanding or judgment but
to the light of God which surrounded him with a visible radi-
ance; for otherwise the passion to destroy the name and glory
of Christ would not have allowed him either to recognize that
voice or to follow it.

John says (I John 2): "Ye need not that any man teach you:
but as the same anointing teacheth you of all things, and is
truth, and is no lie, and even as it hath taught you, ye shall
abide in him." Now first note that this anointing is the same
as the enlightenment and gift of the Holy Ghost. You will
see, then, that once God has taught us with this anointing,
that is, his Spirit, we do not need any other teacher, for there
is no more error, but only the pure truth in which we are to

[29] *Cüntz*—a wag, used as a representative name for the lower orders.

abide. But at this point our opponents[30] say: How can I know that my belief is of the Spirit of God unless it is known and recognized to be of God or to be the teaching of God by those whose office it is to do this? (29) Answer: I will give you the same answer as Jesus did to the Jews, when they asked him by what authority he worked miracles, and he retorted with a counter-question, but one which revealed an understanding of their intention, saying: "The baptism of John, whence was it? from heaven, or of men?" So I will ask you the counter-question: Tell me, you fools,[31] when the rabble of carnal divines[32] that you call fathers and bishops pronounce upon a doctrine about which there is a doubt, are you enlightened, and do you know with absolute certainty that it is as they say? You answer: Yes. Oh, like the foolish Galatians, who hath bewitched you, that you believe deceitful men and do not believe those words of God which are the truth itself? How are you ever to overcome your obtuseness, that you do not believe the Spirit of God who offers you the truth, but put your trust in fallible men, who can do nothing without the grace and spirit of God, subscribing and defending the abuses of which they are guilty? You believe that men can give you certainty, which is no certainty, and you do not believe that God can give it you. Do you not know that the mind[33] and understanding of every man must be brought into captivity to the obedience and service of God, and not of men? But I see your error, and in God's name I will show it you. You do not know that it is God himself who teaches a man, nor do you know that when God has taught him that man has an inward certainty and assurance. For you do not know what the Gospel really is. He that hath ears to hear, let him hear. The word Gospel is the equivalent of good news or tidings which God gives to men in matters of which they are either ignorant or doubtful. Illustration: (30) A man is longing for his soul's salvation, and he asks a Carthusian: (31) Dear brother, what must I do to be saved? And the answer will undoubtedly be this: Enter our order, and you will assuredly be saved, for it is the most rigorous. But ask a Benedictine (32) and he replies: It is worth noting that salvation is easiest in our order, for it is the most ancient. But if you ask a Dominican (33) he will answer: In our order salvation is certain, for it was given from heaven by our Lady. And if you ask a Franciscan, (34) he will say: Our order is the greatest and most

30 die vorgenannte rott, adversarii (G).   31 du tolle rott.
32 der fleischlich geistlichen.   33 aller gedanck, intellectus (G).

famous of all; consider then whether you will find salvation more easily in any other. And if you ask the Pope he will say: It is easiest with an indulgence. And if you ask those of Compostella (35) they will say: If you come here to St. James you will never be lost and you will never be poor. You see, they all show you some different way, and they all contend fiercely that their way is the right one. But the seeking soul cries out: Alas! whom shall I follow? They all argue so persuasively that I am at a loss what to do. And finally it can only run to God and earnestly pray to him, saying: Oh God, show me which order or which way is the most certain. You fool, you go to God simply that he may distinguish between men, and you do not ask him to show you that way of salvation which is pleasing to him and which he himself regards as sure and certain. Note that you are merely asking God to confirm something which men have told you. But why do you not say: Oh God, they all disagree amongst themselves; but you are the only, unconcealed good; show me the way of salvation? And the Gospel gives us a sure message, or answer, or assurance. Christ stands before you with open arms, inviting you and saying (Matt. 11): "Come unto me, all ye that labour and are heavy laden, and I will give you rest." O glad news, which brings with it its own light, so that we know and believe that it is true, as we have fully shown above. For the one who says it is a light of the world. He is the way, the truth and the light. In his Word we can never go astray. We can never be deluded or confounded or destroyed in his Word. If you think there can be no assurance or certainty for the soul, listen to the certainty of the Word of God. The soul can be instructed and enlightened—note the clarity—so that it perceives that its whole salvation and righteousness, or justification, is enclosed in Jesus Christ, (36) and it has therefore the sure comfort that when he himself invites and calls you so graciously he will never cast you out. And if you try to turn your soul away from him, saying: Here is Christ, or there, with the soul of the lover in the Song of Songs it will reply: "I held him, and would not let him go." With Magdalene, (37) it has chosen that good part, which is the Lord himself, whose Word alone can give it encouragement and comfort. The orders may rest in their foolish and arrogant boasting; it is we who are the true sons of Mary Magdalene and who lead the contemplative life. [34] They may say what they like, but that is the view of Christ himself. It was the habit of Christ always to move from earthly

[34] *das schowlich leben, vita contemplativa* (G).

things to the necessary doctrine of the Spirit. Illustration: When one said to him: "Thy mother and brethren are without, desiring to speak with thee" (Matt. 12), he drew their attention away from the physical relationship [35] to the relationship with God, and he stretched forth his hand toward his disciples, and said: "Behold, my mother and my brethren. For whosoever shall do the will of my Father which is in heaven, the same is my brother, and sister, and mother." Similarly, when the woman who had been healed cried out: "Blessed is the womb that bare thee, and the paps which thou hast sucked," he gave them instruction about a spiritual and divine birth: [36] "Blessed are they that hear the word of God, and keep it." It was not that he disowned his mother, but he showed the significance of what she had done. She had received the Word of God, and in the same way those who hear his Word are received and born of the Spirit of God. She bore him as a pure virgin, and in the same way those who receive the Word of God and exercise and nourish themselves in it bring forth wonderful fruit. And so too when he was with the two sisters they both acted rightly, but he took Mary Magdalene as the starting-point for his lesson, that to choose the good part which shall never be taken away is to receive him and to seek him: for none will ever allow himself to be taken away from him. And for that reason he says to Martha: "Thou art careful and troubled about many things," and then proceeds to the discernment of the one good thing: But one thing is necessary to salvation, and Magdalene has found it; hold it fast. And do you see what that one thing is which is necessary to salvation? Or rather, who that one thing is? You answer, Christ. You have judged rightly. Hold fast to him and never forsake him. But do you imagine that only you who are cloistered and cowled can find Christ and hear his Word? On the contrary, you are the very last to hear his teaching.(38) For you have laid hold of other things, and you hold fast to those things and find comfort in them. It says of Magdalene: She heard his Word: that was the good part which she had chosen. And so it is with every soul. Once it is enlightened by God, it can find no assurance or consolation or encouragement in the word of man, but only in the Word of God; and like the disciples in John 6 it says: "Lord, to whom shall I go? Thou hast the word of life," that is, Thy Word quickens and restores and gives life, so that the soul is comforted and bound to thee, and cannot trust in any other word but thine.

[35] früntschafft. [36] gotzbürtige schwengre, divina nativitas (G).

But when you are called of God you say: How am I to prepare myself, so that I may be certain to attain his grace? I
reply: Put all your trust in the Lord Jesus Christ, that is, rest
assured that as he suffered for us there is atonement before
God for us to all eternity (I John 1). The moment you believe,
know that you are drawn by God, and that which you regard
as your own work is that of the Spirit of God secretly at work
within you. For in John 6 Christ says; "No man can come to
me except my Father which is in heaven draw him." Note
that if you seek him and find him and cleave fast to him you
are drawn by the Father, otherwise you could never have
come to him.

The reason why I have spent so long over this proof [37] is
this: Those who defend the doctrines of men say: It is quite
true that above all other doctrines we ought to esteem the
evangelical doctrine, that is, the doctrine which is declared and
taught by God—so much they will allow, praise be to God—
but we understand the Gospel in a different way. And if there
is a conflict between your understanding and ours, someone
will have to decide between us and have authority to silence
the one who is in error. And this they say in order to subject
the interpretation of God's Word to men, thus making it
possible to rebuke and suppress the evangelical preachers by
Caiaphas and Annas.(39) In direct contradiction to the teaching of Paul, that all interpretation and thought and experience
should be made captive to the will and service of God, they
try to subject the doctrine of God to the judgment of men.
Now take note of the answer: In the first place, by the Gospel
we do not mean only the writings of Matthew, Mark, Luke
and John, but, as we have said, all that God has revealed to
man in order that he may instruct him and give him a sure
knowledge of his will. But God is one, and he is a Spirit of
unity, not of discord. Hence we may see that his words have
always a true and natural sense; (40) may God grant it, no matter how we may wrest them this way or that. And here I beg you
in the name of God not to take it amiss if I draw your attention
to a common error. It is that of the majority of those who in
these days oppose the Gospel—for although they dare not
admit to doing this in public, in secret they do everything
within their power to that end. Listen to what they say. Not
everything, they say, is told us in the Gospels. There are many
good things which are never even thought of in the Gospel.(41)

37 *bewärnus, argumentum* (G).

Oh you rascals—you are not instructed or versed in the Gospel, and you pick out verses from it without regard to their context, and wrest them according to your own desire. It is like breaking off a flower from its roots and trying to plant it in a garden. But that is not the way: you must plant it with the roots and the soil in which it is embedded. And similarly we must leave the Word of God its own proper nature if its sense is to be the same to all of us. And those who err in this way we can easily vanquish by leading them back to the source, though they never come willingly. But some of them are such confirmed dunces[38] that even when the natural sense is expounded in such a way that they cannot deny it, they still allege that they cannot presume to understand it thus unless the Fathers allow that it may so be understood: on the ground that many expositors will always have a better understanding than one or two.(42) Answer: If that is the case, then Christ himself was in error, which God forbid, for most of the priests of the time held quite a different view and he had to stand alone. And the apostles were also mistaken, for they were opposed by whole nations and cities. And even today the number of unbelievers far outweighs the number of believers: are we to conclude then that their view is right and ours wrong simply because they are more numerous than we? No. Consider for yourselves; truth is not necessarily with the majority. What then of the argument? It has no force in the present controversy. Indeed, I see that even popes and councils have sometimes fallen into serious error, especially Anastasius, and Liberius in the Arian heresy.(43) Will you concede that? Yes. Then your case is lost,[39] for you must allow that if they erred once there is always the fear that they will err again, and therefore we cannot trust in them with any certainty. Once we have discovered that— for: *omnis homo mendax*, all men are liars, deceiving and being deceived—we see that ultimately only God himself can teach us the truth with such certainty that all doubts are removed. But you say: Where can I find him? Answer: Seek him in your chamber (Matt. 6), and ask him in secret: he will see you and give you the understanding of divine truth. For as our earlier illustrations show, the doctrine of God can never be learned with greater certainty than when it is taught by God himself, for it comes from God, and he alone is truthful, indeed, he is the truth itself. This is proved by the words of I John 2

38 *so tuff in die eselshut vernäyt*, lit. so tightly sewn up in their ass's hide.
39 *So ist der sach der hals ab*—i.e., it is broken off at the neck.

to which we have already referred: "Ye need not that any man should teach you." You hear that? We do not need human interpreters, but his anointing, which is the Spirit, teaches us of all things—all things, notice—and therefore it is truth and is no lie. But at this point they say: I have prayed to him and I am still of the same mind as before. You will not take it amiss if I say: You lie. I allow, of course, that you prayed, but not as you ought. How then should I approach him and pray to him? In this way: First, put away that view of your own which you want to read into Scripture, for it is quite valueless, as I shall clearly show. I know that you will reply that you have worked through the Scriptures and discovered texts which support your opinion. Alas! here we come upon the canker at the heart of all human systems.(44) And it is this: we want to find support in Scripture for our own view, and so we take that view to Scripture, and if we find a text which, however artificially, we can relate to it, we do so, and in that way we wrest Scripture in order to make it say what we want it to say. Illustration: most of us have our doctrines and interpretations all ready, like someone asking a favour found axe in hand, as though to say: Grant it, or the axe will speak for me. And that is how we come to Scripture. The popes and foolish emperors and kings—suffer me, lords, to speak the truth—have made the majority of our German bishops into temporal princes (beggar-princes as the common man[40] would call them). And in that way they have acquired power. They have a sword in their hands. And with that sword they go to Scripture. And they quote I Peter 2: *regale sacerdotium*: a royal priesthood. And with the sword they now force Peter: what he meant was that the clergy can be temporal princes and wield secular authority.[41] (45) That is what the axe can do. But Peter's real meaning was that the Lord Jesus Christ has called all Christians to kingly honour and to the priesthood, so that they do not need a sacrificing priest to offer on their behalf, for they are all priests, offering spiritual gifts, that is, dedicating themselves wholly to God. Note, then, that we must not approach Scripture like that. But how are we to come? In this way: If you want to speak on any matter, or to learn of it, you must first think like this: Before I say anything or listen to the teaching of man, I will first consult the mind of the Spirit of God (Ps. 84 (A.V. 85)): "I will hear what God the Lord will speak." Then you should

40 *Cüntz*. See note on p. 82.   41 *nach der welt herschen.*

reverently ask God for his grace, that he may give you his mind and Spirit, so that you will not lay hold of your own opinion but of his. And have a firm trust that he will teach you a right understanding, for all wisdom is of God the Lord. And then go to the written word of the Gospel. But at this point there are many who turn up their noses,[42] not believing that if they have called upon God he will give them a different understanding, his own understanding, for they set so much store by their own human understanding that they are sure there cannot possibly be any other. But note how falsely you speak. You must be *theodidacti*, that is, taught of God, not of men: that is what the Truth itself said (John 6), and it cannot lie. If you do not believe, and believe firmly, leaving the wisdom of men and resting only in the divine instruction, you have no true faith. And this is not merely my own view, but St. Hilary was of the same opinion,(46) though we do not heed his help: Christ and Peter and Paul and John were all of this opinion. Thus the whole philosophical system called *theologica scholastica* falls to the ground, for it is merely a system evolved by man; and if it occupies the mind of a man, he thinks that the divine teaching is to be judged and perverted in accordance with the infallible teaching received of men. That this is the case may be seen from the tag: "Where the philosopher leaves off, the theologian begins," which clearly means that when a man is thoroughly instructed in the human doctrine he is better able to interpret the divine, as though our light could illuminate and enlighten the divine light, and in spite of the fact that Christ says, John 5: "I receive not light from men, but I know you, that ye have not the love of God in you." For if they had had his love in them, they would not have believed any word but his: for he is the light that lighteth every man that cometh into the world, and philosophy is not such a light. Proof: who was the philosopher who taught the disciples? They were weak and foolish things when God chose them to proclaim his doctrine and, as St. Paul says (I Cor. 1), to overthrow and confound the wise of this world. Similarly today worldly or human wisdom is confounded and overthrown by those who have attained to the divine doctrine by inward longing and faith. We see, then, that the simplicity of the disciples was instructed only by God, which is an example to us, that we might seek the form of divine doctrine from God alone. The doctrine of God is never formed more clearly than

[42] *werffend sy die nasen uff.*

when it is done by God himself and in the words of God. Indeed, I make bold to say that those who make themselves, that is men, the arbiters of Scripture, make a mockery of trust in the Spirit of God by their design and pretension, seeking to wrest and force the Scriptures according to their own folly. For whenever anyone offers to arbitrate or testify he lays himself open to suspicion. Much more so in this particular case, in which there is one who bids us come to himself, and it is from him that the Word comes, and we resist, not because of the weakness of the Word, but because of the bondage of sinful lusts [43] deceiving us and wresting the Word according to their own caprice.

When you say then that an arbiter is needed to decide the issue and to compel those who are defeated, I deny it: for even the most learned of men are fallible except in so far as they are led by God. If they are not certain, God will guide them, but I myself can come to the same teacher and guide, and he will undoubtedly guide me also.(47) You say: How do you know whether he will teach you or not? Answer: From his own words in Matthew 21 and Mark 11: "All things whatsoever—that is, all things which it is right and proper for God to give—ye shall ask in prayer, believing, ye shall receive." Then, St. James teaches me to go to God for wisdom (James 1), saying: "If any of you lack wisdom, let him ask of God, that giveth to all men liberally, and upbraideth not; and it shall be given him. But let him ask in faith, nothing wavering." Note that James points us to God and not to men. You say: But today we have men to preach to us: should we not ask of the preachers and doctors? Answer: No matter who a man may be, if he teaches you in accordance with his own thought and mind his teaching is false. But if he teaches you in accordance with the Word of God, it is not he that teaches you, but God who teaches him. For as Paul says, who are we but ministers of Christ and dispensers or stewards of the mysteries of God? Again, I know for certain that God teaches me, because I have experienced the fact of it: and to prevent misunderstanding this is what I mean when I say that I know for certain that God teaches me. When I was younger, I gave myself overmuch to human teaching, like others of my day, and when about seven or eight years ago I undertook to devote myself entirely to the Scriptures I was always prevented by philosophy and theology. But eventually I came to the point where led by the

[43] anfechtungen, vitio affectuum (G).

Word and Spirit of God I saw the need to set aside all these
things and to learn the doctrine of God direct from his own
Word.(48) Then I began to ask God for light and the Scriptures
became far clearer to me—even though I read nothing else—
than if I had studied many commentators and expositors.
Note that that is always a sure sign of God's leading, for I
could never have reached that point by my own feeble understanding. You may see then that my interpretation does not
derive from the over-estimation of myself, but the subjection.
You were going to speak, but I will forestall you. What you
wanted to say was this: It is a great error to think that you
understand a matter perfectly and not to accept advice.
Answer: it is indeed if we rest in our own understanding. And
that is what you do, for you will not leave your human understanding, but would rather shape the divine understanding
to it, if you will forgive me saying so.(49) Hear the words of Paul
(I Cor. 2): "But the natural man receiveth not the things
of the Spirit of God: for they are foolishness unto him: neither
can he know them, because, they are spiritually discerned.
But he that is spiritual judgeth all things, yet he himself is
judged of none. For who hath known the mind of the Lord,
that he may instruct him." These words of Paul are more
precious than all the gold upon earth.[44] The natural man is
he who brings his own mind: the spiritual man he who does
not trust any mind but that which is given by God: he is pure
and simple, and quite free from worldly ambition or covetousness or carnal lust. The spiritual man judges all things, that is,
he sees at once whether the doctrine is of God or not. But he is
judged of none, that is, even if he is judged, which for this
reason he cannot be, he will not let himself be torn or turned
aside. No matter how great the human wisdom opposed to him,
he replies: Who has told you the mind of God, that you declare
things which God himself has not said, that is, you say that you
have received them from God, but you lie, otherwise God
contradicts himself, for elsewhere he says something quite
different. But you would teach God and force him according
to your own desires, etc. Illustration: in Matthew 18 God
instituted excommunication: sinners who commit flagrant sin
and offend their neighbours are to be cut off from their fellows,
just as a dead branch is cut off from a tree or a corrupt member
from the body. But when the bishops undertake to collect the
debts of usurers by condemning poor Christian people,(50) I

44 *uff unnd in dem erdtrich.*

do not believe that those people are really bound or excommunicated before God. And why? Because God said: "When thy brother sins," not: "When thy brother is in debt, thou shalt cut him off." And I am certain that that is the teaching of God, and you will not change my view even if you bring against me all the lies and inventions of the canonists or the hypocrisy of the monks [45] or the wrath of bloated prelates or the poison of Rome or the fire of Etna or indeed of hell itself. And even if God did take away his grace and for fear of death I said otherwise with my lips, yet I should still know that this abuse is not pleasing to God and that it has no authority by the divine institution. But hear the fine way in which they cloak their action. They say: It is not for debt that we excommunicate them, but for disobedience, as if it were possible to discharge a debt at the very moment the excommunicator demands. And yet that is not our real answer, but this: On what grounds does a Christian owe any obedience to you in a matter of this kind? Did God command you bishops to be the world's debt-collectors? You reply: "*Obedite prepositis vestris*," "be obedient to them that guide you." But does that mean: "Excommunicate men for debt"? In this and in other matters we shall not go astray if we seek only the mind of the Spirit. But if we do not, if we apply our energies to find scriptural support for our own opinions, though they are nothing but leaves and grass, [46] we shall constantly be in error. The will of God is this, that he alone should be the teacher. And I intend to be taught by him and not by men, that is, in respect of doctrine: for in respect of sin and disobedience I will be subject to all. For it is not for us to sit in judgment on Scripture and divine truth, but to let God do his work in and through it, for it is something which we can learn only of God. Of course, we have to give an account of our understanding of Scripture, but not in such a way that it is forced or wrested according to our own will, but rather so that we are taught by Scripture: and that is my own intention. Paul says (I Cor. 4): "For with me it is a very small thing that I should be judged of you, or of man's judgment. Yea, I judge not mine own self. For I know nothing by myself; yet am I not hereby justified: but he that judgeth me is the Lord." The Lord, who addressed and instructed Paul and all the apostles and all who proclaim his truth, he is to be their judge. We speak of Scripture, and this came from God and not from men (II Pet. 1). How then can

45 *kappenfritzen—Kapuzenträger*—those who bear the cowl.   46 *loub und gras.*

man be its judge? Paul describes it as *theopneuston*, that is, inspired or uttered by God (II Tim. 3).(51) He admits that even the lowliest can speak on Scripture when the leading prophets—that is, teachers—have missed the truth, so long as he is inspired thereto by God (I Cor. 14). At this point you might ask: Who is to tell me whether he is divinely enlightened or not? The God who enlightens him will enable you to perceive that what he says is of God. You may say: That is not my experience, but if so, take heed lest you be of those who have ears and hear not, as Christ shows from Isaiah (Matt. 13). Even if God does leave you unenlightened in your own hostile opinion, he will still use you for good. How? In this way. Paul says (I Cor. 11): "For there must be also heresies among you, that they which are approved may be made manifest among you." Your contentiousness is the means of revealing that which otherwise would neither be sought nor asked of God. And now finally, to make an end of answering objections, our view of the matter is this: that we should hold the Word of God in the highest possible esteem—meaning by the Word of God only that which comes from the Spirit of God—and we should give to it a trust which we cannot give to any other word. For the Word of God is certain and can never fail. It is clear, and will never leave us in darkness. It teaches its own truth. It arises and and irradiates the soul of man with full salvation and grace. It gives the soul sure comfort in God. It humbles it, so that it loses and indeed condemns itself and lays hold of God. And in God the soul lives, searching diligently after him and despairing of all creaturely consolation. For God is its only confidence and comfort. Without him it has no rest: it rests in him alone (A.V. Ps. 77): "My soul refused to be comforted; I remembered God, and was refreshed." Blessedness begins indeed in this present time, not essentially, but in the certainty of consoling hope. May God increase it in us more and more, and never suffer us to fall from it. Amen.

I (52) thought it might be good at this point to give some instruction in the way to come to a true understanding of the Word of God and to a personal experience of the fact that you are taught of God. For if we are not versed in Scripture, how are we to tell whether the priest who teaches us is expounding the pure truth unadulterated by his own sinful desires?

First, we must pray inwardly to God, that he will kill off the old man who sets such great store by his own wisdom and ability.

Second, when the old man is killed off and removed, that God will graciously infill us, and in such measure that we believe and trust only in him.

Third, when that is done we shall certainly be greatly refreshed and comforted, and we must constantly repeat the words of the prophet: Lord, God, strengthen that which thou hast wrought in us. For "let him that thinketh he standeth take heed lest he fall," as Paul says.

Fourth, the Word of God does not overlook anyone, and least of all the greatest. For when God called Paul, he said to Ananias: "He is a chosen vessel unto me, to bear my name before the princes and kings of the earth." Again, he says to the disciples (Matt. 10): "And ye shall be brought before governors and kings, that ye may testify unto them concerning me."

Fifth, it is the nature and property of the Word to humble the high and mighty and to exalt the lowly. That was the song of the Virgin Mary: "He hath put down the mighty from their seats, and exalted them of low degree." And again, John proclaimed concerning Christ (Luke 3): "By him shall all the hills be brought low, and the valleys filled, etc." (53)

Sixth, the Word of God always attracts and helps the poor, comforting the comfortless and despairing, but opposing those who trust in themselves, as Christ testifies.

Seventh, it does not seek its own advantage: for that reason Christ commanded his disciples to take neither scrip nor purse.

Eighth, it seeks only that God may be revealed to men, that the obstinate may fear him and the lowly find comfort in God. Those who preach in that manner are undoubtedly right. Those who cautiously beat about the bush [47] for their own advantage, defending the teaching of man instead of holding and expounding the doctrine of God, are false prophets. Know them by their words. They make a fine outcry: The holy Fathers! Is it nothing that man can do? and the like. But for all their complaining they do not complain that the Gospel of Christ is slackly proclaimed.

Ninth, when you find that the Word of God renews you, and begins to be more precious to you than formerly when you heard the doctrines of men, then you may be sure that this is the work of God within you.

Tenth, when you find that it gives you assurance of the grace of God and eternal salvation, it is of God.

[47] *hüpschlich strychend, wie ein katz umb ein bry:* lit. cautiously prowl around like a cat round a (hot) mash.

Eleventh, when you find that it crushes and destroys you, but magnifies God himself within you, it is a work of God.

Twelfth, when you find that the fear of God begins to give you joy rather than sorrow, it is a sure working of the Word and Spirit of God.

May God grant us that Spirit.[48] Amen.

[48] *Den welle uns got geben*—to achieve the precise reference of the German it is necessary either to translate *den* by "him" or to repeat "that Spirit."

Of the Education of Youth

INTRODUCTION

THE SHORT ESSAY ON THE ESSENTIALS OF A CHRIS-
tian education belongs to the year 1523,[1] when Zwingli
was actively engaged in the reformation of church life
in Zurich. Ostensibly it was written as a personal gift for his
future step-son,[2] Gerold Meyer von Knonau, who had just
returned from a visit to the baths at Baden. It is significant,
however, that the time when it appeared, August 1, 1523,
was the very time when Zwingli was at work upon the reorganization of the Great Minster and the Minster school.
The particular importance of the latter lay in the fact that
Zwingli looked to it both as an agency to disseminate Reformed
truth and also as a place of training for future pastors of the
Reformed Church.[3] In these circumstances it is not illegitimate
to regard the essay as something more than a personal admoni-
tion. It is a statement of the principles underlying the projected
educational reform. That the essay is for the most part impersonal in tone and that it was obviously written with a view
to publication makes it quite certain that something of this
was in the mind of Zwingli himself at the time when he wrote.[4]

Zwingli's pronounced stress upon the need for education and
the fact that he had very definite ideas concerning it are
hardly surprising when we remember that he had himself
come to a knowledge of evangelical truth partly by way

---

[1] Cf. C.R., II, pp. 526 f.
[2] Strictly, Gerold was already his step-son, for a secret marriage between
Zwingli and Anna Meyer seems to have taken place prior to the official
ceremony on April 2, 1524.
[3] Cf. D.C.R. 194.
[4] C.R., II, pp. 526 f.

of the Renaissance learning.[5] It may be recalled, too, that he had had some experience as a teacher during his university days in Basel, and that at Glarus and to some extent at Einsiedeln and Zurich he had held classes for the more promising young men of the congregation.[6] Again, in Zurich Zwingli had quickly pressed for the introduction of Greek studies, more particularly with a view to a better knowledge of the New Testament,[7] and already in 1522 he had brought in the well-known scholar Ceporinus[8] to take classes in Greek and Hebrew. It seems that Zwingli himself attended the Hebrew course, for his efforts to learn this language had not previously been attended by any great success. Unfortunately Ceporinus was not able to stay in Zurich more than a few months, for he had to return to Basel to superintend the publication of his Greek Grammar, a work which he dedicated to Zwingli. However, in June, 1523, Zwingli was able to introduce his programme for the reorganization of the Minster school, and this was formally accepted by the Council on September 29. After its reconstitution, the school consisted of two main sections, the one a grammar school, providing instruction in the rudiments of a classical education,[9] and the other a theological seminary, providing more advanced theological teaching for ministers and ordinands.[10] In both cases the main emphasis was upon those humanistic and biblical studies which form a basis for general Christian education and which have also a particular value in training for the work of the ministry. Ceporinus himself returned in 1525 to lecture in Greek and Hebrew, but in December of the same year he died at the early age of 26.

A point worth noting is that in the essay, although Zwingli touches on all aspects of training, he gives the place of pre-eminence to a definite instruction in Christian and evangelical truth. The suggestion has sometimes been made that Zwingli was more of a humanist than a Reformer, or at any rate that he was a Reformer because he was first a humanist.[11] Now it

---

[5] Although the extent of Renaissance influence is an open question. Cf. O. Farner, *Huldrych Zwingli*, II, esp. pp. 152 f.
[6] *Ibid.*, I, p. 194 f.; II, esp. pp. 152 f.   [7] C.R., II, *loc. cit.*
[8] Ceporinus (Jakob Wiesendanger) was born *c.* 1499, had studied at Winterthur, Cologne, Vienna and Ingolstadt and gained proficiency in Greek and Hebrew as well as Latin. In Basel he worked as a Greek proof-reader.
[9] D.C.R. 194, 7.   [10] *Ibid.*, 5.
[11] Cf. S. M. Jackson, *Zwingli*, pp. 77 f.

can hardly be denied that his Renaissance contacts and studies did help Zwingli towards an apprehension of New Testament truth. But it is easy to exaggerate this humanistic aspect at the expense of the deeper theological and spiritual needs which drove Zwingli to the Bible and evangelical truth.[12] In his thinking as in his actions Zwingli was fully aware of the primacy and centrality of the Gospel itself. For that reason the first and most important task of the teacher is to inculcate a knowledge of theological truth and ethical duty. All other aims are subservient to that primary and ultimate goal. Education does not consist only in making good scholars, not even good classical scholars. It consists first of all in making good Christians. And for that reason the first section of Zwingli's essay is devoted to an exposition of the main teachings of the Gospel, and even in the two succeeding sections, in which he treats of the more detailed matters of curriculum and conduct, the individual themes are constantly related to Christian faith and discipleship.

Of course, the work is not meant to be an exhaustive treatise, but for that very reason the emphases and judgments of Zwingli have a particular interest and value. On the more purely academic side he gives pride of place to the three ancient languages, Latin, Greek and Hebrew: [13] Latin because of its indispensability to the scholar, Greek and Hebrew because of their usefulness in the more intensive study of Holy Scripture. He has not a great deal to say concerning other subjects. The ability to speak effectively he regarded as essential—no doubt he had the pulpit in view—and he included some interesting advice on this difficult art. A certain value could be accorded to mathematics, but it appears that the mathematician occupied a lowly status and could not count on any certain livelihood in the sixteenth century, and Zwingli could not recommend any serious study of this subject. Indeed, by present-day standards the most serious deficiencies of the whole programme are on the scientific and to some extent the modern side. Apparently Zwingli did envisage a limited consideration of natural science because of its then theological value,[14] but there is no evidence of any interest in science as such, and history and geography seem to be entirely ignored. Similarly,

12 Farner, *op. cit.*, II, pp. 127 f., 234 f., 347 f.
13 The ordinance of reform instituted lectureships in these three languages, D.C.R. 194, 5.
14 I.e., to prove the existence and providence of God.

there is no place for a study of the vernacular—spelling at least might have been a help—for Latin still remained the universal language of scholarship and literature. Of course, it must be remembered that Zwingli had in mind the type of training that would be most suitable for the theologian, and with all its limitations the suggested programme undoubtedly forms a useful course for the particular purpose in view.

Apart from the academic side, the essay has further points of interest. It testifies to the fact that Zwingli's concern was not narrowly religious or scholastic. He could see the need for recreation and physical exercise as well as doctrinal and academic training. In this respect the ideal of Zwingli represents all that is best in the Renaissance-Reformation movement. As Zwingli saw it, ideal manhood can be attained only by the full and proper development of the three main aspects of man's nature. It is not enough merely to cultivate the soul or spirit, though that must be the first priority. Nor it is enough to cultivate the soul and the mind together. The mind must be trained, and even the mind must have interests outside the purely academic. For that reason all games which had an intellectual or cultural value—chess for example—were commended by Zwingli, so long, of course, as they were not allowed to become ends in themselves. But in addition, Zwingli saw that the body must be trained and fit as well as the mind and spirit. Bodily exercise might not profit greatly if divorced from godliness, but that did not mean that it could be dismissed as completely worthless. In this matter Zwingli retained a right sense of proportion, and he could advocate strongly all bodily exercises which contributed to physical health and vigour, notably running, jumping and wrestling. Rather strangely, he had no great enthusiasm for swimming, the utility of which he seemed slow to recognize in spite of the frequent disasters in many of the Swiss lakes and rivers.[15] In this same connection Zwingli pointed out the value of plain and wholesome foods and the need for moderation in eating and drinking. The whole emphasis upon physical fitness contrasts favourably with that comparative neglect of the body which was a characteristic feature of much mediaeval piety.

The remarks on morals and manners again bear witness to the sane and balanced outlook of the Swiss Reformer. Zwingli would not tolerate dicing and card-games, no doubt because of their evil associations, but on the other hand he saw the

15 Cf. Farner, II, p. 24.

need for social gatherings in which the young (and old) of both
sexes might freely mingle in public. Nothing could be more
foolish or dangerous than to attempt to suppress entirely the
instincts which find expression in public festivities. As concerns
marriage, Zwingli regarded it as the normal fulfilment of one
aspect of human life. Rightly, he deprecated any laxity in
sexual relationships, but rightly too, he found the cure in a right
use rather than attempted repression. In this respect he was
taught by his own difficult experiences when bound by the
ecclesiastical law of chastity.[16] Zwingli's remarks on war are
also of interest, the more so as the manner of his death has left
the impression of a certain lack of scruple in the use of military
force. Zwingli did stress the advantages of martial training, but
he justified such activities only on the grounds that the unsettled
state of Europe demanded defensive precautions. The truth
is that although Zwingli was more ready than Luther to make
use of diplomatic and military weapons, his experiences in
Italy had taught him the bitterness and futility of war,[17] and
he could not accept it except when compelled by patriotic or
evangelical duty.

The essay as a whole is marred by that disjointedness which
characterizes almost all Zwingli's writings, but in content it is
a fine statement of the Reformation ideal not merely for education but for life as a whole. In the essay we see the faith and
piety of the Reformation informed by all that was best in the
humanist movement. The narrowness, obscurantism and disproportionate other-worldliness which had marked so many
mediaeval writings had yielded before the breadth of interest,
the more vital scholarship and the balance in the understanding
of human life which were the special gifts of the Renaissance.
Yet Zwingli avoided the danger of anthropocentricity which
was the peculiar temptation of the humanist. When all is
said, the Zwinglian basis of education and life is an inward
faith in God and an acceptance of the obligations of faith.
Upon that foundation a larger and more spacious building
was erected, but the foundation itself remained substantially
the same.

Editions[18]

The *Education of Youth* was originally written in Latin and
in this form it was first published at Basel in 1523. Ceporinus

16 *Ibid.*, pp. 140 f.   17 *Ibid.*, pp. 180 f.; C.R., XII, p. 267.
18 C.R., II, pp. 526 f.

arranged the publication and also contributed a Preface. The book was well received, and there were fresh editions in 1524 (Augsburg), 1525 (Zurich) and 1561 (Zurich). There is a fifth edition without name or date, probably deriving from Augsburg. Ceporinus made the first translation into German, and this was published in 1524, most likely at Augsburg. A revised translation appeared at Zurich two years later, and this version has an added interest because it is almost certainly the work of Zwingli himself.[19] There is no direct evidence in favour of this supposition, but it is strongly suggested by the personal nature of the dedication, the use of many characteristic words and phrases, and the freedom with which the Latin original is expanded, compressed or altered. An early translation into English was made during the reign of Edward VI under the title *Certain Precepts* (London 1548).

The basis of the present translation is the original Latin text of 1523 (A), but Zwingli's German version of 1526 (B) is also used. The latter text is particularly valuable, partly because it provides a counter-check in the construing of the Latin, and partly because it offers some useful variations, usually expansions of the original. On the whole it has been thought better to retain the classical allusions mainly abandoned in the German versions. The main variations between A and B are indicated in the textual notes, and where helpful, reference is made to Ceporinus' more literal rendering of 1524 (C).

[19] So W. Koehler in his selections 1918–1919.

Of the Upbringing and Education of Youth in Good Manners and Christian Discipline: An Admonition by Ulrich Zwingli

THE TEXT

To the noble and pious youth Gerold Meyer,(1) I, Ulrich Zwingli, wish grace and peace from God and our Lord Jesus Christ. On your return from the baths[1] at Baden (2) you have been received everywhere with presents, some honouring you in one way and some in another. It would therefore be regarded as most discourteous[2] on my part, my dear Gerold,[3] if I too did not welcome you with a gift: the more so as it is the usual custom amongst friends to honour in that way those who return from or are still at the baths. I number you amongst my friends for two reasons: first, because you are seriously and (as I hope) not unprofitably devoted to learning; [4] and second, because you are one of those who serve under our Glareanus.[5](3) I have considered at length what gift would be most acceptable to you, and I have reached the conclusion that that which will serve you best must be either religious or literary in character, or perhaps both. For by nature you are born to divine favour and virtue, and already you reveal the acceptable fruits of discipline and culture. However, no matter how diligently I applied myself to the task I could never achieve anything of literary merit. Therefore I thought it might be profitable both for yourself and others if I fulfilled my obligation towards you by setting out certain precepts (4) which would be wholesome and helpful for

[1] A, *a thermis*; B, *von Baden*.
[2] A, *incivilis*; B, *eine grosse grobheyt und unvernunft*.
[3] A, *Gerolde adolescens suavissime*.
[4] A, *literis*; B, *der leer und kunst*; C, *die schrifft*.
[5] A, *sub Glareani nostri signis meres*; B, is much expanded: *under unserem Glareano als under einem gelerten und berichten houptmann unnd leerer in der zal siner jungen helden dich arbeitest*.

N.B.—The capitals refer to the editions as lettered on preceding page.

102

both body and soul and which would serve to the advancement of virtue and piety. For some time I have been planning a book on the right upbringing and education of youth, but my plans were hindered by the many distracting matters which came up (as things then were). But as I have considered what gift I should make my earlier project has taken shape again. I notice that many writers, when they have finished their work, are anxious to dedicate it to someone who is truly worthy of it. But with us the very opposite is the case. For the one to whom this book will be dedicated is already found, but I myself lack the time and leisure, the nine years which a workman should spend upon his work.(5) Being in a strait between the two demands, the first, that I must have something to give you, and the second, that I have had neither the time nor the leisure to fulfil the task properly, I have found, I think, a way to satisfy both of us. I have stolen sufficient time hurriedly to gather together some precepts and admonitions—but not too many, and all carefully selected so as not to drive away, for it is often the case that when little is poured out, the desire to drink is all the greater.(6) You must not weigh and judge these counsels according to their outward form, but according to their content, and the spirit which has given them birth. For anyone who is not ungodly can promise a godly work: but even the most learned would be ashamed to promise a work of art. These precepts of mine fall into three parts:

The first tells how the tender mind of youth is to be instructed in the things of God;

The second, how it is to be instructed in the things which concern itself;

And the third, how it is to be instructed in conduct towards others.

It is not my purpose to set out the directions which ought to be given from the cradle or during the earliest years at school,[6] but those which are suitable for young men who have already attained to discretion and can stand on their own feet.[7] I count you amongst this number. You will, I hope, diligently read these directions and so model yourself upon them that you will be a living example to others. May God[8] himself do this work in you.(7) Amen.

Zurich, August 1, MCXXIII

---

[6] A, neque . . . a cunis ordiri, neque a rudimentis; B, söliche underwysungen, die man den kinden von den wiegen an geben sölle, ouch not wie man die anfahenden schüler erstlich berichtet.

[7] lit. "swim without corks."   [8] A, Christus optimus maximus; B, gott.

PART I

First and chiefly, it is beyond our human capacity to bring the hearts of men to faith in the one God (8) even though we had an eloquence surpassing that of Pericles.[9] (9) For that is something which only our heavenly Father can do as he draws us to himself. Yet it is still the case, in the words of St. Paul, that "faith cometh by hearing, and hearing by the Word of God," though this does not mean that very much can be accomplished by the preaching of the external word apart from the internal address and compulsion of the Spirit.(10) Therefore it is necessary not merely to instil faith into the young by the pure words which proceed from the mouth of God, but to pray that he who alone can give faith will illuminate by his Spirit those whom we instruct in his Word.

It seems to me to be quite in keeping with Christ's own teaching to bring young people to a knowledge of God in and through external phenomena.(11) For as we bring before them the fair structure of the universe, pointing them to each part in particular, we learn that all these things are changing and destructible,[10] but that he who conjoined them (and many other things besides) in so lasting and marvellous a whole is necessarily unchanging and immutable. Again, we learn that he who has so skilfully [11] ordered all these things need never be suspected of forgetting or disregarding his handiwork, for even with men it is counted a reproach if the head of the household [12] does not keep a careful watch over all domestic matters.(12)

Thus the young man is taught that all things are ordained [13] by the providence of God: for of the two sparrows sold for a farthing not one can fall to the ground except by decision of the divine providence (which has also numbered the very hairs of our head), nothing being too insignificant for its care.

Hence it is clear that the divine providence appoints the things necessary for the body as well as the soul. We see that by it the ravens are liberally fed and the lilies gloriously arrayed. By such forms of the divine providence the spirit of man is

[9] B expands: *den hochberümpten und wol beredten Periclem.*

[10] A, *esse mutatione obnoxia*; B, *dass die ding alle wandelbar und zerstörlich sygind.*

[11] A, *tanta solertia*; B, *so klüglich, so artlich.*

[12] B, *hussvater*—this is an expansion of A.

[13] A, *destinare*; B, expands: *fürsieht, fürordnet und bescheert.*

taught that it ought never to give way either to anxiety or to ignoble greed. And if the temptation to greed or anxiety is hewn down and uprooted as soon as it begins to spring up, we shall keep our soul from a harmful poison.[14]

For we shall then know in our heart that God is not only the Lord but also the Father of all those who trust in him. We shall know that men ought to run to him for help no less than they do to an earthly father. We shall know that in his words he has promised us that help, indeed he wills that we should make our prayer to him. If, then, we are afflicted by sickness of mind or body, we are taught to look only to him for healing. If we are oppressed by enemies or harassed by envy and hatred, we learn to flee only to him. If we desire wisdom or learning, we are taught to ask it of him alone. Indeed, it is from him that we are to seek even our wife and children, and if riches and honour are showered liberally upon us, we ought to pray to him that our heart may be kept from corruption or from turning aside from him.

I need not say more. Instructed in this way,[15] the soul knows that it ought to ask all things from God. And it knows how shameful it is to ask anything which God cannot fittingly give. In fact, it will be ashamed either to ask or to have anything that it cannot fittingly receive from God. It will keep before it and lay up for itself only the things which are a true source of blessing.

The young man whom we teach will know and understand the mystery of the Gospel as follows.(13) First, he must know the original estate of man, how he transgressed the commandment of God and became a prey to death, how by his transgression he infected and corrupted his offspring—the whole human race—for the dead cannot give birth to the living and we do not find Moors born in Britain.[16] (14) From this the young man will learn and acknowledge his own sickness. And he will see that sickness, too, when he realizes that everything that we do has its origin in frailty, lust and temptation, but God himself is far above all such temptation,[17] for in him

14 B, *und wo wir dise anfächtung* (C, *bewegung*) *dess gyts und sorgfaltiger angst, glych so sy anfacht grünen, abhauen und ussrüten, werdend wir unsere gemüt vor einem schädlichen gifft verhüten.*
15 B expands: *wo und gemüt sölicher mass, wie obergesagt, bericht ist.*
16 A, *nec Aethiopem vidimus imquam apud Britannos natum*; B, *als wir dann by den Britanniern nye kein Moren geborn gesehend habend.* Ethiopian is used in the sense of black man. Cf. Erasmus, *Adagiorum Chil. I, Centur. IV, Prov. 50.*   17 Following the expanded version in B.

is no temptation. Hence it follows that if we would dwell with God, we must be set free from all temptations. There can be no fellowship between the godly and the wicked, nor can the wicked bear with the godly (for the Neros order the Senecas to be punished, and the Ennii and the Scipios are covered by the same tomb).[18] (15) Similarly, only those can dwell with God who are holy (as God himself is holy), whose lives are without blemish and whose hearts are pure: "Blessed are the pure in heart, for they shall see God."

But beset on every hand by gross temptations, how can we attain to such purity? for we are set between the hammer and the anvil, half beast and half angel.[19] God requires of us a perfect righteousness, but we are corrupted and full of sin and whether we will or no we can do nothing but evil. Therefore we have no choice but to give up ourselves into the hand of God, to abandon ourselves entirely to his grace. And here it is that there breaks forth the light of the Gospel, the good news proclaimed to us [20] that Christ releases us from the desperate plight in which we were held.[21] And Christ redeems us far better than any Saviour Jupiter.[22] (16) First he restores the conscience, which is reduced almost to despair. He unites it with himself in an unshakable hope, thus setting it at rest. For he himself is free from all the pollutions and onslaughts of sin, being conceived of the Holy Ghost and born of a pure Virgin. And first he puts forth his righteousness [23] (17) for us, bearing our griefs and sicknesses: then he redeems all those who steadfastly believe. For those who believe in the bountiful gift which God has made our poor race in Christ are saved and made co-heirs with Christ, to enjoy eternal felicity with the Father: for he wills that where he is, there his servants may be also.

The righteousness [24] of Christ, put forth for us who are sinful and lost, releases us from sin and the guilt and suffering of sin[25] and makes us worthy before God. And it does so for this reason, that Christ is able to attain the standard of divine righteous-

18 B omits both these allusions.
19 Conflating the variant forms in A (*inter malleum et incudem*) and B (*zwüschen tür und angel*).
20 "proclaimed to us" is added by B.
21 B expands this thought.
22 B omits the title "servator."
23 A, *innocentia*; B, *unschuld und frombkeyt.*
24 A, *innocentia*; B, *die unschuld, frombkeyt und reynigkeyt.*
25 Following the slightly expanded version in B.

ness,[26] (18) being free from all corrupt affections. And he, the righteous and more than righteous, that is, God himself, was made like one of us. Hence it follows that his righteousness (which lacked in us) was made ours: "for of God he is made unto us wisdom, righteousness, sanctification and redemption."(19) Now therefore we have access by him to God, for he is ours, a sure token of divine grace, an advocate, a pledge, a security, an intercessor, a mediator, the first and the last,[27] the alpha and omega, our all.[28]

Those who understand and believe the mystery of the Gospel thus far are born of God: for blinded by human folly the mind cannot of itself attain to the deep counsel of divine grace. By this we learn that those who are born again of the Gospel do not sin: for "whosoever is born of God sinneth not," and whosoever believes the Gospel is born of God.(20) Hence it follows that those who are born again of the Gospel do not sin, that is, sin is not imputed to them to death and perdition, for Christ has redeemed them [29] at the price of his death.

As long as we are absent from the Lord in this mortal body we cannot be free from temptations. Therefore we cannot be entirely without sin. But Christ himself is ours and makes good all our deficiencies. For he is an eternal God and Spirit. And that means that he is of sufficient value to redeem the offences of all men, more so indeed than the offences themselves can possibly require.(21)

But such confidence in Christ does not make us idle.[30] (22) On the contrary it equips and constrains us to do good and to live rightly, for such confidence is not of man. For in most things the human mind depends upon the external senses. But how can it come to put its confidence in something which none of the senses can perceive? In view of this, we can very well see that such faith and confidence in Christ can derive only from God. Now where God works, you need have no fear that things will not be done rightly.

For God is an entelechy,[31] (23) that is, a perfect and immutable force which moves all things and itself remains unmoved. And as such, he will never allow the heart which he has drawn

---

26 A, justitia; B, frombkeyt und unschuld.   27 A, prora et puppis.
28 The different versions are here conflated: A, prora et puppis, α et ω; B, unser all; and C, which adds der anfang und das end after das Alpha und Omega.
29 B adds: "and cleansed."   30 A, segnes; B, ful, noch farlässing.
31 A, endelechia; B, ein vollkommnende, yemerwärende bewegnus oder bewegende kraft.

to himself to be unmoved or static. This statement has to be confirmed, not by proofs but by practice. For only believers know and experience the fact that Christ will not let his people be idle. They alone know how joyful and pleasant a thing it is to engage in his service.

Therefore those who have rightly understood the mystery of the Gospel will exert themselves to live rightly. As far as possible, then, we should learn the Gospel with all exactness and diligence. And as occasion offers we should study what services will be most pleasing to God: and undoubtedly these are the very ones which he himself renders to us, righteousness, fidelity and mercy.[32] For God is a Spirit, and he can be truly worshipped only with the sacrifice of a consecrated spirit. The young man should see to it, then, that he studies to grow up a man of God, righteous in life and as nearly like God as possible. For God does good to all and is profitable to all. He does hurt only to those who first do hurt to him. So, too, the man who is most like God is the one who studies to be profitable to all, to be all things to all men, and to keep himself from all forms of evil. When we consider our own powers, these things are very difficult, but "to him that believeth all things are possible."

PART II

Once a young man is instructed in the solid virtue which is formed by faith,(24) it follows that he will regulate himself and richly adorn himself from within: for only he whose whole life is ordered finds it easy to give help and counsel to others.(25)

But a man cannot rightly order his own soul unless he exercises himself day and night in the Word of God. He can do that most readily if he is well versed in such languages as Hebrew and Greek,(26) for a right understanding of the Old Testament is difficult without the one, and a right understanding of the New is equally difficult without the other.

But we are instructing those who have already learned the rudiments, and everywhere Latin has the priority. In these circumstances I do not think that Latin should be altogether neglected. For an understanding of Holy Scripture it is of less value than Hebrew and Greek, but for other purposes it is just as useful. And it often happens that we have to do the business[33] of Christ amongst those who speak Latin. No Christian

32 B adds to this short list of virtues.
33 A, *negotium*; B, *gschäfft*; C, *sach*.

should use these languages simply for his own profit or pleasure: for languages are gifts of the Holy Ghost.

After Latin we should apply ourselves to Greek. We should do this for the sake of the New Testament, as I have said already. And if I may say so, to the best of my knowledge the Greeks have always handled the doctrine of Christ better than the Latins.(27) For that reason we should always direct our young men to this source. But in respect of Greek as well as Latin we should take care to garrison our souls with innocence and faith, for in these tongues there are many things which we learn only to our hurt: wantonness, ambition, violence, cunning, vain philosophy and the like. But the soul, like Ulysses,(28) can steer safely past all these if it is only forewarned, that is, if at the first sound of the voices it pays heed to the warning: Hear this in order to shun and not to receive.

I put Hebrew last because Latin is in general use and Greek follows most conveniently. Otherwise I would willingly have given Hebrew the precedence, for in many places even amongst the Greeks those who are ignorant of Hebrew forms of speech have great difficulty [34] in attempting to draw out the true sense of Scripture. But it is not my purpose to speak exhaustively of these languages.

If a man would penetrate to the heavenly wisdom, with which no earthly wisdom ought rightly to be considered, let alone compared, it is with such arms that he must be equipped. And even then he must still approach with a humble [35] and thirsting spirit.(29)

If he does come, however, he will everywhere find patterns of right conduct, that is, he will find Christ himself, the perfect exemplar of all virtues. And if he knows Christ fully both in his words and deeds, he will know that in all his acts and counsels, so far as human frailty [36] allows, he must venture to manifest some part of the virtues of Christ.

He will learn of Christ both in speech and in silence, each at the proper time. In early youth, he will be ashamed to speak those things which are more fitting in adults, for he will note that Christ did not begin to preach until about his thirtieth year. It is true that when he was only twelve he attracted the attention of the doctors of the law, but from this instance we do not learn to rush in hastily, but from early

[34] A, *sudet*; B, *gross arbeit haben muss.*
[35] A, *humili*; B, *niderträchtigem.*
[36] A, *tenuitati*; B, *blodigkeit*; C, *unvermügen.*

youth to exert ourselves in the high matters which are worthy of God.

For as silence is always the greatest adornment of a wife, so nothing is more becoming to youth than to try to be silent for a time, so that mind and tongue may be instructed both individually and together, and thus learn to co-operate with each other. It is not my intention to enforce a five years' silence, like that which Pythagoras demanded of his disciples,(30) but to warn against a too great readiness in speech. And I forbid a young man to speak at all unless he has something useful and necessary to say.

Quite naturally, a young man acquires the manner of speech of his teacher. He must be careful, then, not to follow him in what is bad, for even in speech there is sure to be some defect.[37] And this warning must not be treated too lightly, for amongst the ancients it is recorded that some imitated their masters' defects not only in speech but in life. To recognize deficiency in language is easy, but in expression and enunciation (we are not speaking technically, for which this is not the place) the common faults are these: the rate of speaking is either too fast or too slow; the tone is either too low and weak or too high and strong, irrespective of the subject matter; the style is monotonous: and the accompanying gestures are hackneyed, or perhaps the gesticulation is not appropriate to what is being said.(31)

It has been observed that when elephants are alone they anxiously apply themselves to learn things for which they are beaten.[38] (32) In the same way the young man should constantly practise how to compose his mouth and features, and also how to use his hands, so that he may rightly indicate whatever is required and not merely beat the air.

And in all these things he must study moderation, that what he does may serve the truth and not merely please men: for how can the Christian soul countenance such meretricious devices? So then, when I ask that the young man should practise, I mean only that each one should learn privately to master or to eliminate his external faults, which are always the sure marks of an undeveloped or defective spirit.

Above all else, the spirit itself must be sound and ordered.[39] Where such is the case, it is easy to control the external movement of the features, so that instead of knitting our brows or

37 A, *vitii*; B, *lastren oder prästen*.   38 B expands the original.
39 A, *integram*; B, *styff*; C, *rechtschaffen*.

twisting our mouths or shaking our heads or tossing our hands hither and thither we direct all our gestures with the simple and unaffected moderation of the peasant. Thus far concerning speech and silence.

Superfluity of wine (33) is something which the young man must avoid like poison. In the young its effect is to inflame the body, which by nature is already prone to violence and lust. It also brings to premature age. And from the very outset it so corrupts the body that instead of finding in age the peace which we supposed we meet with nothing but trouble. For those who are accustomed to excess of wine will inevitably succumb at length to some dangerous sickness, epilepsy,[40] paralysis,[41] dropsy,[42] elephantiasis and the like. Therefore if you would be old long, be old betimes.

Other foods ought to be plain,[43] (34) for in youth the stomach is naturally designed to be fit, and what need is there of partridge, thrush, titlark, goat, roebuck and other delicacies? Much better to leave such things until old age, when the teeth and jaws are worn out and the throat has hardened with long use and the stomach has grown cold and the body is half-dead; it is then that these things are needed. For how shall we nourish our old age if for lack of self-control wanton youth has grown weary of the very things which age desires and in which it delights?

Hunger we should stay by eating but not banish completely. For it is written that Galenus (35) lived for a hundred and twenty years because he was never satisfied when he left the table. I do not mean that you should starve yourself to death, but that you should not give rein to a voracious appetite (beyond what is necessary for life). I know quite well that in this matter there are faults on both sides. On the one hand there is the man who is wolf-like in his voracity: and on the other hand the man who makes himself useless for lack of sustenance.(36)

I can think of nothing more foolish than to seek fame by way of expensive apparel. If we are to judge only according to outward appearance, we shall have to ascribe glory and honour to the papal mules, which are so strong that they can carry more gold and silver and precious stones than any Milo.[44] (37) But who will not be ashamed of such costly attire when he

[40] B, *siechtag*.   [41] B, *lämmy*; C, *gicht*.
[42] B, *malatzy*; C, *aussatz*.
[43] A, *parabilis*; B, *nochgültig*; C, *gemain*.
[44] B omits the reference to Milo.

hears of the Son of God and of the Virgin crying in the manger, with no more clothes in which to be swaddled than those which the Virgin Mary had taken with her (not yet expecting his birth).

Those who make daily display of new clothes give sure evidence of an inconstant, or (if that is too strong) an effeminate or childish [45] turn of mind. They are not Christians. For while they array themselves after this fashion they allow the destitute to perish with cold and hunger. So then the Christian must guard against excessive and wanton apparel as against any other form of evil.(38)

It is when the young man begins to fall in love that he must show true nobility of spirit. And as in war others exercise their arms with weapons and feats of strength, so the young man must now apply all his forces in defence against senseless passion. That he should fall in love is inevitable. But let him be careful not to give way to despairing passion, but to single out as the object of his affection someone whose ways he can always bear with in lawful wedlock.[46] Let him approach that one, but let his union with her be so pure and undefiled that apart from her he knows no other.

What need is there to forbid the Christian youth all desire for fame or wealth when such evils are castigated even by pagan writers?(39) He is no Christian who gives way to covetous ambition, the ambition which not only engulfs ones and twos and threes but overthrows flourishing kingdoms, devastates powerful cities and attacks and overturns the very foundations of government. Once this evil takes hold of the spirit, right conduct becomes impossible. Ambition is a deadly poison. And today it has gained the mastery and is rampant everywhere.[47] (40) Only through Christ can we destroy this evil, by seeking diligently to follow him: for what was Christ's work except to destroy this evil?

I advise the young man not to despise mathematics [48] (with which we may also reckon music),(41) but he ought not to devote too much time to this subject. It is useful to those who know it and an obstacle to those who do not. But it does not yield any great profit to those who grow old in its service, and they are reduced to wandering from place to place in order not to perish for lack of activity.

[45] A, tenerae; B, kindlich; C, waychen gemüts.
[46] Following the expanded version in B.
[47] Following B.
[48] A, mathematicae disciplina; B, die zal.

I do not blame anyone for learning the art of war,[49] but I should judge differently if I did not see other kingdoms fleeing the pursuits which are beneficial to the life of the community. A Christian should avoid the weapons of war as far as the security and peace of the state allow. For God made David to triumph when he was unskilled in arms and went against Goliath with a sling.[50] And he protected the unarmed Israelites against the invading enemy. Undoubtedly, then, he will help and protect us—or if he sees fit he will put weapons in our hands. For "he teaches our hands to fight." But if the young man does undergo military training, he must see to it that his only purpose is to protect his own country and those whom God approves. (42)

It is my wish that all men (and especially those who are commanded to preach the Word of God) should make it their aim to be able to emulate the ancient city of Marseilles,[51] (43) which numbered amongst its citizens only those who were masters of a trade and could support themselves. If that were so with us, then idleness, which is the root and seed of all forms of wantonness, would be excluded, and our bodies would be healthier and stronger and would live longer.

PART III

The noble spirit must first consider the fact that Christ gave himself up to death on our behalf and became ours: therefore we ought to give up ourselves for the good of all men, not thinking that we are our own, but that we belong to others. For we are not born to live to ourselves, but to become all things to all men.

From early boyhood, then, the young man ought to exercise himself only in righteousness, fidelity and constancy:[52] for with virtues such as these he may serve the Christian community,[53] the common good, the state and individuals. Only the weak are concerned to find a quiet life: the most like to God are those who study to be of profit to all even to their own hurt.

In this connection, however, we must be careful to see that the things undertaken for God's honour or the state or the common good are not corrupted by the devil or by self-pleasing,

---

[49] A, *palaestram*; B, *fächten*; C, *ringen und fechten*.
[50] Following B, which adds *mit der schlingen*.
[51] A, *Massilia*.   [52] B increases the list of virtues.
[53] A, *rei publicae Christianae*; B, *gemeiner Christenheyt*.

so that in the long run we turn to our own interest that which we want to be regarded as undertaken in the interests of others. For many begin well at the first, but they are quickly perverted and turned aside from all that is good by that vainglory which is the bane of all good counsels.

As regards the good or evil fortunes of others, a Christian spirit will conduct itself as if they were his own. When fortune comes to another he will think of it as coming to himself, and similarly with adversity. For he will look upon the whole fellowship [54] only as one household or family, indeed as one body, in which all the members rejoice and suffer together and help one another, so that whatever happens to one happens to all.

So then he will "rejoice with them that do rejoice and weep with them that weep," looking upon the fortunes of others as his own; for as Seneca says, What happens to one can happen to everyone. (44)

Yet the Christian ought not to show joy or grief after the common manner, being carried away by good fortune and plunged into despair by evil. On the contrary, seeing we must always be affected either by the one emotion or the other, we ought so to moderate them (if we are wise) that we never trespass the bounds of due decorum. And that is how we are to rejoice at the prosperity of others as at our own, and that is how we are also to weep, bearing all things with moderation and self-control.

I do not believe that a young man should be debarred from seemly pleasures, for instance at those times when the sexes are accustomed to come together publicly, [55] the marriage of relatives, annual games, carnivals and festivals: (45) for I note that Christ himself did not despise the wedding feast. Seeing such things are necessary, I am better pleased if they are done publicly and not in corners or secretly, for the multitude of witnesses is more frightening to some than their own conscience; and if there are any who are shameless enough to conduct themselves indecorously in public, no good can be expected of them. [56]

When communal gatherings of this kind do take place, the young man ought always to study to profit by them, so that he will not return home any the worse (which was the com-

[54] A, *rem publicam*; B, *gmeind*.
[55] Following the expanded version in B.
[56] This sentence is paraphrased and expanded in B.

plaint of Socrates). To that end he should mark those who are behaving honourably and decorously, that he may be able to follow them, and also those who are behaving scandalously and dishonourably, that he may avoid them.

But these things are not suitable for adults. For that reason it is my advice that the young ought to be allowed to attend such gatherings as infrequently as possible. Inevitably there is an almost frantic enthusiasm for associating with others in this way, but recovery from this enthusiasm should be swift. To help toward recovery, reasons can be offered which will satisfy those who realize that we are intent always upon better things.

When a neighbour is in trouble, we ought not to allow anything to hinder us from going. We should be the first there and the last away, and we must exert ourselves to weigh the hurt, treating it and removing it and proffering counsel.

Next to immortal God our parents ought to be held in highest esteem, as is customary even amongst pagans and unbelievers.(46) To our parents we ought always to yield.(47) And though at times they may not act according to the mind of Christ (which is our mind), we must not oppose them violently, but tell them as gently as possible what they ought to say and do.(48) And if they will not listen, it is better to leave them than to insult or reproach them.

Anger (as the natural scientists tell us) is a product of heat; and as youth is the time of heat, the young man ought to keep a careful watch against anger, that his words and actions may not be impelled by it. Since anger continues with us, we ought to mistrust anything that might give rise to it.

If an insult is offered which we cannot swallow because it is too bitter,[57] it is better to bring the matter before a magistrate or to take it to court. For if we give back word for word or reproach those who reproach us, we only make ourselves like those whom we reproach.

At the proper time there is no reason why you should not play games with your equals, but they ought to be useful either educationally or as bodily exercise. Games with educational value are those which involve numbers (from which we learn arithmetic), or strategy, as for example chess, which teaches how to advance and retreat, and how to keep careful watch behind and before; for the main lesson we learn from this game is not to assume anything rashly.(49) But even in this, moderation is to be observed, for there are some who push aside the

---

[57] A, *prae amaritudine*; B, *dass es ja uns zu bitter dunckt.*

serious affairs of life and give themselves to this one thing alone. For my part, I would allow such recreations only occasionally and as a pastime. Dicing and card-games I condemn absolutely.[58]

The games which exercise the body are running, jumping, throwing, fighting and wrestling, but the latter only in moderation, for it often takes on a serious character.[59] Such sports are common to almost all peoples, but especially amongst the Swiss,[60] who find them useful in many different circumstances.(50) I do not find the same value in swimming, though at the proper time it is pleasurable to stretch one's limbs in water and imitate the fish. And on occasion swimming has also proved useful, as with the man who swam from the Capitol and told Camillus of the pitiable state to which the city had been reduced by covetousness.(51) Chloelia too escaped to her own people by swimming.(52)

Our conversation and speech should all be of a kind to profit those with whom we live. If we have to reprove or punish, we ought to do it wisely and wittily, and so good humouredly and considerately that we not only drive away the offence but win over the offender, binding him more closely to us.

We ought to follow after truth with such consistency and single-heartedness that we weigh not only our own speech but that of others, lest it contain any deceit or falsehood. A man of noble spirit is never more perturbed than when he involuntarily lets slip an untruth—not to mention his shame and horror when he lets out a flood of idle and empty gossip invented by himself or repeated from others. The Christian is commanded to speak truth with his neighbour. Christ himself is the truth. Therefore the Christian must cleave steadfastly to the truth. "A double-minded man is unstable in all his ways." A man who is inconsistent in his speech cannot be trusted. The heart declares itself in speech. If the speech be empty and untruthful and inconsistent, it is a sure sign that things are far worse inwardly. At the same time, lies cannot be concealed indefinitely, although they may be for a long time. For that reason it is foolish to cherish or mitigate a secret evil by hoping that it will remain secret.[61]

But we must study to be truthful not only in our words but

[58] Lit. to the gallows; B, *an ryffen hinuss*; C, *verwirf ich gar.*
[59] In B this clause follows the next sentence.
[60] A, *Helvetios*; B, *Eydgnossen.*
[61] Following the paraphrase in B.

in all our actions. We must never do anything which is manifestly false.[62] The face and hands and all the external features must not pretend to be other than the heart, which is the source of all our actions. If someone enters in a way quite different from that which his nature demands, his affected walk is quite enough to show us what manner of man he is, frivolous, and of a dissolute spirit.

But what need I say more? The young man ought to fix his whole attention upon the fullest possible absorbing of Christ himself. Where that is done, he will be a rule to himself.[63] And acting rightly, he will never be lifted up or cast down. He will increase daily, but he will see to it that he himself decreases. He will progress, but he will always reckon himself the least of all. He will do good to others, but he will never hold it against them, for that was the way of Christ. And to be perfect, we must set ourselves to follow Christ alone.

These then, my dear Gerold,[64] are what appear to me to be the essentials in the instruction of a young nobleman. I need not draw attention to the disjointedness of their presentation, for that is easily perceived.(53) It is for you to ponder them in your mind and then to express in your conduct that which I have roughly sketched out on paper. In so doing, you will give order to that which is scattered and disorderly, and you will be a living example of the rule[65] which I have written out for you. Indeed, if you apply yourself to them, may it not be that you will attain a greater completeness and perfection than I have been able to show in words. But you will have to stretch every nerve, which will have the useful result of banishing indolence, the mother of all mischief, to which so many are of evil custom shamefully addicted, as though their only ambition were to live upon others and to fulfil all manner of wickedness. But turn your own youth to good account, as the poet said,(54) for the time passes quickly and the latter days are seldom better than the former.[66]

The true Christian is not the one who merely speaks about the laws of God,[67] but the one who with God's help attempts great things. And for that reason, noble youth, see to it that

---

[62] A, *ficte*; B, *välschlich*.
[63] A, *ipse sibi regula erit*; B paraphrases: *wirt inn Christus wol wysen zu läben, zu reden, zu handeln.*
[64] A, *elegantissime Gerolde.*
[65] A, *formulae*; B, *des leysts*; C, *dieses musters.*   [66] B paraphrases.
[67] A, *dogmatis*; B, *von gott*; C, *von den gesetzen.*

you adorn more illustriously and with true adornment the fair gifts of race, physique and patrimony with which you have been endowed. I say less than I ought? (55) Rank, beauty and wealth are not genuine riches, for they are subject to chance. The only true adornments are virtue and honour. May God so lead you through the things of this world that you may never be separated from him.[68] Amen.

[68] Following the expanded version in B.

Of Baptism

INTRODUCTION

THE DOCTRINE OF BAPTISM HOLDS AN IMPORTANT position in Zwingli's theology, partly because it helps to an understanding of his sacramental teaching as a whole, but more particularly because of its inter-connection with such basic themes as the covenant and the election. The period of Zwingli's more active concern with the topic may be dated from the outbreak of Anabaptism in Zurich in the year 1523. The champions of the new movement were all supporters of the Reformation, and at first Zwingli seems to have been impressed by their appeal to Scripture. Indeed, he went so far as to concede to Balthasar Hubmaier, the pastor of Waldshut, that normally baptism ought to be preceded by instruction.[1] It is difficult to say what brought about the decisive change in Zwingli's view of the matter. Perhaps he was influenced by the sectarianism of the Anabaptists, or their revolutionary tendencies,[2] or more likely their tendency to depreciate the Old Testament. It may even be that he gained something from Luther's resolute opposition to the Zwickau prophets.[3] Above all, he must have seen that the appeal to Scripture meant something far bigger and deeper than simply the citation of one or two proof-texts. Certainly by the year 1524 he had constituted himself the defender of infant baptism, and in the development of his defence he had necessarily to work out the whole subject in relation to the text and teaching of both Old and New Testament Scripture.

[1] Cf. Füsslin, *Beyträge*, I, p. 252 f.; Zwingli, *Opera*, I, p. 260.
[2] The Swiss Anabaptists were in correspondence with Thomas Müntzer. Cf. D.C.R. 210.
[3] *Ibid.*, 52–54.

During the following year events began to move swiftly in Zurich. Two conferences were held on January 10 and 17, but the Anabaptists, who were represented by Hubmaier, Grebel and Manz, refused to abandon their position. On January 18 the Council passed a decree ordering the baptism of infants and silencing the opposition.[4] In defiance of this decree the first re-baptism took place at Zollikon on February 7,[5] and it was followed by others at Schaffhausen and Waldshut. A further disputation was held on March 20, but again without effect. In an attempt to enforce recantation, the authorities committed several of the more prominent Anabaptists to prison, but they made a successful escape on April 5. A final disputation took place in November, and when this failed to achieve its object the Council took the drastic step of decreeing death by drowning as the penalty for all those who persisted in the heresy.[6] During the months which followed the Anabaptist leaders were all imprisoned, executed or banished.

In the meantime, however, Anabaptist teachings had been widely propagated in neighbouring districts, and it was this more widespread challenge which stimulated Zwingli to declare his position in a published writing. Already in the *Commentary on True and False Religion* he had announced his intention of writing a special treatise on the subject,[7] and by the spring of 1525 he had worked out his views and was confident that he could put the matter in a completely new light. The first direct reference to the proposed work was in a letter to his friend Vadian at St. Gall, the date being March 31, 1525.[8] The work went ahead with Zwingli's usual speed and it was published on May 27. Originally he had intended to dedicate it to the church at Berne, but during May the Anabaptist menace became particularly acute in St. Gall,[9] and the issue was still in the balance at the time when the essay on baptism was ready. On May 19 the Anabaptists had been allowed a fortnight in which to study a long written statement by Vadian, and at the end of that time the issue was to be debated before the Council. There is no real evidence that Vadian made an appeal to Zwingli,[10] but the two were in close touch and in order to help

[4] Egli A.S., 622–624; D.C.R. 211.   [5] Egli A.S., 636; D.C.R. 212.
[6] D.C.R. 213.   [7] C.R., III, p. 773.
[8] *Ibid.*, VIII, 336.
[9] For a history of Anabaptism in St. Gall, see E. Egli, *Die St. Galler Täufer.*
[10] This is suggested by Egli, *op. cit.*, p. 33.

his friend at this time of crisis he determined to dedicate his new work to St. Gall, dedicating to Berne his projected Latin work on the Eucharist, *Subsidium seu Coronis de Eucharistia.* On May 28 he sent copies of the new treatise to St. Gall. A messenger who was already in Zurich delayed his departure until the edition was ready.[11] He also wrote a dedicatory epistle exhorting the people of St. Gall to stand fast against the new error. He gave a special warning against the type of subterfuge practised in the disputations at Zurich[12] and quoted the decision of the Zurich Council as a precedent for St. Gall to follow.

Indirectly as well as directly Zwingli's work played a not inconsiderable part in the events which followed. Grebel had heard of the despatch of the book, and he retaliated at once by sending a letter to Vadian in which he warned him against Zwingli and complained of Zwingli's actions especially in relation to tithes.[13] Vadian showed this letter to the Council and there was much indignation at Grebel's intervention. In the meantime Zwingli's book was being widely circulated. One of the pastors, a certain Dominico Zili, began a public reading of it in church. He was interrupted by the Anabaptists, who first demanded that Grebel's letter should also be read and then complained that they wanted the Word of God, not the word of Zwingli.[14] In the upshot, the arguments of Vadian and resentment against Grebel resulted in a triumph for the ortho- dox teaching, and there can be no doubt that Zwingli's treatise contributed in part to this triumph.

On the other hand, Zwingli did not succeed in his primary object, the winning over of the Anabaptists to his own position. Neither in St. Gall nor in Zurich did the work result in any abandonment by the Anabaptists of their basic tenets. In Zurich, indeed, it gave rise to a considerable literary warfare, for Hubmaier replied with his work, *The Christian Baptism of Believers,* and a series of replies and counter-replies followed which terminated only with Zwingli's *Refutation of the Tricks of the Catabaptists* in 1531.

For obvious reasons, Zwingli was now forced to consider some of the deeper problems of baptism as well as the surface-questions

---

11 There is nothing to show that this messenger had originally come with a request for help.
12 Some illuminating anecdotes are included in the main text.
13 See the *Vadian Briefsammlung,* 430.
14 Kessler, *Sabbata,* p. 149.

of exegesis and history which had figured so prominently in the disputations. He divided his work into four main sections: baptism, the institution of baptism, rebaptism and infant baptism. To make his arguments more pointed, he appended a short list of conclusions. He also added the purified service of infant baptism then in use at Zurich.[15] Theologically, the main interest of the work is as a positive statement of the Reformed position. From this standpoint the more essential points are contained in the first two sections, and it is hardly necessary to include the two final sections and the baptismal order[16] in the present translation. A short summary will be enough to make plain the scope and teaching of the work as a whole.

In the first section Zwingli began by repudiating the traditional doctrine that external baptism can of itself cleanse from sin. Properly understood, the sacrament of baptism is simply a covenant sign. In the New Testament the term baptism was used in many different ways, and Zwingli distinguished four main uses: immersion in water, baptism by the Spirit, baptismal instruction and the faith which accompanies baptism. Zwingli did not think it necessary either that all these elements should be present in any given administration or that they should succeed each other in any particular order. Water baptism might well be given without the baptism of the Spirit, and instruction might just as well follow water-baptism as precede it.

After this short analysis, Zwingli turned to consider in more detail the meaning and value of baptism as a covenant sign. He could not agree that the purpose and effect of such a sign is to confirm faith. The signs which confirm faith are miraculous signs, and even in their case the confirmation is really the work of the Holy Spirit. A covenant sign is a sign which pledges to faith and discipleship. It does not pledge to a life of absolute perfection, as the Anabaptists demanded. Nor is the pledge the culminating point of Christian knowledge, as they seemed to intend. Baptism is an initiatory sign, symbolizing although

---

[15] This was the second reformed order. The first, by Leo Jud, had been little more than a translation of the existing service. Cf. C.R., IV, pp. 707 f.

[16] A translation of the order may be found in D.C.R. 192. It may be noted that there are two slight mistranslations in the opening prayer: the words *selb acht* indicate that Noah was one of eight persons, but *selb* is rendered "Thyself" and the eight are not mentioned; and the word *grundlos* is translated "unmerited" instead of the more likely "unbounded" or "fathomless."

not itself effecting an inward change in those who receive it. This understanding is supported by the correct exegesis of Matthew 3 and Romans 6. Zwingli could allow that the Anabaptists had done excellent work by their attacks upon the baptismal ceremonies and their insistence upon the ineffectiveness of the external element to purify the soul. But he claimed that they were quite mistaken when they tried to connect the inward change with the moment of baptismal administration, and their attempt to enforce complete righteousness upon the baptized resulted in a new and oppressive legalism and ultimately in self-righteousness and hypocrisy.

In the second section Zwingli attempted to date the institution of Christian baptism from the baptism of John and not from the commission of Matthew 28. Mediaeval theologians had allowed an institution of the sacrament prior to the passion, but they could not agree that it had the same force, and the identification with the baptism of John was completely new. In defence of his view Zwingli argued that the preparatory work of John was a beginning of that which Christ continued and completed. In his teaching, for example, John exhorted to repentance and he also gave a first testimony to Christ as Saviour. Thus his preaching contains the two basic elements in all Christian proclamation. Again, Zwingli pointed out that the One whom we follow as our great example was baptized by John and not by himself or the apostles. If it was objected that John did not baptize in the Triune name, Zwingli replied that "in the name" means "into the name or power," and it was "into" the Trinity or power of the Trinity that John baptized even if he did not use the prescribed form of words. The argument from the supposed rebaptism at Ephesus Zwingli dismissed as based upon a misunderstanding of the narrative. The statement that the twelve knew only the baptism of John really meant that they knew only the baptismal teaching of John, and even there their knowledge was partial and defective. Certainly there was no reason to suppose that they had ever received water-baptism.

In the third section Zwingli considered the specific question of rebaptism. His main aim was to prove that his opponents' baptism under the papacy was true and valid. Once this proposition was accepted, the illegality and futility of any subsequent administrations would be plainly demonstrated. First, Zwingli referred back to the controversies about heretical baptism in the time of Cyprian. He deduced that baptism even under the papist heresy is still valid baptism and must not be reiterated. The fact that that baptism was infant baptism did not affect the issue, for, as some of the Anabaptists allowed, the custom of infant baptism could easily be traced back to the period of Augustine. The persistent assertion that it was an invention of Pope Nicholas II Zwingli denounced as an absurd fiction. If the Anabaptists were not satisfied that they had actually been baptized they could easily settle the question by consulting their god-parents or even enquiring where and when they were given their Christian names. It may be noted that the argument is constantly interrupted by forceful but not very helpful denunciations of the arrogance, duplicity and sectarianism of the Anabaptist leaders.

In the fourth and final section Zwingli came to grips with the immediate issue, the baptism of infants. He argued that by nature and institution the covenant sign belongs to the family rather than the individual. This is proved by the clear case of circumcision. But the Anabaptists clamoured for a plain text in the New Testament. In reply to this, Zwingli pointed out that there is no plain text to sanction the admission of women to the Lord's Table. But surely we do not add to Scripture when we settle these details of administration for ourselves. And even if a plain text cannot be adduced, Zwingli felt that many passages favoured at least the probability that the apostles administered baptism to infants. In particular he quoted Christ's blessing of the infants and the household baptisms in Acts. Zwingli refused absolutely to base infant baptism upon the alleged guilt of original sin. He allowed an inherited frailty of our nature which inevitably gives rise to sin, but he did not believe that any guilt attaches to that frailty, at any rate in the case of Christians. When the Anabaptists quoted their stock text in Mark 16, in which faith precedes baptism, Zwingli dismissed it as quite inapplicable where the first preaching of the Gospel has been completed. He then cited Augustine in proof of the apostolicity of infant baptism, and he pointed to Colossians 2: 10–12 as a conclusive proof that baptism has replaced circumcision. Zwingli did not believe that any importance ought to be attached to the external details of administration, e.g., whether baptism should be on the first day, or in consecrated water, but for the sake of order he thought that normally it ought to be given publicly and by the ordained minister. Both pastor and parents were under an obligation to give instruction to the child, and although sponsors were dispensable they answered to the general demand of Scripture for two or three witnesses.

So much then for the general substance of the essay. In the assessment of its value we may note first of all that it is almost the rule to emphasize its defects rather than its merits.[17] This is not altogether surprising, for the defects are obvious and not unimportant. Perhaps the outstanding weakness is the lack of that almost inevitable progression in thought which characterizes all really great writing. The work does follow a conscious and definite plan, but the interconnection of the various themes is not always apparent and there are far too many digressions. In defence of Zwingli it may be pointed out, first that the subject is a difficult one to arrange, and second, that the diffuse character of the treatise derives in large part from his anxiety to give a comprehensive answer to the rather scattered arguments used in the various disputations. It is still the case, however, that he did not take sufficient pains to work out his argument as a logical whole, and he would certainly have done better to concentrate upon a constructive statement, even if this had meant ignoring the more detailed Anabaptist arguments.

A second and closely related defect is the thinness of much of the exegetical argumentation. Here again, the tiresome details of exposition were to a large extent forced upon Zwingli by the deductions which his opponents drew from the literal wording and order of individual texts. In most of the exchanges Zwingli showed a better scholarship, a greater acuteness and a much higher sense of proportion than his adversaries. But it must still be granted that his ingenuity is often wasted in attempts to make Scripture mean something other than that which it appears to mean, and in spite of the outward confidence it is evident that Zwingli himself is not always too assured in his interpretations. His argument is surely strained when he claims that infants were baptized by John in the river Jordan, or that the men who knew only John's baptism had not in fact received water-baptism at the hands of John or his disciples.

A third and final weakness is the failure to show any compelling necessity for infant baptism on theological grounds. Zwingli provides more or less adequate arguments in favour of the traditional practice, and he exposes clearly some of the weaknesses in the Anabaptist case. But Zwingli himself seems

17 Cf. the Introduction in C.R., IV, p. 202.

to lack the beliefs or presuppositions which make infant baptism logically necessary.[18] He does not accept an original guilt in infants of which baptism is the means or sign of remission. Nor does he admit any possibility of a real faith in infants, which would, of course, carry with it a full qualification for the sacrament. Indeed, the thinness in exegesis is matched by a general thinness in the whole theology of baptism, especially as compared with the full-blooded teaching of Luther and the more developed "sacramentalism" of the later Reformed school. It is true that the devaluation of baptism applies only to the external sign and not to baptism in the full sense, but it is also true that Zwingli seems to separate too rigidly the sign from the thing signified. He grasps clearly the basic duality of the sacrament, but he is in danger of losing the essential and underlying unity.

The defects are there, but the treatise has many qualities as well. For one thing, it does achieve its immediate purpose, showing that the Anabaptist case is by no means so plain and straightforward as its exponents believed. It may be that Zwingli does not always have the better of the argument, but at least he makes it clear that the matter cannot be settled either by the insistence upon the detailed wording of single texts or by the ignorant propagation of bad history. And the appeal to the covenant exposed the failure of the Anabaptists to base their faith and practice not merely upon the New Testament but upon the Bible as a whole.

Again, the treatise testifies to Zwingli's sharp awareness of what proved to be a basic point in the whole dispute. He realized that the doctrine of the Church was involved as well as the doctrine of baptism. Acceptance of the Anabaptist view of baptism inevitably carried with it acceptance of the Anabaptist view of the Church. What the Anabaptists were aiming at was a "pure" or "gathered" Church, a Church in which the invisible company of the elect is co-terminous and indeed identical with the visible company of the baptized. Much of the urgency of Zwingli in the defence of infant baptism was undoubtedly due to an anxiety to preserve the state Church, although not necessarily for purely political or ecclesiastical reasons, as his critics have unfairly alleged. Zwingli saw clearly that Anabaptism meant sectarianism, and he could not believe that either the Bible or church history justifies an attempted

[18] This point is well brought out in the Introduction to the C.R. edition, C.R., IV, p. 202.

anticipation in the Church of that final judgment which is the prerogative of God alone. Naturally, Zwingli had neither time nor space to argue this point in detail, but his awareness of the issue is revealed in the repeated charges brought against his opponents and in his appeal to the historical parallel of Donatism.

A further quality of the book is the boldness and consistency with which Zwingli repudiates the mediaeval doctrines of baptismal efficacy. Admittedly, Zwingli goes rather far in his separation of sign and thing signified. On the other hand the mediaeval Church had gone much too far in its identifying of the two. The result was disastrous, for at any rate in popular thinking the effect of the sacrament came to be attributed to the sign itself and not to the Holy Spirit working in and through the sign. Against dangerous and perverted notions of this kind it was right and necessary that a protest should be made. Zwingli knew well enough that he had the testimony of many centuries against him, but he had no hesitation whatever in affirming that which he knew to be the truth. And he had the honesty to admit that the Anabaptists themselves had done good work in drawing attention to the errors and corruptions of mediaeval dogma and practice.

There is one final point. Zwingli failed to work out any fully developed or coherent theology of baptism. But with his definition of baptism as a covenant sign he did indicate the lines along which much profitable work was to be done by the later Reformed theologians. It is easy enough to detect the weaknesses in Zwingli's understanding. He isolates the various aspects of the sacrament. He has no true doctrine of sacramental efficacy. He has little or nothing to say about baptism as a sign of remission and regeneration. He constantly overemphasizes the fact that baptism is a pledge of what we ought to do rather than of what God has already done for us. Yet as Zwingli brought out clearly in other writings, a covenant is necessarily two-sided. In the long run, the baptismal covenant involves a pledge given by God as well as a pledge made by us. The ultimate basis of baptism is not that we are willing to accept God's service. It is rather that God is willing to accept us as his servants. And in the last analysis it is because the divine willingness has precedence over the human that we may rightly administer the sacrament to children within the covenant. The possibilities latent in the concept of baptism as a covenant sign were never fully exploited by Zwingli, certainly not in this treatise, but the best Reformed work on the.subject derived in large part from this source.

Editions

The first three editions of the essay were all published by Hager of Zurich. Between these three there are no differences in substance, but typographical errors are successively eliminated.[19] R. Gwalter translated the work into Latin for inclusion in the collected *Opera* (Tom. II). A version in modern German was made by Raget Christoffel in his *Zeitgemässige Auswahl* (Zurich 1843). The original has been reproduced in the *Corpus Reformatorum* edition (IV), with footnotes to indicate Hager's misprints. More recently the Zwingli-Verlag has republished the treatise in its popular edition of selected works (XI). The translation which follows is based directly upon the orginal text as reprinted in the *Corpus Reformatorum* edition.

[19] For details of these editions see C.R., IV, pp. 203 f.

Of Baptism (1)

THE TEXT

Brethren most dearly beloved in God, above all things I pray our heavenly Father, through Jesus Christ his only begotten Son our Lord, that he will not permit me to say or to write anything which is contrary to his own will and truth. And as I propose to write about baptism, I ask all believers to read and ponder my words with Christian good-will and charity, not allowing themselves to be so hardened by contentiousness or obstinacy that they will not accept that which they clearly perceive, but obscure it by controversy. We do not learn the truth by contention, for contention is like a mountain torrent or spate.(2) Everything that it comes across it carries headlong before it and thereby increases its strength. At first only small stones are disturbed, but with their constant rolling they move larger ones, until the fall becomes so great and powerful that it dislodges and carries away everything that stands in its path, leaving behind only unnecessary distress and suffering and the desolation of pleasant fields and pastures. So too it is with obstinacy and contention. It has its source in some small thing which stimulates the carnal nature to envying and strife. Once these two great boulders fall into the stream, the roaring begins, that is, the clamour and cleverness of controversy. And just as it is impossible to see anything in the torrent except muddied water, though great rocks are concealed in it, so too contentious and turbid speeches carry with them the boulders of hatred, ambition and the like. But we cannot see them, and it is only by the tumult that we are aware of their presence. Again, contention carries before it everything that it reaches, turning it to its own advantage. And at the end the only result is that it prevails, like the mountain torrent. Apart from that, it simply causes unnecessary strife and unrest amongst Christian people. It destroys charity. And all for the sake of external things on which the honour of God does not depend and by which purity and quietness of conscience are not advanced.(3) For contention leaves behind it the desolation of fair and flourishing churches. Therefore I warn my readers not to be impressed by the effects of contention but only by the teaching of truth.

In this matter of baptism—if I may be pardoned for saying it—I can only conclude that all the doctors have been in error from the time of the apostles.(4) This is a serious and weighty assertion, and I make it with such reluctance that had I not been compelled to do so by contentious spirits I would have preferred to keep silence and simply to teach the truth. But it will be seen that the assertion is a true one: for all the doctors have ascribed to the water a power which it does not have and the holy apostles did not teach. They have also misunderstood the saying of Christ about water and the Holy Ghost in John 3. Our present task is to see what baptism really is. At many points we shall have to tread a different path from that taken either by ancient or more modern writers or by our own contemporaries. We shall be guided not by our own caprice but by the Word of God.

When he took upon himself the curse of the Law, Jesus Christ, the very Son of God, deprived us of all external justification. Therefore no external thing can make us pure or righteous. That means that everything ceremonial, all outward pomp and circumstance, is now abolished, as Paul says in Hebrews 9: "This figure was for the time then present, in which were offered both gifts and sacrifices that could not make him that did the service perfect as pertaining to the conscience; which stood only in meats and drinks, and divers washing, and carnal ordinances, imposed on them until the time of reformation" etc. This reformation was accomplished by Christ, as we see in the following passage: but it would take too long to speak of that now. These verses tell us, however, that Christ abolished external things, so that we are not to hope in them or to look to them for justification. Certainly we are not to ascribe cleansing to the external things which are still left. For if in the Old Testament they were only carnal and outward, not being able to cleanse us or to give us peace or to assure the conscience, how much less are they able to accomplish anything in Christ, in whom it is the Spirit alone that quickeneth.

Yet to us, his fellow-members, he has bequeathed two ceremonies, that is, two external things or signs: baptism and the
eucharist (or remembrance).(5) And undoubtedly he has done
this as a concession to our frailty: "for a bruised reed shall he
not break, and the smoking flax shall he not quench".(6) By
the first of these signs, baptism, we are initially marked off
to God, as we shall see later. In the other, the Lord's Supper or
Eucharist, we render thanks to God because he has redeemed
us by his Son.

Before treating of baptism we must first indicate the meaning
of the word sacrament. In our native tongue the word suggests
something that has power to take away sin and to make us
holy.(7) But this is a serious perversion. For only Jesus Christ and
no external thing can take away the sins of us Christians and make
us holy. And as a result of this misunderstanding there are some
who cry out: "They are depriving us of the holy sacraments
whereby our poor souls are comforted." But we have no desire
to take away the sacraments but simply to use them rightly
and not to pervert them. And they are perverted by those who
ascribe to them a virtue which they do not possess. As used
in this context the word sacrament means a covenant sign or
pledge. If a man sews on a white cross, he proclaims that he is
a Confederate.(8) And if he makes the pilgrimage to Nähenfels
and gives God praise and thanksgiving for the victory vouch-
safed to our forefathers,(9) he testifies that he is a Confederate
indeed. Similarly the man who receives the mark of baptism
is the one who is resolved to hear what God says to him, to
learn the divine precepts and to live his life in accordance with
them. And the man who in the remembrance or Supper gives
thanks to God in the congregation testifies to the fact that from
the very heart he rejoices in the death of Christ and thanks
him for it. Of those who complain I ask only this: that they let
the sacraments be real sacraments and do not describe them as
signs which actually are the things which they signify. For if
they are the things which they signify they are no longer signs:
for sign and thing signified cannot be the same thing.(10)
Sacramenta—as even the papists maintain—are simply the
signs of holy things. Baptism is a sign which pledges us to the
Lord Jesus Christ. The remembrance shows us that Christ
suffered death for our sake. Of these holy things they are the
signs and pledges. You will find ample proof of this if you
consider the pledge of circumcision and the thanksgiving of
the paschal lamb.

Of Baptism

All the sacraments and pledges of the Old Testament were with blood, for purifications which were merely carnal were never without blood. In this respect they pointed to the Lord Jesus Christ, whose blood purges the conscience as that of beasts could never do. But with the coming of that blood which, once shed, purified the conscience, the shedding of blood ceased. The two main sacraments of the Jews, circumcision and the paschal lamb, were both with blood. But with the shedding of the precious blood of Christ the shedding of physical blood ceased. Christ transformed the two signs into two more gentle sacraments in which there is no shedding of blood or physical death.(11) On the one hand there was the death and blood of the paschal lamb, with which they thanked him for the passover in Egypt and their deliverance from bondage. This he has now replaced by bread and wine, two most suitable and ordinary things, by which we offer him praise and thanksgiving that he gave up his body for our redemption and his blood for the washing away of our sins. On the other hand there was the blood of circumcision, and this he has now changed to water, another element which is agreeable and common to all men. These most friendly elements and signs, water and wine and bread, have been given to us in order that by the outward signs we may know the grace and loving-kindness of the New Testament, that we are no longer under the Law—the shedding of blood has therefore been abrogated by the blood of Christ—but under grace.

Now in Scripture the word baptism is used in four different ways.

First, it is used for the immersion in water whereby we are pledged individually to the Christian life. Second, it is used for the inward enlightenment and calling when we know God and cleave to him—that is the baptism of the Spirit.

Third, it is used for the external teaching of salvation and external immersion in water.

Finally it is used for external baptism and internal faith, that is, for the Christian salvation and dispensation as a whole.

Because they do not see clearly these different uses of the term, there are many who fall into strange errors, judging that which they neither know nor understand. We will cite specific texts from Scripture in favour of our view.

1. In John 3 it is written: "And John also was baptizing in Aenon near to Salim, because there was much water there: and they came and were baptized." It is evident that the reference here is simply to water-baptism, for it is pointed out that there was much water there, and the value of this is only for external baptism. And there can be no doubt that those who administer this baptism know very well that they are only baptizing with water.

2. Christ himself speaks of the baptism of the Spirit in Acts 1: "For John truly baptized with water, but ye shall be baptized with the Holy Ghost not many days hence." In this verse Christ stresses that there are two kinds of baptism. John baptized only with water or external teaching. And it is exactly the same today. What men can give is only outward baptism, either by external teaching or pouring or dipping in water. In baptism neither the apostles nor John nor anyone else can do more than give external instruction and immersion in water. Hence the dispute about infant baptism is a dispute only about water-baptism and teaching; are we to baptize infants before we teach them or not? For only God can give the baptism of the Spirit.(12) And that is why Christ at once adds: "But ye shall be baptized with the Holy Ghost." This is the baptism of inward teaching, calling, and cleaving to God. And when he says this, Christ does not repudiate the baptism of John. For the external baptism of John is the same as that of Christ and the apostles, as we shall show later. What Christ says concerning John's baptism may be said of every baptism administered by man. Peter and Paul and James did not administer any baptism but that of water and external teaching. They could not baptize with the Spirit, for God alone baptizes with the Spirit, and he himself chooses how and when and to whom that baptism will be administered.

3. Third, the teaching and baptism of the apostles make it plain that the word "baptism" is used for external teaching and baptism, as may be seen in the words of John himself in John 1: "I baptize with water." For John does not baptize with water only: he teaches as well. But the teaching of John, and also that of the apostles, was only external.(13) It had no power to move the heart. And for that reason it was just as much an external thing as pouring or dipping in water. So then, although John himself says: "I baptize with water," he teaches as well as baptizes, for just before he says: "I am the voice of one crying in the wilderness." And that baptism

is used for teaching we see plainly in John 3: "After these things came Jesus into the land of Judaea: and there he tarried with them and baptized." But how did he baptize? Did he do it himself? Immediately following, in John 4, it says: "Though Jesus himself baptized not, but his disciples." But in John 3 it says: "Behold the same baptizeth, and all men come to him." There can be no doubt, then, that in this context the word baptize is expressly used for teach. For as Christ himself said, teaching was his main office, and it it is the main office of all apostles, evangelists, bishops and pastors,(14) as Paul says in I Corinthians 1. It was the disciples who baptized with water. And Christ himself knew how he used that baptism to move the heart. Again, it is clear from Matthew 21 that the baptism of John also meant his teaching, for there Christ said to the leaders of the Jews: "I also will ask you one thing: the baptism of John, was it from heaven, or of men?" In this context Christ could not mean only the baptism of water, for in that case it would have been quite right to have replied that it was given him by men.(15) But he asked them concerning his teaching, whether they thought that it was from men or from God. For his adversaries reasoned with themselves, saying, "If we shall say 'From heaven,' he will say, Why did ye not then believe him?" Note that the Jews knew perfectly well that by his baptism he meant his teaching. And baptism is also used for teaching in Acts 19.

(4)[1] Fourth, baptism is used for the Christian dispensation and salvation, that is, for the inward faith which saves us, as in I Peter 3: "The like figure whereunto doth now save us . . . even baptism." For neither as water nor as external teaching does baptism save us, but faith.

This division is not my own invention but according to the teaching of Scripture, and those who are not aware whether they are speaking of water-baptism, of baptism as teaching, or of the baptism of the Spirit will fall into serious error. Yet every time that we have tried to make the distinction in our discussions with the Anabaptists and Catabaptists they have answered that they are all the same. They would even have denied the possibility of salvation without water-baptism had we not forcibly restrained them by quoting the words of Christ in John 6: "Verily, verily, I say unto you, he that believeth on me hath everlasting life."(16) Christ himself did not connect salvation with baptism: it is always by faith alone.

1 In the first editions this number is omitted.

We will now show that all the three forms of baptism are given separately.

The disciples gave water-baptism without teaching and without the Spirit. We have seen already in John 4 that when Christ taught but did not baptize it was the disciples who baptized. See too I Corinthians 1: "God (Christ) sent me not to baptize, but to preach the Gospel." On some occasions, then, instruction was given by one and baptism by another. And that some were baptized before they believed we see in John 6, for there can be no doubt that none of those disciples which went away was unbaptized. For as we saw in John 4, "he made and baptized more disciples." But later, in John 6, he upbraided them for their unbelief: "Ye also have seen me and believe not." And finally he said: "There are some of you that believe not." Yet he had permitted them to be baptized. Again, Judas did not believe, as we are told in the same passage: "Have not I chosen you twelve, and one of you is a devil?" But from the verse first quoted it is quite certain that he was baptized, for Christ made many more disciples than John, and he baptized them through his disciples. But those who baptized were not unbaptized themselves. Hence it follows that water-baptism was given even when there was no faith, and it was received even by those who did not believe. The same was true in the case of Simon Magus, concerning whom we are told in Acts 8 that "Simon himself believed also." In this context "believed" must be given the sense of "listened to his message" or "reckoned himself a believer," as Augustine somewhere construes it.(17) For shortly afterwards it became clear that he did not believe. Not that this makes much difference. All that we are trying to prove is that water-baptism is sometimes given even where there is no inward baptism or faith. And unfortunately this is frequently the case at the present time, for many who have no faith allow themselves to be baptized, especially Jews.(18) Yet they are truly baptized with the external baptism of teaching and water. It is evident, then, that the two need not be concurrent: for nothing is more foolish than to say that when a man is baptized he necessarily becomes a believer.

The baptism of teaching was often administered externally when no-one believed or accepted water-baptism. In Acts 18, for example, Paul shook his raiment and excluded the Jews at Corinth because they would not receive Christ.(19) And there are many other cases.

The baptism of the Spirit was also given without the baptism of water. Nicodemus, Joseph of Ramoth and Gamaliel were all believers, but in secret. They were certainly not baptized: otherwise they could not have kept their secret. For baptism is given and received for the sake of fellow-believers, not for a supposed effect in those who receive it. In Acts 10 Cornelius and all who heard Peter received the Holy Spirit before they were baptized. Hence the two baptisms are not always concurrent. Indeed, in the Bible as a whole we find more instances of the Spirit given before water-baptism than after. In one case in particular faith was present but not water, and faith was sufficient to save. The thief on the cross believed, and the same day he was with Christ in Paradise, that is, eternal felicity.(20) Now the thief was certainly not baptized with an external baptism. For it is not true that he was baptized in blood, as Jerome asserts in a passage which once misled me.(21) For the thief did not hang there in the cause of God, like the innocents who suffered on behalf of Christ, but because of his act of murder. And Peter says in I Peter 2: "For what glory is it, if, when ye be buffeted for your faults, ye shall take it patiently?"

These passages all serve to show us that in Scripture the word baptism is used in different senses and that there is no salvation in external baptism. We see, then, that water-baptism is a ceremonial sign with which salvation is not indissolubly connected. We have already proved this from the example of the dying thief and others. And we see that the two are not to be connected and used together as the Anabaptists and Catabaptists insist. I hope that no one will complain if for the sake of brevity I call them all Anabaptists.(22) I do this on the ground that they deny the baptism of infants. Baptism itself, please God, they do not deny. My use of the title is not in any sense controversial.

Now in this connection we must speak first and chiefly of the baptism of the Holy Spirit.

This baptism was both outward and inward.

The inward baptism of the Spirit was taught by John in Matthew 3 and Luke 3: "I indeed baptize you with water unto repentance, or amendment: but he that cometh after me is mightier than I, whose shoes I am not worthy to bear: he shall baptize you with the Holy Ghost, and with fire." In this verse we should first notice that when John says: "I baptize you with water," he does not mean that his office was merely to baptize with water. For by water alone he could not have taught the people to know their sin and to repent. It would need a good deal of washing in water for us to know and amend ourselves and to seek Christ as our Saviour and Comforter. What John means is simply this: I am only a weak vessel. The message which I can bear is only outward. I cannot give anything but external baptism in water. I have no power to soften the heart. But the one who comes after me has greater power than I have. He is able to penetrate to the heart. He will baptize you inwardly with his Spirit, setting you on fire with his love and endowing you with the gift of tongues, etc. This baptism of the Holy Ghost is exactly the same as what Christ said in John 6: "No man can come to me, except the Father which hath sent me draw him." And he goes on to tell us what that "drawing" is: "Every man therefore that hath heard, and hath learned of the Father, cometh unto me." The inward baptism of the Spirit is the work of teaching which God does in our hearts and the calling with which he comforts and assures our hearts in Christ. And this baptism none can give save God alone. Without it, none can be saved—though it is quite possible to be saved without the baptism of external teaching and immersion.(23) The proof of this is that the murderer on the cross was externally neither taught nor baptized, and yet he was saved. It follows that the one necessary thing which saves those of us who hear the Gospel is faith, or trust, and this faith none can implant within us save God alone.

The outward baptism of the Spirit is an external sign, the gift of tongues. This sign is not given for the benefit of those who actually speak with other tongues or languages: for they have already learned the way of salvation in their hearts. It is given for the benefit of unbelievers, as we see in I Corinthians 14: "Wherefore tongues are for a sign, not to them that believe, but to them that believe not." And who are these ? The ones to whom tongues are given? No, for they are already believers. They are given to believers as a sign and wonder to unbelievers. Similarly, baptism is not given as a sign to those who receive it, but for the benefit of other believers.(24) And this outward baptism of tongues was appointed by the Lord himself in Acts 1: "Ye shall be baptized with the Holy Ghost not many days hence." Now the disciples were already believers. But the fire of love was increased and tongues were given, as happened on the day of Pentecost. Again, this sign is not necessary to salvation, for it is given infrequently and only to a few. It is a miracle, and like other miracles it takes place only when

God wills. Nevertheless God himself has described the sign of tongues as a baptism. And as this sign is sometimes given before water-baptism, sometimes after, so too the baptism of teaching may be given either before water-baptism or after. This is not the foundation upon which we build infant baptism, but it is a *suasoria*,(25) pointing in the right direction.

We must now examine equally carefully the question of signs in order to expose a mistake which once deceived me as found in certain writers. For some have taught that signs are given for the confirmation of an existing faith in that which we have already learned and to which we are pledged.(26) But this is not so. The danger is that often we are so inclined to accept that which is superficially attractive, and is perhaps attractively presented, that we stumble into it blindly, not paying any heed to the Word of God or the inward man, that is, faith. It is true, of course, that some signs are given the better to confirm faith, or in some sort to reassure the flesh, which does not allow faith any rest. But such signs are not pledges, but miraculous signs, like Moses' rod and Gideon's fleece and innumerable others given to the fathers. At the moment, however, we are not speaking of miracles, but of the seals and pledges which are not miraculous, like circumcision under the old covenant. Circumcision did not confirm the faith of Abraham. It was a covenant sign between God and the seed of Abraham. For circumcision was given to Abraham when by faith he was already accounted righteous by God, as we learn in Genesis 15. And in Genesis 17 God himself makes it quite clear that circumcision is not a sign for the confirmation of faith but a covenant sign: "This is my covenant, which ye shall keep, between me and you and thy seed after thee; every man child among you shall be circumcised." Note that God calls it a contract or covenant. Similarly, the feast of the paschal lamb was a covenant, as we read in Exodus 12: "And ye shall observe this thing for an ordinance to thee and to thy sons for ever." Note that the paschal lamb was a covenant sign. By means of it they were to remember every year that God had passed over in the night that he slew all the first-born in Egypt, both of man and beast, and that he had then led them out and drowned the Egyptians who pursued after them. Similarly, baptism in the New Testament is a covenant sign. It does not justify the one who is baptized, nor does it confirm his faith, for it is not possible for an external thing to confirm faith. For faith does not proceed from external things. It proceeds only from the God who draws us. Therefore it cannot be grounded in any external thing. The same applies to the Lord's Supper as well. It is true that miracles were given to confirm faith,(27) but even this does not mean that they add anything to faith or augment it, but that they satisfy the curiosity of the flesh which is constantly itching to see and to know. And that is why when Jesus answered the Jews and said: "This is the work of God, that ye believe on him whom he hath sent. They said therefore unto him. What sign shewest thou then, that we may see and believe thee?" But what happens is simply this: if there is no faith, and miracles are shown to the flesh, that is, the carnal man, it still does not believe. For that reason Christ severely rebukes the sin of the Jews and indeed of all those who cry out for signs but do not believe even when they see them. Thus Jeroboam did not believe when his arm was dried up, nor did Ahab (28) when God revealed to him the unheard of miracle of the Virgin Birth. But when the Lord gave signs to Gideon and Hezekiah they were much refreshed and the rebellious flesh was quelled. Against those who unthinkingly accept the idea that signs confirm faith we may oppose the fact of infant baptism, for baptism cannot confirm faith in infants because infants are not able to believe. (29) For some time I myself was deceived by the error and I thought it better not to baptize children until they came to years of discretion.(30) But I was not so dogmatically of this opinion as to take the course of many today, who although they are far too young and inexperienced in the matter argue and rashly assert that infant baptism derives from the papacy or the devil or something equally nonsensical.(31) I am always pleased when I see strength and constancy in a Christian, but a senseless fury in which there is neither the love nor discipline of Christian decorum can give pleasure only to those who are violent and rebellious.

Our next task is to see what kind of a pledge baptism is, that is to say, to what does it pledge us?

At this point the Anabaptists claim that only those who know that they can live without sin ought to receive the sign of baptism.(32) In so doing they make God a liar and bring back the hypocrisy of legal righteousness. My proof of the first point is as follows. In I John 1 it says: "If we say that we have no sin, we deceive ourselves, and the truth is not in us". That is what God himself says by the mouth of John. Hence if we claim that we can live without sin, we make God a liar. For us to live without sin—is not that the height of presumption?

As long as we are in the flesh, we are never without sin. For the flesh and the spirit are contrary the one to the other, so that we do not do the things which in the spirit we would do. But if we are never without sin, yet boast that we will live without sin, it follows that we are simply bringing back the hypocrisy of the law. For once a man claims that he is without sin, he has to keep up before men a reputation for sinlessness. The result is that he fulfils a righteousness which is purely external: for internally he has the same carnal nature as all flesh and he is not without sin, for God is not a liar. If he can only conceal it, he does not act any less carnally than other carnal creatures. And if the Anabaptists argue that "to be without sin" means "to be in faith," then as we have often shown in previously published writings there is no occasion whatever for strife or controversy: for there is no point at issue.

But the Anabaptists do hold that they live without sin. This is proved by what they and some others write and teach concerning the *perseverantia justorum*, or perseverance of saints. In this they are committed absolutely to the view that they can and do live without sin. How far that claim is borne out by their envy, lying, clamour, evil-speaking and blasphemy I leave on one side. But the following anecdote will show that they do regard themselves as righteous.(33) The Anabaptists had eventually been granted a disputation by the city council. But after three days of effort, all that one of them could say about baptism was this: I would willingly justify my position from the Word of God but none will understand it except those who are without sin. What answer do you think should be given? That of silence? Not at all, for only the Lord Jesus Christ can say: "Which of you convinceth me of sin?" (John 8). Therefore I spoke up and said: Did you not make a mistake when you said that none will understand you except those who are without sin? He answered: That is what I said, and that is the case. I said: But you yourself understand this question of infant baptism? He answered: Yes. Then I said: Therefore you must be without sin. But as long as you are in the flesh that is impossible, for all those who are in the flesh are sinful. He replied: I would to God that all men were as conscious of their sins as I am. But when he said that he did not mean that he too was a sinner. But all good Christians may judge for themselves whether this boasting is anything but empty words, or any less arrogant than that hitherto made by the monks and nuns.(34)

Clearly, then, baptism cannot bind us in such a way that we must not accept it unless we know that we can live without sin: for if that be the case, baptism was instituted in vain, for not one of us can claim to do that before God. Therefore we will turn to the Word of God and learn there both what baptism is and when it was instituted. As regards the first question, baptism is a covenant sign which indicates that all those who receive it are willing to amend their lives and to follow Christ. In short, it is an initiation to new life. Baptism is therefore an initiatory sign, *ceremonii*, or in Greek *teleta*. It is like the cowl which is cut out for initiates into an order. They do not know the rules and statutes when the cowls are made, but they learn them in their cowls.

We will now adduce passages in proof of this point. The first is the text in Matthew 28 which the Anabaptists allege against infant baptism. In this verse Christ says: "Go ye therefore, and teach all nations, baptizing them in the name of the Father, and of the Son, and of the Holy Ghost: teaching them to observe all things whatsoever I have commanded you." In expounding these words the Anabaptists sadly mislead both themselves and others: for they merely insist upon the order of words and cry: He says, "Teach all nations, baptizing them." They will not see that he goes on to say: "Teaching them to observe all things whatsoever I have commanded you"; from which words it may easily be seen that baptism is an initiatory sign, and only when it is given do we learn to keep the things which Christ has commanded. But they insist upon the letter: It is written: "Teach all nations, baptizing them." And although they would rather break off the controversy at that point, for their sake I too will insist upon the letter. They say: "Teach all nations, baptizing them." And I say: "Baptizing them in the name of the Father, and of the Son, and of the Holy Ghost, teaching them to observe all things whatsoever I have commanded you." Now which of us has the clearer word about teaching, we or they? They have the saying: "Teach all nations, baptizing them"; but there is nothing there about what we are to teach. And we have the clear words: "Teaching them to observe all things whatsoever I have commanded you." And that follows baptism. Again, in the Greek the word for "commanded" is *entilamen*, which might equally well be rendered "entrusted" and "commanded," just as in older Latin the word *mandavi* meant strictly "I have entrusted." And the Greek word for "teach" is *matheteusate*, which might

just as well be translated "make disciples" or "bring to me
as a master." This, then, is the literal sense: "Go ye and make
disciples of all nations"; then there follows the initiation with
which they are to make disciples: "baptizing them in the name
of the Father, and of the Son, and of the Holy Ghost"; and
after the initiation the instruction: "teaching them to observe
all things whatsoever I have entrusted to you." But observe
that although we too can weigh the individual words, in Christ
there is no place for strife about words: therefore I do not
place too great importance upon the literal wording.(35) We
are to study the literal sense, but with moderation. We must
not allow the letter to kill us, for the letter of the Gospel kills
no less surely than the letter of the Law. Yet by the faith which
I have in God, and the sure understanding—however slight—
which I have of his Word, I know that this is the right and true
and proper sense: for previously when Christ called his disciples
he said that he would make them fishers of men. And what is
that but to draw men to him, to make them his disciples?
But I will not strive any more about the wording except to
show that infant baptism cannot be overthrown by this saying.
For even if the order did constrain us, the text does not apply to
children or prevent their baptism. The saying applies only to
those who are instructed. But we do not instruct infants.
Therefore the words do not apply to children or forbid their
baptism. They say: If the words do not apply to them, we
ought not to baptize them, for this is the place where Christ
instituted baptism. Answer: Ye do err, not knowing the Scriptures. Baptism was not instituted here, and that is how you are
misled. We shall soon be treating of the institution of baptism, and the evident truth will then force you to admit that
you have deceived both yourselves and others. For if baptism
was not instituted on this occasion, you have no right to press
the saying against infant baptism even if the literal order of
words did constrain us, which it does not. For if we were
bound by the literal order, we should have to expound many
passages of Scripture quite falsely. In John 1, for example,
it tells us that John pointed to Christ and said: "Behold the
Lamb of God, which taketh away the sin of the world." But
shortly after it says: "And I knew him not." But how could he
not know him when he had just said: "Behold the Lamb of
God," etc.? Again, in Romans 10: "For if thou shalt confess
with thy mouth the Lord Jesus, and shalt believe in thine heart
that God hath raised him from the dead, thou shalt be

saved." In this verse precedence is given to the external confession, but this is worthless without the heart. Hence we must
not press the letter in the text in Matthew 28. For baptism
was not instituted on that occasion as we formerly supposed,
building upon the common error of the older theologians (36)
that the baptism of John was different from that of Christ.
We will therefore continue our exposition of the verse in
Matthew 28.

Already we have made it quite clear that if the words are to
be pressed we gain an easy victory. For only after baptism
does it say: "Teaching them to observe all things whatsoever
I have commanded you." Before baptizing it simply says:
"Teach," without saying what they are to teach. And even
if the Anabaptists say: The latter phrase is simply an exposition
of the former, that is, it tells them what they are to teach, I
reply: But you insist upon the order of the words: you must
take them as they are. And this is not the only place where
baptism precedes teaching, as we shall show later. But if you
do not insist upon the order of the words, how are you going
to overthrow infant baptism, seeing you lose the text in
Matthew 28? Therefore the Anabaptists either have to abandon
the literal order or else they are really on our side and not their
own. For we shall see that at its first institution baptism precedes instruction. You have only to say to the wicked,
slanderous and contentious devil,(37) I resist you, and you will
understand the simple truth. When Christ says: "Go ye
therefore, and teach all nations, baptizing them in the name,"
etc., in the Greek there is no "and" between "teach" and
"baptizing." It does not say "teaching and baptizing" but
"teach ... baptizing them." The use of this idiom makes it
plain that when Christ said this he was not laying any conscious
stress upon the order. The words "baptizing them, etc." are
not closely connected with what precedes but are autonomous.
As far as the letter is concerned they might just as well come
first. This comes out even more clearly in Mark 16. As we have
it the text is: "He that believeth and is baptized shall be saved."
But literally the Greek is this: "He that has believed and is
baptized shall be saved." Note that the words "is baptized" are
quite independent even though they are connected by the
conjunction "and." I do not mean that John administered
water-baptism or immersion before he began to teach, for at
the very outset it is necessary to teach the reason for baptism—
even today children would not be brought to baptism if their

parents had not been taught first.(38) But once instruction has been given, infants are also brought to baptism, as may be seen in times past. But we shall come to this later. In Matthew 28, then, the meaning of Christ's words is this: "Go ye therefore and teach all nations"—for if they believe, I am the Saviour of all. Go, therefore, and bring them to me. "Baptize them"— and the connection with what precedes is so slight that in the original it is simply "baptizing them," as we have seen—"in the name of the Father, and of the Son, and of the Holy Ghost." Properly the Greek is not "in the name" but "into the name." I know that *accusativi* are sometimes changed into *ablativos*, but that does not apply in the present case, as we shall now see.

In Scripture the word "name" is frequently used for "power" or "majesty." We have given many instances of this in previous writings, and a single example will now suffice. In Mark 16 Christ says: "In my name shall they cast out devils." In this verse "in my name" must mean "in my power" or "majesty" or "might." Trust in that name and in my power you will cast out devils. Similarly, to baptize in the name of Father, Son and Holy Ghost is to dedicate, appropriate and bring to the true God, Father, Son and Holy Ghost, those who were straying abroad like sheep without a shepherd, that is, without God. I do not mean that when we give baptism we are not to baptize "in the name of the Father, the Son and the Holy Ghost." But we must speak the truth, and the truth is that when he uttered these words Christ was not instituting the form of baptism, as the theologians maintain.(39) *Probatio*, or proof: the disciples did not use this form, but baptized in the name of Jesus (Acts 10 and 19). This has so confounded the theologians that they do not know where to turn to avoid the force of it. And all because they interpret Christ's words as the form of baptism, although Christ himself never suggested this, but meant simply that by teaching and by the covenant sign of baptism we are to be brought back and pledged to the one true God, Father, Son and Holy Ghost. But accepting the view that the words had been given as a form, they are at a loss to understand why the disciples administered baptism in the name of Jesus, for the disciples did not use the form (as they call it) which according to their view Christ himself had prescribed. So they invent tortuous excuses in an attempt to show that the apostolic custom was not contrary to Christ's command.(40) In those days, they say, the name of Christ was more appropriate than that of the Father or the Holy Ghost, concerning whom there was very little understanding. In this they are just about as right as the simpleton (41) who killed a cat and thought it was a hare. For amongst the Jews no name was more abominated than that of Jesus Christ, and to the Gentiles it was foolishness to speak of a crucified God (I Cor. 1). The Jews would not have been offended at the name of Father, Son and Holy Ghost, for they had frequently heard of the three in Scripture. And the Gentiles would have listened far more readily to the name of the Father than to that of the crucified Jesus. But Christ does not say: When you baptize, pronounce these three names. And that was not what he intended. Certainly I commend the form, but what we understand by the words, "I baptize thee in the name" is this, I dedicate thee to the name, that is, the power, the majesty, the grace of the Father, the Son and the Holy Ghost. When Christ uttered these words his purpose was to teach them to bring unbelievers to the true God and to dedicate them to him. And does that not mean that water-baptism is an initiatory sign dedicating and pledging us to God? That is how the disciples understood it. The whole of Christian life and salvation consists in this, that in Jesus Christ God has provided us with the remission of sins and everything else, and that we are to show forth and imitate Jesus Christ in our lives. For that reason the disciples baptized in the name of Jesus Christ. Hence our name Christians, that is, we are initiated into Christ and dedicated to him. Nowhere do we read that the disciples baptized in the name of the Father, the Son and the Holy Ghost. Therefore it is evident that the words in Matthew 28 were not instituted as a form, and the theologians have made the biggest mistake of their lives in their exposition of this text. Not that I forbid baptism according to that form.(42) Not at all. I am simply pointing out that according to their true and natural sense these words of God do not impose a strict baptismal form. If they did, the disciples would not have used a different form when they baptized. And I am proving what was the real intention of Christ: that in baptism the wandering sheep should be marked for the true God and brought to the true shepherd of our souls, Jesus Christ, to whom we are pledged in baptism, that we might live as he did—but this will be made clear later.

Hence the meaning of the words "baptizing them" is this: with this external sign you are to dedicate and pledge them to the name of the Father, the Son and the Holy Ghost, and to

teach them to observe all the things that I have committed to
you.

Now it is obvious that so long as the Christian lives and continues to believe, he increases in faith and knowledge. Therefore I ask the Anabaptists whether it is lawful to administer
baptism before faith is made perfect or not, and the same in the
case of knowledge. If they say: Baptism must not be administered before faith is made perfect, my reply is this, that we
should all remain unbaptized, for faith is constantly developing.
For in Luke 17 the disciples said: "Lord, increase our faith."
Therefore they have to recognize that we must administer
baptism as soon as instruction commences. Hence they agree
that baptism is a sign initiating into the process of development. Indeed, they admitted as much in the disputations.
All that I am now claiming is this : I have proved that baptism
is an initiatory sign, and that those who receive it are dedicated
and pledged to the Lord God. I am not basing the baptism of
infants upon this fact. I am simply following up my main
argument or thesis, which is to prove from the words of Christ
himself and of all the disciples that baptism is simply a mark or
pledge by which those who receive it are dedicated to God.
And in the dispute concerning Christ's words in Matthew 28
I claim only that we cannot use those words to disallow infant
baptism.

In Matthew 3 we read: "In those days came John the Baptist,
preaching in the wilderness of Judaea," etc. And here they
cry out: Do you not see that John preached before he baptized? We not only see but freely concede it. And we ourselves follow the same practice, for we do not allow children
to be brought to baptism unless their parents have first
been taught. But when it says that John preached, does
that mean that we are not to baptize infants? To me that
seems a strange interpretation. However, we are not treating
of infant baptism but of baptism in general. We are trying to
show what kind of a sign it is and what its effects are. We firmly
confess that John taught first and then baptized. But it cannot
be denied that once his hearers had been taught they had
their untaught children baptized as well, that is, they dedicated
them to God in baptism.(43) The main point at issue is whether
in so doing they were acting according to the will of God,
but we are leaving that question for the moment, as we have
already said. A little later in the same chapter of Matthew we
are told: "Then went out to him Jerusalem, and all Judaea,

and all the region round about Jordan, and were baptized of him in Jordan, confessing their sins." With regard to this verse we may well say that if the whole multitude went out it is evident that children went out as well, for elsewhere where there were similar gatherings, for example at the feeding of the five thousand, we are told that children were present. Our opponents say: It is stated that they confessed their sins, and this cannot apply to children. I might reply that in Scripture there are many examples of synecdoche, that is, inclusive speech, in which that which is done by some is ascribed to all. For example in Matthew 26 we are told that "when the disciples saw it, they had indignation, saying," etc. But none of them actually spoke like this except Judas. Similarly, in the present case I might well say: Even if children were present and were baptized—and we cannot prove this absolutely (44)—it would still be true that the people confessed their sins, for all those who were able and sufficiently enlightened to confess their sins undoubtedly did so. But we will not argue the point: for if the text does not establish infant baptism it does not disprove it. It can be turned to that purpose only for controversial reasons. Like the mountain torrent in our earlier illustration, an angry man snatches up whatever he can lay his hands on and uses it as a weapon, whether it be table, or bench, or stool or anything else that is available. And so too it is with those who are obsessed with this matter of infant baptism. They turn all their writings against it, even those which are not specifically aimed at the practice.(45) However, John himself shows us what is the true nature of baptism when he says: "I baptize you with water unto repentance." But how can he bring them to repentance by means of water? The answer is that he preaches amendment of life and then uses water to mark off those who pledge themselves to a life of repentance. The water does not make them better than they were before. They might easily have amended their lives without immersion in water. Immersion in water is simply a ceremony by which they testify that they are of the number of those who repent. Therefore when he says: "I baptize you with water unto repentance," he makes it quite plain that baptism is an initiatory sign or pledge initiating us to a lifelong mortification of the flesh and engaging or pledging us like the soldier at his enlistment. In Mark 1 it says: "John did baptize in the wilderness and preach the baptism of repentance for the remission of sins." What do the Anabaptists make of this? First, it says: "In the wilderness." And if we are to insist upon the order of words, the victory is on our side, for the "baptizing" precedes the "teaching." But we will not do that: for when the evangelist says: "John did baptize," he means that he gave water-baptism, and when immediately after he says: "And preach the baptism of repentance," he is referring to the teaching which accompanied his baptism. Hence we shall be led astray if we press the order of the words.

The text in Luke 3 also proves that baptism is an initiatory sign, and that many of those who received it—indeed the majority—did not live as the pledge required. But this destroys the contention that none ought to receive baptism except those who know that they can live without sin. Luke writes as follows: "Then said he (John) to the multitude that came forth to be baptized of him, O generation of vipers, who hath warned you to flee from the wrath to come? Bring forth therefore fruits worthy of repentance." Note that the reason why he reproves them is that they take baptism as a sign that they are willing to amend their lives and yet they do not do so. And if you say: This proves that they ought to have done so, you are quite right: but it does not prove that John charged them to examine themselves whether they could live without sin. And it is against that kind of hypocrisy that we are specifically contending. John administered baptism without respect to the persons of those who received it. And if he saw later that they were not living as they ought, he publicly rebuked them. But he did not compel, as the Anabaptists do. For the humility and contentiousness or obstinacy of the Anabaptists are deduced from the virtue of water-baptism, which is to bring back the Law. For if they do the work of God only for the sake of the Law, or their own vows, they are restoring a full monkish system. Indeed, they will even say: I was rebaptized in order that my brethren might compel me to act rightly where I do not do so. Is not that to put ourselves under the very yoke which our fathers were not able to bear? Let your own faith work in you, and not the constraint of the religious men to whom you look. For if you stand under constraint, whenever you can escape the rebukes of the brethren, you will go back to your own ways, dissembling outwardly.

In short, from the words of Luke we see that baptism is an initiatory sign or pledge with which we bind ourselves to God, testifying the same to our neighbour by means of the external sign, and not withdrawing ourselves in any way: for if we do the result will be a sect and not faith.(46)

In John 1 the Jews asked John: "Why baptizest thou then?" And he gave them this answer: "I baptize with water, but there standeth one among you, whom ye know not; he it is, who coming after me is preferred before me, whose shoe's latchet I am not worthy to unloose." Now we see here that the baptism of John and of all those who have ever baptized or taught can only baptize outwardly. None but God alone can baptize inwardly. St. John (47) himself refers to this fact when he says in Luke 3: "He shall baptize you with the Holy Ghost and with fire." Hence it follows that baptism is an initiatory sign which we administer even to those who do not enjoy the inward baptism of the Spirit and without knowing whether they have that inward baptism or not.(48) Why, then, do the Anabaptists say that we must not administer baptism except to those who have the Holy Ghost (Acts 2)? And because infants do not have the Holy Ghost, they are not to be baptized. Of how many do we read that they were baptized by John and Christ and the Apostles and yet had no faith, as we have shown already from Luke? And the false argument that infants do not have the Holy Ghost is vain and foolish, for where are we told the manner of God's indwelling or the time when he implants the gifts which he bestows upon us, whether in the mother's womb, or in early youth or in old age? (49) Jeremiah was sanctified in his mother's womb, and in his mother's womb John the Baptist recognized the Saviour with far more joy than we do as adults. Pharez and Zarah, and Jacob and Esau contended with each other at the very time when they were being born. Yet it was not they who did it, but God. What is the value, then, of the rash assertion which one of them made in the disputation, that infants do not have the Spirit?—he even tried to prove that they cannot have the Spirit. That is the result of contentiousness. For my part, I allow God to work how and when he wills.

In Acts 1 our Lord Jesus Christ says: "For John truly baptized with water, but ye shall be baptized with the Holy Ghost." Excellent. For although the Scripture refers us only to the baptism of John, we may ask how the disciples baptized. Certainly they did not baptize with the Holy Ghost, for only God can do that. There can be no doubt, then, that they baptized in exactly the same way as John, that is, they gave instruction and water, that is, external baptism. First, then, the baptism of the disciples is nothing more than an initiatory sign and ceremony, as is always the case with water-baptism. And second, the baptism of John is the same as the baptism of the disciples and the external baptism of Christ. But we shall have more to say about that later.

We now come to the text from which we learn most surely that water-baptism is an initiatory sign pledging us to a new life before God, a life to which we and all other Christians testify by receiving the sign of water-baptism. In Romans 6 we find these words: "Know ye not, that so many of us as were baptized into Jesus Christ were baptized into his death? Therefore we are buried with him by baptism into death: that like as Christ was raised up from the dead by the glory of the Father, even so we also should walk in newness of life. For if we have been planted together in the likeness of his death, we shall be also in the likeness of his resurrection," etc.(50)

My first task will be to show the true and natural sense of Paul's words. Then I will reply to Anabaptist objections.

The aim of Paul in this passage was to exhort to purity of life those who were saying: All sins are forgiven us through Christ, therefore let us live in sin.(51) And he teaches them that they are quite mistaken, saying: "Know ye not that so many of us as were baptized into Christ"—note that he says "into Christ" and not "in Christ." There is a real distinction here, the same distinction between "into" and "in" which we saw earlier in the words "into the name of the Father" and not "in the name." "Into" is used to signify an entry from outside. For example, when we say: He went into the house, it is quite clear that he was outside and then entered. But "in" is used when we are already inside. When we say: He moved about in the house, we know that he was already in the house when he began to move. So when Paul says: "So many of us as were baptized into Jesus Christ," he must mean that we who were outside Jesus Christ have entered into him by baptism. Necessarily, therefore, baptism is an initiatory sign: "Know ye not that so many of us as were baptized into Jesus Christ were baptized into his death?" It is as though he were saying: Know ye not that when a man is immersed into water (as a visible entry and sealing into Christ), he is immersed into the death of Christ, that is, he is thrust into the death of Christ. This is to be seen clearly from the ceremony of baptism itself. Do you not see that when we are plunged into the water, it is as though we are buried in Christ, that is, in his death, signifying thereby that we are dead to the world. And as Christ was raised from the dead, and dies no more, so we who have been raised up

from the water of baptism must walk in newness of life. For
as we are made like unto him in his death when we are plunged
into the waters of baptism, so we are made like unto him in
his resurrection.(52)

What clearer proof could there be than this text from Paul
that baptism is an initiatory sign which introduces or pledges
us to Christ, that in him we may be new men and live a new
life. Immersion in the water signifies death, that as Christ was
dead and buried, so we too die to the world. Re-emergence
from the water signifies the resurrection of Christ, that as he
rose again to die no more, we too have a new life in Christ, and
can never die, but have passed from death unto life (John 5).
But at this point the Anabaptists object: We must take into
account the preceding verses, and we shall then see that the
Apostle is answering those who were saying: If Christ redeems
us from all sin, and if the grace of God is manifested most clearly
where the sin is greatest, we will continue in sin. Therefore
Paul is not speaking about external baptism, but internal. For
immediately after it reads: "Knowing this, that our old man is
crucified with him, that the body of sin might be destroyed, that
henceforth we should not serve sin," etc. These words make it
quite plain that he is not speaking about external baptism, but
internal, that is, true baptism. Answer: I have taken into
account both what precedes and what follows, and boasting
apart, I knew the meaning of this passage far better than
you (verbo absit invidia) long before you had ever seen it.
But I must give you a more forceful answer than that. No
one denies that in these verses Paul is speaking about the
death of the old man and the new life. But to make his meaning
plainer he introduces water-baptism as a figure or illustration.
It is as though he were saying: How can you live any longer in
sin, you who formerly were dead in sin? For your outward
baptism ought to show you that you cannot continue the old
life. For when you were plunged into the external water, it
signified (53) that you were plunged into the death of Christ,
that is, as Christ died for you, so you too died to the old man.
And when you re-emerged, it signified the resurrection of
Christ, that in him you were raised up again and now walk in
newness of life. Indeed, in all his teaching concerning the death
of the old man and the new life in Christ Paul nowhere makes
his meaning clearer than when he uses the illustration or figure
of water-baptism. And water-baptism must have had the
character which he ascribes to it or else there was no foundation

for the lesson which he based upon it. Necessarily, then, water-baptism is an initiatory sign, pledging us to a new life, and engrafting us into Christ.(54) In this connection note first that Paul uses the sign of baptism as a friendly exhortation to the Christian life and not as a constraint, which is what you do when you identify the external baptism with the internal. I am not thinking now of the constraint of excommunication,(55) by which certain offences are not allowed to go unpunished, but of the constraint imposed by you when you say that you live without sin and force those who are baptized by you to speak and act and dress as you prescribe: (56) which is to form a clique or sect. Baptism must not be used to constrain, as though it were a monastic profession. On the contrary, we must leave every man free to live in the name of God as God himself exhorts, subject only to the ban. Second, I must point out that your words are not substantiated by your actions. If true baptism is the putting off of the old man and the putting on of the new, as indeed it is, why did you begin to reiterate the external baptism of water? Have we not constantly told you: Go and live the best possible Christian life, as the grace of God permits, but leave off rebaptizing: for obviously by rebaptizing you form a sect. The Christian life can be lived just as well and even better without rebaptism; for there is no basis for rebaptization in the Word of God. The only outcome of rebaptism is a constraint which provokes opposition,(57) as was always the case under the monastic system. For "the kingdom of Christ is righteousness and joy and peace in the Holy Ghost" (Rom. 14). Can you not receive that true and saving baptism, that is to say, can you not inwardly fashion yourself upon God, without an external baptism for which you have no warrant? You vacillate from one extreme to the other. If you are forced to receive baptism, you treat it lightly as a thing which is of small account. If for the sake of peace others treat it lightly, you make of it something high and significant.(58) If only others will follow your example, as soon as they are baptized you treat them as those who have begun a new life. And if such were indeed the case, we would be only too pleased to bathe in the Limmat.(59) Let all good Christians note well the arts used by the Evil One in tempting us to division. For he sees that unless we can be divided our cause will prosper. But "he that is with us is greater and stronger" (I John 4). It may be added further that there is nothing new in St. Paul's use of an illustration to teach essential truth. In I Corinthians 10 he uses the communion of the Lord's Supper to show that we ought not to have fellowship with idols. And he bases his teaching upon the illustration in order that in the illustration he may explain to us the correct use of the Lord's Supper. It is the same in the present case. By means of external baptism he gives instruction in internal baptism and the new life, but in such a way that we are instructed also in the nature and character of external baptism itself.(60)

We have now made it sufficiently clear what kind of a sign or sacrament baptism is. Our next task is to consider what it effects or accomplishes.

In this respect I willingly concede to the Anabaptists that the dispute has had many beneficial results. First, it has convinced us of the worthlessness of such human additions as exorcism, spittle, salt, and such like. Many false hopes and beliefs have attached to these things, for they are like a form of magic. True, they have come down to us from the earliest times, but the Fathers did not honour them for the same reasons as we do. And they were not instituted by God, but are a human addition, which could then be permitted on the ground that newly converted Christians, like the children of Israel, looked back to Egypt, and had been used to such ceremonies in paganism. In order to enable them to give up these ceremonies the more easily, the early Christians adapted them to a different use. But better to have abolished them entirely.(61) In any case, that which is allowed temporarily for the sake of infirmity must not be sanctioned indefinitely, for once the truth is learned, the shadow ought to be cast away. Some would even go so far as to reject the Christian prayers offered in baptism. They are quite wrong (I say as much as is Christian), for Christ himself blessed the infants when they were brought to him (Mark 10).(62)

Second, the controversy has shown us that it is not the pouring of water which washes away sin. And that was what we once believed, although without any authority in the Word of God. We also believed that the water of baptism cleanses children from a sin which they never had,(63) and that without it they would be damned.(64) All these beliefs were erroneous, as we shall see later. Water-baptism cannot contribute in any way to the washing away of sin. This is shown by St. Peter in I Peter 3: "In the ark few, that is, eight persons were saved. The like figure whereunto, even baptism, doth also now save us, not the putting away of the filth of the flesh, but the answer of a good conscience towards God," etc. We may see clearly that in this passage Peter commits us to the view that although baptism may wash the body—and that is all that water-baptism can do—it cannot take away sin. Sin is taken away only when we have a good conscience before God. But no material thing can purge the conscience, as we have proved already from the Epistle to the Hebrews. Some early Fathers went astray on the point because they misinterpreted the words of Christ in John 3, when he said to Nicodemus: "Verily, verily, I say unto thee, Except a man be born of water and of the Spirit, he cannot enter into the kingdom of God." These doctors thought that by water he meant material water, and consequently they ascribed more to the water than was justified. Thus it came about that they maintained that the water itself can cleanse, not noticing that the same chapter goes on to tell us: "That which is born of the flesh is flesh, and that which is born of the Spirit is Spirit." From these words they might have seen at once that material water cannot give birth to anything but material things. And for that very reason material water cannot contribute in any way to the cleansing of the soul. If they reply: True, the material water does not do anything, but it is done by the word and the water together, as Augustine says: "The word is made an element, and as such it is a sacrament,"(65) (I do not criticize Augustine,(66) but those who misunderstood him): it is still the case that a spoken or material word has no greater power than that of the water.(67) For none can remit sin but God alone. So then, even if—as they say—the word and the element together constitute the sacrament, the sacrament can never cleanse the soul, for it is only an external thing. The word which saves the soul is not the word outwardly spoken, but the word inwardly understood and believed. And it is to that water that Christ is here referring, as we shall now show. In John 7 Jesus says: "If any man thirst, let him come unto me, and drink. He that believeth on me, as the scripture hath said, out of his belly shall flow rivers of living water." In this verse we see clearly that Christ is speaking of that water which quickens the soul.(68) But that water can be none other than Christ himself. For Christ is the soul's only comfort and nourishment. Therefore the meaning of the earlier text is this: Except a man be made new by coming to know me and believing in me—and that can only take place by the Holy Spirit, for no man can come to me except my Father draw him—indeed, except a man be born again, he cannot enter into the kingdom of heaven. This is the true sense and it is nothing other than the Gospel. Christ preached the same message in many different places and he used many different figures of speech. In John 4 he says to the woman of Samaria: "But whosoever drinketh of the water that I shall give him shall never thirst; but the water that I shall give him shall be in him a well of water, springing up into everlasting life." His meaning here is simply that those who know and believe in him will come to God. Everywhere he proclaimed the Gospel as his hearers could best understand it. It was the Gospel which he taught in John 6: "Labour not for the meat which perisheth, but for that meat which endureth unto everlasting life, which the Son of man shall give unto you." In this verse trust in him is called meat. And later, having pointed to the way of salvation, namely, that the bread or meat which he shall give has been so baked or prepared that it is given up to death on our behalf, he continues: "Except ye eat the flesh of the Son of man, and drink his blood, ye have no life in you." Here too his only purpose is to proclaim the Gospel. Unless we believe that he was given up to death for us and washed us in his blood, unless we trust in that fact (for spiritual eating is trust), we have no life in us. It all amounts to this: "He that believeth on me hath everlasting life" (John 6). And: "No man cometh unto the Father but by me" (John 14). And: "I, if I be lifted up from the earth, will draw all men unto me" (John 12). So, then, in John 3: "Except a man be born of water and of the Spirit, he cannot enter into the kingdom of God," he is simply teaching that evangelical doctrine which alone can quicken the soul as material water refreshes the thirsty heart. And it was no innovation by Christ when he applied water in this way, for we find a similar application in the Old Testament. For in Isaiah 55: "Ho, every one that thirsteth, come ye to the waters, and he that hath no money, yea come, buy without money and drink," etc., the prophet is exhorting us to come quickly to the free gift, in which all that we have to do is to drink, to come to Christ who is the soul's true comfort. Again, in Zechariah 14 we find the words: "And it shall be in that day, that living waters shall go out from Jerusalem," etc. And there are many other places as well. Therefore the passage in question is simply a proclamation of the Gospel, first under the figure of water and then openly and plainly. Read the third chapter of John and you will see that Christ taught Nicodemus the Gospel in the clearest possible fashion.

Nevertheless we will suggest a defence against those who continue to dispute about the text. If you would claim that the "water" here is material water, then you must allow that the "fire" of Matthew 3 is material fire. In that text John says: "He shall baptize you with the Holy Ghost and with fire." But you say: The cases are not the same, for we do baptize with water but not with fire. Answer: There was in fact a baptism with fire, for Christ was not lying in Acts 2 but baptized the disciples with tongues of fire.(69) Hence if the "fire" of Matthew 3 is not to be understood as material fire, the "water" of John 3 is not to be understood as material water. Not that we reject water-baptism. It is based upon other passages of Scripture: John 3,(70) Mark 1, etc. But because they do not understand this point, the Indian Christians err in the administration of external baptism, for first they baptize with water and then they burn a mark upon the head.(71) They do so because they have just as much reason to take the "fire" of Matthew 3 for material fire as they have to take the "water" of John 3 for material water. Indeed, if we take the water for material water, they could easily convince us that their baptism is correct and not ours, for we do not baptize with fire, and yet if the water is understood as material water they have just as clear a text for fire as we have for water. The Fathers were in error in this matter of water-baptism because they thought that the water itself effects cleansing and salvation. In such circumstances error was inevitable, and one result was that they did not find the true foundation for infant baptism, for they grounded it in part upon the external baptism of water.(72) But it is clear that the external baptism of water cannot effect spiritual cleansing. Hence water-baptism is nothing but an external ceremony, that is, an outward sign that we are incorporated and engrafted into the Lord Jesus Christ and pledged to live to him and to follow him. And as in Jesus Christ neither circumcision nor uncircumcision avails anything, but a new creature, the living of a new life (Gal. 6), so it is not baptism which saves us, but a new life. Therefore one of the good results of the controversy has been to teach us that baptism cannot save or purify. Yet I cannot but think that in other respects the Anabaptists themselves set too great store by the baptism of water, and for that reason they err just as much on the one side as the papists do on the other. For though the whole world were arrayed against it, it is clear and indisputable that no external element or action can purify the soul. But in the disputation there were some who maintained openly that they had experienced a great release at the moment of baptism. To this Myconius (73) answered: Did you not come to baptism with considerable apprehension? One of them replied: Yes—for they claim that no one should let himself be baptized unless he knows that he can live without sin. Then said Myconius: The release which you experienced in baptism was simply a cessation of that apprehension which you yourself had created. They affirmed, however, that God had done something quite new towards them—the very experience which at one time we had in penance. For there, too, we were in great fear and distress before we made our confession: but the moment we had made it we said: God be praised, I feel a great joy and refreshing. And all that we really felt was a relaxation of the previous tension. Yet the penitent could easily claim that in penance or papal absolution he experienced within himself a great renewal the moment he made his confession. And it was simply the removal of his apprehension. This is proved by the fact that our lives did not undergo any great change in consequence. Now those who allow themselves to be rebaptized make much of a similar experience. Its true source is the fact that rebaptization has no foundation in the Word of God. Hence the conscience opposes it, and it is anxious and afraid. But as the deed is done we brace ourselves and accept the risk, and then we want everyone else to do as we have done in order to free ourselves from reproach.(74) Oh, but they say, formerly we were sinners, but now we are sinners no longer. Answer: The monks used to talk like that, and we answered, rightly, that in making a statement of that kind they were committing the greatest possible sin. And now the devil is leading us back to the same evil ways. We disclosed his stratagems and revealed the hypocrisy of the monks. And now he is trying a new trick—he is using the light itself to bring us back to darkness. Again, they say: We allowed ourselves to be rebaptized in order that our brethren in rebaptization might have power and authority to restrain us when we have the impulse to sin. Note well that this is nothing other than monkery, separatism, sectarianism, a new legalism. For we Christians do not act rightly under the compulsion of law, but by faith.(75) But it is no longer by faith when a man acts rightly because he is compelled to do so by his brethren in baptism. Naturally there are certain offences which have to be punished, but even there the punishment ought to be administered by the Church and not by the Anabaptist sect. But they say: We are the Church, and those who do not belong to our Church are not Christians. The Church was founded by us: before us there was no Church. Answer: Exactly; it is just as I have said from the very first. The root of the trouble is that the Anabaptists will not recognize any Christians except themselves or any Church except their own.(76) And that is always the way with sectarians who separate themselves on their own authority. It is what the papacy itself did, claiming to be the true Church without either the approval or the consent of genuine churches. Study carefully the passage in Acts 20 which speaks of wolves drawing the people after them, and you will find there a picture of yourselves. No, you despoilers. You should accept as Christians even those who do not re-baptize, and you should rejoice that they too accept you as Christians. For better far not merely to exclude but to banish you than to permit you to despise others.(77) And for this reason: How dare you introduce innovations into the Church simply on your own authority and without consulting the Church? I speak only of those churches in which the Word of God is publicly and faithfully preached. For if every block-head who had a novel or strange opinion were allowed to gather a sect around him, divisions and sects would become so numerous that the Christian body which we now build up with such difficulty would be broken to pieces in every individual congregation. Therefore no innovations ought to be made except with the common consent of the churches, and not merely of a single church. For the judgment of Scripture is not mine or yours, but the churches' (I Cor. 14); for it is to the churches that the keys are committed (John 21).(78) What, then, is the true nature of this revolt or schism? It includes within it all those who want to introduce innovations of this type into congregations which hear and believe the Word of God, and as God permits, obey it. Now as I have said, the devil is too clever for us. He knows how best to check the rising tide of the Gospel. Therefore, good Christians, do not try to push ahead too quickly: for to press on regardless of the weak is the mark not of a strong but a restless spirit which cannot wait until the poor sheep can catch up be-hind.(79) I am speaking only of churches where the Word of God is preached, and of external things. In other matters it is right and proper that each Christian follow Christ in the inner man as the grace of God permits.

But at this point they ask: Is it not right and proper that we live according to the Word of God? By all means, but if you do you will not make innovations in contentious matters, for you will be taught first and foremost not to put a stumbling-block in the way of your brother in things which are external and indifferent (Rom. 14). How much less are we to put a stumbling-block in things which are external and have no warrant in the Word of God, like rebaptism? For in that passage in Romans Paul is speaking about meats, and it may be shown by clear texts of Scripture that meats are indifferent. But that is not so in the case of rebaptism; for unlike meats, baptism is a ceremony or pledge. But they say: Occasions do arise when things ought to be abrogated or initiated and the authorities will not act. But if it is a matter like rebaptism, you ought to deal with it as a thing indifferent, submitting it to the whole Church for amicable discussion, allowing sufficient time for the study of Scripture and loyally accepting the scriptural teaching.(80) But you are trying to coerce the churches: it is for them to try the words of the novice, not for the novice to coerce them. And the Church of Christ would never have authorized you to rebaptize, for it knows of no warrant for rebaptism. The same procedure must be followed in such matters as the choice of meats. If innovation is desired, the bishop or prophet ought first to instruct the Church and then leave discussion and authorization to the congregation. But at this point it might be said: Does not this raise the question of authorities which refuse to accept instruction? That is quite true. In such cases give instruction faithfully and exercise your liberty as a Christian privately amongst those who will not be offended. God will plant his Word in the hearts of believers, increasing it until the authorities are overpowered—but let God himself do the work.(81) And in external matters which serve only to disrupt the congregation, unless you have clear texts, avoid like poison any innovation on your own account without the prior decision of the Church. But note how the Anabaptists stand in this respect. They have made innovations in our midst without saying a word to anyone, not to speak of their public preaching in the congregation, to which they have no lawful calling.(82) In this regard it is hardly necessary to adduce proofs from Scripture. They may be found everywhere if there are any who speak of concealment.

To return to the text in John 3. The Anabaptists might interject: If the word water means the Gospel or refreshment through

Christ, why did you argue in the disputation that according
to this text water precedes the Spirit? Answer: We are forced to
use this type of argument in order that the world may not be
filled with lies by your calumnious speaking. It was the same
once with Leo Jud when he was disputing with an Anabaptist (83) who insisted that we must abide by the literal
words of Scripture and keep to the order in which those words
are written. Therefore Leo answered: Tell me, how do you
understand the word "water" in John 3 when Christ says:
"Except a man be born of water and of the Spirit," etc.? The
man hesitated a long time, but he would not accept the view
that the water here can be anything but the material water of
baptism. He did this out of sheer perversity, for they had often
heard us say that the water here is confession and faith in
Christ. But they would not depart from the letter of the text.
So Leo said: If you must abide by the letter, then in this verse
"water" is put before the Holy Spirit: therefore even according
to your beliefs we may give water-baptism before giving instruction. And they preferred not to give any answer rather
than abandon the letter, for if they once did that the text in
Matthew 28 would be dashed out of their hands and without
it they would not be able to argue the question of infant baptism. Thus they allowed themselves to be worsted in the one
text in order not to be forced away from the other: but most
foolishly, for if their views are refuted by one text, no other
can ever be of the slightest help to them. If any of them did
not even know our interpretation, they have to thank the clever
teachers who have led them astray in so many other matters:
for these latter heard our exposition of the text in two private
discussions held last summer.(84) The text would have been
most useful to us in the defence of infant baptism, and the
Fathers all took the water to be the water of baptism, which
would have been a great help to us. But we refused to do
violence to the text, for when did we ever defend ourselves by
wresting the true sense of Scripture? We opposed them on the
above lines only in order to expose their own obstinacy, but
with the majority of them all to no purpose.

Of the Origin and Institution of Baptism (85)

The occasion of the institution of baptism is something which
the Anabaptists refuse to perceive. They maintain that baptism
was instituted in Matthew 28: "Go ye. Teach all nations, bap-

tizing them in the name of the Father, and of the Son, and of the Holy Ghost, teaching them to observe all things whatsoever I have commanded you." But not so, dear friend. Baptism was not instituted at that time, for by means of his disciples Christ himself had baptized long before, and he himself had already been baptized. Necessarily, therefore, it must have been instituted earlier. Note, then, that God instituted baptism in and through John—hence his name, the Baptist. For God says in Malachi: "Behold, I will send my messenger, and he shall prepare the way before me." This messenger or angel was none other than St. John the Baptist (Mark 1). And when John came he baptized, as we may see quite plainly in all the evangelists. But if he came to initiate and prepare the way of the Lord, and in fulfilling that mission he baptized, then assuredly he initiated the baptism of the Lord. But here the Anabaptists say: The baptism of John and that of Christ are not the same. And they are not alone when they say that, for all the theologians that I have ever read or can call to mind say exactly the same. Therefore it is not easy for me to assert the contrary, for if the Anabaptists and the papists are in league against me, I am inevitably confronted by more formidable adversaries than any theologian of our age has ever previously encountered.(86) What shall I do then? Shall I suppress the truth? I cannot do that, for already it has been abandoned by almost everyone, and the lack of understanding has resulted in much error and discord. So long as the foundation rests not in my own word but in the strong and invincible Word of God, the task of maintaining the truth will be neither too disagreeable nor too difficult for me. And as I do so, I shall show the derivation, institution and initiation of baptism, so that two birds will be killed with the one stone.(87) For if the baptism of John is the same as that of Christ, we have proved already that baptism was initiated when John began to baptize. And if it was initiated then, it was not instituted subsequent to the resurrection of Christ, in Matthew 28. Again, if it can be proved that Christ had already baptized his disciples, it necessarily follows that baptism was instituted prior to the resurrection. Otherwise Christ had two baptisms, which is quite impossible, as we shall see.

Now the text which we have already quoted from the prophet Malachi shows that the external baptism of John is the same as the external baptism of Christ. For if the baptism of John had been different from that of Christ, he would not have

begun to prepare the way of the Lord, as is prophesied in
Isaiah 40, but would have gone his own way. But this would
have been quite out of keeping with his role as a prophet, for the
prophets did not introduce anything novel or strange, but
simply led men to God and did the work of God.

The Anabaptists and papists argue that the baptism of John
is a type of the baptism of Christ.(88) But in this they do
violence and injustice to both Christ and John. To Christ,
because they disregard his own word. For in Luke 16 he says:
"The law and the prophets were until John: since that time the
kingdom of God is preached," etc. But if the law and the prophets were until John, and since that time the kingdom of
God is preached, then necessarily the kingdom of God is more
than a type or shadow. For we have it clearly from Christ
himself that John preached the kingdom of God, that is, the
Gospel. But if John preached the kingdom of Christ, then he
administered the baptism of Christ. For how could his doctrine
be a doctrine of light if his baptism was only the shadow (89)
of some future baptism?

And they also do violence and injustice to John, for they
make of him a type and reckon him with the Old Testament.
But by divine appointment he initiated the Gospel, preaching
and declaring it with no less clarity than the Apostles themselves. Indeed, he was the very first to point to the Lord
Jesus Christ when the time of his manifestation had come,
as we read in John 1: "The next day John seeth Jesus coming
unto him, and saith: Behold, the Lamb of God, which taketh
away the sin of the world. This is he of whom I said, After
me cometh a man which is preferred before me: for he was
before me." In this passage we see plainly that John came in
order to reveal Christ to the people of Israel. It was not his
office to give types and shadows, but to declare the Saviour of
the world, as the words themselves show. But here the papists
and Anabaptists say: John regards his baptism only as a baptism
of water. But the baptism of Christ is more than a baptism of
water. Therefore the baptism of John cannot be the same as
that of Christ. Answer: Were it not that your ears are stopped,
you would have heard the answer already. Did John baptize
with water only? No. Therefore it is evident that when he says
"baptize with water" he is referring not merely to the pouring
of water but to teaching: for by water-baptism alone he could
never have taught the knowledge of Christ. By the baptism of
water he means first and foremost his teaching. And he gave

this teaching in order that men might learn to know Christ and to place their hopes on him. But now the papists and Anabaptist rabble say: The two baptisms could not be the same, for Christ baptizes with the Holy Ghost, as John himself says in Matthew 3, but John could not baptize with the Holy Ghost. Answer: God be praised: for like the fox you have betrayed yourselves. Tell me, when the disciples baptized, and when we baptize today, with what do we baptize? With the Holy Ghost or with water? You have to admit that the disciples and we too can only give external teaching and the external baptism of water: we cannot baptize internally with the Holy Ghost.(90) Tell me then, is the baptism of the disciples the same as the baptism of Christ or not? You cannot deny that it is, for you desire your rebaptism to be the same as the baptism of Christ. But what is it that you give? You merely give water and teaching. I do not allow that when you baptize again you follow Christ, but from your own practice I am demonstrating the true meaning of the baptism of Christ. But if, as we shall see, the baptism of teaching and water which John gave was the same as that of the disciples, and if the baptism of the disciples was the same as that of Christ, how much more is the baptism of John identical with the baptism of Christ—for John was appointed by God to initiate that teaching and baptism.

But for God's sake remember that when we say that the baptism of Christ was the same as that of John we are thinking only of teaching and the baptism of water.(91) For otherwise, even the baptism of the disciples would not be the same as that of Christ, for the disciples could not baptize with the Holy Ghost any more than John.

And now consider whether the two baptisms, the inward and the outward, are necessarily concurrent. For we give outward teaching and the baptism of water. But God moves inwardly according to his own sovereign choice. Hence we may prove that the teaching of John is the same as that of the apostles: that is, he preached the Gospel. And this being the case, it is established that there is only one baptism of water, and no distinction can be drawn between the baptism of John and the baptism of Christ. For if Christ himself had administered water-baptism, his external baptism, and in content his teaching, would have been exactly the same as that of the disciples and John. And inasmuch as the disciples baptized in his name, that is, on his behalf, his baptism was identical with that of the disciples and John so far as teaching and the baptism of water were concerned. I say, in content, that is, in the sum and matter, for in other respects we all agree that his teaching had a force and dignity and power far surpassing that of any other.(92) Our point is proved by the fact that many of those who heard him did not believe, as he himself sometimes complains. But why did they not believe? Because God did not move them inwardly: for he willed their rejection (Matt. 13, Isa. 6). Therefore in respect of its significance and purpose the baptism of Christ was the same as that of John and the disciples, for he could not accomplish anything inward apart from the internal enlightenment which is given by the Father. Do not be misled, good Christian. What the Father does, the Son and the Holy Spirit do also (John 5). But according to his human nature (93) the Son has given us a model of teaching, that the disciples might not despair too easily when they see that men do not believe them, for it was exactly the same in his case as well (John 15).

We will now examine the preaching of John and see whether it was the same or not as that of Christ and the apostles. Mark gives us an exact account of the beginning of the preaching of Christ in chapter 1 of his Gospel: "After that John was put in prison, Jesus came into Galilee, preaching the gospel of the kingdom of God, and saying, The time is fulfilled, and the kingdom of God is at hand: repent ye, and believe the Gospel." Note that St. John the Evangelist gives us a similar account in John 3. He means that Jesus taught and baptized, as we have already shown. But the record in Mark is more exact, for he taught in Galilee as well as Judaea.

And now let us compare the teaching of John with that of Christ. It is described in Matthew 3: "In those days came John the Baptist, preaching in the wilderness of Judaea, and saying, Repent ye; for the kingdom of heaven is at hand." Notice that there are two parts to the Gospel, the one repentance and amendment of life, and the other trust in God through the Lord Jesus Christ. For in Luke 24 Christ himself taught us that in his name repentance and remission of sins are to be preached to all peoples. And later, the Gospel was at one time widely known as repentance, as we see in Acts 11: "Then hath God also to the Gentiles granted repentance unto life." Now only Christ can give life. We may repent for long enough and yet have no rest in our souls. But when we trust in Christ, our souls rejoice and live. In this passage, then, the Gospel is called repentance.(94) And sometimes in Scripture it is called remission of sins, as in Acts 10: "To him give all the prophets witness, that through his name whosoever believeth in him shall receive remission of sins." In this verse the Gospel is called remission of sins. Hence we see that at any rate one part of the Gospel was faithfully proclaimed by John. And for that reason the Anabaptists have no right not to count John an evangelist and preacher of the Gospel. For when it says that repentance was preached it means the whole Gospel, as we have seen. For we read in Mark 6: "And the disciples went out, and preached that men should repent." But quite apart from that we will show plainly that John preached the Gospel as clearly as any apostle. In John 1 he said: "Behold the Lamb of God, which taketh away the sin of the world." And that is the whole sum of the Gospel in its aspect as grace, that is, that Christ is the Lamb of God which taketh away the sin of the world. And immediately after he says: "And I bare record that this is the Son of God." That is the affirmation upon which Christ built his Church. And when we extol the apostles we must extol John as well, that is, we must recognize that John is not less than the disciples.(95) But we will examine the matter even more closely. In his parables Christ often teaches that he is the very Son of God and that all who believe in him have eternal life (John 4, 6, 7, etc.). Is not that the message of the grace of God? I believe so. And if I can show that John preached exactly the same message, I have proved, I hope, that John preached the Gospel no less than the others. Turn to John 3 and read what he said about Christ to the disciples and Jews who had come to question him. It would take too long to quote the whole passage, but these verses make it plain that the baptism of John is the same as that of Christ as we allege. And at the end he says: "The Father loveth the Son, and hath given all things into his hand. He that believeth on the Son hath everlasting life: and he that believeth not the Son shall not see life; but the wrath of God abideth on him." (96) Excellent. For where is the apostle who ever described Christ more plainly as the one to whom the Father has committed all things? Where is the apostle who ever summarized the Gospel more clearly or concisely than the Baptist did in this concluding discourse? Consider the saying: "Go ye into all the world, and preach the gospel to every creature. He that believeth and is baptized shall be saved; but he that believeth not shall be damned." Is not this the same as that of John: "He that believeth on the Son"—notice the emphasis and forcefulness of the expression. He does not call him Son of God but Son of the Father.(97) In this way he makes it all the surer that he is the very Son than if he had merely said the Son of God. For many are called sons of God and yet they are not very Sons. But Christ is the Son of the Father. Of necessity, then, he is of one nature with the Father—"He that believeth on the Son hath everlasting life: and he that believeth not the Son shall not see life; but the wrath of God abideth on him." Yes, it is exactly the same. Again in Acts 19 Paul says: "John verily baptized, that is, taught with the baptism of repentance, saying unto the people, that they should believe on him which should come after him, that is, on Christ Jesus." Excellent. For is not that the true Gospel, to teach sinners to amend and repent? And when the penitent is despairing and without hope, when of ourselves we can find nothing to comfort ourselves to salvation, God sent forth his Son to be our comfort and to be to us a sure pledge of salvation. And John pointed to the Son. John testified that he is the Son of God (John 1). John said of him that he he that believeth in him hath everlasting life, John 3. John exhorted to faith in him. Is not that the whole Gospel, the true Gospel, the plain Gospel? Away then, you Anabaptists, and learn that when Scripture describes the preaching and baptism of John as the baptism of repentance, the meaning is that John began to preach the way of salvation and by repentance we must understand the Gospel. But if the teaching of John is the Gospel, what grounds have we for saying that the baptism of John is different from the baptism of Christ? It is beyond question that there is only one baptism. For the Gospel began with the preaching of John. That is what Christ himself said in Luke 16, as we have seen already. It follows, then, that the baptism of Christ began at the same time. It is not my affair if the theologians failed to perceive this. The teaching of John is the same as that of Christ and the apostles and it points to the salvation of men, Jesus Christ. John both proclaims him as the one who is to come and points to him as the one already present. So, too, do the apostles. Read carefully Matthew 10, Mark 6 and Luke 10. The apostles preached the kingdom of God, that is, salvation through Christ, even before the crucifixion; and Christ proclaimed himself even before his death and passion. I say this in order that those who divide baptism may not argue: John preaches the Christ who is yet to come, but the apostles and we preach Christ crucified.

For he preached Christ in exactly the same way as Christ himself and the disciples did.

But even if we had no other evident proofs, Christ's own baptism by John would be sufficient to prove that the baptism of Christ and that of John were one and the same, for Christ was baptized only with John's baptism and not with any other. Now it is quite certain that Christ was baptized as an example to us. And if there are any who say: Leave off baptizing infants, for they belong to God in any case, let them note in passing that Christ, the very Son of God, took to himself baptism in order that he might give us an example of unity, that we may all enter under the one sign. Therefore we ought not to say that infants do not need baptism, for Christ did not need it. I return to my main point. Was Christ baptized as an example to us? Yes. Then I ask: In what baptism? for you separate between the baptism of Christ and that of John. If by his baptism he wished to give us an example, why was he not baptized in his own baptism? But if he was baptized in the baptism of John, we too must be baptized in the baptism of John. In short, my answer is this: The apostles as well as Christ were baptized in the baptism of John.(98) Of course, it was not his baptism, but Christ's,(99) although then as now ignorant persons regarded it as the baptism of John. But incorrectly, for in I Corinthians 1 Paul will not allow us to speak of the baptism of Cephas, Apollos, etc. If, then, both Christ and the apostles were baptized in the baptism of John, it follows necessarily that there is only one baptism. And if we wish to be baptized according to the example given by Christ, we are baptized in the baptism of John. Hence there is only one baptism. It was initiated by John, and it has continued right up to the present. If the baptism with which John baptized had not continued indefinitely, then Christ and the apostles were not baptized with the same baptism as we are. Away, you blockheads. In Ephesians 4 Paul gives a fine exhortation to unity: they are all one body, they have one spirit, they are all called in one hope, there is one Lord, one faith, one baptism, one God and Father of all things. Break this passage of Paul, you who would divide baptism. For if John taught the same spirit, and gathered into the same body, and taught the same hope in Christ, the same Lord, the same faith, the same God and Father, why will you not allow that the baptism of John is the same baptism and faith as that of Christ and the apostles. May God grant you understanding. But those who divide baptism allege two objections. The first is that we ought to distinguish between the baptism of Christ and that of John because Christ taught us to baptize in the name of the Father, and of the Son, and of the Holy Ghost, but this John did not do. Now tell me whether you believe that these words contribute at all to our salvation or not. If they do contribute to the purifying of the soul, then it is possible for man to help forward the purification of the inner man, for any one man can pronounce these words over another. But that is blasphemy: for only God can purify the soul and inner man. And if the words cannot contribute at all, then why try to distinguish between the baptism of John and that of Christ? For take note, as we have already shown, that according to the Greek the words in Matthew 28 mean simply: "Baptizing them into the name of the Father, and of the Son, and of the Holy Ghost." It is not as though Christ intended that they should actually use the words: "I baptize thee in the name of the Father, and of the Son, and of the Holy Ghost," as though the words themselves could wash away sin. What he intended was that when they baptized they should baptize into the name, that is, the power and majesty and obedience of the Father, and of the Son, and of the Holy Ghost. For if he had been appointing a form of words, as the theologians maintain, it would have gone ill with the disciples, for we do not read that they baptized anyone with such a formula, but simply in the name of Jesus, as we have already seen. Although, of course, all Christians rejoice in these words, for there are no words which we speak with greater readiness than the names of those to whose service we are thereby engaged. But if, as we have seen, St. John in his preaching taught the Father, the Son and the Holy Ghost, if indeed he recognized them—for the Father spoke at the baptism of the Son, and when the Son was baptized by him he saw the Spirit in the form of a dove(100)—it follows that John baptized into God the Father, the Son and the Holy Ghost no less surely than did the disciples, who simply baptized into Jesus Christ. We have no proof that John ever pronounced the threefold name with his lips, but essentially he did lead men to the Father, the Son and the Holy Ghost. For he said: "He will baptize you with the Holy Ghost." The objection that the words are not used counts for very little if the content is there. It would be quite wrong, of course, arbitrarily to despise the given form: "I baptize thee in the name of the Father, and of the Son, and of the Holy Ghost." For all Christians are at one in the use of this form, and the Greek churches do not err when they say: "Be thou baptized in the name of the Father, and of the Son, and of the Holy Ghost": a form closer to the original words of Christ than ours is.(101) But the outward form does not greatly matter so long as we have the right meaning.(102) For Peter says in Acts 2: "Be baptized every one of you in the name of Jesus Christ"—in the Greek it might equally well be "on the name of Jesus Christ." The name means the power or capacity or foundation, so that "in the name" means into the power, or on the power, capacity, foundation or grace of Jesus. The man who does that undertakes to live a new life, and it is the whole nature and character of baptism that in it we dedicate ourselves to God, and indeed pledge ourselves to a new life.

The second objection is the passage in Acts 19: "Paul came to Ephesus: and finding certain disciples, he said unto them, Have ye received the Holy Ghost since ye believed? And they said unto him, We have not so much as heard whether there be any Holy Ghost? And he said unto them, Unto what then were ye baptized? And they said, Unto John's baptism. Then said Paul, John verily baptized with the baptism of repentance, saying unto the people, that they should believe on him which should come after him, that is, on Christ Jesus. When they heard this, they were baptized in the name of the Lord Jesus." Our opponents destroy the unity of baptism and rebaptize themselves simply because they do not understand this passage. We will first convince them that they misunderstand the passage, and then we will show them its true meaning. And in this way. Did John administer baptism as Paul says? Yes, for we cannot accuse Paul of untruth. But if so, then John administered the baptism of Christ, for the baptism of Christ requires us to amend our lives, to turn to Christ and to believe in him. But if he did that, then his action was valid, and the words of Paul must have a different sense from that which they would have if he were denying or belittling the baptism of John.(103) Now it cannot be disputed that in Paul's account of the baptism of John we find the true meaning and content of the baptism of Christ. Therefore the text cannot possibly be used to destroy the unity of baptism. It may be noted that sometimes we are so strongly influenced by the opinions of theologians who have led us astray that we simply accept their directions and do not think out a matter for ourselves. It is as though we had learned to play the lute in the wrong way, and then we try to learn the right way.(104) It costs us a great amount of time and trouble to unlearn the wrong way and to learn the new, for something of the old will always persist. That was why Timotheus (105) asked a double fee when he had to teach someone who played already: the first for teaching him how not to play, and the second for teaching him how to play. In the same way we today are still influenced to some degree by the opinions advanced by the theologians concerning the distinction between the baptism of John and that of Christ. For not only did they not understand this passage, but they corrupted and divided it. They argued that the baptism of John was only a baptism of contrition, meaning that it did not point to salvation in Christ. In proof of this they adduced the first part of Paul's statement: "John baptized with the baptism of repentance," but omitted what follows. Yet there we are pointed to the finest part of the Gospel, for John also taught us to trust in Christ, and in Paul's words we have a short summary of the whole Gospel. The erroneous notion of a distinction between the two baptisms derives from this falsification or ignorance, and it has continued with us right up to the present time, although we ourselves are hardly aware of it. And now I will show you the true meaning of the passage. When Paul came to Ephesus he was met by twelve men who told him that they were of the new faith (I must put it in that way for as yet they knew nothing concerning Christ). But Paul saw that their instruction was deficient and that they lacked any true faith. Therefore he asked them whether they had received the Holy Ghost after they believed, that is, whether they had received in their hearts assurance towards God and joy through Christ. He was not asking concerning tongues, although these proceed from the same source. The proof of this is that this sign is not necessary to salvation: it is given only in a few places. What Paul is asking is this: You profess to be believers, but how is it with your hearts? Are you enlightened by God? Does your consolation rest in God through Christ? He is simply asking whether they are sound in the faith which they profess. But the moment Paul mentions the Holy Ghost they say that they have never even heard whether there is a Holy Ghost. So Paul asks them: "In what then were ye baptized?" We have to note here two small points of style. In Latin we say: "In what" then were ye baptized? But in the Greek it is: "Into what" then were ye baptized? Notice that there is quite a big difference between "in what" and "into what," as we have already shown in our discussion of the words: "Into the name of the Father" and "in the name of the Father." This has been taken into account in the translation of the New Testament,(106) which does not read: "In what," but, "unto what" then were ye baptized? And in Matthew 28 it does not read: "in the name," but "into the name." I did not investigate the matter earlier but I have now taken up the point and examined the translation. And that is how it stands: "Unto what then were ye baptized?" which is much closer to the natural sense of the Greek, that is: "Into what then were ye baptized?" than is the rendering: "In what then were ye baptized?" For "unto what" and "into what" both suggest the same thought: Upon what were you grounded in your baptism? or, Into what were you initiated by it? Furthermore, "into what" suggests that we are speaking only of water-baptism and the external words which accompany it. The other point of style is this: that in this context the word "baptized" is used for "taught." Already we have advanced strong proofs from Scripture that the word must often be understood in that sense, and we will now try to show that that is how it must be construed in the present context. The theologians argue that Paul asks concerning the Holy Ghost because the baptism of John did not make use of the formula: Of the Father, and of the Son, and of the Holy Ghost. But it may easily be seen that this is a complete fabrication, for when the men were baptized a few moments later they were not baptized in the name of the Father or of the Holy Ghost but only of the Lord Jesus. It follows, then, that Paul is not asking them about their external baptism, but about their instruction and faith, as in John 1: for when the priests and Levites said to John: "Why baptizest thou then if thou be not that Christ, nor Elias, neither that prophet?" we have every reason to believe that they were not asking concerning external baptism, for the Jews had many and varied washings (Heb. 9).(107) If it had merely been that John baptized in a different way from those who preceded him, they could hardly have had any objection. But John preached a new Saviour. He pointed to the Lamb of God which taketh away the sin of the world. And that was something which they could not allow, since it abrogated the existing sacrifices. Therefore, when they asked: Why baptizest thou then? the word baptism signified teaching, and they were asking John why he was initiating a new doctrine. Scripture often uses one word for another in this way, and if we do not consider the proper sense we shall be completely misled.

So then, when Paul spoke to them concerning the baptism of John, it was not his intention to repudiate that baptism, but to bring out its fundamental meaning and character. He defined for them the true nature of John's baptism, as though to say: You allege that you are baptized into John's baptism, that is, instructed in the teaching which John gave, but I do not see any signs of it. Therefore I will tell you the content of that baptism, and we shall see whether you have been instructed rightly in the teaching of John. John baptized unto repentance; that is, he taught repentance and baptized unto it, saying—notice that the word "baptism" is used for teaching and preaching. The word "saying" is a note or sign by which we may clearly see that when Paul says: "Unto what then were ye baptized?" he is merely asking them concerning their instruction and faith. He asks them what faith or doctrine they held. And they reply: Unto John's baptism, that is, we are instructed in the doctrine taught by John—saying unto the people that they should believe on him which should come after him. But is not that the whole content of the Gospel? For what is the Gospel but a new life, and faith in God through Christ Jesus, who is himself very God and very man? If that is what John preached—and the fact that the words "baptized" and "saying" are used together means that he preached—then necessarily the words of Paul are a declaration, and a promise, and an enquiry whether or not they were rightly instructed according to the teaching of John. And we must not forget that at four different points the Greek is stronger and more definite than the Latin. First, Paul does not say: "In what then were ye baptized?" but, "Into what then were ye baptized?" Second, it does not read: "In John's baptism," but, "Into John's baptism." Third, it does not say: "John baptized with the baptism of repentance," but, "John baptized the baptism of repentance." Note the phrase and ask yourself how else the word baptized can be construed except as taught. And fourth, it does not say: "They were baptized in the name of Jesus," but, "They were baptized into the name of Jesus."

Now the context of the whole matter was as follows: Apollos was an excellent scholar, and in Acts 18, just prior to this incident, we are told that "he was not fully instructed in the way of the Lord, knowing only the baptism of John"—the word baptism being used for teaching. But someone might say: From this passage it is plain that the baptism of John is inferior to that of Christ. Answer: It is beyond question that John's teaching was the teaching of the Gospel. We have seen that already. Therefore when it says: "Knowing only the baptism of John," we must take it that he knew the baptism, that is, the teaching of John only in the way that he knew the baptism, that is, the teaching of Christ. In other words, he knew only the rudiments: he had received very little instruction even in the baptism or teaching of John. For if he had fully understood the teaching of John he would have known the Gospel. The true meaning is as follows: The little that Apollos did know he had learned from John or the disciples of John and not from Christ or the disciples of Christ.(108) And what Apollos did know he taught faithfully and diligently, for he was mighty in the Scriptures. But when Aquila and Priscilla came, they expounded unto him the way of the Lord more perfectly. Notice that that which was previously described as baptism is now called teaching. Now there is every reason to suppose that the twelve men who are mentioned immediately afterwards in Acts 19 had been instructed by Apollos. And if Apollos did not know the way of the Lord either fully or clearly, there can be little doubt that the twelve had even less knowledge: for it is evident that they would not have outstripped their learned master in so short a time. So when Paul came to Ephesus, Apollos had been there before him, and had now sailed to Achaia. According to his usual custom Paul preached the Gospel. There then met him the twelve men who professed to be disciples of Christ. He saw the inadequacy of their knowledge and he asked them whether they had received the Holy Ghost, that is, whether they were in a right relationship with God and believed in their hearts. As we have said, he was not asking concerning the sign of tongues, which is not essential to the completeness of the Gospel. The question revealed their ignorance, for they had never even heard of the Holy Ghost. Then said Paul: "Into what then were ye baptized?" that is, into what then were ye instructed? as we shall show later. They replied that they had been instructed in the baptism, that is, the teaching of John. Notice that they do not tell us what they were taught: they simply name the teacher whose doctrine they knew, but imperfectly, just as today there are vagrants who profess to be Lutherans or Evangelicals, but whose only knowledge of the life and teaching of the Gospel is to live easily off pious Christians without doing a hand's turn.(109) If I compare the twelve with rascals of this kind, it is not in respect of any deception, but in respect of their fear: they were not willing to reveal their ignorance, professing to be Christians or disciples. But when Paul saw their hesitation he exposed the very thing which they would not acknowledge. For he knew the teaching of John far better than they did, and he told them: "John baptized the baptism of repentance." Note that in this context the words "baptize" and "baptism" cannot have any other meaning than teach and teaching, in other words, John taught the doctrine of repentance, and together with it the certainty of the grace of God—note the two parts of the Gospel—"saying unto the people that they should believe on him which should come after him", that is, on Christ. Up to this point there has not been anything to show that the twelve were ever baptized with water: for it cannot be shown that Apollos baptized with water, but only that he taught diligently that which he knew of the baptism of John, baptism in the sense of teaching (Acts 18). And the evangelists usually mentioned the baptism of water when it was given. John both taught and baptized with water. Christ taught and he also administered water-baptism at the hands of his disciples. Hence if Apollos had baptized with water, Luke would certainly have mentioned it. On this point I might say to the Anabaptists: If you insist that Apollos baptized with water, you are turning against yourselves your strongest possible weapon against the baptism of infants. Your argument runs as follows: We do not find that the apostles baptized infants: therefore we ought not to baptize them. But if that is the case, you should also argue: We do not find that Apollos baptized: therefore he did not baptize. For you must reason with yourselves in the same way as you do with others. Not that I justify your strife and argumentation. The argument is without foundation, as we shall see later. All that we are seeking to establish is that we cannot find any record at all that Apollos baptized with water. But it is quite evident that the twelve were taught by Apollos, for Luke mentions that he had just been in Ephesus and that the instruction which he gave was imperfect. He does this in order to show that it was Paul who first planted the doctrine of Christ in Ephesus. Apollos had been there before him, but his teaching had so little value that Paul had to begin again from the very foundations. Again, the twelve were not baptized by Aquila and Priscilla, for these two had been taught the Gospel so clearly and fully that they could instruct Apollos more perfectly. Even if we did contend that they were baptized by Aquila and Priscilla we should still have to admit that the disciples of

Christ gave baptism prior to instruction, and that would at once give us an easy victory in the matter of infant baptism. In respect of the teacher, then, it is evident that the men were not baptized by Apollos. And in respect of the baptized the words make it quite clear that "baptize" is used here in the sense of teach. Clearly Apollos did not baptize with water, and Paul was not referring to the baptism of water. On what grounds, therefore, do ignorant and foolish, not to say presumptuous, rebels and agitators use this passage in Acts as a cloak for rebaptizing, when rebaptism is against Christ and against the whole mystery and content of his passion.(110) Of this we shall treat later. But when the twelve understood that which Paul expounded to them, they were baptized into the name of Jesus. Notice that this makes it even more evident that they had not previously been baptized into the water-baptism of John. For if they had, they would already have been baptized in the name of Jesus; for it was the sole office of John to lead men to Christ Jesus. The fact that the Holy Ghost then came down with tongues all goes to show that the twelve had not previously been instructed or baptized.(111)

On the Lord's Supper

INTRODUCTION

DURING THE VERY PERIOD WHEN HE WAS ENGAGED in bitter internal controversy with the Anabaptists Zwingli was also active in the development and exposition of his apparently novel doctrine of the Lord's Supper. Already in the *De vera et falsa religione commentarius* he had given a brief statement of his position, and it was evident that he could not accept either the Lutheran or the Renaissance alternatives to traditional teaching. During the following year (1525) the Mass was abolished in Zurich,[1] and Zwingli wrote two Latin treatises in defence of his views: the *Subsidium sive coronis de eucharistia* in August,[2] and the *Responsio ad epistolam Joannis Bugenhagii* in October.[3] As the doctrine of Zwingli became known it provoked hostility on the part of the Lutherans and active suppression on that of the Romanists. In many places the Zwinglian position was officially condemned, and in the canton of Uri and the city of Nuremberg Zwingli's writings were proscribed. Bitter controversies developed with both the Romanists on the one hand and the Lutherans on the other, and even in Zurich itself Zwingli was opposed by an exponent of the Renaissance understanding, a certain Joachim am Grüt.

It was in these circumstances that Zwingli felt the need for a more popular work on the subject in order that his position should be made clear not merely to theologians but to the Church at large. On the one hand the work was necessary for the

---

[1] D.C.R. 205.
[2] This was the work dedicated to Berne in place of the treatise on baptism.
[3] This answer was directed against the Lutheran view as represented by Johann Bugenhagen of Wittenberg.

purposes of defence. It was known generally that the doctrine of Zwingli had been disowned by all parties, but so long as that doctrine was expounded only in Latin the ordinary reader had no means either of knowing that doctrine or of judging for himself whether it was true or false. Hence there was a very real danger that in some districts the new teaching would be condemned unheard. On the other hand, the work was also necessary for the purposes of attack. Zwingli could see clearly that the eucharistic doctrine held a key position in the whole mediaeval system. Much of the ignorance and superstition which afflicted the pre-Reformation Church derived from this source. And the reinterpretations suggested either by Erasmus on the one hand or Luther on the other did nothing to remove the root-cause of the error: the belief in a literal and corporal presence of Christ either in or with the elements. So long as that belief remained, dark shadows would continue to obscure the pure light of the Gospel. It was urgently necessary, therefore, that the true and scriptural doctrine of the Lord's Supper should be propagated as widely and forcefully as possible, and a pamphlet in the national tongue was indispensable to that purpose.

The first mention of such a work appears in a letter to Vadian which is dated January 17, 1526.[4] Zwingli had not yet made a start, but the project must have been fully formed in his mind. Certainly he set to work almost immediately afterwards, for Capito and Bucer both refer to the matter in letters at the end of January (28 and 29),[5] and the treatise was finished on February 23. Early in March copies were already on their way to Vadian and Oecolampadius, and Bucer was eagerly awaiting the arrival of the work in Strassburg.[6]

Notwithstanding the interest with which it was received, and the definiteness of the statement, the treatise did not play any notable part in the complicated controversies which followed. A reply was written by Joachim am Grüt, who advocated a real presence of the ascended body of Christ, thus avoiding the crasser literalism of the traditionalists. However, Zwingli now found himself engulfed in more detailed argumentation with Luther and his disciples and he did not find time to write his projected answer. In the bitter and protracted struggle with the Lutherans the treatise on the Supper did not figure directly, although it had a certain general value as a clarification of Zwingli's teaching.

[4] C.R., VIII, 442.   [5] *Ibid.*, 444, 446.   [6] *Ibid.*, 458.

The central issue in the essay, as indeed in all the ensuing controversies, was that of the nature of the presence of Christ in the sacrament of Holy Communion, and especially in relation to the doctrines of the Ascension and Session. For the most part the battle was fought out over the exegesis of the words of institution: "This is my body." In answer to the controversial requirements the work is divided into four sections. In the first of these Zwingli states the false interpretations which have been advanced. In the second he offers proof of their falsity. In the third he expounds and supports the correct understanding. And finally he answers some objections which might be lodged against it.

The three false interpretations which he attacks are of course the traditional, the Renaissance and the Lutheran. According to the traditional view the words: "This is my body" imply that the bread literally becomes the crucified body of Christ. The Renaissance alternative is that the bread becomes not the crucified but the resurrected body of Christ. The Lutheran view is that the bread remains, but the body of Christ is present in and with it. As Zwingli saw it, all these interpretations rested upon a misunderstanding of the true nature of a sacrament, and they were defended by ill-grounded assertions concerning the omnipotence of God. They also had the disadvantage of being mutually exclusive. The Lutheran doctrine had the further disadvantage that it is illogical and self-contradictory. It claims that the word "is" must be taken with absolute literalness, but it then explains that the phrase: "This is my body" really means: "This is bread and my body." Far from resting on simple Scripture, it rests on Scripture interpreted in the most confused and unintelligible manner.

Having stated his general criticisms of the prevailing views, Zwingli then went on to develop his more detailed and positive arguments against them. He had two main points to make: first, that a proper exegesis of John 6 makes it plain that faith is the true feeding upon Christ, and second, that the doctrine of the Ascension of Christ, confirmed by Scripture, Creeds and Fathers, destroys all possibility of a literal presence of Christ's body. On this latter point Zwingli could not accept either the Lutheran argument from the communication of attributes, i.e., that the attributes of the divine nature of Christ, including ubiquity, are imparted to the human, or the Renaissance argument from the transfigured character of the resurrection body, i.e., that after the resurrection the body of Christ is no longer subject to the ordinary limitations of time and space. Against the Lutheran view Zwingli maintained that the communication of attributes is true only in a logical sense but not in actuality. This is proved by the death and passion: for although the one who suffered was God, he did not suffer as God—otherwise God died, which is quite impossible. Against the Renaissance view he pointed out that it would prove the ubiquity of all the resurrected, and in any case it is directly contradicted both by the teaching on the Ascension and also by the fact that Christ instituted the Supper prior to his death and passion.

The rest of the treatise was devoted to the statement and defence of Zwingli's own interpretation. As he saw it, the words: "This is my body" were plainly figurative or symbolical.[7] Zwingli had no intention of denying a spiritual presence of Christ in the sacrament. Indeed, in the course of the Christological discussion in the second part he had freely allowed a presence of Christ after his divine nature. This presence certainly means that the communion is more than a "bare" sign, at any rate to the believing recipient. But what Zwingli cannot allow is that the presence is in any way to be identified with the element itself. The importance of the elements is that they are a sign of the body and blood of Christ offered up for us: and that is why they are called a sacrament. This does not mean that the elements are necessarily nothing more than a reminder of the death and passion of Christ. For in the sacrament we have to do not merely with the elements but with the spiritual presence of Christ himself and the sovereign activity of the Holy Spirit. What it does mean is that in themselves the elements are nothing more than a representation of the body and blood of Christ. The words: "This is my body," simply mean: "This represents my body." There is no literal identity between the sign and the thing signified.

In support of this interpretation Zwingli could adduce many examples of figurative language drawn from other parts of Scripture. Perhaps the most interesting and instructive of these was the description of the Paschal Lamb as the Lord's Passover: a relating of the Old and New Testament signs which his Romanist opponents could hardly concede. But parallels could also be found in the New Testament, and even in the Pauline narrative of institution in I Corinthians 11 the cup is

[7] He seems to have been helped towards this interpretation by a letter from Cornelius Hoen of the Hague, 1523–1524.

called the "new testament in my blood", a statement which can
hardly bear a strictly literal interpretation. Having explained
and defended his figurative understanding Zwingli concluded
by replying to two objections which might be made against
it. The first was that the exponents of this understanding did
not agree in their interpretation of the verse. Zwingli himself
took it to mean: "This represents my body," but Oecolampadius construed it: "This is a representation of my body."
Zwingli had little difficulty in showing that these are merely
two different ways of saying precisely the same thing. The
second objection was that the text I Cor. 10:16 speaks
of a communion of the body and blood of Christ, which implies
a literal feeding upon the substance of the body and blood.
But Zwingli did not accept the traditional exegesis of the verse.
As he understood it, the word translated "bless" does not mean
"consecrate" but "praise" or "honour," and the word translated "communion" really means "the community," i.e.,
the Church. In any case, he could always claim that the fellowship which we have with Christ is not physical but spiritual.

Taken as a whole the treatise forms a clear and forceful
statement of Zwingli's doctrine. Like many writings of the
period, it suffers from the disproportionate amount of space
devoted to detailed and rather wearisome exegesis. But in
the eucharistic debate the exegetical battle was undoubtedly
the crucial one, and if we remember the setting we can hardly
blame Zwingli for doing that which the demands of the controversy inevitably required of him. The whole doctrine of a substantial presence rested upon a particular interpretation of
the words: "This is my body," and of related statements such
as those contained in the all-important sixth chapter of St.
John. If Zwingli wished to combat error and to establish what
he held to be the truth, he was compelled to investigate the true
sense of these passages of Scripture. And in face of the detailed
and complicated exposition of his opponents—for nowhere did the
subtlety of the schoolmen find greater scope—he could find no
short cuts to the vindication of his apparently novel teaching.

Again, even if we allow that much of the exegetical discussion
is tiresome and artificial, this at least may be urged in favour of
Zwingli's treatment, that he did contend for a sensible and in
the main a true exegesis of the texts relevant to the question.
His opponents could appeal to the superficial straightfor-
wardness of their understanding, but surely they betrayed a
lack of perception and even intelligence when they attempted

to derive a substantial presence and literal partaking from the words of institution and the parallel discourse in John 6. Indeed, on analysis even their supposedly straightforward exegesis involves all kinds of logical difficulties. It may well be that the detailed discussions with which Zwingli sustained his thesis appear trivial and tiresome, but the thesis itself is still for the most part a valid one, and it is an apparent truism to the modern Protestant only because Zwingli and his supporters laboriously penetrated through the hard crust of traditional misinterpretation.

A more serious criticism of the statement is that it fails to develop any consistent or constructive doctrine to replace the discarded mediaeval, Renaissance and Lutheran teachings. The truth is that Zwingli does the negative work of criticism far better than he does the positive work of reconstruction. Certainly he reveals serious weaknesses in the prevailing interpretations. Certainly he gives adequate exegetical and doctrinal reasons for suspecting and perhaps rejecting those interpretations. Indeed, he goes further, and suggests a true line of interpretation which is in harmony with his general conception of the nature and function of the sacrament. But beyond that Zwingli does not go. He tears down the false structures of his opponents. He uncovers the true and solid basis upon which the doctrine of the sacrament must be built. But he does not make any large-scale contribution towards the actual work of reconstruction. And it is that failure to advance a developed positive understanding which makes it appear that he has nothing at all to offer except a bare sacramentarianism, i.e., the sacrament is a sign, and no more.

Now it is must be admitted that in the doctrine of the Supper, as in that of baptism, Zwingli does tend to separate overharshly between the two aspects of the sacrament: the sign and the thing signified. True, in the doctrine of transubstantiation he had to meet a virtual obliteration of the sign by the thing signified, which meant the end of the sacrament in any meaningful sense. But in his own expositions Zwingli concentrated almost exclusively upon the sign, that is to say, the sacrament in its purely external sense. Naturally, he had no great difficulty in showing that the presence of the sign is no guarantee of the presence of the thing signified. As he understood it, the presence of the thing signified depended entirely upon the sovereign will and working of Almighty God. For that reason it was incalculable, although not, of course, unreal. And in his reaction against the identification of sign and thing signified he failed to give any very coherent account of the relationship between the two. He did not deny that God can and does use the sacrament as a means of grace, but he so isolated the sovereign operation of God that for all practical purposes there was no connection between the internal and the external work. The sign was one thing, and in itself it was only a sign. The thing signified was quite another, and it had no necessary connection with the sign except that it was represented by it. A possible link was true faith in the recipient, but even this was ultimately the gift of God and independent of the external sacrament. The fact remains that while Zwingli had a strong sense of the two "natures" of the sacrament, he did not show any clear sense of its unity. This does not mean that he was necessarily a sacramentarian in the full sense, but it certainly does mean that he was a sacramentarian in effect.

But two points must be made in Zwingli's defence. The first is that his primary task was to meet a false and dangerous interrelating of sign and thing signified. Inevitably, then, the main drift of his work was to isolate the two in order to make it plain beyond all doubt that they are not identical. Whether he saw the need for a more correct interrelating or not, he certainly could not run the risk of a possible misunderstanding. The exigencies of the situation forced him to lay the whole stress upon the distinctness of the external and internal aspects.

But second, Zwingli did incidentally suggest many lines of thought which were to lead to something more positive in sacramental understanding. For one thing, he was always conscious of the fact that there is an objective thing signified. In the strict sense the sacrament is only a sign, but it is more than the expression of a subjective experience. It is a sign which points us to something else. Therein lies its value and necessity. And that objective something is not merely a given fact of history. The sacrament does bring before us the historical work of Christ, but it also points us to the present activity of God. That activity may not bear any necessary relationship to the outward administration of the rite, but it is still the underlying reality represented and proclaimed by it. But again, that activity of God is linked up with the spiritual presence of Jesus Christ, who is known in the sacrament not merely as the one who was crucified for our redemption, not merely as the one who is risen and ascended and will come again to judge the quick and the dead, but also as the ever-present Son of God:

"Lo, I am with you alway, even unto the end of the world."
For Zwingli does not dispute that Christ is truly present in
the Supper. What he disputes is that he is substantially present,
present in the substance of his flesh and blood, present after his
human nature. As the Bible itself testifies, the Ascension brought
a break in the form of Christ's presence: but it did not end the
presence itself. Prior to the Ascension, Christ was present
locally, in the body. After the Ascension he was still present,
but spiritually. That thought of the spiritual presence of Christ
is not emphasized, indeed it is almost taken for granted, for
it was not a point at issue. But the fact that Christ is indeed
present in that way formed an obvious starting-point for a more
positive understanding.

Against Zwingli's view of the presence the Lutherans could
argue that it rested upon a faulty Christology. The divine
nature of Christ cannot be present apart from the human—
otherwise the unity of the person of Christ is negated. Now it
must be admitted that Zwingli did tend towards that isolation of
the distinctive natures or aspects both of Christ himself and also
of the Word and sacraments. But it must be stressed that in
this case a real distinction has to be made, and the Bible itself
certainly gives us good reason to make it. In his humanity
Jesus Christ is not present in the world in the same way as he
was even during the forty days or as he presumably will be at
his coming again. Logically he is present in his humanity
wherever he is present at all, and to that extent the Lutherans
contend for a real truth of Christology. But in actual fact he is
not present according to his human nature, and there does not
seem to be any meaningful sense in which we can say that the
body and blood of Christ are literally present in the Supper.
Even if Zwingli was wrong, it is still true that he had no wish
to deny the presence of Christ altogether, and the reality of
the spiritual presence of Christ involves something far more
than a bare memorialism. The Supper cannot be merely a
commemorative rite when the one commemorated is himself
present and active amongst those who keep the feast.

One final point: the activity of God is not only linked with
the spiritual presence of Christ but it is also related to the
internal ministry of the Holy Spirit. At this point, the doctrine
of Zwingli joins hands with its opposite, the *ex opere operato*
doctrine of sacramental efficacy, for at bottom both of them
are concerned to emphasize the divine transcendence and
sovereignty. In the one case, the divine transcendence and

sovereignty is seen in the freedom of God to work only how and where he chooses. In the other it is seen in the faithfulness of God to work how and where he has promised to do so. With Zwingli the inward operation of God is not related in any clear or definite way to the outward sacramental rite, but the separation between the two need not be so complete or final as it perhaps appears to be in his own statement. Without any sacrifice of the divine sovereignty the outward sacrament can itself be an instrument used by the Holy Spirit, not automatically, but according to his own free appointment. That, at any rate, was the positive sacramental doctrine developed by Calvin, and the seeds of it were all present already in Zwingli's work.

Editions

The first edition of this treatise was published by Hager of Zurich in 1526, and it was quickly followed by an edition by Froschauer of Zurich in the same year. A third anonymous edition also appeared in 1526. Since this is in all respects identical with a fourth edition (again 1526) which bears the name of Köpfel of Strassburg there is every reason to suppose that it was published by the same house. Between these originals there are very few differences apart from the variations in spelling and the correction of occasional printers' errors. The original text has been reproduced by Schuler and Schultess (II, 1, pp. 427–468), and more recently in the *Corpus Reformatorum*, Zwingli IV, No. 75, and the *Volksausgabe* XI, 1948. Gwalter translated the essay into Latin in his *Opp. Zw.*, Tom. II, and a version in modern German was included by Raget Christoffel in his *Zeitgemässige Auswahl*, 1843.

There do not appear to have been any early translations into English. The following translation is based on the *Corpus Reformatorum* edition of the original text.

On the Lord's Supper

THE TEXT

Hear the words of Christ in Matthew 11: "Come unto me, all ye that labour and are heavy laden, and I will give you rest."

To all Christian believers Huldreich Zwingli offers grace and peace from God and our Lord Jesus Christ.

May God, who sent into this world his only begotten Son, the true light which penetrates all darkness, grant unto us such light and truth that we may speak only those things which will serve his glory, the setting forth of the truth and the good of our neighbour. We make that prayer to him by the faith which we have in him and by the strict judgment which he will exercise over the whole of the human race.

He has promised that if we pray he will hear us: and that which he has promised he will surely perform.

Fellow-believers in Christ, in the space of a single year I have written some three or four times concerning the sacrament of the body of Christ.(1) So far I have never written in German,(2) but only in Latin, as the situation in our own and other lands then demanded.(3) But I now see that in some parts my writings are being refused entry and proscribed(4)—with what kind of conscience I leave to the judgment of those concerned, who once proclaimed earnestly the words of Paul: "Prove all things; hold fast that which is good." But they publicly speak of my works as heretical, and in their writings they call upon God to deliver us from the error. For although we know from the Word of God that in this sacrament there is no partaking of the corporal body and blood, they say that we cannot have any certainty in the matter, and they decry our opinion as a monstrous error. They will not suffer themselves to be taught, but with every word they rate us soundly. In

these circumstances I thought it necessary to gather together
from the Word of God the more essential texts and passages
which point us to the basic meaning of this sacrament, and
together with them some pronouncements of the primitive
doctors and of the papal canons or decrees.(5) My purpose is
that the ordinary and simple Christian may learn the truth for
himself, so that those who are accounted preachers of the Gospel
will not be able either to withhold or to misrepresent it: (6)
for these latter plunged into deep water at the very outset, and
they refuse to see that it is better to return to land than to press
further and further into the deep, and consequent darkness.
For what is darkness if not the delusion that the bread is flesh
and the wine blood, and that we partake of the flesh and blood
really or essentially? The transubstantiation of the bread has
long been disputed. Some argue that we take the body and
blood of Christ as they hung on the cross; (7) others that we
take the resurrection body.(8) The Word of God shows us that
all these opinions are erroneous. And yet in spite of that fact
these false teachers claim that it is we who are in error, and
that we constantly shift our ground. That that is not the case
we shall make as clear as daylight in what follows. In the name
of God, therefore, I warn all dignities, princes, lords, dominions
and powers not to allow themselves to be embittered against
the truth, but as is particularly fitting in rulers to do all things
advisedly and quietly, and indeed to restrain all wicked and
violent action and to weigh the matter with a serious and
mature judgment. For in this matter they are confronted by the
articles of our Christian Creed: "He ascended into heaven, And
sitteth on the right hand of God the Father Almighty; From
thence he shall come to judge the quick and the dead." Therefore they must either abandon the false doctrine of the presence
of the essential body of Christ in this sacrament, or else they
must at once renounce these three articles, which God forbid
that anyone should ever dream of doing. In all justice, then,
we ought not to yield to that papal arrogance which orders
princes to protect the Christian faith under the guise of flesh
and blood. For those who think that in so doing they are
safeguarding the faith are really jeopardizing it, as we shall
see. And I also warn scholars not to handle this matter with
craftiness and subtlety, but if they desire to dispute, let them
come out boldly and openly, for it is our aim to avoid all
sophistry, philosophizing and rhetoric, except in so far as we
are forced to give answer along such lines. And let them also

cease from unworthy tirades, and the pouring out and heaping up of abusive words. Not that we quake before such storms. I am used to them, thank God, and I stand upon a rock which does not shake under me and prevents me from being swept away. But I would rather see the truth standing by itself than see it despoiled by unmeasured words which necessarily suggest arrogance. I know well how Christ himself spoke sharply and administered severe rebukes. But I am speaking only of those who at the very first glimpse of truth and irrespective of all reasoning take to themselves blustering and deceitful words and smite their way in, misleading the simple by crying: They are agitators—to whom we are as little partial as to Lucifer. If the matter were only investigated, it would soon appear who were the instigators of past tumults—or, They root about in Scripture merely out of a spirit of mischief or the desire for notoriety—if it were notoriety we were after we should have to seek it some other way— or, They have no faith—but if we had no faith we should never have discovered that the flesh profiteth nothing—and so on. With these and similar words they cause the simple people to flee from the truth before they have ever even considered it. But I know that the ordinary Christian will listen more readily to the truth when it comes to him in its own garb and without over-much adornment or arrogant noise. And I know too that the blame for the wicked speeches which meet us in all quarters is due in no small measure to the writings of certain scholars who have presented the whole matter in the most bad-tempered and shameless fashion.(9) If it were merely a matter of a rebuke, I should have no cause for complaint. However little I might expect such a rebuke, either from God or from true believers, I realize that there is a controversy in this matter, and that that controversy will not be settled in a day. But if we blacken our opponents with rough words, the stain may well become so great that the truth is lost, as in the old saying: In the multitude of strife, the truth is forfeit. For that reason I ask scholars not to overload the matter with their hostile clamour, but to conduct themselves with sobriety. Otherwise as much evil will issue from the roughness of the words as good is wrested from their meaning and force.

The whole question has its source in the misunderstanding of the text: "This is my body." Therefore our first task will be to consider these words in the light of the various misinterpretations and to see what errors result.

As our second article we will turn to the Scriptures and the articles of the Creed in order to prove that the text cannot have the meaning which a wresting of the words has given to it.

As our third, we will establish out of the Scriptures the true and natural sense.

And as our fourth we will answer some apparent objections.

THE FIRST ARTICLE

Amongst those who believe that in this sacrament we partake of the literal body and blood of Christ there are three groups. First there are those who say that we partake of his body and blood as they hung on the cross, the corporal substance of the bread and wine being transubstantiated into that of the corporal body and blood.(10) Then there are those who say that we eat the body of Christ under the bread. All the time the bread remains bread, and we are not to ask how we eat Christ's body, but simply to confess the fact and rejoice that we eat: for Christ said: "This is my body," and therefore it must be so.(11) Finally, there are those who say that we eat of the body of Christ as it was in the resurrection when he came to his disciples through closed doors, etc.(12)

Now for the sake of the ordinary reader, before we expound and refute these opinions, we must first make it clear what a sacrament is and what it signifies.(13)

A sacrament is the sign of a holy thing. When I say: The sacrament of the Lord's body, I am simply referring to that bread which is the symbol of the body of Christ who was put to death for our sakes. The papists all know perfectly well that the word sacrament means a sign and nothing more, for this is the sense in which it has always been used by Christian doctors. Yet they have still allowed the common people to be deceived into thinking that it is something strange and unusual, something which they cannot understand and which for that reason they have come to equate with God himself, something which they regard as holy in that sense. But the very body of Christ is the body which is seated at the right hand of God, and the sacrament of his body is the bread, and the sacrament of his blood is the wine, of which we partake with thanksgiving. Now the sign and the thing signified cannot be one and the same. Therefore the sacrament of the body of Christ cannot be the body itself.

We come now to the first group who say that in this sacrament the substance of the bread is changed into the substance of the real body of Christ, that body which lay in the crib and hung on the cross. They defend their position in this way: The power of the Word of God is so great, so present, so living, that everything that God says is as he says, for heaven and earth must pass away, but not the Word of God, not even a single tittle of his Word (Luke 16). (14) For example, at the beginning of creation, in Genesis 1, God said: "Let there be light: and there was light."(15) Hence we see that the Word of God is so living and powerful that the moment he commands, things which are not spring forth out of nothing. How much more is the substance and essence of bread changed into the essence of the body of Christ when he says: "This is my body"; for it is easier to change one substance into another than to create a substance out of nothing. Therefore when Christ says: "This is my body," it literally is his body. For he says that it is, and therefore it is so, and all things must give place and allow this bread to be the true and essential body of Christ. For when he says: "Is," it is so. In Matthew 8, when Christ said to the leper: "Be thou clean," he was clean from that very hour. And again, when he said to the blind man: "See," he saw from that very hour. In the same way, when he says: "This is my body," the bread is his body and the wine his blood.(16)

Answer: Notice, good Christian, how the eyes of the simple are obscured by this fabrication, and they are asked to believe falsehoods. Yet if only we can open their eyes there is nothing easier than to refute these errors, as we shall now proceed to do. For it is our intention to answer these assertions from the assertions themselves. Thus: I do not deny that which is adduced concerning the power of the Word of God. I confess that when God says a thing it is so. For the Word of God is a living command. But note that there are two flaws in the argument. The first is that we are not given any reason to believe that when the Pope or some other man says: "This is my body," then the body of Christ is necessarily present. It is of no avail to say that Christ himself said: "Do this in remembrance of me": therefore the body of Christ is there. For the Pope does not say: "This is the body of Christ," but: "This is my body." Therefore only his own body would be present.(17) But since this answer involves much futile wrangling, we will pass on, not using the first flaw as the basis for what we have to say, as well we might: for there are many who do use it. The second flaw is the failure to see that before we use the Word of God

to justify anything we must first understand it correctly. For
example, when Christ says: "I am the vine," we have to consider first that he is using figurative speech, i.e., he is like a vine,
for as the branches are nourished by the vine and cannot bear
fruit without it, so believers are in him, and without him they
can do nothing. Now if you object against this interpretation:
He said: "I am the vine," therefore he must be a real vine,
you make Christ a vine. In the same way, when you come to
the words: "This is my body," you must first make sure that
he intended to give his flesh and blood in bodily form. Otherwise it is quite futile to argue: He said it, and therefore it is so.
For it is so only as he himself understood it to be so, and
not as you misunderstand it.(18) And how can you prove
from Scripture that he gave his flesh and blood in bodily form
when he says in John 6: "The flesh profiteth nothing," meaning,
to eat, etc. We will come to this in the next article. For the
moment let us consider the basis of the doctrine. If in Christ's
saying: "This is my body," we take the little word "is" *substantive*, i.e., literally, then it follows necessarily that the substance of the body or the flesh of Christ is literally and essentially present.

But this gives rise to two manifest errors.

The first: If he is present literally and essentially in the flesh,
then in the flesh he is torn apart by the teeth and perceptibly
masticated. We cannot evade the issue by saying: "With God
all things are possible." For as you yourself showed at the outset, it is not possible that the light which he created by the Word
should not be a literal and perceptible light. On the contrary,
when he spoke the Word, the light was there, a literal, perceptible, present and visible light, as it still is. In the same way,
if we take the word "is" literally, it is not possible that the flesh
should not be perceptible, for the light was not an imperceptible
light. Similarly, the cleansing given to the leper and the sight
to the blind were not imperceptible. The leper and the blind
perceived their wholeness as something which they actually
possessed. But in this sacrament no one has ever partaken of
the body literally and perceptibly; for although fables have
been invented and proclaimed to that effect, they do not prove
anything; for even if it did occasionally take place by fraud,
that is not enough: it must be the same in the mouths of all
who communicate, for the word and the partaking are in all
cases the same. It is evident, then, that the flesh is not there
literally and corporally. For if it were, its mass and substance

would be perceived, and it would be pressed with the teeth. In short: It would be there just as literally as the firmament and light which God also commanded: for these are not imperceptible, but perceptible. Therefore, if the "is" is to be taken literally, the body of Christ must be visibly, literally, corporally and perceptibly present. For that reason even in the erroneous teaching itself there is proof that the words cannot possibly mean that we partake physically of flesh and blood: for I maintain that if God says literally: "This is my body," then the body ought to be there literally and corporally, just as the light was there literally when he commanded it to be so. And since we do not experience or perceive any such presence, it follows that the words of Christ cannot refer to physical flesh and blood. For if that were the meaning, we should constantly perceive them, for he cannot lie. You see, then, that the argument for a literal presence merely turns to their own confusion.(19)

The second error resulting from a literal interpretation corresponds to that second opinion which we mentioned alongside the first, namely, that we eat the body of Christ in or under the bread, the bread itself remaining bread.(20) If we take the word "is" *substantive*, i.e., literally, then it is an obvious mistake to say that the bread remains bread and to deny transubstantiation, the changing of the substance of bread into that of flesh. And for this reason: I apply the argument used in the first error. The Word of God is living. He said: "This is my body." Therefore it is his body. But if we take the word "is" literally, as the second error obstinately maintains, then necessarily the substance of bread has to be changed completely into that of flesh. But that means that the bread is no longer there. Therefore it is impossible to maintain that the bread remains, but that in or under the bread flesh is eaten. Notice how utterly unreasonable this position is. On no account will it allow that Christ's words: "This is my body," are figurative or symbolical. It insists that the word "is" must be taken literally. But it then proceeds to set that word aside and to say: "The body of Christ is eaten in the bread." Yet Christ did not say: "Take, eat, my body is eaten in the bread." He said: "This is my body."(21) How fearful a thing it is to get out of one's depth. If it were I who perverted the words of Christ in that way, surely the axe of judgment would smite me down.(22) The second error is easily perceived, then, and we have only to compare the two and they cancel each other out. For the first maintains that the flesh and blood are present by virtue of the word "is." But if we take that word literally, it destroys the second, which tries to take it literally but still asserts that the bread remains bread. For if the word is taken literally, the bread is not bread but flesh. Conversely, the second error does at least perceive and recognize that the substance of bread is not turned into the substance of flesh. In so doing, it safeguards the truth that the word "is" cannot be taken literally. If it were literal, the flesh would be no less perceptible than the bread. For as prior to the consecration (as they term it) the bread is perceptible as bread, so from the moment of consecration it would have to be perceptible as flesh. Hence the first error is destroyed, and we may conclude that they are both manifestly false. For when the second maintains that the "is" is to be taken literally, it is adopting a quite unwarrantable position, as we have seen: for there is no alternative way of avoiding a figurative interpretation. Yet when we forcibly expose this defect, pointing out that there is no foundation for such fancies, they simply cry: We abide by the simple words of Christ,(23) trusting that those Christians who follow the simple words of Christ will not go astray. But what you call the simple meaning of those words is the most doubtful, the most obscure, the least intelligible of all. If the simple meaning of Scripture is that which we maintain through a misunderstanding of the letter, then Christ is a vine, or a silly sheep, or a door, and Peter is the foundation-stone of the Church. The simple or natural sense of these words is that which obtains in all similar instances, that which the minds of all believers find the most natural and the most readily comprehensible, that which is not contradicted by the truth, as are the two views expounded above, of which neither the one nor the other can prove the truth of its assertions. For the first cannot prove that the body is present. If it were, we should be able to see and perceive it like all the creatures which God has made. And the second cannot prove that the body is present under the bread. For Christ does not say: "This is my body under the bread." Therefore in Scripture the simple or natural sense is that which is grounded and secured in the truth, that is, in the Word of God, not standing in any possible contradiction to it.(24) The papists might complain that we do not abide by the natural sense when it is a matter of the saying: "Thou art Peter, that is, a stone, or rock, and upon this rock I will build my Church." Does that mean that we fall into error if we do not abide by the simple or natural sense, as the second view alleges? Not at all. For we find that Christ alone is the rock, Christ alone is the Head, Christ alone is the vine in which we are held secure. Therefore Christ himself is the rock upon which the Church is built, and that is the natural sense of the words. As applied by the papacy, the words are not natural. They are contrary to faith and reason, and quite unacceptable to the believing heart. So too with Christ's words: "This is my body." To refer them to his physical flesh is not the natural interpretation. To the believing heart it is the least intelligible of all. And it has no basis in the Word of God, as we shall see later. According to their proper signification, the words cannot bear this sense, as we have already seen. The third error, that we eat the body of Christ as risen from the dead, we shall oppose under the second article.

We will now turn to the papal canons in order to show that there is no justification in Christ's words for the view that in this sacrament we partake physically of the body and blood of Christ. When I appeal to the papal law, it is not my intention to use that law to prove anything to true believers, but simply to show those who accept the papacy that it is possible to reach the truth even by way of the papal canons.(25) For God has ordained that even in those writings which Antichrist has exalted there should be found that which subverts the erroneous doctrine of Antichrist. The text *De consecr. dist. 2 ca. Ego* (26) is as follows: "I, Berengarius,(27) an unworthy servant of the church of St. Maurice of Angers, confessing the true, catholic and apostolic faith, anathematize all heresy, including that of which I myself have been long suspected, which maintains that the bread and wine which we place upon the altar is after consecration only a sacrament, that is, a sign—notice how even the papacy uses the word sacrament—and that it is not the very body and blood of our Lord Jesus Christ, and that it (that is, the body) is handled and broken by the priests and pressed by the teeth of the faithful only symbolically and not essentially and literally. But now I agree with the holy Roman church and the apostolic see, and both with my lips and in my heart I confess that in respect of the sacrament of the Lord's Table I hold the same faith as that which my noble lord Pope Nicholas (28) and holy synod (29) prescribed and confirmed on evangelical and apostolic authority, namely, that after consecration the bread and wine on the altar are not merely a sacrament (that is, a sign, etc.) but the very body and blood of our Lord Jesus Christ, and that manifestly not merely the sacrament but the very body and blood of Christ are handled and broken by the priests and pressed or crushed by the teeth of the faithful." Now first let the thoughtful believer consider how the devil may transform himself into an angel of light. This Berengarius lived about 1080 years after Christ. He felt that there had been serious error in relation to this sacrament, for there have always been those who have perceived the error. But the Pope intervened to prevent this window being opened, and he forced him to make a ridiculous public recantation, in which it is quite obvious that what is said concerning the physical flesh of Christ is utterly false. And there are some historians who testify that Berengarius was so pious that after his death many princes said that they would rather follow Berengarius than the Pope,(30) notwithstanding the fact that he was under suspicion right up to the time of his death: as though in his heart he had never really abandoned the view which is stated in the first part of the recantation. He made what is obviously a false recantation in the face both of his own conscience and of that of all men. Second, let us consider what is involved in the recantation. It involves the confession that with his lips and in his heart he believes that the body of Christ is perceptibly taken by the priests, perceptibly broken, and perceptibly pressed or crushed by the teeth of the faithful. But these three affirmations are all of them manifestly false, like the devil's words to Eve: "Ye shall not surely die, but ye shall be as gods." For where is the priest who ever took the body of Christ perceptibly? For if the body were really there, how could they elevate it? And is it not an outrage upon Christ to enclose him in a damp and stinking tabernacle? (31) For if the priest can perceive Christ, then surely he can perceive himself. And if so, then surely, too, he suffers the cold and discomfort. But here they argue that we are not to take the word "perceptibly" quite so baldly or literally,(32) but to read the gloss.(33) Answer: Tell us then how we are to understand the word. You reply: as it says in the gloss. And the gloss says the same as you do, that we must understand the words properly, and then it goes on to say that these things are to be understood of the two forms of bread and wine. But what else was it that Berengarius maintained when he said that the body is broken sacramentally? Is not that to refer only to the forms of bread and wine? But he was forced to confess that the very body of Christ is truly taken, and broken, and

pressed with the teeth. Do not these words make it quite plain
what is meant by the word "perceptibly"? For it is clear that
if they insist upon a literal interpretation of the word "is" in
the saying of Christ: "This is my body," they must inevitably
maintain that Christ is literally there, and therefore they must
also maintain that he is broken, and pressed with the teeth.
Even if all the senses dispute it, that is what they must inevitably
maintain if the word "is" is taken literally, as we have already
shown. Hence they themselves recognize that the word "is"
is not to be taken literally. If the sky is red at dawn, we can
say: It will be stormy by evening; and if it is red at sunset,
we can say: It will be fair tomorrow; and yet we are quite
blind to the fact that if in the flesh Christ is miraculously present in the bread, or if the bread is actually flesh, we must
be able to perceive it. And if we say that although the bread
is flesh and the flesh is literally eaten, this takes place miraculously so that the flesh and blood are not perceived, is it not
evident that we are lying and deceiving ourselves? For God
never performed miracles or manifested them to the world
without someone either seeing them or in some way perceiving
them. The recantation then goes on to say that the body of
Christ is literally handled and broken by the priests. But how
is it broken? Without doubt they will reply: As it was broken on
the cross, that is to say, as it was put to death: for there can be
no doubt that this is the basis of their doctrine of the eucharistic sacrifice. But what of the verse which tells us that Christ
dieth no more? Or perhaps they say: Only the bread or
"species," that is, the form, is broken. Our grateful thanks!
For that is what Berengarius said when he claimed that Christ's
body is not broken in the flesh, but only in the sacrament of
the flesh. So the words "literally broken" are just as meaning-
less as the words "literally handled or taken." Next, the recantation states that the body of Christ is perceptibly pressed
and chewed by the teeth of the faithful. But who is the believer
who ever perceived any such thing? And who is the believer
who would not shudder to perceive any such thing? Is the
Word of Christ no longer valid (Matt. 15): "Whatsoever
entereth in at the mouth goeth into the belly, and is cast
out into the draught?" What nonsense this erroneous statement
leads us to imagine, nonsense for which there ought not to be
any place in the hearts of believers. But here some thinkers
have felt that an answer needs to be given to sceptics like
Rabanus for example.(34) But it is grounded in the same false

teaching. Yes, we say, it all takes place miraculously, and with that one word all our difficulties are resolved, as though God worked miracles which could not be perceived. If only those tiny pieces of bread and wine were actually perceived to be flesh and blood, that would be a miracle indeed. The manna which came down from heaven was of the same size and shape as coriander seed, but its taste was quite different. Here the case is otherwise, for what we see and what we taste are exactly the same, bread and wine. And how can we say that it is flesh when we do not perceive it to be such? If the body were there miraculously, the bread would not be bread, but we should perceive it to be flesh. Since, however, we see and perceive bread, it is evident that we are ascribing to God a miracle which he himself neither wills nor approves: for he does not work miracles which cannot be perceived. And the uninstructed who read the gloss must not press it too hard, for it is mere words without any real meaning, for the one who wrote the gloss *De consecratione di. I cap.* 1(35) says himself that it is harmful and even dangerous to speak the truth concerning the sacraments. It looks as though Gratian (36) was afraid to speak the truth, but simply alluded to it through the Fathers, not pronouncing or legislating in his own name as was his usual custom elsewhere. Good Christian, that is how even a papistical commentator speaks. He knows that in face of the papacy it is dangerous to speak the truth concerning the sacraments. But it is not dangerous to say that the flesh and blood are present, for that is what the papacy requires. The dangerous thing is to say what we say. And that is the truth as the commentator understood it: for he says that it is dangerous to speak the truth concerning the sacraments.(37) If he had merely said: It is dangerous to speak of them, there would have been no great significance in the words. But when he says: It is dangerous to speak the truth concerning them, it is evident that the truth concerning them was not spoken in his day. I have had to say all this about the gloss for the sake of some foolish people with whom I should have dealt quite differently had I not spared them in the Lord's name.

But at this point there are some who say: I do not believe that we eat the physical flesh with our mouth and teeth, but that we eat it quite apart from external perception.(38) Of such I have good hopes that they will soon receive the truth with joy: for when they say that, they are in effect renouncing the papal doctrine, although they do not want to be thought to do so. For the papacy maintains that we perceptibly press or chew with the teeth. Again, they make it quite clear that they do not understand the word "is" literally as they allege, for if they did understand it literally they could not deny that the flesh of Christ must be literally present.

It is a fair assumption that the truth contained in Gratian's book—which was called the Papal Decretals because the papacy itself endorsed it and used it over a long period (39)—was in fact suppressed. For as we have already shown from the commentator, it is obvious that Gratian himself did not hold to the papist view, even though he lived about A.D. 1160 when the darkness of ignorance was at its worst. After the recantation of Berengarius, this Gratian introduces as his sixth canon some words of Augustine, which the papacy also affirmed. The words are these: "What need of teeth and stomach? Believe and thou hast eaten. For to believe in him is to partake of the bread and wine. He who believes on him feeds on him."(40) Now obviously these words contradict the previous words in the recantation of Berengarius. For in the one it says: "What need of teeth and stomach?" but in the other it says: "The body and blood of Christ are perceptibly pressed with the teeth." In the one the teeth are unnecessary, in the other indispensable. It was not the intention of Gratian that the truth should be suppressed. The whole basis of the sacrament is contained in these words of Augustine. For when he says: "What need of teeth and stomach?" he gives us to understand that we are not eating anything physical, for if we were there would be need of teeth and stomach. And when he says: "Believe and thou hast eaten," he makes it perfectly clear that to feed on Christ is simply to trust in him, to confide oneself to him. But our opponents say: The word: "Believe and thou hast eaten," must be understood in this way: If you believe or trust that the body and blood are present, you will then partake of the body and blood. Those who believe partake, and those who do not believe do not partake. Here I should like to ask: How many are there who actually perceive that they are partaking of flesh and blood? From the time of the institution by Christ they cannot point to a single one, and therefore they have to confess that no one has ever believed. And here we catch them out, for this means that they themselves do not believe that they partake of the body of Christ, etc. But I will avoid provocation and make this answer: The words which follow are these: "To believe in him is to partake of the bread and wine," and from these words we may learn the correct understanding of the first part of the saying. Augustine says first: "Believe in him," teaching us that the object of trust or faith is not the bread or the body, but Christ alone. And then he says: "To believe in Christ is to partake of the bread and wine." How does that happen? We have here two hard sayings: how are we to interpret them? On the one hand there are many who have a constant faith in Christ yet seldom partake of the sacrament, the wine and the bread. On the other, Augustine still speaks of believers as partaking of wine and bread. Note, then, that what he means is simply this: If we believe in Christ, we go to communion, we partake of the bread and wine, in the right way: we make a right use of the sacrament. For immediately after he says: "He who believes on him feeds on him." It follows then that to feed on Christ's body is to believe in him who was given up to death on our behalf. But the deluded say that what Augustine means is that those who believe on him feed on his flesh and blood. Answer: the previous saying: "To believe in him is to partake of the bread and wine," makes it quite plain that Augustine did not mean: He who believes on him feeds physically on his flesh and blood, for already Augustine has shown that the partaking which is needed is to believe in him. Indeed, at the very outset he said: "Believe, and thou hast eaten." And what we eat physically Augustine refers to as bread and wine, called by Christ his body and blood in order that in our act of thanksgiving they might be the significant signs of his body and blood, as they are also described by Paul. Briefly, then, the whole meaning of Augustine is this: When you come to this thanksgiving you need neither teeth to press the body of Christ nor stomach to receive that which you have chewed, for if you believe in him you have already partaken of him. And when in the thanksgiving, in company with the congregation, you partake of the two elements of bread and wine, all that you do is to confess publicly that you believe in the Lord Jesus Christ. Therefore when we take the signs of bread and wine the principal thing to which we must look is to believe in Christ. For he who believes on him feeds on him. To feed on him is simply to believe on him. The papists have altered the whole meaning and have done violence to these sacred words—which are none other than the words of God himself, John 6—as may be seen further in *De con. di.* 2 *c. Credere,*(41) quoting Augustine: "To believe in Jesus Christ is to eat the living bread. He who believes eats," etc.

Thus far the first article, in which we have shown what serious difficulties are caused by taking literally Christ's words: "This is my body," and how the words themselves make it clear that the saying is not literal but figurative and symbolical. For if the "is" is to be taken literally, then we must eat the body of Christ with its flesh, bones, veins, nerves, marrow and other members which I will forbear to mention: for God cannot lie. If Christ spoke literally and not figuratively, then of necessity it follows that his body is eaten literally and perceptibly, as Berengarius was forced to confess: but all believers know very well that they do not eat the body of Christ in that way. Hence the very nature and truth of the matter will not allow us to take the words literally. And by nature and truth I do not mean only the nature of our human understanding, but that of the Word of God, which is, that where God speaks literally his words are fulfilled literally, i.e., in such a way as may be seen and touched and known and experienced. But since that does not obtain in the present case, we have conclusive evidence that God did not speak literally: for God never deceives us. If he did speak literally, we should perceive the body. Hence we have clear proof that the saying is not to be taken literally.

The Second Article

In the first article we have, I hope, seen quite clearly from the nature and property of God's Word that the saying of Christ: "This is my body," cannot be taken literally. In the second article we will further demonstrate and prove that the words cannot have the literal sense ascribed to them, first from the evident teaching of the Word of God and then from the articles of the faith as set forth in the introduction.

The primitive Fathers, and we ourselves in the *Commentarius* and *Subsidium*,(42) have shown quite clearly that in the teaching brought before us in John 6,(43) when Christ referred to eating his flesh and drinking his blood he simply meant believing in him as the one who has given his flesh and blood for our redemption and the cleansing of our sins. In this passage he is not speaking of the sacrament, but preaching the Gospel under the figure of eating and drinking his flesh and blood. In case there are any who are not yet aware of this fact, I will briefly recapitulate the main points, indicating the clear signs by which we know that throughout the discourse Christ is simply declaring the Gospel, that is, the salvation which

God has given us in him. Now Christ usually prefaced or
introduced his teaching by taking something external and
upon that as upon a simile he built up and taught the heavenly
and spiritual message. For example, when someone told
him: "Thy mother and thy brethren stand without desiring
to speak with thee" (Matt. 12), he uses the incident as an
opportunity to teach the lesson that all believers are his
members and brethren, saying: "Who is my mother? and who
are my brethren? And he stretched forth his hand toward his
disciples, and said, Behold my mother and my brethren. For
whosoever shall do the will of my Father, which is in heaven,
the same is my brother, and sister, and mother." There is a
simple case in Matthew 16. The disciples had forgotten to take
bread across the sea, and in that fact he saw an opportunity
or opening to teach them to avoid the leaven of the Pharisees.
And so too it is in John 6. He had provided them with such
an abundance of food that the disciples had taken up twelve
baskets full of fragments. The people ran to him. But he saw
that they pursued him because they marvelled at the sign and
not because they longed for salvation. Therefore he held out
salvation to them. They went after him for the sake of physical
food and he taught them concerning the spiritual food, which
is himself. But he uses the physical food which they were seeking
as an introduction or opening, saying: "Verily, verily, I say
unto you, Ye seek me, not because ye saw the miracles, but
because ye did eat of the loaves, and were filled. Labour not
for the meat which perisheth, but for that meat which endureth
unto everlasting life, which the Son of man shall give unto you:
for him hath God the Father sealed (that is, given him as an
infallible pledge)." "Then said they unto him—i.e. because he
had called them to labour for a lasting food—What shall we
do, that we might work the works of God?" "Jesus answered
and said unto them, This is the work of God, that ye believe on
him whom he hath sent." (Note that this is clear proof that
everything which he says about eating and drinking is meant to
lead them to belief in him, which is the true nourishment of
the soul.) "They said therefore unto him, What sign shewest
thou then, that we may see, and believe thee? what dost thou
work?" (Note how it is with the crowd. Some understand
one thing and some nothing. And they all cry out according
to their own desire or understanding. And when they saw that
he was preaching faith in himself they scorned him, crying out
that he should show them a sign in order that they might believe

on him. And they pointed him to a great work of the past, saying: "Our fathers did eat manna in the desert," etc.) But Jesus answered: "Verily, verily, I say unto you, Moses gave you not that bread from heaven; but my Father giveth you the true bread from heaven. For the bread of God is he which cometh down from heaven, and giveth life unto the world." (Note how he still keeps to the same figure of bread, and under the image of the heavenly bread he teaches them that he himself is sent down from heaven to give new life to the world. Even if we had no clearer words, the single saying: "The bread of God is he which cometh down from heaven, and giveth life unto the world," would be sufficient to prove that Christ is described as bread because he gives life to the world. And he did that by means of his death. Hold fast to Christ, and you have nourishment and life. But hold fast to him, not as eaten but as crucified for you. For that alone is how he gives life. To eat Christ physically does not help to give life). "Then said they unto him, Lord, evermore give us this bread," for he had said that this bread gives life to the world. "And Jesus said unto them, I am the bread of life: he that cometh to me shall never hunger; and he that believeth on me shall never thirst." (But how is he life, crucified or eaten? Crucified, as we shall see later. But note how appropriately his words follow up the introductory figure: "I am the bread of life," that is, I am the only food which can nourish the desolate soul and give it life. "He that cometh to me shall never hunger." Note that it is he who comes that is nourished, not he who eats physically. The necessary thing is to come to him, to believe on him, as he himself immediately says: "And he that believeth on me shall never thirst." The little word "and" is here used after the Hebrew manner to denote explanation, namely, that to come to him is simply to believe on him. And why do those who would partake of flesh and blood in this sacrament speak of a hunger and thirst after the physical flesh and blood in addition to faith? For Christ says that he that cometh to him, that is, he that believeth on him shall not hunger or thirst for anything else, for any other hope or ground of comfort. This is confirmed by the words which follow, when he says: "But I said unto you, that ye also have seen me, and believe not." Here we see clearly that he does not demand any other eating but faith, setting aside entirely any external or physical perceiving or partaking, for he says; "Ye have seen me, and believe not". This completely overthrows the childish statement which is sometimes

put out to the simple: "I believe, and therefore I will partake
of him. I will have both my belief and also that in which I
believe." For the Jews could see him plainly enough, but their
seeing did not help them. Similarly eating does not help us,
for eating and seeing are both on the same plane, they are
both experiences of the senses.) Christ then goes on to teach that
no one can believe in him except he is drawn of the Father:
which means that the flesh does not profit anything whether it
is eaten or seen: for he says: "All that the Father giveth me shall
come to me; and him that cometh to me I will in no wise cast
out." (That is, no man can receive him, except the Father
draw him, as will appear later.) "For I came down from
heaven, not to do mine own will, but the will of him that sent
me." (We shall speak of the two wills of Christ, the divine and
the human, later in this section.) "And this is the Father's will
which hath sent me, that of all which he hath given me I
should lose nothing, but should raise it up again at the last
day." And that is simply to say, This is the will of him that sent
me, that he that seeth the Son—that is, knoweth the Son, for
in all three languages the word "see" is frequently used for know,
or recognize, or understand, and we have already made it
sufficiently clear that physical seeing does not help us—and
believeth on him hath eternal life, and I will raise him up
at the last day. Now first, note that Christ explains his own
words. For twice he says: "This is the will of him that sent me,"
but the second time he speaks more plainly than the first.
Second, note that in Scripture words like "resurrect" and
"resurrection" are used not only of the general resurrection
of the dead but of the life of the soul after this present age,
as may be seen in I Corinthians 15 and also in this passage.
But this is not the place to speak at large on that topic.(44)
Again, the last day refers not merely to the day of judgment
but to our departure from this present world. Hence in this
context the words of Christ: "I will raise him up at the last
day," do not mean only: I will summon him to the final
judgment, but: I will give him eternal life the very moment
that he departs this life, as is clearly stated in John 5. "The
Jews then murmured at him, because he said, I am the bread
which came down from heaven. And they said, Is not this
Jesus, the son of Joseph, whose father and mother we know?
how is it then that he saith, I came down from heaven. Jesus
therefore answered and said unto them, Murmur not among
yourselves" (Note his kindness in not allowing them to err

through ignorance). "No man can come to me, except the Father which hath sent me draw him: and I will raise him up at the last day." (That is, From the last hour of this present time I will keep him to life everlasting.) "It is written in the prophets, And they shall be all taught of God. Every man therefore that hath heard, and hath learned of the Father, cometh unto me." (Note what is meant by the earlier sayings: "All that my Father giveth me," and: "My Father draweth him": As he himself reveals, they mean simply this, that by his Spirit the heavenly Father teaches the knowledge and faith of Christ to those whom he has willed to save through him.) "Not that any man hath seen the Father, save he which is of God, he hath seen the Father." (He is referring to himself.) "Verily, verily, I say unto you, He that believeth on me hath everlasting life." This is one of the clear places which teach us that by eating his flesh and blood Christ simply means believing in the one who gave his flesh and blood that we might live. It is not eating or seeing or perceiving him which saves, but believing on him. And here too we see clearly what he meant earlier when he spoke of coming to him: to come to him is simply to believe on him. He then begins to reveal to them the mystery of his passion, and he answers the objection which they brought against him when they said: "Our fathers did eat manna in the desert," saying: "I am that bread of life." (Undoubtedly that food of eternal life to which he had just referred: "He that believeth on me hath everlasting life." Hence it follows that in this context the bread and flesh are simply believing on him, for it is faith which carries with it eternal life. If he is the bread of life, he gives everlasting life to those who believe on him.) "Your fathers did eat manna in the wilderness, and are dead. This is the bread which cometh down from heaven, that a man may eat thereof, and not die. I am the living bread which came down from heaven: if any man eat of this bread, he shall live for ever." (Note that the first time he had spoken obscurely: "Of all that the Father hath given me I shall lose nothing, but shall raise it up again at the last day." Then he used rather plainer speech: "Everyone which seeth the Son, that is, knoweth him, and understandeth his work, and believeth on him, hath everlasting life, and I will raise him up at the last day." And now the third time he again takes up the main point, using the same illustration as that with which he introduced his message, that in giving himself up to death he is a spiritual food or bread, saying: "He that eateth of this bread shall never die," which is the equivalent of what he said earlier: "I will raise him up again at the last day.") "And the bread that I will give is my flesh, which I will give for the life of the world." Note first that he now gathers his meaning into one short sentence, as if to say: I have been telling you that I am the living bread, but I have not yet told you how. In this way: I am about to give my flesh in death. In so doing I shall propitiate the righteousness of my heavenly Father, and as a result man will be raised up again to a new life and will attain to divine grace. Note further that he is the lifegiving bread as put to death, not as pressed with the teeth or eaten. For he does not say: The bread is my flesh which I will give you physically to eat, but, "The bread that I shall give you is that I will give my flesh for the life of the world." And that is what nourishes the soul as bread nourishes the body. Third, we learn that the flesh is not itself a satisfaction or payment, but it stands for the payment of death.(45) The death and passion which Christ bore in the flesh are the means of our redemption. Hence we see the meaning of Christ's words: "This is my body which is given for you." The word "body" stands for the suffering which he bore in the body, as the phrase "which is given for you" specifically shows us. The body of Christ is redemptive in so far as it is given up to death. We are not to look for any other kind of physical eating. "The Jews therefore strove among themselves, saying, How can this man give us his flesh to eat?" And why did they strive among themselves? Because they neither saw with their eyes nor heard with their ears nor understood with their hearts. Christ had spoken a good deal about food and bread, and he had just shown them that this food is simply his being given up to death for the world, saying: "The food or bread of which I speak is my flesh which I will give for the life of the world." But they try to seize upon the first part of his saying: "The bread that I will give is my flesh", ignoring the latter part: "which I will give for the life of the world." And they strove among themselves because they did not see that what Christ was teaching was that his death is the only consolation and nourishment of the believing heart. Therefore Jesus said to them: "Verily, verily, I say unto you, Except ye eat the flesh of the Son of man, and drink his blood, ye have no life in you. Whoso eateth my flesh, and drinketh my blood, hath eternal life; and I will raise him up at the last day. For my flesh is meat indeed, and my blood is drink indeed. He that eateth my flesh, and drinketh my blood, dwelleth in me, and I in him." (There is no need to oppose specifically those who claim that Christ now begins a fresh discourse on the subject of the sacrament: for if they take note of the opening word, "then" or "therefore," they will see that this saying of Christ is connected with the one which preceded it, and whenever he speaks of eating his flesh and drinking his blood he simply means believing in the worth of that suffering which he bore for our sakes. For here he says: "Whoso eateth my flesh, and drinketh my blood, hath eternal life." And just before he said: "He that believeth on me hath everlasting life." Therefore to eat his flesh and to believe on him are one and the same, otherwise there are two ways of salvation, the one by eating and drinking the flesh of Christ and the other by believing on him. And if that is the case, then the crucifixion was not necessary, for the disciples were children of everlasting life the moment they partook of his flesh and blood in the Last Supper. To such calumniating of the truth does the misinterpretation of Scripture lead. But the aim of Christ is simply to teach us that he is our consolation and salvation, having given his flesh and blood to death on our behalf.) And now follows: "As the living Father hath sent me, and I live by the Father: so he that eateth me, even he shall live by me." (Here is another passage in which he is clearly speaking of faith in himself: for that is what makes the soul live, that is, live by him.) "This is that bread which came down from heaven: not as your fathers did eat manna, and are dead: he that eateth of this bread shall live for ever." (Note that what he had just described as flesh and blood he now calls bread, and for two reasons, first, to adhere to his original illustration and point of departure, and second, to explain and to make it quite clear that when he speaks of bread or flesh and blood he means that the one bread, food, nourishment, growth and life of the soul is to know that for our sakes God has given his Son to death in the flesh, that is, in his true humanity. In short, whether it is bread, or flesh, or faith, it is all one and the same, as those who have ears to hear will quickly perceive.) "These things said he in the synagogue, as he taught in Capernaum. Many therefore of his disciples, when they had heard this, said, This is a hard saying; who can hear it? When Jesus knew in himself that his disciples murmured at it, he said unto them, Doth this offend you? What and if ye shall see the Son of man ascend up where he was before? It is the spirit that quickeneth; the flesh profiteth nothing: the words that I speak unto you,

they are spirit, and they are life. But there are some of you
that believe not. For Jesus knew from the beginning who they
were that believed not, and who should betray him." And note
what ignorance does. The less it understands a matter, the more
arrogantly it draws aside and holds aloof. Therefore Christ
says: "Doth this offend you?" that is, Are you so violently
incensed against me because I explain myself so clearly?
You know perfectly well that I am not forcing you to eat
my physical flesh, but teaching you to believe on me. But if
you do not, then take as a token of your unbelief that physical
eating of my body by which you hope to lay upon me the
scandal of your apostasy. And when you see me ascend up
where I was before, then the unbelief which refuses to receive
me will be confounded. For my Ascension will show you clearly
that I am the Son of God, the Saviour of the world, the Way
of life. And there will then be brought to light that secret sin
of unbelief which you now falsely excuse by alleging the difficulty of a literal partaking of my flesh (John 16). Moreover,
when you see me ascend up to heaven, you will see clearly
that you have not eaten me literally and that I cannot be eaten
literally. It is the spirit which gives life. I speak of the life of
the spirit, the life of the soul. There can be no doubt that only
the spirit can give life to the soul. For how could the physical
flesh either nourish or give life to the soul? To partake of the
flesh does not profit anything if you do it as something necessary
to the life of the soul. But the words which I have spoken to
you: "He that believeth on me hath everlasting life," and,
"Whoso eateth my flesh, and drinketh my blood, hath eternal
life", and similar sayings, should all be interpreted in this
sense, that I am the nourishment and consolation of the soul
as I was put to death for the world, not as I am eaten with the
mouth: for only then do we interpret them spiritually, and only
then are they life. Now note, dear reader, that when the ancient
doctors speak here of the spiritual and carnal sense, they do
not mean carnal in the sense of sinful, as some maintain, nor
do they mean by spiritual that which is frequently described
as the spiritual sense, as when the enemy in Matthew 13 is
referred to as our enemy the devil. But when they speak of the
carnal and spiritual sense, by carnal they mean that sense in
which it is supposed that we eat the flesh and blood, and by
spiritual they mean the interpretation and understanding of
Christ himself, which is, that the soul must believe on him. (46)
To quote passages in proof of this statement would take up

too much space. But with his own words Christ teaches us that everything which he says concerning the eating of flesh or bread has to be understood in terms of believing, and that those who expressed repugnance at the idea of eating flesh did so in error, and in order to have a pretext for departing from him, for he said: "There are some of you that believe not." Note how salutary is the saying: "There are some of you that believe not," or have no faith in me, but try to fasten their aversion upon my flesh, which I do not literally give to eat. Yet it is their unbelief which drives them away: that is the true cause of their departing. Obviously he would have been quite satisfied with them if they had believed on him, like Peter, who later said in the name of all the disciples—and with this I will conclude my exposition—"We believe and are sure that thou art the Christ, the Son of the living God." He does not say: We believe that we eat thy flesh and blood, but, they believe that he is Christ, the Saviour, the Son of the living God. It was that that saved them. And it was surely the purpose of all the prior discourse of Christ to reveal to them the purpose of the incarnation and the value of his death. And that is the sum of the Gospel.

I have thought it most necessary to indicate the true meaning of what Christ said in John 6 in order that the uninstructed should not be misled by those who support the papacy. And I trust that the proper sense has been so securely established from the words themselves that no further arguments can be brought against it. We will now see whether this is the true sense according to the papal canons, not in order to prove anything to the believer from such a source, but in order to be able to confront the papacy itself with its own canons. For in those canons the interpretation for which we are anathematized is contained just as clearly as it is in our own statement. You will say: Then why does not the papacy abide by its own canons. Answer: That is the complaint which is made by all true believers. For side by side with the truth the papacy says: Let the truth perish, let it be no more held. You may see for yourself how arrogant and dishonest and unbearable that is to true Christians. And the words of the canon or papal decree are those of St. Augustine. It is his words which they have made into the canon or decree.

The words are as follows:

De consecr. di. 2 ca. prima: (47) "The first heresy (that is, schism) arose amongst the first disciples of Christ (not meaning the twelve, but the many others), and it seemed to derive from the obscurity of his sayings. For he said: Except ye eat my flesh and drink my blood, ye have no eternal life in you. And they did not understand his words, but they all said: That is a hard saying, for who can eat his flesh? And with those words: That is a hard saying, they departed from him, and only the twelve remained with him. But when some had departed, he taught the rest, saying: The spirit giveth life; the flesh profiteth nothing. The words which I have spoken unto you are spirit and life. If you understand them spiritually they are spirit and life." (Note that here too "spiritually" means "in the sense in which Christ understood them," which was, that we are to believe in him who gave up his flesh and blood to death for our sakes.) "If you understand them carnally, they are still spirit and life. But they are not spirit and life to you, for you do not understand them spiritually." (Note that here to understand them "carnally" is to interpret them in the same way as those who departed from him. Therefore Augustine says that the words of Christ were still spirit and life even though those who departed from him would not receive them spiritually: but they were not spirit and truth to them. From this we may clearly gather that the carnal understanding in terms of flesh and blood does not give life. But now Augustine and the papacy add, still in the name of Christ): "The things which I have said unto you you must understand spiritually. You do not eat the body which you see, nor do you drink the blood which is to be poured out by those who crucify me. I have given you a sacrament (that is, a sign) which spiritually understood will give you life: but the flesh profiteth nothing. But they made answer according to their understanding. They thought of flesh in terms of the flesh which is sold and cut up in the market (and at this point, good Christian, do not let yourself be led astray or seduced by the papists, as though Augustine were speaking loosely or even representing their view. For he simply reverses the order. The first point is that the Jews applied to the carnal flesh that which Christ spoke only in respect of his suffering; the second, that if the carnal flesh is there, it may be handled and seen and perceived. As Augustine uses the words he is simply thinking of "carnal flesh".) But when Jesus saw it, he said: Does it offend you that I said: I give you my flesh to eat and my blood to drink? What and if ye shall see the Son of man ascend up where he was before? What does this mean? He resolves that which provokes them and explains that which scandalizes them: for they believed that he would give them his body, but now he says that he will undoubtedly ascend up whole and entire into heaven. And when you see the Son of man ascend up to heaven where he was before, you will know for certain that he does not give his body as you now imagine. For you will perceive that his grace is not given by eating."(48) Now here, good Christian, you see how the first Christians thought concerning the body of Christ. On what grounds then do they cry out, Heretic, Heretic, when we do not say anything but that which is contained in their own decrees? And how can anyone put it more plainly: "You do not eat the body which you see, nor do you drink the blood which is to be poured out by those who crucify me?" Where then are the papists who say: We eat him as he was present in the crib and at the wedding-feast, and as he hung on the cross? Can that mean anything else, as Augustine observed, but the eating of his flesh in the same way as all other flesh is eaten, the view which Berengar too was forced to confess? And is not that a necessary view if the word "is" has to be taken literally, as we have already seen? But no: even of itself the text in John 6: "The flesh profiteth nothing" (meaning the flesh as it is eaten, not as it is crucified) is quite enough to prove that Christ's words: "This is my body," cannot possibly refer to the literal, carnal flesh. For if the flesh profiteth nothing, then Christ did not give it.

But at this point we are informed by some of whom we should least expect it that when Christ says: "The flesh profiteth nothing," we are not to think that he is speaking of his own flesh, but of the nature and frailty of the flesh in general, as in Isaiah 40: "All flesh is grass."(49) Hence we must interpret his words as follows: A carnal understanding profiteth nothing. For he does not say: "My flesh profiteth nothing": Indeed, how could he say that when it is the means of our salvation? Answer: This objection is the source of many others which we can now pass over because they have no sure basis in the Word of God. And why should we answer childish objections without any scriptural basis when they will not accept the solid and unshakable text: "The flesh profiteth nothing," and are unable to make any reply when we show them the true interpretation of the words: "This is my body?" For taken literally these two texts cannot stand together. However, for the sake of Christian courtesy we will reply to all objections.

As regards the first, it is quite true that a carnal understanding profiteth nothing and is indeed harmful. But Christ is not speaking of the carnal understanding as you maintain. For to begin to speak in this critical way about the carnal understanding would not have been sufficiently adapted to the needs of his disciples, the point then at issue being the carnal eating of his flesh. If they were to avoid misunderstanding, then necessarily his answer had to refer to the carnal eating of his flesh. Otherwise Christ was not meeting the error but introducing something completely new concerning the material or carnal understanding. But that was not his custom, for normally he explained sayings which they did not understand. Indeed, his own words show specifically that he was answering their murmuring against the carnal flesh. For it says that "when Jesus knew in himself that they murmured at it, he said unto them," etc. These words make it perfectly clear that it was his aim to elucidate that which had given them offence. Again, the fact that his intention was still the same is shown by many of the things which he said, for example: "Therefore said I unto you, that no man can come unto me, except it were given unto him of my Father." Three times already he had brought this saying, or the drift of it, to their notice. In short, then, the subject of the controversy was his carnal flesh. Therefore the teaching refers to the carnal flesh. And Christ says that literally to eat that flesh profiteth nothing.

As regards the second point, we must not be led astray by the fact that Christ does not say: "My flesh profiteth nothing." For he was not referring to any flesh except his own. He does not say: "My spirit giveth life," but simply: "The spirit." But every believer understands that he is referring to his own spirit, even though he does not say: "My spirit."

As regards the third, the flesh of Christ does indeed profit us greatly as it was put to death for us. But that was something which the Jews and the disciples refused to accept, for they were thinking in terms of a carnal eating. Therefore he says that eaten it profiteth nothing, although crucified it is the greatest blessing ever experienced or received by our miserable race. Thanks be to God that our opponents cannot bring forward any other arguments apart from feeble sophistries.

But they return to the attack, saying: In this sixth chapter of John there is no reference to the sacrament. Why then do you relate it to that subject? Answer: Because you have introduced into the sacrament a carnal eating of the flesh and blood.

Now seeing this passage tells us that the carnal eating of

Christ's flesh and blood profiteth nothing, and you have introduced such a carnal eating into the sacrament, how refute the error more appositely than by quoting the very words with which Christ himself refuted the same error? It is true that in that discourse Christ was declaring the Gospel. But the Jews and the disciples went astray, conceiving this notion of a literal eating of his flesh. And when today we find the same false idea that his flesh is literally eaten in the sacrament, it is only right that we should seek the remedy in the very place where the idea first arose.

So much for the first of those plain Scriptures which strongly forbid a literal or carnal interpretation of the words of Christ: "This is my body."

The second plain Scripture is in I Corinthians 10: "Moreover, brethren, I would not that ye should be ignorant, how that our fathers etc. . . . did all eat the same spiritual meat; and did all drink the same spiritual drink: for they drank of that spiritual rock that followed them: and that rock was Christ." The sense of this passage is wrested this way and that by those who do not examine closely the intention of Paul himself. For what Paul was trying to convey was this: that our fathers were just as precious as we are, and that they had the same God as we have and the same Christ as we have, although they fixed their hopes on one who was still to come, we on one who has already come. But in spite of all that they displeased God when they fell into disobedience. He tells us that amongst the other things which our fathers had no less than we was the same spiritual food and the same spiritual drink as we now enjoy. Now there cannot be the slightest doubt that they did not partake of the literal body and blood of Christ, for Christ did not come in the flesh until sixteen hundred years later. Therefore in their case this eating was simply believing in the one who was to give his flesh and blood to death on their behalf. Similarly in our case the eating and drinking of his body cannot be anything else but believing in the one who has already given his flesh and blood. For he says *to auto*, that is, "one and the same food." This text is sufficiently firm and clear to make it plain to the uninstructed that to feed on Christ is simply to believe on the one who offered up his body and blood for our sakes. It does not make any difference if there are some who scoff. For the text has been misunderstood even by many who are of some account in the Gospel of Christ. The fact is that those who came before had the same faith as we have, for they had the same God. If they looked to a Christ still to come, whereas to us he has been given, that does not make any difference to faith, for we have the same spirit of faith as they had (II Cor. 4, Gal. 3). That is how Augustine interpreted this passage of Paul, *Tract. XLV in Johannem*, clearly teaching that "although we have other signs, they still partook of the same Christ as we do." And that partaking cannot be anything else but believing in him.

The third plain Scripture is to be found in the three articles of the Creed, which are based upon the Word of God, otherwise they would not be articles of faith. And the three are as follows: "He ascended into heaven, And sitteth on the right hand of God the Father Almighty; From thence he shall come to judge the quick and the dead." The first two are found in Mark 16: "He was received up into heaven, and sat on the right hand of God." And he is there literally, for Stephen saw him there (Acts 7). But some are so sure of themselves that they make the matter a subject for jest, saying: In Matthew 28 he said just as clearly: "Lo, I am with you alway, even unto the end of the world." And they refer these words to the body of Christ, which cannot possibly be the case, as we shall show clearly in what follows.

For note well, good Christian, that in Christ there are two different natures, the divine and the human: and yet the two are only the one Christ.(50) According to his divine nature Christ never left the right hand of the Father, for he is one God with the Father, and that is why he says: "I and the Father are one" (John 10), and again, "No man hath ascended up to heaven: but the Son of man which is in heaven" (John 3). According to his divine nature he did not need to ascend up to heaven: for he is omnipresent. Even where two or three gather together in his name, he is there in the midst (Matt. 18). Again, according to this nature he is always at the right hand of the Father, for he says that he is in heaven even when in the body he is upon earth (John 3). That was possible only according to his divine nature. The other nature is Christ's human nature. For our sakes he took this upon him in the pure body of Mary by the receiving and fructifying of the Holy Spirit, and he carried it truly in this present time. According to this nature he increased and grew both in wisdom and stature. According to it he suffered hunger and thirst and cold and heat and all other infirmities, sin only excepted. According to it he was lifted up on the cross, and with it he ascended up into heaven. This nature was a guest in heaven, for no flesh had ever previously ascended up into it. Therefore when we read in Mark 16 that Christ was received up into heaven and sat on the right hand of God we have to refer this to his human nature, for according to his divine nature he is eternally omnipresent, etc. But the saying in Matthew 28: "Lo, I am with you alway, even unto the end of the world," can refer only to his divine nature, for it is according to that nature that he is everywhere present to believers with his special gifts and comfort.(51) If without distinction we were to apply to his human nature everything that refers to the divine, and conversely, if without distinction we were to apply to the divine nature everything that refers to the human, we should overthrow all Scripture and indeed the whole of our faith. For what can we make of a saying like: "My God, my God, why hast thou forsaken me?" if we try to refer it to his divine nature? And the same is true of countless other Scriptures, although I know that by virtue of the fact that the two natures are one Christ, things which are said of only the one nature are often ascribed to the other. Nevertheless, the proper character of each nature must be left intact, and we ought to refer to it only those things which are proper to it. For instance, it is often said that God suffered on our behalf. This saying is tolerated by Christians and I myself do not object to it: not that the Godhead can suffer,(52) but because he who suffered according to his human nature is very God as well as very man. Yet strictly speaking, the suffering appertains only to the humanity. Similarly the Ascension can be ascribed properly only to his humanity. And do not make of this a matter for jest, for according to his divine nature he no more needed to ascend up into heaven than he was capable of suffering, for John says in John 1: "The only begotten Son, which is in the bosom of the Father"— and yet in the flesh he was at that time on the earth and not at the right hand of the Father. Therefore in respect of his divine nature he did not need to ascend up into heaven, although we are not at fault but speak quite rightly if we say: The Son of God ascended up into heaven, for he who ascended up is God. Strictly speaking, however, the Ascension is proper only to his human nature. Let the ordinary reader hold fast to that truth and not puff himself up with mischievous subtleties, for much contention has arisen in relation to this question and it all comes back ultimately to what I have briefly set out concerning the two natures.

Hence the content of the two groups of texts must not be confused. That which is said concerning the Ascension must be referred specifically to the human nature, as, for example, in Mark 16: "He was received up into heaven, and sat on the right hand of God." And that which is proper to his divine nature must be referred specifically to that nature, as for example, his omnipresence, his abiding fellowship with us, his presence in all our hearts, and that all things consist in him, etc. In our reading of Scripture this distinction must always be made. But if Christ is now seated at the right hand of God, and will sit there until he comes at the last day, how can he be literally eaten in the sacrament? You say: He is God. He can be everywhere. But note with what circumspection you say this. First you say: He is God. You give it to be understood that it is the property of God to be everywhere. But it is not the property of the body. I will elucidate. In John 16 Christ says: "I came forth from the Father, and am come into the world: again, I leave the world, and go to the Father." Note that these words contradict his saying: "Lo, I am with you alway, even unto the end of the world," for here he says: "Again, I leave the world." How then does he leave the world? With his divine presence and protection and grace and goodness and loving-kindness? God forbid: it is not for any creature to say that. But necessarily he has left us, for he said so himself, and he cannot lie. It follows, then, that he has departed from us at any rate in the body, he has left us in the body. And there is nothing singular in that, for in Matthew 26 he said even more plainly: "Ye have the poor always with you; but me ye have not always." Now if the saying: "Lo, I am with you alway, even unto the end of the world," refers to the body of Christ, it follows that he is with us in the body, but not with divine grace and power, for he said: "Me ye have not always." But that saying is incredible and misleading if we refer it to his divine nature. Therefore we have conclusive proof that the two sayings: "Again, I leave the world," and: "Me ye have not always," both refer to the departure and absence of his human nature. But if he has gone away, if he has left the world, if he is no longer with us, then either the Creed is unfaithful to the words of Christ, which is impossible, or else the body and blood of Christ cannot be present in the sacrament. The flesh may fume, but the words of Christ stand firm: he sits at the right hand of the Father, he has left the world, he is no longer present with us. And if these words are true, it is impossible to maintain that his flesh and blood are present in the sacrament.

These three Scriptures are of themselves quite sufficient to establish the articles of the Creed and to expose the falsity of the alleged presence of the flesh of Christ in the sacrament. But in order to answer the contentious we will say something more concerning them.

At this point we are attacked by those who say: (53) Note their blasphemies, for they speak as if God were not able to restore to us the body of his Son. Is not that to deny the divine omnipotence? And there are others to whom we have already referred who say: It is the nature and property of the resurrection body to be present at one and the same time both in heaven and also in the sacrament, and indeed everywhere.(54)

To the former group we return this threefold answer.

First, it is those who make God a liar who blaspheme him; for the supreme Good cannot be a liar. Yet God is a liar if he acts contrary to his own Word. But he does not do so. For God has said: "I will not alter the thing that is gone out of my lips" (Ps. 88 (A.V. 89)). Therefore if he has said: "Again, I leave the world," and: "Me ye have not always," and if those sayings are to be taken literally, as we have seen, then we make him a liar if we say that he is still here in the body and that he will remain here in the body until the last day. And if they say: We too have a clear word: "This is my body," that is not the case. For the saying is obscure, and it is contradicted by the clear sayings which we have already noted. Therefore we cannot take it in the sense which they ascribe to it, for the Word of God is not self-contradictory. But the whole context and force both of Scripture and the Creed show us that it cannot bear that crudely literal sense. For if it did, it would be impossible to reconcile it with these other passages. For the whole context and meaning show us that Christ's aim was to teach them that he would ascend up bodily into heaven and sit at the right hand of the Father until the last day. The omnipotence of God accomplishes all things according to the Word of God: it never does that which is contrary to that Word. Therefore it cannot possibly be as they say: for God does not do anything contrary to his own Word. And that is not impotence, but true omnipotence.(55) For because a thing is possible to God it does not follow that it is. It was quite possible for God to make the seven lean years into years of plenty,(56) but the fact that it was possible did not actually make them into years of plenty, as we have shown in the *Subsidium sive coronis.*

Second, we point out that until the last day Christ cannot be anywhere but at the right hand of God the Father. In Psalm 110 it is written: "Sit thou at my right hand, until I make thine enemies thy footstool." Paul refers to this text in I Corinthians 15 when he teaches that Christ will sit at the right hand of the Father until the last day. But if Christ is seated there, he is not present here. And if he were here, we could not speak of his return, for he would have returned already. The proof of this is in Matthew 26: "Hereafter shall ye see the Son of man sitting on the right hand of power, and coming in the clouds of heaven." What could be clearer than that? The word *ap arti*, "hereafter," is of itself quite enough to show us that we must seek him at the right hand of the Father until that day when he returns in the clouds to judgment. That "hereafter" extends to the last day. And that is the basis of the third article in the Creed: "From thence he shall come to judge the quick and the dead." This article requires that he shall not come from thence until he comes to judge. For it says: "From thence he shall come to judge," not, "From thence he shall come into the bread." It follows, therefore, that he will not come from the right hand of the Father until he comes to judge. That is what David says in Psalm 110, it is what Christ himself tells us, and it is what we are taught by this article of the Creed, which it would be a heresy to deny. Again, Christ himself says in Matthew 25: "When the Son of man shall come in his glory, and all the holy angels with him, then shall he sit upon the throne of his glory: and before him shall be gathered all nations," etc.

But if he is present in the bread, or if the bread is the body of Christ, then the last day has already come, he is already present, he is already seated on the judgment throne. But if the last day has not yet come, he is not present in the flesh: for when he does come in the flesh, he will sit in judgment. I know quite well how the foolish try to evade this: The judgments and penalties of God are daily with us, and therefore the body of Christ is present daily. Answer: We have no right to obscure the matter in this way. For it is evident that Christ is speaking here only of the last judgment, to which the whole world will come, from the first man to the last. He is not speaking of daily judgments at which his presence in the flesh is neither required nor promised.

Third, Christ cannot come in any way but visibly. For in Acts 1 it is written: "While they beheld, he was taken up; and a cloud received him out of their sight. And while they looked steadfastly toward heaven as he went up, behold, two men stood by them in white apparel; which also said, Ye men of Galilee, why stand ye gazing up into heaven? this same Jesus, which is taken up from you into heaven, shall so come in like manner as ye have seen him go into heaven." This text will not cause any difficulty to the ordinary reader. If he came in the bread in the same visible form as the disciples saw him go up, we would believe that he is there: for the angels said that he would so come in like manner as they saw him go. But if he does not come openly and visibly, we will not expect his bodily return until he does come as he said by the angels. And no matter what protestations may be made of his bodily presence, we will believe neither angels from heaven, nor men, nor devils, until we see him come in the same visible form as the disciples saw him go. It was to this that St. Paul referred in I Corinthians 11 when he said: "Ye do shew the Lord's death till he come." If Paul had believed that we eat the body of Christ in the Supper he could not have said "till he come." And he knew perfectly well that according to his divine nature he is with us always. Therefore in these words he is necessarily referring to his human nature. In the same way Christ himself says in Matthew 24: "For as the lightning cometh out of the east, and shineth even unto the west; so shall also the coming of the Son of man be." When we see him as clearly as the lightning we shall have every reason to believe that he is really present. When we do not see him, we are not exercising faith by believing something for which we have no clear word of Scripture. Again, in Luke 17, when his disciples asked him concerning the time of the last judgment, Jesus said: "Wheresoever the body is, thither will the eagles be gathered together." By giving them this illustration as his answer, he meant to teach them that as the eagles gather together where the body is, so where his body is we shall be also.(57) He is really present when we are with his body in the same sure and visible way as the eagles are with their prey. As long as that is not so, we must be content to await his coming until we can see him with the same openness and certainty as he himself has taught.

To the others,(58) who say: After the resurrection the body of Christ can be wherever he himself wills: therefore he sits at the right hand of God and yet at the same time he is eaten by us.

For if he can be wherever he wills, then he is present everywhere, even though we do not know either the cause, manner or mode of his omnipresence. He was born of the Virgin Mary without violation of her maidenly purity. He passed through closed doors. Twice he made himself invisible and escaped the hands of his enemies. All these things are beyond our comprehension. Yet we firmly believe that his body has in fact been transformed in this way. To such we give the following answers.

First, they make all these statements without any warrant in God's Word. For the thesis upon which their doctrine is grounded is merely a theological deduction, namely, to say that it is the property of Christ's resurrection body to be wherever he wills. And this is a mischievous assertion for which there is no basis in the Word of God, although they do try to make it more plausible by saying that the transformation applies only to the bodies of the elect and not of the reprobate. But if that is the case, then it follows at once that it is not the property of the resurrection body as such, for otherwise all the resurrected could be wherever they willed. And then they add: But the elect will to be where God wills, of which I have not the slightest doubt. But if so, it follows necessarily that Christ is where his heavenly Father wills, and nowhere else. But as David tells us in Psalm 110: the Father said that he should sit at his right hand until he made his enemies his footstool, that is, until the last day, as St. Paul tells us in I Corinthians 15 and as we have made as clear as the day in our previous exposition. Therefore he is nowhere else: for by the word "until," which the theologians (59) have never been able properly to explain, we see that a clear reference is made to the fact that he is now seated above and that we shall not see him until the last day. Hence it is quite evident that the view under discussion is only an opinion of men, so that we are not really under any obligation to answer it. Nevertheless it is only right that we should try to meet its exponents with charity and truth. And it is also right that we should expose the futility of their evasion. Consider, then, that notwithstanding his birth of a pure virgin, Mary, the body of Christ was not ubiquitous, as we shall see. He did not always pass through closed doors. In short, he is only in the one place at the one time, as we shall show in our second answer from God's Word. The fact that he is wherever he wills does not mean that he is everywhere at once. For in the body he does not will to be anywhere except at the right hand of the Father.

Second, it belongs only to the divine nature of Christ to be ubiquitous. Otherwise Christ could not have ascended up bodily into heaven, as we have seen, for he would be there already. Note that in the early Church there was an obstinate heretic named Marcion who refused to believe that Christ was very man.(60) In defence of his opinion he alluded to the passages already mentioned. Christ was born of a virgin. He made himself invisible. Without support he walked miraculously on the water. He appeared to his disciples, etc. But Marcion found his main prop in the text: "This is my body," which he expounded in the following way: It cannot be his body that is eaten, because he did not have a substantial or natural body; for we could not eat such a body. Hence it follows that it is only an incorporeal and spiritual body. To that interpretation the pious teachers and evangelists of the time made this reply: that he did not give us his material body to eat, but in the bread and wine he appointed a sign or sacrament of his very flesh and blood which he truly bore and truly offered up to death.(61) I mention this point only in passing. And now I come to the answer. If we wish to argue that Christ's body is in the bread in the same way as it was born of the Virgin Mary and passed through closed doors, etc., then we either have to say that his passion did not cause him any hurt, that he did not experience it, or else we have to accept the heretical doctrine of Marcion. And for the following reason. If we partake of him miraculously, in the same way as he was miraculously born of Mary without violation of her virginity, or miraculously put to death without any suffering: for as he left the virginity of Mary inviolate, so he himself remained inviolate, for his words are these: "This is my body which is broken, that is, put to death for you" (62)—if, then, we partake of him as he was put to death, and if we also partake of him as he was born of the Virgin and passed unhindered through closed doors, it follows necessarily either that he did not experience his passion or that he had only an incorporeal and spiritual body, as Marcion heretically maintained. But to believe this is to offer the most grievous and outrageous insult to the Christ who suffered so bitterly for us miserable sinners. And that is what happens when we oppose the evident truth with our human reason and the words and subtleties of man. But no: Let us look only to the truth and we shall see clearly the error of those who would tell us that the partaking of the body of Christ takes place invisibly and imperceptibly, saying: We eat him corporally *modo quodam ineffabili*, that is, in a way which defies expression. And for this reason : If they tell us that the words: "This is my body," must be interpreted literally, then consider the words which follow: "Which is broken, that is, put to death for you." For if he suffered death visibly and perceptibly, not invisibly and imperceptibly, and if he gave his body to be eaten as he gave it to his passion, then necessarily his body is pressed with the teeth visibly, perceptibly and materially: for that was how he was pierced and smitten by the cruel thorns and the lash and the nails and the spear so that even the sun and earth and stones could not withold their pity. This, then, is our answer to those who maintain that we eat his flesh invisibly and imperceptibly, or as he rose again from the dead: We have to concede either that he suffered imperceptibly, or that his disciples did not eat in the same way as we do: for he had not yet risen again when he instituted this act of thanksgiving. For he does not say: "This is my body which is to rise again from the dead," but: "which is given up to death for you." And here we must leave the point.

The third answer we have already outlined, namely, that those who maintain that we partake of the body of Christ as he rose again from the dead are already opposed by the fact that Christ is speaking of his mortal body: "which is broken, that is, put to death for you." For as we have already said, if we wish to refer the words: "This is my body," to the literal flesh, as if he were giving us that to eat, then the words which follow are: "which is given, that is, put to death for you," and we have to partake of him as he was put to death and not as he rose again. Hence their speculations are shown to be groundless and even mischievous, obscuring and confounding the Word of God. But in order to counter them thoroughly we will now prove to them from the Word of God that it is not possible for the body of Christ to be in many or all places at one and the same time, but that even after the resurrection it is possible for his body only to be in the one place. In this way we shall deprive their philosophy of the *ubi* or *locus* (63) with which they sustain themselves. Now we have already made it sufficiently clear that although Christ was born without any violation of the virginity of his mother, the pure Virgin Mary, that does not mean that his body could be in many places at one and the same time, for there is no record of anyone being in different places simultaneously. We will now prove that even after his resurrection he could not be in many places at one and the same time. First, it is the same thing to be in many places and to be everywhere, which is proper only to his divine nature. With that in mind let us consider the words of the angel in Matthew 28 when he told those that sought him, Mary Magdalene and the other Mary: "I know that ye seek Jesus, which was crucified. He is not here," etc. But if the body of Jesus was everywhere, then the angel was not telling the truth, for necessarily he was there also. But if he was not there, it is a sure sign that he cannot be in more than one place, for he was not at the place where the women sought him. Yet he says that where two or three are gathered together in his name he is there in the midst. Seeing then that he was not there, it follows that he is omnipresent only according to his divine nature and not his human. Similarly Christ himself says in Matthew 24: "There shall arise false Christs, and false prophets, and shall shew great signs and wonders," etc. "Wherefore if they shall say unto you, Behold, he is in the desert; go not forth: behold, he is in the secret chambers; believe it not," etc. In this and in other passages already mentioned we are given clearly to understand that we must not seek him in the body, for if we do we are acting like those who say: I have seen the Lord God here or eaten him there, etc. If he is in many places at once he is in all places at once, and in that case he would not have taught us not to believe those who show him in this place or that. Do not let yourself be misled, good Christian, by the fact that some interpret the passage differently, for he specifically teaches us not to allow ourselves to be deceived when we are told that he has come in this place or that. Read Luke 17 on the point and you will get a full understanding. Similarly in John 12 he says: "Where I am, there shall also my servant be." The text refers to both natures, but it refers primarily to the human. For his sake the disciples would have tribulations, but he consoled them with the fact that they were finally to be with him. And if they are where he is, that is, in heaven, where he is seated at the right hand of the Father, then it follows that in the body he is only in one place: otherwise the disciples would be in more than one place, seeing they are with him. Similarly in John 14: "I will receive you unto myself; that where I am, there ye may be also." This can refer only to his human nature, for otherwise the creature cannot be where the Creator is, or they would be everywhere as God is, which is a heresy. But if the disciples are where he is, it follows that in the body he is only in one place, otherwise the disciples would be in many places, and indeed they would be in the host, as they call it. Again, in John 17 he says: "Father, I will that they also, whom thou hast given me, be with me where I am." This verse teaches us that according to his humanity he cannot be in more than one place even after his resurrection, for in the same passage he speaks of his ascension into heaven and of their being left physically in the world. You may be told, ordinary reader, that in this verse we are doing violence to the text of Scripture, but do not be concerned no matter who it may be that tells you. Let him state his view in writing and with the help of God we will prove that what we teach is the truth and that the word of truth is in us.

We will now prove to the papacy from their own canons that the risen body of Christ cannot be in more than one place at one and the same time. For in *De consecra. dist. 2 ca. prima, paragr. finali,*(64) it is written: "The Lord himself is above until the end of the world; but the faithfulness (65) of the Lord is still with us. For the body which is risen is necessarily in one place: but his faithfulness or grace is poured out everywhere."(66) Thus far from the papacy's own book. And what could be clearer? You will see that by the Lord he means Christ. Therefore if the body of the risen Christ is necessarily only in the one place, without doubt that place cannot be any other than at the right hand of the Father. And if so, how can he be here below in the bread? The papists will try to win you over to some other interpretation, as we have shown, but do not allow yourself to be outwitted. Hold fast to the words: The body which is risen is necessarily in one place, and you will counter all their objections.

If God wills, all men of piety will now perceive the honesty of those who allege against us that like the Jews we are going about to cast down from heaven the Lord Jesus Christ, the very Son of God our Saviour, and to deny him and the like. For it will be evident to them that in large measure we deduce our understanding of the partaking of his flesh from the fact that he sits unchanged at the right hand of the divine majesty until the last day, and then eternally. To whom be praise and glory, world without end. Amen.

THE THIRD ARTICLE

In the first article, God willing, it was made clear from the nature of Christ's words that the saying: "This is my body," cannot be taken literally, otherwise we tear his flesh with our teeth in the very same way as it was pierced by the nails and the spear. In the second we considered the clear Scriptures which will not permit of the literal presence of his flesh and blood in this sacrament, a necessary procedure if we are not to rush to the details of the letter of Holy Scripture but in everything to test the meaning which Scripture as a whole will bear. For if Scripture is spoken by God, as is taught by Peter and Paul, then it cannot contradict itself. If it appears to do so, it is because we do not rightly understand it, comparing Scripture with Scripture. In this connection it has been made perfectly clear that the three articles of the Creed, "He ascended into heaven, And sitteth on the right hand of God the Father Almighty; From thence he shall come to judge the quick and the dead," cannot be maintained if we accept the view that he is eaten in the body. Our present task is to indicate that interpretation of the words: "This is my body," which will best harmonize with the rest of Scripture and the three articles of the Creed. With the help of God we will do this no less forcefully in this third section. O Lord open thou our eyes.

Now first we must understand that throughout the Bible there are to be found figures of speech, called in the Greek *tropos*, that is, metaphorical, or to be understood in another sense. For instance, in John 15 Christ says: "I am the vine." This means that Christ is like a vine when considered in relation to us, who are sustained and grow in him in the same way as branches grow in the vine. Similarly the words: "Ye are the branches," are a trope. We have to take them metaphorically, that is, we are like branches, as we have seen already. Similarly, in John 1: "Behold the Lamb of God, which taketh away the sin of the world," the first part of the verse is a trope, for Christ is not literally a lamb. Necessarily, then, it has quite a different meaning, namely, that he is the pure offering which takes away the sin of the whole world. Similarly in John 6: "I am the living bread," the word "bread" has to be taken metaphorically, namely: I am the living food, nourishment or consolation of the soul. Similarly in Matthew 21, when Christ refers to himself as a stone: "Whosoever shall fall on this stone shall be broken," there is a twofold trope or metaphor: in the word "stone", which signifies Christ in his unshakable constancy, and in the words "fall on it" which are a figure for "do him violence," etc. Now the word "is" is used with particular frequency in a figurative or metaphorical sense.

For example, in Luke 8 Christ says: "The seed is the Word of God." The sense here is necessarily a non-literal one, namely, that the seed of which he has been speaking signifies the Word of God. In this instance, then, the word "is" is used for "signify," that is: "The seed signifies the Word of God." Similarly in Matthew 13, in his exposition of the parable of the wheat and the tares, Christ says: "He that soweth the good seed is the Son of man," that is, the man of whom it is said that he soweth the good seed signifies the Son of man. Again, "the field is the world" means "the field signifies the world." Again, "the good seed are the children of the kingdom" means "the children of the kingdom are signified by the good seed." Again, "the tares are the children of the wicked one," means, "the children of the wicked one are signified by the tares." Again, "the enemy that sowed them is the devil," means, "the enemy signifies the devil." "The harvest is the end of the world"—"is" is used for "signifies." "The reapers are the angels"—"are" for "signify." In all these sayings "is" means "signifies," or "are" "signify." But someone says: Yes, but this is only in parables. Answer: Not so, it is in the exposition of parables, when everything must be as clear as possible. And where it is does not really make the slightest difference. We are simply trying to show that there are innumerable passages in Scripture in which the word "is" is used for "signifies." And to those who have briefly opposed this fact, but in Latin, (67) I will make this short answer: If I may be allowed to say so, they observe neither grammar nor logic. We may find another example in the Old Testament, in Genesis 41, when Joseph is expounding the dream and says: "The seven good kine and the seven good ears are seven fruitful years," and again, "The seven thin kine and the seven empty ears are seven years of famine": in both these cases by virtue of the trope or figure the word "are" is used for "signify." But it is objected that in the Hebrew there is no word for "are." Answer: And do you know how it is that there is no word for "are"? But this is no time for childish frolic. There is no word for "is" and "are" simply because the Hebrew language is not the same as the German. If it were, the words "is" and "are" would be present when occasion required. But in Hebrew there are expressions which have the same sense as in German, as shown above. A more detailed answer will be given in Latin. (68) We will now omit as superfluous the many other instances which might be cited, for we have already furnished an adequate number of incontrovertible passages.

Our next task is to see whether Christ's words in Matthew 26: "This is my body," can also be taken metaphorically or *tropice*. It has already become clear enough that in this context the word "is" cannot be taken literally. Hence it follows that it must be taken metaphorically or figuratively. In the words: "This is my body," the word "this" means the bread, and the word "body" the body which is put to death for us. Therefore the word "is" cannot be taken literally, for the bread is not the body and cannot be, as we have seen already. Necessarily, then, it must be taken figuratively or metaphorically; "This is my body," means, "The bread signifies my body," or "is a figure of my body." For immediately afterwards in Luke 22 Christ adds: "This do in remembrance of me," from which it follows that the bread is only a figure of his body to remind us in the Supper that the body was crucified for us. And now out of the Old Testament we will show how exactly the trope or metaphor corresponds to the words used. In Exodus 12 we are specifically told that in one night God smote all the first-born in the land of Egypt, both of man and beast, but spared the children of Israel, for he instructed them to take a lamb and to kill it and to cover with the blood the two side-posts and the upper door post of their houses, that he might see the sign and not smite there. And before that awful night they were to eat the lamb roast with fire: "And thus shall ye eat it: with your loins girded, your shoes on your feet, and your staff in your hand; and ye shall eat it in haste: it is the Lord's passover." Note that the lamb itself is here called a passover, although when they first ate the lamb the passover had not yet taken place. And apart from that, a lamb is not a passover, for a passover is forbearance to smite, whereas a lamb is flesh and blood, etc. Yet God himself says: "It is the passover." Therefore in this context the little word "is" is necessarily figurative, that is, it is used for "signify": the lamb signifies the passover, that is, it is to do so in the night which follows: and this passover was later celebrated every year by the children of Israel. The fact that the words are wrested by some scholars merely serves to confirm our interpretation, for nothing can be gained by wresting the verse, as we shall show in our Latin work. No type of Christ is more precious, more exact or more evident than that of the Paschal Lamb: and that is why Christ shared it with his disciples with such joy just before his death (Luke 22). And for that reason, when we ponder and investigate the figurative meaning of Christ's words, there is no text to which we may turn more confidently than that which speaks of the Paschal Lamb: for everything corresponds. The Paschal Lamb was eaten the night before the smiting and passing over, and yet then and in years to come it was to be the representation of the Lord's Passover. In the same way Christ instituted the remembrance of his death the night before he died, and that remembrance of his death, instituted before he died, is to be observed by all believers until he comes. In the former the Egyptians were smitten and the children of Israel were passed over. In the latter Christ is taken and put to death and the murderer Barabbas is passed over, our guilt being borne by the righteousness of Christ, as we have shown at greater length in the *Subsidium*. (69)

And now compare the two texts: The Paschal Lamb is the passover, that is, the Paschal Lamb represents the passing over of the angel of God; and, "This is my body," that is, This represents my body, the eating of this bread being the sign and symbol that Christ, the soul's true consolation and nourishment, was crucified for us. But some argue: In the text about the former Paschal Lamb the word "it" or "this" does not refer to the lamb but to the feast, thus: The feast is the passover, the word "this" referring then to the feast. To such we make this reply: It is not at all the case that the word "this" refers to the feast, as they maintain, but it refers to the Paschal Lamb, as the text itself makes perfectly clear. But even assuming that the word "this" does refer to the feast: The feast is the passover, we still have to make enquiry concerning the origin of the feast, for all feasts derive from something. And they are forced to answer: it derives from the lamb and the passover. But if it is found that it derives from the lamb and the passover, the victory is with us, for the words: The lamb is the passover, relate to the original lamb. You see then that there is no solid foundation for some of the epistles now circulated so widely. (70) But again, even assuming that the word "this" refers to the feast: The feast is the passover, we have still to explain the word "is," for a feast cannot be a passover. Necessarily the word "is" is used for "represents" or "signifies," and even if they try to argue that the Paschal Lamb is a feast, we have still to ask of what it is the feast, and again we are brought back to the passover: the lamb is a figure of that first passing over. But further, if we allow that it is a feast, and do not press the enquiry into the derivation— although the origin ought to be investigated and discovered—then we have every right to take the words of

Christ: "This is my body," to mean, This bread is a feast, just as we take the words: The lamb is the passover, to mean, the lamb is a feast. For it is indeed a feast of thanksgiving, as Paul shows us in I Corinthians 5, and as Origen describes it in his exposition of Leviticus, basing his statement upon the most primitive Fathers.(71) In short, once we have proved that the words: "This is my body," are necessarily figurative or metaphorical, it is self-evident that they bear a similar sense to the words: "This is the Lord's passover," namely, The bread represents my body which is given for you, and, The lamb represents the passover of the Lord. That this is the true and natural sense we are clearly taught by various points in the context.

The first of these is the clear saying of Christ himself in Matthew 26, when after instituting the sacrament he said: "But I say unto you, I will not drink henceforth of this fruit of the vine, until that day when I drink it new with you in my Father's kingdom." Note that even after Christ had given them the wine, describing it as his blood, he could still point to it and call it the fruit of the vine. This is a clear indication that when he said: "This is my blood," he was not speaking literally but metaphorically: This wine represents my blood, for immediately after he himself calls it the fruit of the vine. And he used the word "fruit" deliberately, for it shows us plainly that literally and according to its true nature and kind this drink is really wine, and comes from the vine. Why then cannot we accept it as the fruit of the vine as Christ himself does? The fact that Luke puts the saying earlier helps to serve the same purpose, for Luke puts it first in order to prevent any misunderstanding of the saying which follows, as though the wine were really blood.

The second point is the perfect calm of the disciples. They were not at all excited or perturbed. They did not begin to question and argue amongst themselves. Yet only a few moments previously, in a matter of far less importance than this is, if it is as we are supposed to picture it, the very same disciples had been greatly agitated and slow of understanding, and even Peter had tried to find reasons for not allowing his feet to be washed. But in this matter there is not the least hint of any word of incredulity. But surely we have good grounds to think that it is here rather than when he was with him in the boat in Luke 5 that Peter would have said: "Depart from me, for I am a sinful man O Lord," if he had really understood Christ to mean that he was eating him in the flesh?

Surely all the disciples would have echoed amongst themselves the words of the centurion in Matthew 8: "Lord, I am not worthy that thou shouldest come under the roof of my sinful mouth." But this was not the case. We are told neither that they exclaimed violently nor that they recoiled and shrank back from him in awe. And for this reason: Being Jews, they did not find anything novel in the words: "This is my body." For every year when they ate the Paschal Lamb they heard the similar words: "The lamb is the passover," and they had always taken it that these words meant simply that the lamb represents the passover. Hence they perceived that the Lord was instituting a similar feast of thanksgiving and using not dissimilar words. The result was that they did not feel any particular surprise, or awe, or sense of novelty at that which Christ said and did.

The third point is that none of the apostles ever taught specifically that in this sacrament the bread becomes the body and the wine the blood of Christ. Yet surely the very contrary is to be expected, for if they had preached concerning this sacrament as is done today all kinds of curious questions would have arisen and to these they would have had to make some answer. But that was not the case, and even after he has given a full account of the institution St. Paul still calls the elements bread and wine, as Christ himself did.

We will now examine the incident word by word as described by Luke in chapter 22 and Paul in I Corinthians 11. In the light of these narratives I hope before God that we shall be able to understand with the same clarity as the disciples themselves the words recorded in Matthew 26 and Mark 14. The text in Luke 22 is as follows: "And he took bread and gave thanks, and brake it, and gave unto them, saying, This is my body which is given for you: this do in remembrance of me." We must not separate the two phrases, "This is my body," and, "which is given for you," but keep them together: for only when they are kept together is the saying of Christ complete. Hence it follows that Christ is speaking only of that body which is given for us in death. It follows, too, that the bread itself is not the body, otherwise the body would be given for us in the form of bread: for the words are these: "This— and he points to the bread—is my body." If then the bread is his body, it is also given for us, for he says that the bread is his body which is given for us. Therefore if the bread is his body which is given for us, the bread is given for us. But that is not the natural sense of the words of Christ. For the word "is" cannot possibly connect bread and body in a literal sense, but must be understood metaphorically, that is, the bread represents my body which is given for you, or, the bread is a figure of my body. But in what way? How does the sacramental bread represent the body of Christ? Answer: When Christ himself says: "Which is given for us," what he means is simply this, that the bread is a sign that his body is given for us, and his next words make this perfectly clear, for he says: "Do this in remembrance of me." These words tell us why it is that he has instituted this symbolical bread, for the remembrance of Christ and his self-offering for us. Hence it follows once again that the bread is the body in the sense that it signifies the body, for by it we are reminded of the body, the body itself not being present. In I Corinthians 11 Paul gives us the words in this form: "This is my body, which is broken for you." "Given for us" and "broken for us" are one and the same. It is simply that Paul wishes to touch on an analogy concealed at this point, namely, that as Christ is broken, that is, put to death for us, so in remembrance of him we offer one another the bread and break it, each representing and communicating with the other, as Christ did for us all.

The institution of the cup is given by Luke as follows: "This cup—the word 'vessel' or 'cup' is used for its contents, just as we often say that we have drunk a cup or beaker of wine, although we do not in fact drink the vessel—is the new testament in my blood, which is shed for you." To elucidate this saying, let us turn to the words of I Corinthians 11, where Paul says: "The wine, the new testament, is in my blood," etc. And briefly the meaning is this: The wine is the new testament. The new testament is in my blood. And my blood is shed for you. Note that neither in Luke nor Paul are we told that the wine is the blood of Christ. By this we may see clearly that the other two evangelists merely intended to say the same as these two. For although they say: "This—that is, the wine—is my blood," what they mean is that the wine is a sign, a figure, a memorial of the blood of the new testament which was shed for us. And seeing there is an evident trope or metaphor in this case, the same principle has to be applied in the case of the bread. But some argue: (72) If the wine is the new testament, it is also the blood of Christ. For the blood of Christ is the new testament. Answer: The new testament is not the blood of Christ. It is the free and gracious remission of our sins. That is the new covenant of Jeremiah 31 and Hebrews 8. And that remission is wrought for us by the blood of Christ. It is free, but it not free to Christ, for he purchased it dearly enough. Yet God gave it to us without any merit on our own part, of his own free grace. Hence it follows that Christ's blood is not the new testament itself, but the blood of the new testament, that is, the blood by which the new testament, the free remission of sins, is wrought and won. Similarly in the Old Testament the blood sprinkled upon the people and the law is called the blood of the covenant, or testament, but it is not the testament itself (Exod. 24), for the testament is that which is preached to them. Therefore we never find the blood of Christ described as a testament but only as the blood of the testament. And when the wine is called the new testament we have to see that this is a manner of speech, like that which we find in Genesis 17, where circumcision is called the covenant, although properly it is only the sign of the covenant. Similarly in the Eucharist the wine is referred to as the new testament because it is a sign of the blood of Christ with which the new testament was won for us, as we have already seen. If you wish to pursue the point further you may consult my *Subsidium*.(73) The words, "which is shed for you," form an additional answer to the objection, for it is not the wine which is shed for us but the blood of Christ. And if the blood itself is not called a testament, how much less can that which represents it be a testament? That it is called a testament is in line with the common practice in Scripture of giving to signs the names of the things which they signify, as we have shown.

Reading on in I Corinthians 11 we now come to the verse which teaches us clearly both what the remembrance is and to what it refers: "As often as ye eat this bread, and drink this cup—note that even after the institution he still calls the elements bread and wine, which he would not have done had he thought of them as we once did—ye do shew the Lord's death till he come." In this verse the word "shew" simply means to praise, honour, give thanks, as in I Peter 2 and many Old Testament passages. This is clear proof that Paul regarded it as a public thanksgiving. "Till he come" necessarily refers to the body, for according to his divinity he is always with us. But he is not with us if he is still to come. And Paul's meaning is that the Christian Church must not cease to give thanks until he comes at the last day.

In order to be brief we will omit the other passages in Paul except for the saying: "But he that eateth unworthily is guilty of the body and blood of Christ, not discerning the Lord's body." What Paul has in mind here is that we must all go to the Supper worthily, that is, with a true faith, for those who do not go with a true faith are guilty of the body and blood of Christ, not the body which we eat, but the real body which Christ gave in death.(74) For if a man professes a true faith in Christ and yet all the time he is dissembling before God, he is guilty of that innocent blood in which he does not believe, although outwardly he appears to do so. This is how the words were understood by Augustine in *Jo. tractatu* LXII and also by Ambrose on I Corinthians 11.

Our next task is to show that the Christians and Fathers of the first five centuries all understood Christ's words: "This is my body," in a figurative and not a literal sense. However, the learned and pious Oecolampadius has already published a most Christian book (75) in which he has proved this interpretation at great length out of the early Fathers, and seeing this book has now been translated (76) I will here refer to only three of these Fathers, the three who are best known to the ordinary and uninstructed Christian: Jerome, Ambrose and Augustine.

Jerome speaks of the words: "This is my body," in the following terms: (77) "When the figure of the passover had been fulfilled and he had eaten the flesh of the lamb with his disciples, he took bread, which strengthens the heart of man, and followed the pattern of the passover, that as Melchisedek, a priest of the Most High God, had done in type when he brought forth bread and wine, he represented and signified the reality of his body and blood." Thus far Jerome, and do not be misled because he speaks of the offering of Melchisedek, for that is a difficulty with which we have frequently dealt. But note with what clarity Jerome at once describes the bread as simply a sign or sacrament of the Paschal Lamb, that is, Christ. He sees clearly that it is the intention of Christ to signify or represent his very body and blood. Hence Jerome takes the words of Christ: "This is my body," to mean: The bread represents my body, the very body which I give for you.

Ambrose comments on I Corinthians 11 as follows: (78) "Seeing we are redeemed by the death of the Lord, we remember it constantly; and when we eat and drink the flesh and blood, we represent the things which are offered up for us." The papacy includes these words of Ambrose in the canons *de cons. di. 2 c. Quia morte,* but they are there ascribed to Augustine, although they are not really his.(79) I have translated the words as the papists themselves interpret them, lest they should have any cause for complaint. But they might equally well be translated: "Seeing we are redeemed by the death of Christ, we remember it constantly; and when we eat and drink (i.e., the sacramental bread and wine of which he is speaking), we represent the flesh and blood which are offered up for us."(80) By misinterpreting the words of Ambrose the papists can say: We eat the flesh and blood of Christ in remembrance of the flesh and blood offered up for us, for he says that when we eat and drink the flesh and blood we represent the things which are offered up for us. Our answer: If I have heard you rightly, there is a twofold flesh and blood, the first, that which was put to death for us and now sits at the right hand of the Father; the second, that which we eat in remembrance of the true flesh which was put to death for us. For it is impossible to deny that the flesh and blood which was put to death for us ascended up into heaven, as Christ himself said in Luke 24: "Behold my hands and my feet, that it is I myself; handle me and see; for a spirit hath not flesh and bones, as ye see me have." In these words it was the express purpose of Christ to show that the body which had been raised was the same as that which had died. And that means that it was the same body which departed from them into heaven, for immediately after it says: "And it came to pass, while he blessed them, he was parted from them, and carried up into heaven." Note that the body which ascended up into heaven was the same as that which he had just commanded them to touch. Therefore we cannot possibly regard the resurrection body as a representation of that which was crucified, as some would maintain; for the resurrection body is identical with that which was crucified: otherwise the resurrection of Christ was vain, which it is an outrage against our most holy faith (81) even to suggest. At this point we may note that in the phrase: "When we eat and drink the flesh and blood we represent the things which are offered up for us," Ambrose is necessarily using the words "flesh and blood" for "bread and wine," that is, the thing signified for the significant sign. In Greek this form of speech was called *metonymia* or *catachresis*, that is, the use of one word for another: for Christ called the bread his body when what he meant was that it is a representation of his body.(82) And that this is Ambrose's view is shown by the words: "We represent the things which are offered up for us." We do not eat the things which are offered up for us. We merely represent them. For if we were to eat them, we should eat them as they were offered up: for he says: "This is my body which is given for you." Note that "offered up" and "given" are equivalent. But this is unnecessary, for what Ambrose means is simply that when we eat and drink the bread and wine, which are the signs of the flesh and blood, we show thereby that the flesh and blood were offered up for us. For just before he had called it a remembrance of our redemption, etc. From the words of Ambrose it may be clearly seen that for him "is" had the force of "represents," *est* of *significat*. It should also be noted in this connection that when the early doctors called the bread and wine flesh and blood, they were speaking in exactly the same way as Christ himself, meaning that the bread and wine were the signs of the very flesh and blood which were given for us. I myself used the term "sacrament of the sacred body and blood of Christ" in just the same way in the exposition of my theses: (83) for the very body of Christ sits at the right hand of the Father, but the sacrament, that is, the sign of that sacred and living body is now eaten by us in Christian fellowship in thanksgiving and remembrance that his body was slain for us. And because it represents that body, it is often called the body and blood of Christ, for that is what it was called by Christ himself.

The words of Augustine may be found in *de cons. di. 2 c. Semel Christus,*(84) and they are as follows: "Christ once died, the just for the unjust. And we know, and are sure, and have a constant hope, that Christ being raised from the dead dieth no more: death hath no more dominion over him. These are Paul's words. But that we might not forget that which once happened we are to keep it annually in remembrance in the Paschal feast. Is Christ slain again on these occasions? No: but the annual remembrance signifies or represents that which once happened, thereby recalling it as though we actually saw the Lord present on the cross." (85) All these are the words of Augustine, and they make it plain that the sacrament is simply a recalling or representing of something which happened only the once: for in the preface to his exposition of the third Psalm he says: "Christ took Judas with him to the Last Supper, in which he gave his disciples and bade them observe a representation or sign of his body and blood." (86)

It is hardly necessary to give any further extracts from the early Fathers, for Oecolampadius has given a sufficient number of references in his little work. There are some with more impudence than erudition who venture to assert that we do violence to the Fathers, but we will deal with such in our reply to their writings. Those who are more erudite than impudent will see that the Fathers held exactly the same view as we do. And they use exactly the same speech as we do, for they call the bread and wine the body and blood of Christ, although what they really mean is that they are the representation and memorial of his body and blood, just as a faithful wife, whose husband has left her a ring as a keepsake, frequently refers to the ring as her husband, saying: This is my late husband, although what she means is that it recalls her husband.(87) Or again, as Augustine shows in his epistle to Boniface,(88) we often say: Today is the Lord's ascension or the Lord's resurrection, or the annunciation of Mary, and yet the annunciation of Mary and the resurrection and ascension of her Son took place only once. But to the anniversaries of what took place only once we give the same names as were given at the time of their occurrence and institution. That is why in our act of remembrance we have retained the words of Christ and of Paul in exactly the same form as originally given,(89) and together with them we have given the following words of explanation to point to a right understanding: "That on the night that he gave himself up to death, by which death he brought to an end the blood of the Old Testament and abrogated all carnal offering, our Lord Jesus Christ purposed to institute a remembrance of that his death, and his grace and redemption. The deliverance and exodus from Egypt was a type of his redemption, and in that deliverance a lamb was slain and eaten as a sign of the passover and the blood was sprinkled on the side posts and the upper door posts, all which expressly typified and represented the Lord Jesus Christ. In the same way he himself instituted a remembrance of that deliverance by which he redeemed the whole world, that we might never forget that for our sakes he exposed his body to the ignominy of death, and not merely that we might not forget it in our hearts, but that we might publicly attest it with praise and thanksgiving, joining together for the greater magnifying and proclaiming of the matter in the eating and drinking of the sacrament of his sacred passion, which is a representation of Christ's giving of his body and shedding of his blood for our sakes. And this he signified by the words: 'This is (that is, represents) my body,' just as a wife may say: 'This is my late husband,' when she shows her husband's ring. And when we poor creatures observe this act of thanksgiving amongst ourselves, we all confess that we are of those who believe in the Lord Jesus Christ, and seeing this confession is demanded of us all, all who keep the remembrance or thanksgiving are one body with all other Christians. Therefore if we are the members of his body, it is most necessary that we should live together as Christians, otherwise we are guilty of the body and blood of Christ, as Paul says." And if only the sacrament had been administered after this sort, it would have been impossible for so much unfaithfulness and arrogance and envy and hatred and all manner of tares to take root and to ripen amongst Christian people. Therefore in Zurich we have left the words of Christ unaltered, but we have added some words of explanation to point to the right understanding which was held by Christ and the disciples and the early Church, as already indicated.

May God reveal the truth to us all, and make it dear to us, and never suffer us to fall from it. Amen.

THE FOURTH ARTICLE

In this section we will answer some objections, although only one or two, for those who have followed the expositions already given will be able to make a good answer to any arrogant criticisms.

One objection is as follows: We who know that the flesh and blood are not literally eaten in the sacrament are divided amongst ourselves: the one part saying that Christ's words: "This is my body," mean, This represents my body; the other that they mean: This is a representation of my body. And if we are not agreed about the words of Christ, we do not have the same Spirit.(90) Answer: Note the extraordinary nature of this complaint. For as long as the sense is the same and the words mean the same thing, it does not matter in the least whether different words are used, if only the sense remains the same. For similar differences may be seen not only between the different evangelists and apostles but even in the different writings of the same author. It would take too long to demonstrate this fact, but compare Romans 6 and Colossians 2, where Paul is stating exactly the same view but uses different words. Again, with reference to the wine both Matthew and Mark give this version of the words of institution, "This is my blood of the new testament." But in Paul and Luke the words are as follows: "This cup is the new testament in my blood." Note that the words are not identical and yet the sense remains the same, as we have already seen. And it is the same in our case: what does it matter if the one says: "This bread represents my body," and the other: "This is a representation of my body," so long as it is quite clear that there is no difference in the sense. To such well-worn stratagems do some have recourse, and yet they themselves understand neither the words nor the sense, as we have shown above.

The second objection is on the grounds of I Corinthians 10, which they construe as follows: "The cup of blessing which we bless, is it not the communion of the blood of Christ? The bread which we break, is it not the communion of the body of Christ? For we being many are one bread and one body, for we all partake of the one bread." They think that in this verse Paul says that we partake of the body and blood of Christ. But this he does not do, as we may show unmistakably even from passages in the papal canons. For one thing, it is wrong to translate "blessing" and "bless"—as they construe the word—but what it ought to be is "thanksgiving" and "to give thanks" or to "honour," for that is the true meaning of the Hebrew and the Greek, as we shall now show. The words *barach* and *eulogein* mean "to give thanks" or "to praise," which is also the true sense of the Latin, for the Romans "blessed," that is, honoured those who had made some big contribution to the public good or well-being. For example, in Genesis 47 it says: "And Joseph brought in Jacob his father, and set him before Pharaoh: and Jacob praised Pharaoh, that is, he gave him thanks." Those who are ignorant of the speech-forms of Scripture translate the last words: "And Jacob blessed Pharaoh," but it was far from the purpose of that wise and capable and godly man to bless an unbelieving and idolatrous king who would only have made a mockery of his blessing. The real meaning is: "He praised him," that is, he gave him thanks for all the honour and favours which he had shown to himself and to Joseph and to all his house. Similarly Psalm 145 ought not to be translated: "I will bless thee daily," but, "I will daily give thee praise or thanksgiving." Once we see this point it is easy to understand the word "communion", for we have simply to give it the sense of "community."(91) Now consider the meaning of the words: "The cup of praise or thanksgiving, with which we give praise or thanks, or which we praise, or drink with thanksgiving, is it not the community of the blood of Christ? The bread which we break, is it not the community of the body of Christ? For we are one bread and one body, one company, or community, seeing we all partake of the one bread." It is the aim of Paul to draw the Corinthian Christians away from the worship and sacrifice of idols, and the main point which he makes is this: You are not a community which ought to eat in the company of idol-worshippers: for you are the community of the body and blood of Christ. For when you offer thanks with the cup and the bread, eating and drinking together, you signify thereby that you are one body and one bread, namely, the body which is the Church of Christ, which in this sacrament confesses its faith in the Lord Jesus Christ, who gave his body and blood on our behalf. And Paul calls believers the community of the blood of Christ, as we may see clearly in the words: "For we are one bread and one body, one company, or community, seeing we all partake of the one bread." Note that he quite obviously calls us one bread and one body because we partake together of the one bread. Study Paul afresh and you will see that we are right.

We will now refer to the papacy's own book to show that our interpretation is correct. The paragraph *consecr. di 2 ca. Quia passus est* (92) contains these words of Augustine: (93) "Because the Lord suffered for us, he entrusted his body and blood to us in the sacrament—that is, the remembrance that his body and blood were given for us. And he has made us that body and blood. For we are made his body, and by his grace we have become that which we have received." That is to say, by the grace of God we have received as our Saviour the Son of God according to his human nature, for he became man (John 1). And we have been made his body, for the Church is his body (Col. 1).

Again, in *eadem dist. c. Commendavit*: (94) "In this sacrament Christ entrusted to us his body and blood, and we are made that body and blood: for we have become his body." The other objections have no foundation in the Word of God and are therefore without force.

So much concerning this sacrament, in which we are just as certain that Christ cannot be present bodily as we are that he is bodily seated at the right hand of God: although we have always stated our position with moderation and reserve in order not to give an example of self-assertion in the Church of God. Yet I have no more doubt than I have in the God who made heaven and earth, or in Jesus Christ the true Son of God, that the body of Christ cannot possibly be present in this sacrament unless we are to set aside the articles of the Creed already mentioned. And for that reason I will not make any attack upon that most learned man, Martin Luther, unlike the anonymous writer (95) who in a published work rightly defended me against Luther and Carlstadt.(96)

In this matter, good Christians, do not allow the scholars to entangle you to your own vexation and hurt. For they plunged in at the outset, and now they will neither maintain the truth nor acknowledge their error: for either the Creed must be shattered or our teaching is true. May God give us grace to surrender to the truth and not to defend that which is against God. Amen. Zurich, February 23.

The question of a simple layman:

> Tell me, if thou know'st,
> How Father, Son, and Holy Ghost,
> And bread and wine, and flesh and blood,
> Can all together be one God?

An Exposition of the Faith

INTRODUCTION

The "Exposition of the Faith" was a direct product of the political developments and policies of the closing period of Zwingli's life. In 1529 the Protestant cantons of Zurich and Berne had been involved in a short struggle with the Five Forest Cantons, which rigorously maintained the traditional position.[1] The "war" had ended in an apparent victory for the evangelical party, but the fundamental hostility was resolved neither by conquest nor conciliation.[2] Furthermore, the edict of the Diet of Speier which had preceded the First Peace of Cappel,[3] and the temporary pacification of Europe which immediately succeeded it,[4] created a situation most unfavourable both to the Protestant cause as a whole and to the Reformed party in particular. It was against this threatening background that Zwingli not merely accepted the invitation to try to reach agreement with the Lutherans at Marburg,[5] but took active steps to create a wider anti-imperial alliance. He began by seeking a closer union with Hesse and Venice in the autumn of 1529,[6] and in 1530 he not only made a successful approach to Strassburg but made the first overtures for a far more advantageous alliance with France.[7]

The idea of a French alliance was in basic contradiction with Zwingli's earlier teaching, for in 1522 and again in 1524 he had inveighed bitterly against the Swiss engaging in mercenary service on behalf of the French.[8] At this juncture, however,

[1] Strickler, *Aktensammlung*, II, No. 46 f.
[2] Cf. *Opera*, VIII, p. 296; Bullinger, II, p. 314.
[3] D.C.R. 105.   [4] *Ibid.*, 108.   [5] *Opera*, VIII, p. 286, 662.
[6] *Ibid.*, p. 665.   [7] *Ibid.*, p. 397.
[8] *Zwingli-Hauptschriften*, VII, pp. 1 f., 105 f.

Zwingli's racial prejudices had to yield to political necessities, and the presence of evangelical communities in France encouraged him to hope that first Francis and ultimately the whole country might be won for the Reformed faith. Already in 1525 Zwingli had dedicated his *Commentarius* to Francis, and although the latter had continued his sporadic persecution at home, his rivalry with the Emperor gave him good cause to look more favourably on the Protestant states and municipalities abroad.

Yet Francis had no wish to alienate the papacy by incurring the suspicion of flirtation with dangerous heresy. Accordingly, in pursuance of the suggested understanding, he dispatched Lambert Maigret to Switzerland to conduct preliminary investigations, especially in relation to the faith of the Civic Alliance.[9] When in Zurich Maigret informed Zwingli that Francis had serious doubts concerning the evangelical movement not only from the theological but also from the political and social standpoint. He advised Zwingli to submit to the French Court a clear statement of his beliefs in order to clear away any suspicions or misunderstandings.[10] In the meantime the situation abroad had been steadily deteriorating, for the Diet of Augsburg had enhanced the dominance of Charles, and the eucharistic controversy separated the Swiss from the main Protestant body, even the four cities of the Tetrapolitan Confession preferring to enter into the League of Schmalkald.[11] Faced with the prospect of complete isolation, Zwingli adopted the suggestion of Maigret, and in the early summer of 1531[12] he composed his *Exposition of the Faith* and despatched it to the French Court by the hand of Rudolf Collin, the then professor of Greek at the Minster school and a close friend of Zwingli[13] Whether Francis ever read the work or not is not known,[14] but it certainly had no influence on the course of events, for persecution continued in France and Zurich was unable to stave off the disaster of the Second War of Cappel and the resultant death of Zwingli himself. Indeed, the only result of the *Exposition* was to increase the bitterness already existing between the Lutheran and Zwinglian parties, for Luther was incensed by the inclusion of pious heathen in the

9 *Ibid.*, XI, p. 297.   10 *Loc. cit.*
11 D.C.R. 124.
12 The exact date of composition is not known.
13 *Zwingli-Hauptschriften*, XI, p. 297.
14 The MS. is still preserved in the National Library at Paris.

number of the elect and regarded it as yet another sign of the basic infidelity of his Swiss rival.

The *Exposition* was never published by Zwingli himself, partly perhaps because of the circumstances of its origin, but more particularly because of the supervention of Zwingli's death. The publication was eventually undertaken by Bullinger in February, 1536. The work appeared at the same time at the First Helvetic Confession, and Bullinger no doubt issued it at that time in order to demonstrate his own loyalty to Zwingli's teaching especially in relation to the Lord's Supper.[15] In a preface which he himself contributed he described the *Exposition* as Zwingli's ripest and finest theological study, a kind of "swan-song" before his approaching death. He also appended a further note on the Lord's Supper and the Mass, together with the form of liturgy used by the churches of the Civic Alliance. These are not part of the original and therefore are not included in the present translation.

In form and content the *Exposition* is not unlike the *Fidei ratio*, the apology presented by Zwingli at the Diet of Augsburg.[16] It has the character both of a confession of faith and also of a defence against the slanders and misunderstandings to which he was subjected. The *Exposition* is built up upon the Apostles' Creed, which Zwingli no doubt adopted as a basis in order to demonstrate his essential orthodoxy. He did not touch on all the articles of the Creed, however, but only on those which were particularly apposite to his purpose. Thus he did not say anything at all about the Holy Spirit. On the other hand he devoted a good deal of attention and space to the much controverted topic of the Holy Communion. The arguments used are substantially the same as those presented in greater detail in the treatise on the Supper, but while there is nothing new they are summarized in a convenient and forceful way. Zwingli also introduced a comparatively long section on the question of civil government and a concluding attack upon the Anabaptists. He did this in order to make it quite clear that he did not share either the perverse doctrines or the revolutionary social and political programme which made the Anabaptists an object of fear and suspicion to all governments.

An interesting characteristic of the *Exposition* is its very pronounced humanistic colouring. We see this at once in the opening paragraph upon the doctrine of God, in which Zwingli draws as much from classical philosophy as he does from

[15] *Zwingli-Hauptschriften*, XI, p. 298. [16] *Opera*, IV, pp. 1 f.

specifically biblical and Christian sources. Again, in the section on civil government he bases his teaching upon the analyses made by Aristotle and adduces examples from Scripture only to prove the duties and responsibilities of rulers. The humanistic emphasis reaches its climax in the discussion of eternal life, for not only does Zwingli use a classical argument to rebut Anabaptist teaching concerning the sleep of the soul, but he asserts the salvation of such heroes of antiquity as Hercules, Theseus, Socrates and Aristides.

It can hardly be questioned that the greater humanistic colouring of his work was largely due to Zwingli's desire to win the interest and approval of the French king who was renowned as a patron of the Renaissance. At the same time, it was not entirely a matter of policy, for in all his writings Zwingli gives evidence of the same humanistic influences and interests, and to that extent the *Exposition* reflects a fundamental element in his thinking. The fact is that although Zwingli adopted a more radically Reformed position in sacramental teaching and also in ecclesiastical practice, he did not break so decisively with the scholastic synthesis as did the in some respects more conservative Luther. In the specifically Christian doctrines he made an exclusive appeal to Scripture, but in those matters which are the concern of philosophy as well as theology he was ready to be instructed by reason no less than by revelation. In other words Zwingli was never the consistent theologian of the Word of God that Luther aimed to be, and if it is true that the most vital and interesting aspects in his teaching derive from evangelical sources, it is also the case that his thinking always included a persistent, and fundamentally perhaps an alien, humanistic element.

Yet the point must not be pressed too far, for even in his assertion of the salvation of the pious heathen Zwingli was not departing from his evangelical presuppositions. It is not merely that on occasion Luther too had hinted at a similar possibility, although that is a valid consideration. The real point is that Zwingli could make the assertion because it was congruent with his whole conception of the divine sovereignty and the election of grace. The redemptive purpose and activity of God was not limited by the chronology or the geography of the incarnation and the atonement. The decree of election upon which all salvation depends was a decree from all eternity, enclosing men of all generations within its embrace. Chronologically the patriarchs and pious Israelites preceded the coming of the Saviour, but this did not prevent their salvation by anticipatory faith. Similarly the pious heathen might well be the recipients of divine grace and redemption even though they remained outside the temporal reach of the Gospel. They were not saved because of their piety, but because of the eternal activity of God in election and atonement. The temporality of the Redeemer's life and death did not set any limit to the possibilities of God's eternal grace. In outward form, no doubt, the assertion was determined by Zwingli's humanistic predilections, but its theological foundation was uncompromisingly Reformed.

The case is much the same in relation to Zwingli's doctrine of God. It is true that Zwingli uses concepts and arguments which he had found in classical philosophy, but it is also true that the God to whom he applies them is the living Trinitarian God of the Bible, and that he derives all his faith from belief in that God and the acceptance of his revelation and work. It is upon this that the certainty of Zwingli's faith rests: if truth were simply a matter of human reason then there would be room for endless diversity and error, but when it is something given by God himself, a full assurance is possible. Rational arguments may be used at this or that point either to substantiate the truth or to repudiate error, but in the last analysis reason is employed as the handmaid of truth and not as its mistress.[17]

In his handling of such controverted themes as justification, purgatory and the Church Zwingli does not differ substantially from the other Protestant leaders. He teaches justification by faith, but is careful to point out that the man of true faith will fulfil the works of the law by an inward compulsion. Purgatory is rejected out of hand as inconsistent both with the text of Scripture and also with the scriptural doctrine of justification and forgiveness. The usual evangelical distinction is drawn between the so-called invisible Church, the company of the elect, and the Church visible, which is the outward assembly of those who profess faith in Jesus Christ. There is nothing particularly original or striking in these sections, but the presentation has all the vigour and clarity which characterize Zwingli's writings. It is worth noting, too, that Zwingli makes constant appeal to the texts of Scripture in support of

[17] Since the above was written, G. W. Locher has argued the same point in the first volume of his work *Die Theologie Huldrych Zwinglis im Lichte seiner Christologie*, Zurich, 1952.

his teaching. His handling of Scripture is keen and logical, but at times he seems to miss that larger insight into the biblical message which is so characteristic of Luther.

To sum up: the *Exposition* admirably fulfils the purpose for which it was written. It is a clear and reasonably concise statement of the main doctrinal positions of its author, and it reflects faithfully his interests and methods. Little or nothing is said which had not been said before, but as an epitome of Zwingli's theological teaching it could hardly be bettered.

Editions

The *Exposition of the Faith* was written in Latin, and the original may be found in the Schuler and Schultess edition. There is a German version in the *Volksausgabe* (XI). An English rendering is included in the three-volume translation of selected Latin works of Zwingli published in America (1912-1929). The present version is an independent one based upon the original Latin and German texts.

An Exposition of the Faith (1)

THE TEXT

PREFACE

Of all the things produced by this tempestuous epoch, there is nothing more useful, most pious king, than dangerous *falsehood* falsehood! For one thing, it is only the good seed of the harvest which the author of evil, the devil, is always attempting to choke (Matt. 13:24 f.); for another, the divine husbandman of souls uses wickedness and unbelief to nurture and increase faith and virtue, like the Spartans, who when they had captured a town with much sweat and blood, forbade its utter destruction in order that they might have somewhere to exercise their soldiers in close combat.(2) In the same way, the Lord God allows us too to be threatened in unexpected ways in order that we may be proved usable before him. For how can we learn bravery or temperance except where there is the stress of danger or ample scope for self-indulgence? And so too, now that the truth has begun to raise its head, it shines all the more brightly and boldly by reason of falsehood. For as falsehood attacks her on every side, shooting out its poison upon her, she is forced to rouse herself and to wipe away the poisonous stains and to protect her members. In this way the mask of falsehood and the dear face of truth are the more clearly revealed and illuminated. But I must bring this preface to a close.

I am afraid that by their more than empty and lying insinuations certain faithless persons will attempt to win your clemency.(3) For I know in truth that it can never be exhausted. The more deceitful they are, the more they not only do not reveal but actively defame the truth. And on every possible pretext they charge us with treading religion under foot and despising the holy office and the dignity of kings and magistrates.(4) How little truth there is in all their actions I request

245

your justice to decide when you have heard me expound
as best I can the principles of our faith,(5) the laws and
customs of our churches, and the respect which we offer to
princes.

And nothing is of more concern to a man than to give an
account of his faith. For if faith, as the apostle describes it, is
the strength and assurance and certainty whereby the soul
trusts inflexibly in the unseen God (Hebrews 11: 1), what man
is there so foolish or dullwitted that he cannot explain whether
he believes a thing or not? Especially when faith is the daughter
of truth: for everyone trusts in what he confesses to be the absolute truth. And since God alone is true, if a man has attained
to a knowledge of this in his own experience, how shall he
not be able briefly to describe that trust?

Concerning God and the things of God this is what we hold:

OF GOD AND THE WORSHIP OF GOD

All being is either created or uncreated. God alone is uncreated, for only one thing can be uncreated. For if there were
many uncreated things there would be many eternal: for uncreated and eternal are closely interrelated, so that the one is also
the other. And if there were many eternal things there would
be many infinite, for these too are very similar and interrelated, so that if a thing is eternal it is also infinite, and if it is
infinite it is also eternal. But only one thing can be infinite,
for once we allow that there are two infinite substances, the
one is immediately limited by the other. Hence it is certain
that God alone is uncreated. And this is the origin and source
and basis of the first article of the Creed: when we say, "I
believe in God the Father Almighty, Maker of heaven and
earth," we state emphatically that ours is an infallible faith
because it rests upon the one and only God. Pagans and unbelievers and all those who trust in what is created have to
admit that they may be deceived in their belief or opinion
because they trust in what is created. But those who build
upon the Creator and beginning of all things, who never began
to be but caused all other things to exist, can never fall into
error.(6) Certainly no creature can be the object and basis
of the inflexible and never-wavering power which is faith. For
that which has a beginning at one time did not exist. And when
it did not exist, how could anyone trust in what was not?
That which has a beginning cannot therefore be the natural

object or basis of faith. Only the eternal and infinite and uncreated God is the basis of faith.

Hence the collapse of all that foolish confidence with which
some rely upon most sacred things or the most holy sacraments.(7) For it is in God that we must put our firm and sure
trust. If we were to trust in the creature, the creature would
have to be the Creator. If we were to trust in the sacraments,
the sacraments would have to be God. Not the Eucharist only,
but baptism and the laying on of hands would be God. And
how absurd that is may be judged not merely by scholars but
by all intelligent people. To help divines to the truth we gladly
hold out to them this ray of light. When they maintain that
we are to employ creation but to enjoy (8) only God, they say
exactly the same as we do except in so far as they unwittingly
disregard their own words. For if we are to enjoy only God,
we must trust only in God: we must trust in what we are to
enjoy and not in what we are to employ.

By this, most gracious king, you will see plainly that we do
not disregard or set aside either the saints or the sacraments,
as some falsely allege, but rather that we maintain and keep
them in their proper place and dignity, thus preventing abuse.
We do not dishonour the Mother of God, the Virgin Mary,
simply because we do not allow her to be worshipped (9) in
the same way as God: for if we tried to attribute to her the
dignity and power of the Creator, she herself would not allow
such worship. For true piety is the same everywhere and in all
men, having its source in one and the self-same Spirit. Hence
it is quite unthinkable that any creature should be truly pious
and yet allow the worship which is due to God to be paid to
it. The more highly the Mother of God, the Virgin, is exalted
above all other creatures and the more reverently she is devoted
to God, her Son, the less will she accept that worship which is
due to God alone. For it is the delusion of godless men and
demons to allow divine honours to be accorded to them. This
is demonstrated by the images of demons and the pride of
Herod. The first led the world into error by teaching that they
ought to be worshipped. The second did not refuse the divine
honours paid to him and was stricken by phthiriasis,(10)
that he might learn to recognize the helplessness of man
(Acts 12).

The sacraments we esteem and honour as signs and symbols
of holy things, but not as though they themselves were the
things of which they are the signs. For who is so ignorant as to

try to maintain that the sign is the thing which it signifies? If that were the case I would need only to write the word "ape" and your majesty would have before him a real ape. But the sacraments are signs of real things: things which once took place really, literally (11) and naturally they now (as I say) represent and recall and set before our eyes. Please do not misunderstand me, O king. Christ atoned for our sins by his death: and the Lord's Supper (12) is a commemoration of this fact, as he himself said, "This do in remembrance of me." By this commemoration all the benefits which God has displayed in his Son are called to mind. And by the signs themselves, the bread and wine, Christ himself is as it were set before our eyes, so that not merely with the ear, but with eye and palate we see and taste that Christ whom the soul bears within itself and in whom it rejoices.

As the true reverence for the saints and sacraments we transmit and teach that which Christ himself transmitted and taught. "If ye are the children of Abraham," he said (John 8:39), "do the works of Abraham." This is the example which we should follow in respect of all the saints and all holy men. For instance, if as the mouthpiece (13) of God some prophet or saint has communicated to us divine warnings, we must receive that which is set before us by the Holy Spirit with the same honour as they themselves when they received and imparted it. And if they have adorned their religion with holiness of life, we must follow in their steps and attain the same piety and holiness and purity as they did.

Concerning baptism, he says: "Baptize them in the name of the Father, and of the Son, and of the Holy Ghost." Concerning the Supper, he says: "This do in remembrance of me": and by the mouth of Paul: "We are one bread and one body, the whole multitude of believers." Neither in regard to the reverence of the saints nor the institution of the sacraments is it maintained that they have the power and grace which belong to God alone. But if God himself did not give to created things the power which we ascribe to them, it is clearly frivolous to teach that the saints or the sacraments can remit sins or confer blessings. For who can forgive sins save God alone? Or from whom cometh every perfect gift, as St. James confesses, except from the Father of lights and of every good thing?

We teach therefore that the sacraments should be reverenced as holy things because they signify most holy things, both those which have already happened and those which we ourselves are to produce and do. Thus baptism signifies that Christ has washed us with his blood and also that we are to put on Christ, that is, to follow his example as Paul teaches. Similarly the Supper signifies all the divine favour bestowed upon us in Christ, and also that in thankfulness we are to embrace our brethren with the same love with which Christ has received and redeemed and saved us. The question whether we eat Christ's natural body in the Supper is one which I will discuss more fully later.

To sum up: the source of our religion is to confess that God is the uncreated Creator of all things, and that he alone has power over all things and freely bestows all things. This chief principle of the faith is destroyed by those who ascribe to the creature that which belongs only to the Creator. For in the Creed (14) we confess that we believe in the Creator. Therefore it cannot be the creature in whom we are to believe.

Moreover, we think of God as follows: Since we know that God is the source and Creator of all things, we cannot conceive of anything before or beside him which is not also of him. For if anything could exist which was not of God, God would not be infinite: he would not extend to where that other is, seeing that it exists apart from him. In the Scriptures, as we see, Father, Son, and Holy Ghost are all described as God, but they are not creatures or different gods, but the three are all one, one essence, one *ousia* or existence, one power and might, one knowledge and providence, one goodness and loving-kindness. There are three names or persons, but each and all are one and the self-same God.

We know that this God is good by nature, for whatever he is he is by nature. But goodness is both mercy and justice. (15) Deprive mercy of justice, and it is no longer mercy, but indifference or timidity. But fail to temper justice by kindness and forbearance and at once it becomes the greatest injustice and violence. Therefore when we confess that God is good by nature, we confess that he is both loving, kind and gracious, and also holy, just and impassible. But if he is just and righteous, necessarily he must abhor all contact with evil. Hence it follows that we mortals cannot have any hope of fellowship or friendship with him, since we are not only guilty of sin, but actually participate in it. On the other hand, if he is good, he must necessarily temper every resolve and act with equity and grace.

It was for this reason that he clothed his only Son with flesh, not merely to reveal to, but actually to bestow upon, the whole earth both salvation and renewal. For inasmuch as his goodness, that is, his justice and mercy, is impassible, that is, steadfast and immutable, his justice required atonement, but his mercy forgiveness, and forgiveness newness of life. Clothed therefore with flesh, for according to his divine nature he cannot die, the Son of the Most High King offered up himself as a sacrifice to placate irrevocable justice and to reconcile it with those who because of their consciousness of sin dared not enter the presence of God on the ground of their own righteousness. He did this because he is kind and merciful, and these virtues can as little permit the rejection of his work as his justice can allow escape from punishment. Justice and mercy were conjoined, the one furnishing the sacrifice, the other accepting it as a sacrifice for all sin.

From what class of creatures could such a sacrifice be chosen? From angels? But how did man's transgression concern them? Or from men? But all men were guilty before God, so that if any man had been selected to make the sacrifice, he would have been unable to do so because of original sin. For the lamb which typified this sacrifice had to be without blemish, that is, absolutely sound and pure and spotless. Therefore the divine goodness took of itself what it would give to us: for God clothed his Son in the frailty of our flesh in order that we might see that his grace and mercy are no less supreme than his holiness and justice. For he who has given us himself, what has he not given us, as St. Paul declares (Rom. 8:32)? Had he made an angel or man the sacrifice for sin, the gift would have been outside himself. There would always have been something greater that he could have given but had not given, that is, himself.(16)

Therefore when supreme Goodness willed to give the supreme gift, it gave the most costly of all its treasures, namely itself, so that the soul of man which is always seeking that which is greater should not be able to wonder how it is that the sacrifice of angel or man can have sufficient value to avail for all, or how it is possible to put undisputed trust in any creature. Thus the Son of God is given to us as a confirmation of mercy, a pledge of grace, a requital of justice and an example of life, to assure us of the grace of God and to give us the law of true conduct. Who can sufficiently estimate the magnanimity of the divine goodness and mercy? We had merited rejection, and he adopts us as heirs. We had destroyed the way of life, and he

has restored it. The divine goodness has so redeemed and
restored us that we are full of thanks for his mercy and just and
blameless by reason of his atoning sacrifice.

OF THE LORD CHRIST

We believe and teach that this Son of God, who is of God,
so took to himself the nature of man that his divine nature was
not destroyed or changed into that of man: but that each nature
is present truly, properly and naturally: his divine nature
has not in any way been diminished so as not to be truly,
properly and naturally God. Nor has his human nature passed
into the divine so that he is not truly, properly and naturally
man, except in so far as he is without the propensity to sin.
According to his divine nature, in every respect he is God with
the Father and the Holy Spirit, not forfeiting any of the divine
attributes by the assumption of human weakness. And according to his human nature he is in every way man, having all
the properties which belong to the true and proper nature of
man save only the propensity of sin, and not lacking any of them
by reason of union with the divine nature.

Hence the attitudes and properties of both natures are
reflected in all his words and works, so that the pious mind is
able to see without difficulty which is to be accredited to
each,(17) although everything is rightly ascribed to the one
Christ. It is quite correct to say that Christ hungered, for he is
both God and man: yet he did not hunger according to his
divine nature. It is quite correct to say that Christ healed all
manner of sickness and all manner of disease: yet if you consider it more closely, this is something which concerns the
divine power and not the human. But the difference of natures
does not involve a division of the person any more than when
we say that a man thinks and yet also sleeps. For although
the power of thought belongs only to the mind and the need
of sleep to the body, yet the man does not consist of two persons,
but one. For the unity of the person continues in spite of the
diversity of the natures.(18)

And everywhere we confess that God and Man are one
Christ, just as man subsists of a reasonable soul and an earthly
body, as St. Athanasius taught.(19) But Christ assumed the
nature of man into the hypostasis (20) or person of the Son
of God. It is not as though the humanity taken by him was one
person and his eternal deity another, but the person of the

eternal Son of God assumed humanity in and by its own power, as holy men of God have truly and clearly shown.

We believe that this human nature was received when the Holy Spirit quickened the Virgin, being manifested without any violation of her virginity, (21) that the redeemer and healer of souls might be born into the world of a virgin-mother, he who from all eternity was Lord and God begotten of the Father without mother, to be a holy and spotless sacrifice, to whom the smoke of beast-laden altars ascended in vain. And on his account men should cease from offering up beasts and be moved to offer spiritual sacrifices, seeing that God has himself prepared and offered up for them the sacrifice of his own Son.

We believe that Christ suffered, being nailed to the cross under Pilate the governor. But it was only the man who felt the pangs of suffering, and not God, for God is invisible, (22) and therefore is not subject to any pain, that is, suffering or passion. The cry of pain (23) is this: "My God, my God, why hast thou forsaken me?" But, "Forgive them, for they know not what they do," that is the voice of inviolable deity. To make atonement for our sins he suffered the most ignominious form of execution, so that there is no humiliation which he has not experienced and borne.

If he had not died and been buried, who would believe that he is very Man? And for the same reason the apostolic Fathers added to the Creed the words, "He descended into hell." They used this expression periphrastically, to signify the reality of his death—for to be numbered amongst those who have descended into hell means to have died—and also to make it clear that the power of his atonement penetrates even to the underworld. (24) This is confirmed by St. Peter when he says that the Gospel was preached to the dead, that is, to those in Hades who from the beginning of the world had believed the divine warnings, like Noah, even when the wicked had despised them. On the other hand, if he had not risen again to newness of life, who would have believed that he is very God, having been put to death and being without life or power? Therefore we believe that according to his human nature the very Son of God truly died to give us assurance of the expiation of our sins. But we also believe that he truly rose again from the dead, to give us the assurance of eternal life. For all that Christ is is ours and all that he does is ours. For God so loved the world that he gave his only begotten Son that he might give us life. If he rose again, he rose again for us, thereby initiating our resurrection. Hence Paul describes him as the *Paul* first-fruits of them that slept, that is, of the dead. For if he lives who was dead, he makes it plain that we shall live though we die. In Hebrew the word "to rise again" strictly means "to remain", "continue" or "endure". Therefore Paul's argument has a double bearing. Even when he was thought to be dead Christ rose again, that is, he lived, and again assumed his body. *resurrection* And if that is the case, then undoubtedly there is a resurrection of the dead.

Notice, most courteous sovereign, that the force of the affirmation is in the fact that Christ and all his work is ours. Otherwise it would no more follow to say: Christ rose again, therefore we shall rise, than it would to say: The king has power to pardon the sentenced, therefore everyone has the same power. But the converse is that if Christ is not risen, we shall not rise. For Christ can live and rise of his own power, which we cannot do. There cannot then be any doubt that he allows us and all men to participate in the power of his resurrection. That is what the holy Fathers had in view when they said that the body of Christ nourishes us to the resurrection.(25) They simply wanted to show that if Christ is altogether ours (26) and he rose again, we are assured that when we die in the body we too shall live on in the spirit and that one day we shall live again with the same body. And inasmuch as this Christ of ours ascended into heaven and is seated at the right hand of the Father (as we firmly believe) we have the promise that we too who ascend up thither the moment we die shall one day enjoy there eternal felicity in the body. And as he is seated there until he comes again to judge the whole earth, so our souls and the souls of all the blessed are with him apart from the body until the judgment. And when the judgment begins we shall again put on the garment of the body which we had laid aside, and with it we shall go either to the eternal marriage-feast of our bridegroom or to the everlasting torment of the enemy, the devil.

At this point, most gracious king, I will give my opinion on two further questions:

OF PURGATORY

The first is that since Christ did not suffer the pains of hell, as St. Peter teaches in Acts 2, but after his death ascended up into heaven, so we when we are freed from the body shall go up thither without any delay, postponement or renewed affliction if only we have maintained our faith inviolable. Hence those who have held the threat of purgatorial torment over men who are already quite wretched enough without it have been far more concerned to satisfy their own greed than to feed the souls of the faithful.

For first, they utterly invalidate and reject the work of Christ. If Christ died for our sins (as he himself taught, and so too did apostles imbued with his Spirit, and as the doctrine of our religion obliges us to confess, since it tells us that salvation is by the grace and goodness of God), then how can we allow any man to force us to make satisfaction for ourselves? According to the judgment of Paul, those who trust in works know nothing of Christ. How much more is Christ compromised and injured by those who teach that sin must be atoned by our own sufferings. For if good works could not merit salvation, but suffering does, the goodness of God is called in question, as if God took pleasure in affliction and distress and refused to know anything of gentleness and pity.

Second, if Christ does not bear the punishment and penalty incurred by our sins, why did he become man and to what purpose did he suffer? The distinction made by some theologians, that we are redeemed only from guilt and not from punishment, is a frivolous invention, and indeed insulting to God. For no human judge will inflict a penalty where there is no guilt. Once the guilt is pardoned by God, the penalty is also remitted.

Third, inasmuch as Christ himself taught that those who believe in him have eternal life, and that those who believe in him that sent him will not come into condemnation but have already passed from death to life, it is manifest that the period of purgatorial torment laid by the papists upon the souls of those who depart this life is a figment of their own invention.

The Presence of the Body of Christ in the Supper

The second thing which I have undertaken to expound at this point is this, that in the Lord's Supper the natural and essential body of Christ in which he suffered and is now seated in heaven at the right hand of God is not eaten naturally and literally but only spiritually, and that the papist teaching that the body of Christ is eaten in the same form and with the same properties and nature as when he was born and suffered and died is not only presumptuous and foolish but impious and blasphemous.

First, it is quite certain that Christ became a true man consisting of body and soul and in all points like as we are except for the propensity to sin.(27) Hence it follows that all the endowments and properties which belong to our physical nature were most truly present in his body. For what he assumed for our sake derives from what is ours, so that he is altogether ours, as we have explained already. But if this is the case it follows indisputably, first, that the properties of our bodies belong also to his body, and second, that the properties of Christ's body are also peculiar to our bodies. For if his body possessed something physical which is lacking to ours, it would at once give rise to the impression that he had not assumed it for our sake. But *Athanasius* why then did he assume it? for in the whole realm of the physical only man is capable of eternal blessedness.

That is why we mentioned earlier that Paul proves our own resurrection by Christ's and Christ's by ours. For when he says: "If the dead rise not, then is Christ not raised," how else *Par.* can his argument be valid? For since Christ is both God and man, it might be objected at once: You are beside yourself,(28) theologian. For Christ's body can and must rise again, being conjoined with his divinity. But our bodies are not able to rise again, because they are not united with God. But Paul's argument is valid for this reason, that whatever nature and endowments and properties the body of Christ may have, it has as an archetype for us. Hence it follows: Christ's body rose again, therefore our bodies shall rise. We rise again, therefore Christ is risen.

It was from these sources that that pillar of theologians, Augustine, drew when he said that the body of Christ has to be in some particular place in heaven by reason of its character as a true body. And again: Seeing that the body of Christ rose from the dead, it is necessarily in one place. The body of Christ is not in several places at one and the same time any more than *apostolic* our bodies are.(29) This is not our view, but that of the apostles and Augustine and the faith in general: for even if we had no witnesses to it, it would be proved by the fact that Christ became in all points like as we are. For for our sake he took to himself human frailty and was found in fashion as a man, that is, in endowments, attributes and properties. In this way, most excellent king, I believe that incidentally I will have

made it plain to you with what injustice we are branded as
heretics in respect of the sacrament of the Lord's Supper,
although we never taught a single word that we have not taken
from Holy Scripture or the Fathers.

But I return to my main theme. On the basis of Holy Scripture it is established that the body of Christ must truly,
naturally and properly be in one place (unless, of course, we
hazard the foolish and impious assertion that our bodies too
are in several places). But if this is the case, our adversaries (30)
must allow that according to its proper essence the body of
Christ is truly and naturally seated at the right hand of the
Father. It cannot therefore be present in this way in the Supper:
if anyone teaches the contrary, he drags Christ down from
heaven and from his Father's throne. For all scholars have
condemned as untenable and impious the view which some
have ventured to assert, that the body of Christ is no less omnipresent than his divinity. For only that which is infinite can be
omnipresent, and that which is infinite is eternal. The humanity
of Christ is not eternal, therefore it is not infinite. If it is not
infinite, it is necessarily finite. And if it is finite, it is not omnipresent. But leaving these matters, which I have introduced
only to meet the requirements of such philosophical reflection
as may happen to engage you, O king, I will now turn to
the unassailable testimonies of Scripture.

I have already made it sufficiently plain that in Holy Scripture all the references to Christ relate to the whole and un-
divided Christ, even when it can easily be seen to which nature
the saying applies. Christ is never divided into two natures,
although that which is proper to each nature is ascribed to it.
For the possession of two natures does not destroy the unity of
the person, as is shown in the case of man. And conversely,
even though that which is proper to his divinity is ascribed to
his humanity, and that which is proper to his humanity is
ascribed to his divinity, yet the two natures are not confused,
as though the divinity had deteriorated and degenerated into
humanity or the humanity had been transformed into divinity.
We must now make this clearer by the testimonies of Scripture.
"And she brought forth her first-born son and laid him in a
manger." The unity of the person has never been used as an
argument against the fact that Christ became very man and
was born of the Virgin. That is why in my judgment it is right
that the Virgin should be called the Mother of God,
Θεότοκος.(31) Yet the Father alone begat his divine nature,

just as in the case of man the mother bears the body but God alone begets the soul.(32) Yet a man is said to be born of his parents. Again, the fact that the one who controls both heaven and earth was laid in a manger also applies to his humanity. But it does not give rise to any difficulty if his being born and laid in a manger are referred to the whole Christ, on account of the agreement and conjunction of the two natures in the one person.

"He ascended into heaven." This relates primarily to his humanity, although the humanity was not borne up thither without the divinity: it was the latter which bore and the former which was borne. As we have already said, the humanity continues finite, otherwise it would cease to be true humanity. But the divinity is always infinite and unfettered: therefore it does not move about from place to place but remains eternally the same.

"Lo, I am with you even unto the end of the world." This refers primarily to his divinity, for his humanity has gone up into heaven.

"Again, I leave the world and go to the Father." Truth itself compels us to refer this saying primarily and quite literally to Christ's humanity. For it is God who says it, and what he says must be true. Which nature is it that leaves the world? Not the divine, for the divine nature is not confined to one place and therefore does not leave it. Consequently it is the human nature which leaves the world. You will see then, O king, that as regards a natural, essential and localized presence the humanity is not here, for it has left the world. Hence the body of Christ is not eaten by us naturally or literally, much less quantitatively, but sacramentally (33) and spiritually.

"Henceforth I shall not be in the world." This is the true signification of the phrase, καὶ οὐκ ἔτι εἰμὶ ἐν τῷ κόσμῳ, "now I am no more in the world." And it completely dispels any mists of uncertainty. Inasmuch as he is man, Christ is not to be expected in the world with a natural, essential and corporal presence, but only with a spiritual and sacramental.

"Ye men of Galilee, why stand ye gazing up into heaven? This same Jesus, which is taken up from you into heaven, shall so come in like manner as ye have seen him go into heaven." This passage shows us clearly that he was taken up from the disciples into heaven. He has gone away, therefore, and is not here. But how did he go away? Corporally and naturally, and according to the essence of his humanity. Therefore when they say, "He shall so come in like manner," it means corporally, naturally and essentially. But when shall he so come? Not when the Church celebrates the Supper, but when she is judged by him at the last day. Therefore the view is irreligious which maintains that the body of Christ is eaten in the Supper physically, naturally, essentially, and even quantitatively, for it is not in agreement with the truth, and that which is opposed to the truth is impious and irreligious.

Your nimble wit is quick to seize a matter, and I believe that these few brief remarks will be sufficient to show you that by the Lord's own words we are forced to enquire in what sense the body of Christ is present in the Supper. I have frequently treated of the same theme in innumerable writings addressed to various persons, indeed Oecolampadius and I have been engaged in lengthy disputes which it would be tedious to recount. (34) But the truth emerges victorious and is daily advancing. I will simply show what it is to eat spiritually and sacramentally, and then I will leave the matter.

To eat the body of Christ spiritually is equivalent to trusting with heart and soul upon the mercy and goodness of God through Christ, that is, to have the assurance of an unbroken faith that God will give us the forgiveness of sins and the joy of eternal salvation for the sake of his Son, who gave himself for us and reconciled the divine righteousness to us. For what can he withhold from us when he delivered up his only begotten Son?

If I may put it more precisely, to eat the body of Christ sacramentally is to eat the body of Christ with the heart and the mind in conjunction with the sacrament. I will make everything clear to your highness, O king. You eat the body of Christ spiritually, but not sacramentally, every time your soul puts the anxious question: "How are you to be saved? We sin every day, and every day we draw nearer to death. After this life there is another, for if we have a soul and it is concerned about the future, how can it be destroyed with this present life? How can so much light and knowledge be turned into darkness and oblivion? Therefore if the soul has eternal life, what sort of life will be the portion of my poor soul? A life of joy or a life of anguish? I will examine my life and consider whether it deserves joy or anguish."

But when you think of all the things which we men habitually do either in passion or desire, you will be terrified, and so far as your own righteousness is concerned, in your own judgment you will declare yourself undeserving of eternal salvation and will completely despair of it. But then you assure your anxious spirit: "God is good: and he who is good must necessarily be righteous and merciful and kind. For justice without kindness or mercy is the height of injustice, and mercy without justice is indifference and caprice and the end of all order. If God is just, his justice demands atonement for my sins. But because he is merciful I cannot despair of pardon. Of both these things I have an infallible pledge, his only begotten Son our Lord Jesus Christ, whom of his own mercy God has given to us that he might be ours. On our behalf he has sacrificed himself to the Father to reconcile his eternal justice, that we might have assurance both of the mercy of God and of the atonement made to his justice for our sins by none other than his only begotten Son, whom of his love he gave to us." When your soul is troubled by anxiety and despair, confirm it with this confidence: "Why are you cast down, O my soul? The God who alone gives salvation is yours, and you are his. You were his handiwork and creation, and you fell and perished. But he sent his Son and made him like yourself, except only for sin, that resting on all the rights and privileges of so great a brother and companion you might have boldness to lay claim to eternal salvation. What devil can frighten or terrify me when this helper stands by me to assist? Who can rob me of that which God himself has given, sending his own Son as pledge and surety"? When you comfort yourself in Christ in this way, then you spiritually eat his body, that is, trusting in the humanity which he assumed for your sake, you stand unafraid in God against all the onslaughts of despair.

So then, when you come to the Lord's Supper to feed spiritually upon Christ, and when you thank the Lord for his great favour, for the redemption whereby you are delivered from despair, and for the pledge whereby you are assured of eternal salvation, when you join with your brethren in partaking of the bread and wine which are the tokens of the body of Christ, then in the true sense of the word you eat him sacramentally. You do inwardly that which you represent outwardly, your soul being strengthened by the faith which you attest in the tokens.

But of those who publicly partake of the visible sacraments or signs, yet without faith, it cannot properly (35) be said that they eat sacramentally. By partaking they call down judgment upon themselves, that is, divine punishment, for they do not honour the body of Christ, that is, the whole mystery of the incarnation and passion, and indeed the Church of Christ, as the faithful have always done, and rightly so. For we ought to examine ourselves before we partake, that is, we ought to search our hearts and ask ourselves whether we have confessed and received Christ as the Son of God our Redeemer and Saviour, so that we trust only in him as the infallible author and giver of salvation; and whether we rejoice in the fact that we are members of that Church of which Christ is the head. For if we join with the Church in the Lord's Supper as though we held this faith, but falsely, are we not guilty of the body and blood of the Lord? Not as eaten naturally and corporally, but because we have falsely testified to the church that we have partaken spiritually when there has been no spiritual partaking. Those who make use of the signs of thanksgiving, but without faith, receive as it were sacramentally. But they are judged more severely than other unbelievers because they act as though they do receive the Lord's Supper while the rest ignore it. For those who celebrate the Supper feignedly are guilty of the two-fold sin of unbelief and presumption, while unbelievers perish like fools simply because of their unbelief.

Now for some time there has been bitter contention amongst us as to what the sacraments or signs themselves either do or can do in the Supper. Our adversaries (36) allege that the sacraments give faith, mediate the natural body of Christ, and enable us to eat it as substantially present. But we have good cause to think otherwise.

First, because no external things but only the Holy Spirit can give that faith which is trust in God. The sacraments do give faith, but only historical faith.(37) All celebrations, monuments and statues give historical faith, that is, they remind us of some event, refreshing the memory like the feast of the passover amongst the Hebrews or the remission of debts at Athens,(38) or it may be that they commemorate some victory like the stone at Ebenezer.

Now the Lord's Supper, too, does create faith in this way, that is, it bears sure witness to the birth and passion of Christ. But to whom does it bear witness? To believers and unbelievers alike. For whether they receive it or not, it testifies to all that which is of the power of the sacrament, the fact that Christ suffered. But only to the faithful and pious does it testify that he suffered for us. For it is only those who have been taught inwardly by the Spirit to know the mystery of the divine goodness who can know and believe that Christ suffered for us: it is they alone who receive Christ. For no one comes to Christ except the Father draw him. And Paul settles the whole dispute with a single word when he says: "Let a man examine himself and so let him eat of that bread and drink of that cup." Therefore if we are to examine ourselves before we come, it is quite impossible that the Supper should give faith: for faith must be present already before we come.

Second, we oppose the erroneous teaching of our adversaries when they argue that the natural body of Christ is presented to us in the symbols because that is the force and effect of the words: "This is my body." The argument is met by the words of Christ already adduced, which deny the continued presence of his body in the world. And if that was the force of the words, the body presented would be his passible body. For when he spoke the words he still had a mortal body: hence the disciples partook of his mortal body. For he did not possess two bodies, the one immortal and impassible, the other mortal. And if the apostles ate his mortal body, which do we eat? Naturally, the mortal body. But the body which once was mortal is now immortal and incorruptible. Therefore it follows that if we eat his mortal body he necessarily has a body which is both mortal and immortal. But this is impossible: for the body cannot at one and the same time be both mortal and immortal. Therefore he must have two bodies, the one mortal, which both we and the apostles eat, and the other immortal, which remains at the right hand of God. Otherwise we are forced to say that the apostles ate the mortal body but we the immortal. And that is plainly ridiculous.

Finally, we oppose our adversaries when they assert that it is the present, natural and essential body of Christ which is eaten: an assertion which is clean contrary to all religion. At the miraculous draught of fishes, when Peter became aware of the presence of Christ in divine power, he said, "Depart from me, for I am a sinful man, O Lord," for he was astonished. And do we desire to feed on his natural body like cannibals? As if anyone loved his children in such a way that he wished to devour and eat them. Or as if cannibals were not regarded as the most bestial of men. The centurion said: "I am not worthy that thou shouldest come under my roof." But Christ himself testified concerning him that he had not found so great faith, no, not in Israel. The greater and holier faith is, the more it is content to feed spiritually. And the more content it is with spiritual feeding, the more does the pious heart recoil from physical feeding. Ministering women used to honour the body of the Lord by washing and anointing it, not by feeding upon it. The noble councillor, Joseph of Arim, and the pious secret disciple, Nicodemus, wrapped it in spices and linen clothes and laid it in the sepulchre: they did not partake of it naturally and physically.

Of the Virtue of the Sacraments

These difficulties make it evident, O king, that even under the guise of piety we ought not to ascribe either to the Supper or to baptism anything that might jeopardize religion and truth. But does that mean that the sacraments have no virtue or power at all?

The first virtue: they are sacred and venerable things instituted and received by the great High Priest Christ himself. For not only did he institute baptism, but he himself received it. And he not only commanded us to celebrate the Supper, but he himself celebrated it first.

The second virtue: they testify to historical facts. Of all laws, customs and institutions it may be said that they proclaim their authors and origins. Therefore if baptism proclaims symbolically the death and resurrection of Christ, it follows that these events did actually take place.

The third virtue: they take the place, and name, of that which they signify. The passover or sparing in which God spared the children of Israel cannot itself be exhibited to us, but the lamb takes its place as a sign of the passover. Similarly, the body of Christ and all that happened in relation to it cannot be exhibited to us, but its place is taken by the bread and wine which we consume instead.

Fourth: they represent high things. The value of all signs increases according to the value of that which they signify. If it is something great and precious and sublime, the sign is all the more highly valued. The ring (39) with which your majesty was betrothed to the queen your consort is not valued by her merely according to the value of the gold: it is gold, but it is also beyond price, because it is the symbol of her royal husband. For that reason she regards it as the king of all her rings, and if ever she is naming and valuing her jewels she will say: This is my king, that is, the ring with which my royal husband was betrothed to me. It is the sign of an indissoluble union and fidelity. In the same way the bread and wine are the symbols of that friendship by which God is reconciled to the human race in and through his Son. We do not value them according to their intrinsic worth, but according to the greatness of that which they represent. The bread is no longer common, but consecrated. It is called bread, but it is also called the body of Christ. Indeed, it is in fact the body of Christ, but only in name and signification, or, as we now say, sacramentally.

The fifth virtue is the analogy (40) between the signs and the things signified. In the Supper there is a twofold analogy. The first is to Christ. For as the bread supports and sustains human life, and wine makes glad the heart of man, so Christ alone sustain and supports and rejoices the soul when it has no other hope. For who is the man who can yield to despair when he sees that the Son of God is his, and he guards him in his soul like a treasure, and for his sake he can ask anything of the Father? The second analogy is to ourselves. For as bread is made up of many grains and wine of many grapes, so by a common trust in Christ which proceeds from the one Spirit the body of the Church is constituted and built up out of many members a single body, to be the true temple and body of the indwelling Spirit.

The sixth: the sacraments augment faith and are an aid to it. This is particularly true of the Supper. You know, O king, how continually our faith is tested and tempted, for the devil sifts us like wheat, as he did the apostles. And how does he attack us? By treachery within: for he sets up the scaling-ladders of passion against our senses, and then he tries to overthrow us by way of the body as by an ancient and crumbling part of the wall. But when the senses are called away elsewhere so that they do not give ear to the tempter his attack is less successful. Now in the sacraments the senses are not only turned aside from the enticements of the devil, but they are pledged to faith, so that like handmaidens they do nothing but what is commanded and done by their master faith. Hence they support and strengthen faith. I will speak openly and freely. In the Supper the four most important senses, indeed all the senses, are at once released and redeemed from the desires of the flesh and placed under the obedience of faith.

With the hearing it is no longer the music of strings and the harmony of varied sounds that we hear, but the heavenly voice: "God so loved the world that he gave his only-begotten

Son for its life." And we are present there as brothers to give thanks for this benefit towards us. For we rightly do this at the command of the Son himself who when he approached his death instituted this thanksgiving as a perpetual memory and pledge of his love for us. And he took bread, and gave thanks, and brake it, and gave it to his disciples, uttering from his most holy lips the sacred words: "This is my body." "Likewise after Supper he took the cup," etc. I say, when the hearing receives things of this nature, is it not completely dumbfounded, and in its astonishment does it not pay heed to the one thing which is proclaimed: hearing as it does of God and of God's love, that the Son was delivered up to death for us. And when it pays heed in this way, does it not do what faith does? For faith rests upon God through Christ. Therefore if hearing looks in the same direction, it is the servant of faith, and it no longer hinders it by its own frivolous imaginings and exertions.

With the sight we see the bread and wine which in Christ's stead signify his goodness and favourable disposition. Is it not therefore the handmaid of faith? For it sees Christ before it as it were, and the soul is enflamed by his beauty and loves him most dearly. With the sense of touch we take the bread into our hands and in signification it is no longer bread but Christ. And there is also a place for taste and smell in order that we may taste and see how good the Lord is and how blessed is the man that trusts in him: for just as these senses take pleasure in food and are stimulated by it, so the soul exults and rejoices when it tastes the sweet savour of heavenly hope.

Thus the sacraments assist the contemplation of faith and conjoin it with the strivings of the heart, which is something that could not happen to the same degree or with the same harmony apart from the use of the sacraments. In baptism sight and hearing and touch are all claimed for the work of faith. For whether the faith be that of the Church or of the person baptized, it perceives that Christ endured death for the sake of his Church and that he rose again victorious. And that is what we hear and see and feel in baptism. Hence the sacraments are like bridles which serve to check the senses when they are on the point of dashing off in pursuit of their own desires, and to recall them to the obedience of the heart and of faith.

The seventh virtue of the sacraments is that they act as an oath of allegiance. For in Latin the word *sacramentum* is used of an oath. And those who use the same oaths are made one race and alliance, coming together as one body and one people, to betray which is perjury. So, too, the people of Christ are brought together as one body by the sacramental partaking of his body. And if anyone presumes to intrude into that fellowship without faith, he betrays the body of Christ both in its head and also in its members, for he does not discern, that is, he does not rightly value the body of Christ either as he delivered it up to death for us or as it was redeemed by death.(41) For we are one body with him.

Therefore whether we like it or not, we are forced to concede that the words: "This is my body," cannot be taken naturally or literally, but have to be construed symbolically, sacramentally, metaphorically or as a metonymy,(42) thus: "This is my body," that is, "This is the sacrament of my body," or, "This is my sacramental or mystical body," that is, the sacramental and representative symbol of the body which I really assumed and yielded over to death.

But it is now time to proceed lest by forgetting brevity I offend your majesty. However, what I have said so far is so sure, most noble king, that although many have attempted a refutation none has ever been able to shake it. Do not be disturbed, therefore, if some who are more ready with their tongues than they are with unassailable Scriptures proscribe this view as impious. They boast of the fact with bold but empty words, yet when the matter is investigated they have no more value than the sloughed off skin of a serpent.(43)

The Church

We also believe that there is one holy, catholic, that is, universal Church, and that this Church is either visible or invisible. According to the teaching of Paul, the invisible Church is that which came down from heaven,(44) that is to say, the Church which knows and embraces God by the enlightenment of the Holy Spirit. To this Church belong all who believe the whole world over. It is not called invisible because believers are invisible, but because it is concealed from the eyes of men who they are: for believers are known only to God and to themselves.

And the visible Church is not the Roman pontiff and others who bear the mitre, but all who make profession of faith in Christ the whole world over.(45) In this number there are those who are called Christians falsely, seeing they have no inward faith. Within the visible Church, therefore, there are some who are not members of the Church elect and invisible. For in the Supper there are some who eat and drink to their own condemnation, although their brethren do not know who they are. Consequently the visible Church contains within itself many who are insolent and hostile, thinking nothing of it if they are excommunicated a hundred times, seeing they have no faith. Hence there arises the need of government for the punishment of flagrant sinners, whether it be the government of princes or that of the nobility.(46) For the higher powers do not bear the sword in vain. Seeing, then, that there are shepherds in the Church, and amongst these we may number princes, as may be seen from Jeremiah, it is evident that without civil government a Church is maimed and impotent. Far from undermining authority, most pious king, or advocating its dissolution, as we are accused of doing,(47) we teach that authority is necessary to the completeness of the body of the Church. But consider briefly our teaching on this subject.

GOVERNMENT

The Greeks reckon three kinds of government and their threefold corruption. The first is monarchy, in Latin kingship, in which the control of affairs is vested in one man according to the direction of piety and equity. The antithesis and corruption of this is tyranny, which the Romans describe rather less aptly as force or violence, or because there is no proper word in Latin they usually borrow the Greek word *tyrannis*. This arises when piety is despised, justice is trampled underfoot, all things are done by force, and the one who stands at the head rules by caprice.

Next, they recognize aristocracy—in Latin the rule of the best people—in which the best possible men are in charge of the state and maintain justice and piety amongst the people. When this form is corrupted it becomes an oligarchy—which the Romans aptly describe as the rule of the few. In this case a small number of nobles rises up and seizes power, not with a view to the public good but to their own advantage, subjugating the state and using it to accomplish their own ends.

Finally they recognize democracy—which the Romans call "republic," although this word has a broader meaning than democracy—in which the state, that is, the direction of affairs is in the hands of the public or the whole people, and all administrative offices and honours and posts of responsibility are under

the control of the whole people. When this form is corrupted
the Greeks call it conspiracy or tumult,(48) that is, uproar,
sedition and disturbance, in which all restraint is thrown off
and obedience is given to the individual will rather than to the
authority of the state, an authority which each individual
claims for himself, seeing he is a member and part of the whole
people. In this way there arise unlawful conspiracies and
factions, which are followed by murder, plunder, injustice and
all the evil results of treason and riot.

The distinctions made by the Greeks in respect of government we recognize and commend as follows: If the ruler is a
king or prince, we teach that he must be obeyed and honoured
according to the command of Christ: "Render unto Caesar
the things that are Caesar's, and unto God the things that are
God's." For by Caesar we understand every ruler to whom
authority has been given or transferred either by right of
descent or by election and custom. But if the king or prince
becomes a tyrant we set a limit to his pretension and censure it
in season and out of season. For that is what the Lord says to
Jeremiah: "See, I have set thee over the nations and over the
kingdoms." If he pays heed to the warning, we have gained a
father for the whole kingdom and country: but if he resorts
all the more to overweening violence we teach that although
his acts are wicked he must still be obeyed until the Lord removes him from the seat of authority or a way is found whereby
those whose duty it is may deprive him of his functions and
restore order. In the same way we are alert and vigilant lest
aristocracy or democracy should begin to degenerate into
conspiracy and confusion.

We have examples in Scripture to illustrate what we teach
and demand. Samuel bore with Saul until the Lord took away
both his kingdom and his life. David returned to a right judgment when he was rebuked by Nathan, and in spite of many
attacks he retained his throne. Ahab and his wife both for-
feited their lives because they would not turn from their godless
way at the rebuke of Elijah. Herod was boldly censured by
John because he did not feel the least shame at his incestuous
union. However, it would take too long to adduce all the
examples from Scripture. Those who are learned and pious
will know that what we say derives from this source.

To sum up: In the Church of Christ government and prophecy (49) are both necessary, although the latter takes precedence. For just as man is necessarily constituted of both

body and soul, the body being the lesser and humbler part,(50) so there can be no Church without government, although government supervises and controls those more mundane circumstances which are far removed from the things of the Spirit.

For that reason, if the two brightest luminaries of our faith, Jeremiah and Paul, both command us to pray the Lord for the powers that be, that we may be enabled to live a godly life,(51) how much more is it the duty of all men in the different kingdoms and peoples to attempt and accomplish all that they can to safeguard Christian quietness. We teach, therefore, that tributes, taxes, dues, tithes, pledges, loans and all kinds of obligations should all be paid and that the common laws should generally be obeyed in such matters.

THE FORGIVENESS OF SINS

We believe that by faith the forgiveness of sins is most assuredly granted to us when we pray to God through Christ. For if Christ told Peter that we are to forgive unto seventy times seven, that is, without limit, necessarily he himself will always pardon our offences. But we said that it is by faith that sins are forgiven. By this we simply meant to affirm that it is faith alone which can give the assurance of forgiveness. For even if the Roman pontiff were to say six hundred times, Thy sins are forgiven thee, the soul can never be at rest or enjoy the certainty of reconciliation with God until it knows within itself and believes without doubt and indeed experiences the fact that it is pardoned and reconciled. For as it is only the Holy Ghost that can give faith, so it is only the Holy Ghost that can give the forgiveness of sins.

Before God restitution, satisfaction and atonement for sin have been obtained once and for all by Christ who suffered for us. He himself is the propitiation for our sins, and not for ours only, but for the sins of the whole world, as his relative, the evangelist and apostle tells us.(52) Therefore if he has made satisfaction for sin, I ask who are the partakers of that satisfaction and reconciliation. Let us hear what he himself says. "He that believeth on me, that is, trusteth in me or relieth on me, hath everlasting life." But none can attain to everlasting life except he whose sins are remitted. Therefore it follows that those who trust in Christ have the remission of sin.

Now since none of us knows who believes, none of us knows

whose sins are remitted except the one who by the illumination and power of grace enjoys the assurance of faith,(53) knowing that through Christ God has forgiven him and having therefore the assurance of forgiveness. For he knows that God cannot deceive or lie and therefore he cannot doubt his grace to the sinner. For God spoke from above: "This is my well-beloved Son in whom I am well pleased, or, by whom I am reconciled." And that means that all who believe in God by Christ the Son of God and our Lord and Brother, know for a certainty that the remission of sins is given to them. Hence it is futile to use words like, I absolve you, or, I assure you of the remission of sins. For the apostles preach everywhere the forgiveness of sins, but it is obtained only by the believing and elect. Therefore, seeing that the election and faith of others is always concealed from us, although the Spirit of the Lord gives us the certainty of our own faith and election, it is also concealed from us whether the sins of others are forgiven or not. How then can any man assure another of the forgiveness of his sins? The popish inventions concerning this matter are all deceits and fables.

FAITH AND WORKS

Since we have touched upon the subject of faith, we would like to give your majesty a short account of our teaching concerning faith and works. For there are those who unjustly slander us as though we prohibited good works, although in this as in all other matters we teach nothing but what is directed by the Word of God and suggested by common sense.(54) For who is so little versed in these matters as not to maintain: Good works must proceed from intention, and works without intention are not works but accidents. Now the place of faith in the human heart is the same as that of intention in conduct. If the act is not preceded by intention, the result is unpremeditated and therefore worthless. If there is no faith to keep the city and direct all our actions, all that we undertake is irreligious and futile.(55) For even we men take more account of fidelity and faith in a work than of the work itself. If fidelity and faith are lacking the work depreciates in value. Supposing someone has performed a great service for your majesty, but not sincerely. Do you not say at once that you owe no debt of gratitude to the one who performed it because he did not do it from the heart? Indeed, do you not feel rather that in any service performed insincerely there lurks some concealed perfidy, and for that reason the one who performs a service insincerely will always be suspected of dishonesty and will appear to you to have acted only in his own interests and not in yours? The same norm and standard applies in relation to good works. The source of works must be faith. If faith is present, the work is acceptable to God. If not, then whatever we do is full of perfidy and not only not acceptable to God but an abomination to him. That is why St. Paul says in Romans 14: "Whatsoever is not of faith is sin," and there are some amongst us who have paradoxically (56) maintained that all our works are an abomination. By this they mean exactly the same as we do, that if a work is ascribed to us and not to faith, it is unbelief and therefore abominable to God. Now faith comes only from the Spirit of God, as we have explained already. Therefore those who have faith look to the will of God as a standard for all their works. That means that they reject not only those works which are directed against the law of God, but also those which are done apart from the law of God. For the law is the eternal will of God. Therefore what is done apart from the law, that is, apart from the Word and will of God, is not of faith. What is not of faith is sin: and if it is sin it is abhorrent to God. Hence it is clear that even if a man does something which God has commanded, the giving of alms for instance, but not of faith, that work is not acceptable to God. For if we enquire what is the source of those alms which are not of faith we shall find that they proceed from vainglory or the desire to receive more in return or some other sinful motive. Who then can deny that such a work is displeasing to God?

It is quite evident that works done apart from the will of God are done without faith, and if they are done without faith then according to Paul's judgment they are sin, and because they are sin God abominates them. Therefore the things which without any warrant or witness of the Word of God the Romanists have declared to be holy and pious and acceptable to God, feigned indulgences, the extinguishing of purgatorial fire, (57) enforced chastity and the variety of orders and superstitious practices (which it would be tedious to relate): these things are all sin and abomination in the sight of God. As regards those works which are done according to the law of God, for example when we feed the hungry and clothe the naked and comfort the prisoners, it is difficult to say whether or not they are meritorious. In proof that they are our opponents quote the saying : "Whosoever shall give anyone a cup of cold water in my name, he shall in no wise lose his reward." But the Word of God also testifies that they are not: "When ye shall have done all these things, say, we are unprofitable servants." For if our works merit salvation, there would have been no need of the death of Christ to reconcile the divine justice. It would no longer be grace that sins are remitted, for we could all merit remission. St. Paul states the matter quite unanswerably in Romans and Galatians. For it is necessarily the case that none comes to the Father except by Christ. Hence it follows that eternal salvation is only by the grace and favour of God as it is superabundantly poured out upon us in Christ.

But what are we to say then to the above and similar texts concerning the reward promised for a draught of cold water? Obviously this: The election of God is free and gratuitous. For he elected us before the foundation of the world, before ever we were born. Consequently God did not elect us because of works, for he executed our election before the foundation of the world. Hence works are not meritorious. If he promises a reward for works he is merely speaking after the manner of men. "For what dost thou recompense, O good God," says Augustine, "except only thine own work? For in that it is thou that makest us to will and to do, what remains that we may ascribe to ourselves?" (58)

Now while there are some men who are incited to good works by promises, there are others who are so generous and good that when they do anyone a favour they say: I owed you that, you thoroughly deserved it, or something similar. Thus the one who receives the gift is spared the humiliation of feeling that he is a suppliant (for if we love our neighbour, we shall be careful not to cause him discouragement). And that is how it is with God. Of his goodness he magnifies those whom he loves, so that they will not be despised but esteemed and honoured. And he attributes to us the things which he does through us, rewarding them as though they were our own works, although not merely our works but all our life and being are his. Again, God usually speaks to men in the language and fashion of men. Therefore, seeing that men give gifts to those who have merited them, and they call those gifts rewards, so too God calls his gifts a reward or recompense. There can be no doubt, then, that the words "merit" and "reward" appear in Holy Scripture, but they are used of the free gift of God.

For how can a man merit anything when it is by grace that he lives and by grace that he receives all that he has?

But we must add at once that the pious will not cease from good works simply because it is impossible to gain any merit by them. Rather, the greater our faith, the more and greater our works, as Christ testifies in John 14: "Verily, verily, I say unto you, he that believeth on me, the works that I shall do shall he do also, and greater works than these shall he do." And again: "If ye have faith as a grain of mustard seed, ye shall say unto this mountain, Be thou removed hence and cast into the sea, and it shall obey you."

Therefore those who claim that we restrain from good works because we preach faith are not kindly disposed towards us. And making mockery of the truth they misrepresent us: This is the doctrine for us, friends. We are saved by faith only. We shall not fast or pray or help the needy. By calumnies of this sort they merely betray their own lack of faith. For if they only knew what a wonderful gift of God faith is, how effective is its power, how tireless its work, they would not despise that which they cannot have.(59) That confidence with which a man reposes upon God with all the powers of his soul can think and purpose only those things which are divine, indeed it cannot do anything but that which is pleasing to God. For since faith is inspired by the Holy Spirit, how can it be slothful or inactive when the Spirit himself is unceasing in his activity and operation? Where there is true faith, works necessarily result, just as fire necessarily brings with it heat. But where faith is lacking, works are not true works but only a futile imitation of works. Therefore those who arrogantly demand a reward for works, saying that they will cease from works if no reward is given, still have the mind and outlook of servants. For it is the servant and idle person who works only for reward. But those who stand in faith are tireless in the work of God like the son of the house. It is not by good works that the son merits his position as heir to the estate, nor does he toil and labour to become the heir: but the moment he was born he was heir to his father's property not by merit but by right of birth. And even when he is tireless in his labours, he does not demand a reward, for he knows that everything is his. Similarly the children of God who stand in faith know that by their divine birth, that is, the birth of the Spirit, and on the basis of free election, they are the sons of God and not servants. Therefore as children of the house they do not ask for a reward. For all things are ours as heirs of God and joint-heirs with Christ. Therefore it is willingly and gladly and without grudging that they do their works: (60) indeed there is no work so great that they do not believe that it can be accomplished, not by our power, but by the power of the one in whom we trust.

In the Church, however, there are various sicknesses like unbelief and debility of faith. On the one hand there are some who absolutely do not believe, those who in the Supper eat and drink to themselves damnation, like Judas and Simon Magus. On the other hand there are those whose faith is half-hearted, those who hesitate when danger threatens, those whose faith is choked by thorns, that is, by cares and worldly ambitions, with the result that they do not produce any fruit or work of piety. Therefore like Christ himself and Paul and James we warn them that they must show forth their faith by their acts, if they have faith. For faith without works is dead, the good tree brings forth good fruit, the children of Abraham do the works of Abraham, in Christ nothing avails but faith which works by love. Hence we preach the law (61) as well as grace. For from the law the faithful and elect learn the will of God and the wicked are also affrighted so that they either serve their neighbour through fear or reveal all their desperation and unbelief.

But at the same time we give warning that those works have no value which have simply been devised by human wisdom for the purpose of serving God. For they are no more pleasing to God, O king, than it would be to you if someone tried to serve you in a way of which you did not approve. Therefore if you must be served in the way in which you yourself will, how much more have we to be careful not to bring before God works which he neither commands nor desires. When we teach faith, then, we open up the source from which good works proceed. Conversely, when we insist on works, we require them as a debt which we all owe to God but are unable to pay without compulsion.

ETERNAL LIFE

Finally, we believe that after this existence, which is captivity and death rather than life, there is for saints and believers an everlasting life of joy and felicity, but for the wicked and unbelieving, of misery and wretchedness. In this regard we do not accept the view of the Anabaptists that the soul as well as the body sleeps until the resurrection. We maintain that the

souls of angels and men can never sleep or rest. For their
teaching is contrary to all reason. The soul is so vital a substance
that not only does it have life in itself, but it gives life to the
dwelling-place in which it resides. Whenever an angel assumes
a body, whether it be of air or one specially created, he at once
imparts to it life, so that it moves and works and acts and is
acted upon. The moment a human soul enters a body, that body
lives and grows and moves and performs all the other functions
of life. But that being the case, how can the soul lie rigid
and asleep when it is released from the body? Because its force
and power are so alive and awake, that is, purposeful, philosophers (62) have described the soul as motion or activity. The
Greeks have a more exact term for it. They call it *entelechy*, (63)
that is, an inexhaustible power, operation, activity and
purpose. The visible things in the world are so ordered by
the divine providence that from them the spirit of man can
rise to a knowledge of the invisible. Among the elements fire
and air occupy the same place as the soul among bodies. Just
as air is present throughout the whole body of the universe,
so the soul permeates the whole body of man. Just as fire is
always active, so the soul is always at work. This applies even in
sleep, for we dream and we remember our dreams. Consequently sleep is something which concerns the body and not
the soul. For during sleep the soul nourishes and quickens and
restores the tired body, and so long as it is in the body it never
ceases to act and work and move. As there is no fire without
light, so the soul never grows old, it is never weak or confused,
it never decays or sleeps. It is always alive, wakeful and strong.

Thus far I have spoken only in terms of philosophy. Now we
will turn to the Scripture-texts which prove that the soul does
not sleep. "He that believeth shall not come into condemnation, but is passed from death unto life." If this is the
case, then he who believes in this present life experiences
already how good the Lord is and enjoys a foretaste of the life
of heaven. But if the soul which now lives in God were to fall
asleep the moment it left the body, the life of a Christian would
be better in the world than when he has left the world, for then
he would be asleep whereas now he is awake and has a
conscious enjoyment of God. "He that believeth on me hath
everlasting life." But life would not be never-ending—which is
what everlasting means here—if the life which the soul enjoys
in this world were to be interrupted by sleep in the world to
come.

"Father, I will that where I am, there shall also my servants be." If the Blessed Virgin and Abraham and Paul are with God, what kind of a life is it in heaven, and what sort of a God, if they are all asleep there? Is God asleep too? But if he is asleep he is not God. For the one who sleeps is subject to change, and he does so to refresh his weariness. But if God grows weary, he is not God. For no toil or labour is too great for God. On the other hand, if God does not sleep, then it is no more possible for the soul to sleep than for the air not to be clear and transparent when the sun arises on the earth. Hence this notion of the Anabaptists is foolish and presumptuous. For it does not satisfy them to delude men, but they must also pervert the sure and certain testimony of the living God. There are many other passages which we might quote: "This is life eternal, that they might know thee," etc., and "I will receive you unto myself, that where I am, there ye may be also," and others too, but we must study to be brief.

We believe, then, that as soon as they depart the body the faithful fly away to God, joining themselves to God and enjoying eternal felicity. Therefore, most religious king, if you discharge the office entrusted to you, as David, Hezekiah and Josiah did, you may look forward first to seeing God himself in his very essence and majesty and with all his attributes and powers. And this you will enjoy, not sparingly, but in full measure, not with the satiety which always accompanies abundance, but with that agreeable fulfilment which no surfeit can destroy, like rivers which flowing unceasingly to the sea and returning through the heart of the earth never become displeasing to men but constantly bring them profit and gladness, watering and fertilizing and bringing forth the seeds of new life. The good which we shall enjoy is eternal: and the eternal can never be exhausted. For that reason surfeit is impossible, for it is always new and yet constantly the same.

After that you may expect to see the communion and fellowship of all the saints and sages and believers and the steadfast and the brave and the good who have ever lived since the world began. You will see the two Adams, the redeemed and the Redeemer, Abel, Enoch, Noah, Abraham, Isaac, Jacob, Judah, Moses, Joshua, Gideon, Samuel, Phinehas, Elijah, Elisha, Isaiah and the Virgin Mother of God of whom he prophesied, David, Hezekiah, Josiah, the Baptist, Peter, Paul; Hercules too and Theseus, Socrates, Aristides, Antigonus, Numa, Camillus, the Catos and Scipios; (64) Louis the Pious and your predecessors the Louis, Philips, Pepins and all your ancestors who have departed this life in faith.(65) In short there has not lived a single good man, there has not been a single pious heart or believing soul from the beginning of the world to the end, which you will not see there in the presence of God. Can we conceive of any spectacle more joyful or agreeable or indeed sublime? Is it not right to direct all our soul's energies to the attainment of such a life? And let the dreaming Anabaptists deservedly sleep in the nether regions that sleep from which they will never awake. The source of their error is their ignorance of the fact that in Hebrew the word to sleep is used as the equivalent of "to die," as is often the case with Paul too when he has occasion to use the word.

Of the Anabaptists

Now that we have mentioned the Anabaptists, O king, we will briefly describe to you the life and conduct of that sect. They consist for the most part of men of a decadent type, vagrants by necessity, whose trade is the enticement of old women by grandiose speeches on divine things, by which they procure for themselves both a livelihood and also considerable monetary gifts. In all respects they affect the same holiness of life as that which Irenaeus reports concerning the Valentinians (66) and Nazianzus concerning the Eunomians.(67) Counting upon this they teach that it is unlawful for a Christian to execute the office of a magistrate, that he must not kill, not even according to the law or in the case of an evil-doer, that he must not participate in warfare, not even if tyrants or wicked and violent men or indeed brigands engage daily in robbery, slaughter and destruction, that he must not take an oath, that he must not exact tolls or taxes, that he is to have all things in common with his brethren, that on departing this life his soul will sleep with the body, that he may have several wives in the spirit and also enjoy carnal intercourse with them,(68) that he must not pay tithes and dues, and innumerable other things.

Indeed, not a day passes but that they scatter new errors like weeds amongst the good seed of God. And although they have gone out from us because they were not of us, there are still some who ascribe their heresies to us. For that reason we are their most bitter enemies and in all the matters mentioned we take the opposite view. Therefore, most excellent king, if it is ever reported to your majesty from any quarter that we aim to abolish the magistrates and forbid the oath and all the other things snarled out to the world by the Anabaptist rabble, I implore and beseech you in the name of that truth to which you are said to be so attached not to believe any rumours of this type concerning us, that is, concerning preachers of the Gospel in the cities of the Christian Civic Alliance.(69)

We do not instigate tumult, nor do we undermine the dignity or laws of magistrates: we are against all failure to redeem promises or to pay debts. Yet we are still accused of these things in some circles, not merely in secret rumour but in public writings. We do not make any specific answer to the charges because the world is already full of inflammatory books, and every day the facts themselves reveal the duplicity of those who spread abroad such reports concerning us, not of course with any regard to the honour of Christ but only to their own honour and their own bellies. But the fact is that the Anabaptist pest has spread for the most part in those places where the clear doctrine of Christ had begun to gain a footing. And by this very fact you may see the more clearly, O king, that it is sent by the evil one in an attempt to root out the good seed from the harvest field. We have seen whole cities and townships which had begun to receive the Gospel well, but were then infected and hindered by this pest and could make no further headway, both spiritual and civic affairs being wholly neglected in the resultant confusion.

For that reason I warn your majesty—Do not misunderstand me, for I know that you are surrounded by the most excellent counsellors. Yet it is impossible to take precautions against that which is not foreseen.(70) I know that your advisers could easily provide against the danger if they were aware of it. But as they will not perhaps recognize the peril, I know that you will not take the warning amiss. Therefore seeing that some sparks of the reviving faith have been kindled in your realm,(71) I warn your majesty not to allow the good seed to be choked by the papists, whose power has increased beyond all measure. For in place of that good seed the tares of the Anabaptists will grow up without your being aware of it. And the result will be such general confusion throughout the whole kingdom that it will be extremely difficult to find a remedy.

That is the sum of our faith and preaching as we execute them by the grace of God, and as we are always ready to give an account of them to any who ask. For we teach not a single jot which we have not learned from the sacred Scriptures. Nor do we make a single assertion for which we have not the authority of the first doctors of the Church—prophets, apostles, bishops, evangelists and expositors—those ancient Fathers who drew more purely from the fountainhead. All who have seen and examined our writings will testify to this fact.

Therefore, most holy king (and why should I not call the most Christian king (72) most holy), prepare yourself to receive with due honour the Christ who is arising again and returning to our midst. For perceive that it was by divine providence that the kings of France were called most Christian, seeing that the renewal of the Gospel of the Son of God was destined to come under your reign, whom friend and foe alike extol as generous and good by nature.(73) For it is necessary that a Christian king should be of a generous and affable disposition, of just and skilful judgment, of a wise and determined spirit. And as we have said, God has wonderfully provided you with these endowments that you might shine forth in this epoch and yourself rekindle the light of divine knowledge. Therefore go forth with these noble virtues, take shield and spear, and fall upon unbelief with all that high-hearted and dauntless courage and with that physical presence which astonishes everyone by its grace. Then when other kings see you, the most Christian, the first to defend the honour of Christ, they will follow your lead and example and drive out Antichrist. Let the doctrine of salvation be purely preached in your kingdom. You are rich in wise and learned men, in resources, and in a people with a leaning to religion. You will not allow their souls to be seduced by superstition when they esteem so highly both God and yourself.

There is no cause whatever to be frightened because of the lying accusations made by slanderers in their opposition to the truth. Not your own subjects only but allied peoples abroad will participate in holy and righteous wars. Preachers as well as people will take the oath without hesitation, which the papists so far have refused to do. And so far are the preachers from teaching that tolls and taxes should not be paid that they will pay them themselves. They will not interfere with any privileges. If faults are committed they will expose them, but not in such a way as to create disorder in temporal affairs. In these matters they always acknowledge the lawful magistrate, no matter how much they may seize on and criticize him when he is at fault.

Believe me, believe me, most noble hero, of all those evils threatened by the papists not one will come to pass. For the Lord protects his Church. Oh that you could only see for yourself the states of some of the princes who have received the Gospel in Germany and the cleanliness and cheerfulness and security of the cities. By reason of the fruits you might well say: I do not doubt that what has come to pass is of God. Consider all these things according to your faith and wisdom, and pardon our temerity in disturbing your majesty after this boorish manner. The matter itself requires it.

Zurich   Your majesty's most devoted servant,
                                             H. ZWINGLI

BULLINGER

Of the Holy Catholic Church

INTRODUCTION

THE SERMON "OF THE HOLY CATHOLIC CHURCH" is the first of the fifth decade of sermons in Bullinger's series on the main aspects of Christian doctrine. The first two decades had appeared in one volume in 1549. The third and fourth constituted a second volume in 1550, and the fifth and concluding decade was published in 1551. A folio edition of the completed series was prepared in 1552, and translations were made fairly quickly not only into English but also into German, Dutch and French.

It is of particular interest to note the close interconnection between the *Decades* and the Reformation in England. The ninth sermon of the second decade was translated and published in the year of its appearance, and the translation carried a dedication to Edward VI.[1] Bullinger himself dedicated the two parts of the second volume to Edward, and the translation of the first of these was set in hand at once.[2] The third volume also had an English dedication, this time to Lord Grey.

The translation of the whole series was not completed until later in the century, but there were three successive editions of this translation, in 1577, 1584 and 1587.[3] The work stood so high in the estimation of the Elizabethan leaders that at the instigation of Whitgift it was granted a quasi-authoritative position as the theological text-book of unlicensed ministers. The question of the exact status of the *Decades* has been much

---

[1] This was the sermon concerning magistrates and obedience. The translation was by Walter Lynne. See *Zurich Letters*, I, p. 396, n. 1.
[2] *Ibid.*, p. 415. The work was done by Thomas Caius.
[3] It is not known who the translator was, but Strype says that it was a "person of eminency in the Church," *Annals*, II, 2, p. 144.

controverted, usually for polemical purposes, but the following appear to be the true facts of the case.

In Whitgift's Register there may be found a record of certain orders drawn up for the better increase of learning amongst inferior ministers. These orders were apparently introduced into the Upper House of Convocation on December 2, 1586.[4] The first of them lays down that all ministers "under the degrees of Master of Arts or Batchelor of Law, and not licensed to be a public preacher, shall . . . provide a Bible, Bullinger's Decade in Latin or English, and a paper-book." Each day they were to read a chapter of the Bible and each week a sermon of the *Decades*, and they were to summarize the contents in the note-book. Provision was made for the inspection of the note-book by authorized preachers, and for the punishment of those who did not regularly perform these beneficial exercises. The whole scheme was undoubtedly an attempt to meet the vociferous Puritan objections against the many clergy who lacked suitable qualifications for a full preaching ministry.

It seems unlikely that these orders were ever formally passed by Convocation,[5] but there can be little doubt that they were approved, for in the seventh session on March 10 the prolocutor of the Lower House "prayed that the articles agreed on by the bishops for the increase of learning in inferior ministers might be read; which was done. And then the Archbishop exhorted all the clergy to do their duty."[6] Again, on November 1, 1588, in a letter to the Bishop of London (probably designed as a circular) Whitgift reminded his reader that at the synod of 1588 "it was thought fit and necessary to me and to the rest of my brethren then present in that synod, although not as a judicial act or conclusion by the authority of the convocation, that the articles of the tenor of the copy herein enclosed should be put in execution by your lordship and all the rest of my said brethren the bishops of this province; forasmuch as it is like it will be looked for at this next parliament, how the same articles have been accordingly used," etc.[7] In the margin of the Register there is a copy of the articles which makes it clear that they are identical with the orders already quoted. From

[4] Tom. I, fol. 131a. See Cardwell's *Synodalia*, II, p. 562.
[5] The earlier records of Convocation were destroyed in the fire of 1666 (Cardwell, *op. cit.*, Preface p. i).
[6] Strype, *Whitgift*, I, p. 499.
[7] *Whitgift's Register*, Tom. I, fol. 151a. Strype (*Whitgift*, I, p. 531) says that the letter was addressed to the bishops, Wilkins (*Concil.*, IV, p. 338) that it was to the Bishop of London.

this letter it seems evident that although the *Decades* were not legally imposed upon the Church, they were at least so highly esteemed that they could be recommended and accepted as a sound and reliable text-book for the purpose required.

The general structure of the *Decades* is not unlike that of the more famous *Institutes* of Calvin, and the fifth and final decade, like the fourth book of the *Institutes*, is devoted to such doctrinal themes as the Church, the ministry, prayer, and the dominical sacraments. There are two sermons on the Church, the first and more important on its nature and characteristics, the second on its unity as the body or bride of Christ and the mother of all true believers. In the latter sermon it is noteworthy that Bullinger, like Calvin, has a high sense of the dignity of the Church and a keen awareness of the dangers of schism. With an evangelical interpretation he approves the Cyprianic dictum that outside the Church there is no salvation, and he insists most emphatically upon the essential unity of the Church and the necessary expression of that unity in external fellowship. The break from the mediaeval Church is defended on the ground that the upstart church of Rome has neither the inward nor the outward marks of the true Church.

In his discussion of the nature and characteristics of the Church Bullinger follows for the most part the orthodox line of Reformation teaching already laid down by Zwingli. He distinguishes between the invisible Church of the elect and the visible Church which comprises all professors of the Christian faith. He explains that the Church of the elect is invisible in the sense that it is known only to God. The two marks or notes of the visible Church are the preaching of the Word of God and the administration of the two evangelical sacraments. Although the Reformed churches cannot trace an episcopal descent, their apostolicity is defended on the ground that they teach apostolic truth. But Bullinger shows how foolish it is for any church to claim inerrancy either in life or doctrine. In all these matters he gives a clear and adequate exposition of the general teaching, but obviously he has nothing very new or striking to say.

Yet there are some interesting features in Bullinger's treatment. In the first place he preserves the traditional distinction between the Church triumphant and the Church militant. The Church triumphant consists of true believers already in heaven, and it is a single not a twofold body. The Church militant consists of Christians upon earth, and it is this Church which may be regarded under the two aspects of the visible and the invisible Church, the former being the totality of those who profess the Christian faith, the latter being the inner company of the elect or true believers. Again, it is to be noted that Bullinger does envisage exceptional circumstances in which true believers may be separated from the fellowship of the visible Church. Hence he cannot believe that membership of the outward body is in every case necessary to membership of the body of Christ. On the other hand he lays the usual stress upon the value and indeed the necessity of the external fellowship in all normal circumstances.

A further point is that in addition to the two notes of the visible Church Bullinger sees three marks or tokens of the invisible: the fellowship of the Spirit, a sincere faith and twofold charity. In the last analysis it is true that the Church of the elect is known only to God, but this does not mean that there are no signs by which true believers may be discerned. As a good tree is known by its fruits, so the genuine believer is known by the quality of his life and conduct.

The attitude of Bullinger to the Roman church is in a sense equivocal. In so far as Rome has preserved the forms of the Church, the Word of God and the sacraments, he finds it difficult to deny it all claim to be counted as a true Church. But in so far as it has perverted the true faith he has no option but to indentify it as the church of the devil rather than the Church of Christ. The champions of the papacy are hypocrites in the sense that the Pharisees were, that is, they trust in their own righteousness of works rather than in the righteousness imputed by faith in Jesus Christ. In this they are to be distinguished from those hypocrites who feign an attachment to the evangelical doctrine, but without any inwardness of personal understanding. The papal claims to inerrancy, overlordship and apostolicity are flatly rejected.

By modern requirements the work suffers from the disproportionate attention to problems raised by the Romanist assertions, but in the circumstances of the time Bullinger could hardly avoid those serious and pressing issues. On the wider points, his introduction of the distinction between the Church triumphant and the Church militant is probably a source of confusion rather than of strength. In itself it is, of course, an obvious and a true one, but it has the disadvantage of obscuring the essential unity between the company of the elect on earth and the company of the redeemed in heaven. On the whole, it would appear to be preferable to include all the elect in the one Church of Christ, of which some are still members of the external churches, while the rest have already passed to their transfiguration.

Again, it may be questioned whether Bullinger has sufficiently grasped that unity which persists in the Church in spite of its twofold nature as an external and an internal body. The point is that while true believers may temporarily or even permanently be deprived of their continued fellowship with fellow-Christians, the cases are almost non-existent where they are not in some sense members of the visible and organized Christian community, even if only by baptism or the confession of their faith. Therefore although it is true that there may well be an external membership without an internal, it is virtually impossible that there should be an internal without an external. The Church has its two aspects or natures, but there is only the one Church, and the point of unity is the common membership of all genuine believers. With all his insistence upon the high dignity and value of the external organization, Bullinger is in constant danger of conceiving of the true Church as in the last analysis a purely spiritual fellowship. On the other hand, the point is a good one that the elect must give perceptible evidence of their faith, for it enables Bullinger to avoid the twin dangers of fatalism and antinomianism, and it brings the invisible Church into more living touch with everyday life and experience.

Although the sermon obviously suffers from its verboseness and inordinate length, it is well-composed and pleasantly phrased, and it is not marred by that harshness and jerkiness which characterize so many of Zwingli's writings. In fact, we have here a competent and quite readable introduction to the general teaching on the Church as found in Reformed circles in the sixteenth century. And since the issues raised are for the most part living issues of the present time, the treatise has still something more than a merely historical value and interest.

The present translation follows fairly closely the Elizabethan translation of 1587 as reprinted in the Parker Society edition (1852). At certain points, however, the English has been brought up to date, and where there are divergences from the Latin, the Latin has usually been preferred, the Elizabethan versions being indicated in the footnotes.

Of the Holy Catholic Church

THE TEXT

The order and course of things so leading us,[1] next after God, the workman and author of all things, we come to speak of his most excellent work, that is, the Church. For so great is the goodness of our good God and most loving Father, that he does not desire to live happily and blessedly alone, but rather to bestow and pour upon us men, his beloved creatures, all kinds of blessedness;[2] and that we should enjoy his goods in every possible way. And to that end he chooses to himself men who live in this world, that he may sometime translate them to himself: in whom also (even while they live here) he may dwell, whom he may enrich with all his goods, in whom he may reign; and that they should be called by his name, that is, a people, a house, a kingdom, an inheritance, a flock, a congregation or Church, of the living God. Of which Church (being aided by your prayers) I will speak such things as the Lord of the Church shall grant unto me to utter.

The word *Ecclesia*, which signifies a church or congregation,[3] is a Greek word, used and received among the Latins, signifying, as I said, a congregation, communion, or assembly (in German *ein Gemeind*), or a people called together to hear matters of the common good; for that is how St. Luke is found to use the word in the nineteenth chapter of the Acts. But it was translated to a holy use, and began to be called a congregation, assembly, or company of the faithful, calling (1) upon the name of the Lord. St. Paul says that he persecuted the congregation or Church of God, and in another place he says: "I received authority from the high priests to bind all those

[1] Lat. *rerum cohaerentium.*   [2] The Lat. adds *et bona sua omnia.*
[3] This clause is not in the Lat.

that call upon the name of Christ." Those whom in the first passage he terms the Church in the second he describes as those that call upon the name of Christ. Elsewhere the word *Ecclesia*, the church or congregation, is indicative of a calling forth together; for in the Greek tongue ἐκκαλέω means to call forth. For God calls forth from all parts of the wide world, and from all the congregation of men, all believers and their seed,[4] that they may be his peculiar people, and he again may be their God; that is to say, that they may be the Church of the living God. In times past the congregation or assembly of the Jewish people, being God's flock, was called a synagogue; for this word synagogue has the same meaning as *Ecclesia*, the congregation. But because of the stubbornness of the Jews, and the unappeasable hatred which they bear towards the Christian religion, this word synagogue is not highly regarded and has mostly gone out of use. But we will keep to our proper order and not discuss the churches of the Jews or the Turks, or other alien churches of the Gentiles,[5] of which we know that there are many sorts and kinds.(2) We will speak of the Christian Church and congregation of the faithful: that which the Germans call *Die kirch*, in allusion perhaps to the Greek word κυριακή. For the Greeks call κυριακήν anything which belongs to the Lord, that is, a house or a people, and similarly the Germans call *die kirchen* both the people of God themselves, and also the place where they assemble together to worship God. But first of all we will describe a little more simply[6] what the church or congregation is.

The Church is the whole company and multitude of the faithful, as it is partly in heaven and partly remains still upon earth: and as it agrees plainly in unity of faith or true doctrine, and in the lawful partaking of the sacraments: for it is not divided, but united and joined together as it were in one house and fellowship.

This Church is usually called catholic, that is to say, universal. For it sends out its branches into all places of the wide world, in all times and all ages; and it comprehends generally all the faithful the whole world over. For the Church of God is not tied to any one region, nation, or kindred; to condition, age, sex, or kind: all the faithful generally and each one in particular, wherever they may be, are citizens and members of this Church. St. Paul the apostle says: "There is neither Jew

---

[4] The Lat. adds *ex hoc mundo*. [5] Lat. *vel aliarum exterarum Gentium.*
[6] Lat. *paulo rudius.*

nor Greek, neither bondman nor free, neither man nor woman: for ye be all one in Christ Jesus."

The Church is distinguished into the two parts, the Church triumphant and the Church militant.(3) The Church triumphant is the great company of holy spirits in heaven, triumphing because of the victory which has now[7] been won against the world, and sin and the devil, and enjoying[8] the vision of God, in which there consists the fulness of all kinds of joy and pleasure, and concerning which they set forth God's glory and praise his goodness for ever. St. John the apostle graphically [9] describes this Church in his Revelation: "After this I saw, and behold, a great company which no man was able to number, of all nations, peoples and tongues, standing before the throne and in the sight of the Lamb, clothed in white garments,[10] and palms in their hands: and they cried out with a loud voice, saying: Salvation belongeth to him that sitteth on the throne of our God,[11] and to the Lamb." And shortly after he says: "And one of the elders answered and said unto me: These which are clothed in white garments, who are they? or from whence come they? And I said unto him. Thou knowest, Lord. And he said unto me, These are they that have come out of great affliction, and have washed [12] their garments and made them white in the blood of the Lamb; therefore are they before the throne of God, and serve him day and night in his temple.[13] And he that sitteth on the throne shall dwell over them. They shall neither hunger nor thirst henceforth any more: neither shall the sun shine on them, nor any heat; because the Lamb, who is in the midst of the throne, shall govern them, and bring them to the living fountains of waters. And the Lord shall wipe away all tears from their eyes." Brethren, you have here a notable [14] description of the Church triumphant in heaven, triumphing truly through the blood of Christ, by whom they conquered and do now reign. For Christ is that Lamb of God that taketh away the sins of the world, by whom all that are sanctified are and shall be sanctified and do live, from the first creation of the world unto the end of all times. And in a certain place St. Paul too gives us a notable description of this Church, telling us that we who

[7] Omitted in the Elizabethan versions (E.V.).   [8] E.V. add "still."
[9] Lat. *graphice*.   [10] E.V., 1584 and 1587, "raiments."
[11] So Bibl. Lat. Tigur, 1544, and Tyndale, 1534.
[12] E.V. "spread forth."   [13] E.V. add "holy."
[14] Lat. *elegantissimam*.

are still busied [15] in the Church militant shall sometime be translated into it, being made fellows with the holy angels of God, received among the orders of the patriarchs, and placed in the company of the blessed spirits, with the most high God himself and the mediator our Lord Jesus Christ. For preaching the greatness of the grace of God brought to us by the Gospel, and exhorting us to receive the same with a true faith, he says: "Ye came not unto Mount Sinai, to a fire, to a whirlwind, a stormy tempest, and darkness; but unto mount Sion, to the city of the living God, to heavenly Jerusalem, and to the innumerable company of angels, and to the church or congregation of the first-begotten which are written in heaven, and to God the judge of all, and to the spirits of the perfect just, and to the mediator of the New Testament, Jesus Christ, speaking better things than the blood of Abel spake." [16] And therefore all the saints in heaven belong to our company, or rather, we belong to their fellowship; for we are companions and fellow-heirs with the saints from Adam unto the end of all worlds, and God's household. And this contains the greatest comfort in all human life, and moves above all things to the study of virtue: for what more worthy thing is there, than to be of God's household? Or what may be thought more sweet to us, than to think ourselves fellows with the patriarchs, prophets, apostles and martyrs, of all angels and blessed spirits? This benefit, I say, Christ has bestowed on us. To him therefore be praise, glory, and thanks for ever and ever. Amen.

The Church militant is a congregation of men upon earth, professing the name and religion of Christ, and still [17] fighting in the world against the devil, sin, the flesh and the world, in the camp and tents and under the banner of our Lord Christ. This Church again must be taken in two ways.(4) For either it must be taken strictly, in which case it comprises only those who are not only called but are in actual fact the Church, the faithful and elect of God, lively members, knit unto Christ not merely with outward bands or marks but in spirit and faith, and often by the latter without the former, of which we shall speak later. This inward and invisible Church of God may well be termed the elect bride of Christ, known only to God, who alone knows who are his. It is this Church especially which we confess when we say as we are instructed in the Apostles'

[15] Lat. *qui versamur.*
[16] Lat. *loquebatur,* as in Bibl. Lat. Tigur, 1544.
[17] E.V. "continually."

Creed:[18] "I believe in the holy Catholic Church, the Communion of Saints." In these few words we understand that there is a Church, what that Church is, and what kind of a Church it is. For first we confess that there always has been and is a Church of God, and that it shall continue for ever. Then, professing what it is, we add: "The Communion of Saints."(5) That is to say: We believe the Church to be simply the company of all those saints who are and have been and shall be, both in this present age and in the world to come, who enjoy in common all the good things granted to them by God. And we also express what is the nature of this Church, that is, holy, the bride of Christ, cleansed and blessed. For St. Paul calls holy those who are cleansed with the Spirit and blood of our God, of whom a large number have received crowns of glory,[19] and the rest labour here upon earth, hoping to receive them in heaven. And certainly, in our consideration of the Church, the most important thing is that through the grace of God we are members of Christ's body and partakers of all heavenly gifts with all the saints;[20] for we confess none more than ourselves to be holy.[21]

Or the Church in the wider sense comprises not only those who are truly faithful and holy, but also those who although they have no true or unfeigned faith and are not clean and holy in the conversation of their lives do acknowledge and profess true religion together with true believers and holy men of God, approving and accepting virtues and reproving evil, and not as yet separating themselves from the unity of this holy Church militant. From this standpoint not even the wicked and hypocrites (as we find that there were in the Church of the time of Christ and the apostles, such as Judas, Ananias and Sapphira, Simon Magus, and also Demas, Hymenaeus, Alexander and many others) are excluded and put out of the Church, which Church may well be described as the outward and visible Church. But this Church again must be thought of either in respect of its individual parts or the whole. It has to be considered both generally and in particular. And the particular Church is that Church which consists of a certain number and is known by the name of some definite place: for it takes its name from the place, being called by the name of some city, like the churches of Zurich and Berne, etc. The Greeks called these

[18] Lat. *Hanc in primis confitentes symbolo edocti apostolico dicimus.*
[19] Lat. omits "of glory." [20] E.V. "with the angels."
[21] E.V. "for we confess none to be more holy than our own selves."

particular churches παροικίας,(6) or as we commonly say, parishes.[22] We call that a parish in which there are houses and streets joined together in a single locality. But both in town and country [23] the various districts are each allotted a church and parish priest to serve them, and the particular circuit is then called a parish,(7) in German, *Ein barchi, oder pfarkirch, oder ein kirchhory.* And formerly the parish priest was a provider, for he provided and distributed necessities to strangers, chiefly salt and wood. By some he is called the maker of the feast, by others the provider of virgins.[24](8) Therefore because the pastors of churches are as it were preparers of virgins for the redeemer and head of the Church, which is Christ, bringing to him a virgin chaste and undefiled; in short, because they themselves provided things most necessary for the people of God, preparing also heavenly feasts and banquets, the pastors of the Lord's flock are very well called parish priests, or the curates of souls.(9) Now it is of the particular church that the Lord speaking in the Gospel says: "If he that offendeth the church will not regard when he is warned, complain unto the church." For the universal Church throughout the world cannot assemble and come together that the rebellious and obstinate should be brought before it: hence judgment is referred to be given to the stubborn by the individual churches. To conclude, the universal Church consists of all individual churches throughout the whole earth, and of all the visible parts and members of them. It is this which we sketched a little while ago when we spoke of it more fully.

But as we began to say, the catholic Church of God has continued with us [25] from age to age from the very first, and at this very time it is dispersed throughout the whole world, both visibly and invisibly; and the Lord's people and God's house shall remain upon the earth to the world's end. For there has never yet been any world,[26] neither shall there be any age, in which God has not sanctified or will not sanctify some men to himself, in whom he may dwell, and that they shall be his flock and holy house; for the testimonies of the old-time prophets also record that the Church is perpetual. For it is written in the 132nd Psalm: "The Lord hath chosen Sion, he hath chosen her for an habitation for himself. This is my resting-place for ever and ever; here will I dwell, because I have chosen

[22] Lat. *Vulgas dicit parochias, alii et rectius dixere paroecias.*
[23] Lat. *et in agro;* E.V. "In cities and towns."   [24] Lat. *paranymphum.*
[25] Lat. *ad nos usque decurrit.*   [26] E.V. Lat. *seculum.*

her." And again: "I have sworn unto David in my holiness, his seed shall remain for ever, and his seat shall continue before me as the sun." But who is not aware that we have to understand all this of Christ, the Son of David, and of his throne and spiritual Sion, which is the Church? And he too, speaking of the continuance of the Church, says in the Gospel: "I will remain with you continually to the end of the world." And again: "I will ask of my Father, and he shall give you another Comforter, the Spirit of truth, that he may abide with you for ever." To the same context there belongs that other saying in the Gospel: "And the gates of hell shall not prevail against the church"; a saying which is indeed a great comfort to the faithful in so many and so great persecutions intended to the utter destruction and overthrow of the Church.

But as Christ has always had his Church here upon earth, and still has, and shall have for ever, so too the devil, as long as the world continues, shall never be without his people in whom he may reign. This church of the devil had its first beginning with Cain, and shall continue to the last wicked person, comprising all those evil peoples that have been in the meantime and shall be between the beginning and the end. But even while they live here upon earth, these have society and communion with those who are tormented in hell. For just as all the goods are one body under the one head Christ, so all the wicked are one incorporate body under one head Satan. This may very well be described as the wicked church,[27] Sodom and Gomorrah, Babylon, the congregation of Chora, Dathan and Abiram, a synagogue, school and stews of the devil, the kingdom of antichrist, or something similar. In this church are reckoned all the wicked and unbelieving, who separate themselves from the society of our holy mother the Church, or forsake its communion: and especially those who are mockers of God and his holy Word, blasphemers and persecutors of Christ and his Church. Of this number today are the heathen, Turks, Jews, heretics, schismatics, and in general all those who are professed enemies of the Christian religion. And to these we may also add hypocrites: for that is no small offence which the Lord himself so earnestly persecutes and blames in the holy Gospel.[28] Amongst other things he says: "The Lord of that servant shall come in the day wherein he looked not for him, and in an hour that he shall not know of, and shall divide him, and shall give him his portion with hypocrites, where shall

27 Lat. *ecclesia malignantium.*   28 E.V. "in every part of the gospel."

be weeping and gnashing of teeth." Beyond all doubt he signifies the greatness of the offence by the sharpness of the punishment. This church follows the motions of the devil, and the
devices and imaginations of its own heart, and is busied and
exercised in all kinds of blasphemy and wickedness, in which
it excels; and at the last it sinks down to hell, that it may be
nowhere separated from that head to which it has so diligently
or rather obstinately joined itself.

I know quite well that you will object that I have reckoned
hypocrites to be of the outward communion and fellowship
of the Church militant, and now number them with the company of the devil's church. And you will say that it is impossible that the same hypocrites should take part in two
churches so different from each other,[29] seeing that the Lord
says: "Either make the tree good and the fruit good, or else
the tree naught and the fruit naught." And St. Paul also says,
that there is no fellowship between Christ and Belial, between
light and darkness, between truth and lying; and that hypocrisy
is lying and darkness.

Here, then, I see a suitable place to show by what means
and to what extent I may reckon hypocrites to be of the congregation of the Church. First, we make a distinction or difference
between hypocrites. For there are certain hypocrites who put
their confidence in their human justice and equity, doing all
their works openly that they may be seen of men, firmly trusting
and stiffly standing to the traditions of men. To these it is a
custom and property not only to fly from the Church which
teaches the righteousness of Christ, but also to curse, detest
and persecute it with all cruelty. Such were the Jews and Jewish
Pharisees with whom our Lord Jesus Christ had much contention, and with whom even today the Church contends and
makes wars. These are the plain and visible members of the
devil's church, and they are not to be reckoned with the outward Church,[30] indeed they are not once worthy to be named
in the Church of God. Again there are those hypocrites who are
dissemblers, not putting any confidence in their own righteousness and justice, nor greatly regarding the traditions of men. (10)
Such people neither hate the Church, nor fly from it, nor
persecute it; but outwardly they agree with it, professing the
same faith, and participating in the very same sacraments; but
inwardly and in mind they neither believe unfeignedly and
sincerely nor do they live holily. Of these, some for a season will

[29] Lat. *diversissimis inter se.*   [30] Lat. *vel exterioris.*

cleave to the fellowship and company of the Church; and then when the pretext arises they will fall from it as heretics and schismatics do and those who instead of friends become enemies. There are others who never fall from the Church, but keep themselves in the fellowship of the Church all their lives, outwardly pretending and feigning religion, but inwardly giving themselves up to their own errors, faults and wickedness: to whom the outward behaviour and fellowship is undoubtedly not of the slightest benefit. For those who desire to live for ever, and to participate in all heavenly blessings, must join in fellowship[31] with the Church of God not only by an outward and visible society, but by inward communion and fellowship, in which there consists life and salvation: but of this we shall speak in the proper place. Such hypocrites or dissemblers, hanging[32] on to the ecclesiastical body, are called members of the body, and are said to be of the Church. And in order that you may all understand this the better, we will expound it in parables.

We say that the wicked or hypocrites are in the Church in the same way as chaff is in the corn, although it is different by nature and is not corn. Again there frequently hang on the human body members which are dry or rotten or feeble. Although these members have no society and do not take part with the living members in the vital spirit, yet they are attached and cleave fast to the living members, so that they too are called by men members and parts of the body. But in order that they may not infect the other parts, men cut them off, or sometimes they let them alone lest by cutting them off the whole body should be endangered. Now in the same way[33] we say that hypocrites are in the Church of Christ, although they are not united to the Church either by the bond of the Spirit or of faith and love, and they cannot be counted living members. But they are tolerated lest some worse mischief should befall the whole body of the Church. And frequently they are cut off in order that better health may come to the body ecclesiastical.

But let us hear what the evangelical and apostolic testimony says. The Lord says plainly in the Gospel that cockle grows up in the Lord's field, being sown by a wicked man, and he forbids it to be plucked up, lest the corn should be plucked up also.

[31] E.V. "For we ought to live for ever and to participate all heavenly gifts with them that desire them, to join in fellowship," etc.
[32] Lat. adds *adhuc*.   [33] Lat. *ratione certa et suo quodam modo*.

Behold, cockle sown by an evil man (I say) by the devil.himself, which is not corn, and yet it increases and it is in the Lord's field. Again, the Lord says in the Gospel: "The kingdom of heaven is like unto a net, which, being cast into the sea, draweth all manner of things up with it; and when it is filled, it is brought to the shore; and there men sitting reserve that which is good in a vessel, and that which is evil they cast away." Behold again, how you may see both good and bad drawn in one and the same net, and therefore both good and evil are to be reckoned in one and the same kingdom. Also in another parable there enters in among the guests one who has not on his wedding-garment. He is tolerated for a time, but finally is expelled by the lord of the feast. In another place it is said that he has a fan[34] in his hand and cleanses the floor and burns the chaff with unquenchable fire. For this reason[35] St. Paul in his epistle to the Corinthians distinguishes between the professed and open enemies of Christ's Church and those impure men who are not as yet absolutely repugnant and adversaries to the name of the Church and of Christ. "If any man (he says) that is called a brother be a thief or a whore-monger, or a covetous person, etc., with such a one see that you eat no meat. For what doth it belong unto me to judge of them that be without? For God judgeth them that be without." Without, that is to say, without the bounds of the Church, he places those who are not called brethren, that is, those who do not acknowledge the name of Christ or of the Church: within, that is to say, in the society of the Church (I mean of the outward Church) he reckons those who still acknowledge the name of Christian, and do not yet withstand ecclesiastical discipline, but who themselves are all the time defiled and spotted with much mischief.[36] Of all men St. John the apostle spoke the most plainly, saying: "They went out from us, but they were none of us; for if they had been of us, they had tarried still with us." This seems to be a new kind of speech. For if those who go out of the Church had not been in the society of the Church, how could they go out of the Church? Therefore if hypocrites and evil men are gone out of the Church, surely at one time they were in the Church, that is, when they had not yet gone out of it but showed plainly of what sort they really were. Again, in that they went out of the Church, they show clearly that they were never really the true and living members of Christ and the Church, but they were numbered for a time

34 Lat. *vannum aut ventilabrum.*   35 E.V. omit.   36 Lat. *sceleribus.*

amongst the members of the Church. The apostle gives us the reason; it is the disposition of the true members of Christ never to forsake Christ and his Church, but to continue and also to prosper and increase daily more and more. The saints and holy men do indeed offend or fall, but they do not forsake Christ utterly.(11) David having committed adultery and manslaughter, cries out, saying: "Make me a clean heart, O Lord, and renew a right spirit within me. Cast me not away from thy presence, and take not thy Holy Spirit from me. O give me the comfort of thy help [37] again, and stablish me with thy free Spirit."[38] St. Peter denies the Lord, and the weak flesh overcame a good spirit: but immediately (the Lord stirring up his heart) he repented, and departing from evil company, he adjoins himself to the good fellowship of the Lord, who foretold him of this great fall, and then added the words: "I prayed for thee that thy faith should not fail; and thou, when thou art converted, confirm thy brethren." The same Peter also in another place when many fell away from Christ, being asked whether he also purposed to depart, answered: "Lord, to whom shall we go? Thou hast the words of eternal life. And we believe and know that thou art Christ, the Son of the living God." Hence St. John says very truly: "They went out from us, but they were none of us." He adds the reason: "If they had been of us, they had still tarried with us." Therefore because they did not continue with us in the society of Christ and the Church, they showed by their defection and falling away [39] what they had previously been: we reckoned them to be members of the Church, but they by their falling away showed that they were chaff in the Lord's corn. For as chaff when it is not [40] stirred or fanned seems to be heavy with a grain of wheat in it, but when it is fanned it is seen to be empty and light and is separated from the corn, so hypocrites, by their light defection,[41] prove clearly that they were never heavy with the seed of God's Word, and that they were never the true corn of Christ.

From this we may gather the general and orthodox [42] opinion that all who are said to be the Church and adorn themselves with the title of the Church are not straightway the Church. For St. John plainly adds: "But that it may be evident, that all be not of us."[43] We read how St. Paul says to the

[37] Lat. *salutaris tui*.
[38] Lat. *spiritu principali*.
[39] Lat. adds *a nobis*.
[40] Lat. *nondum*.
[41] E.V. "being light by reason of their defection."
[42] E.V. "ancient."
[43] Lat. inserts *unde*.

Romans: "They are not all Israelites which came of Israel; neither are they all children straightway, because they are the seed of Abraham: but in Isaac shall thy seed be called." Therefore the faithful are the true and lively members of Christ and the saints. In the meantime, so long as hypocrites or wicked persons do not put off their visors [44] and declare by their sayings and doings what they are, so that they may be lawfully cut off from the Church, so long as they do not break away of their own accord and forsake Christ in the open field and fly to the tents of antichrist or the devil, they are known and taken to be inhabitants of the Church, and are called the Church and members of the Church, although God who sees the hearts of all men judges otherwise concerning them. [45] Once again I will make the matter plain by an example. So long as Judas, the betrayer of Christ and manslayer, did not utter his crafty or rather most wicked device, either by open word or deed, so long as he did not forsake the company of Christ and the apostles, but preached and provided necessary household things for Christ, he was reckoned an apostle and steward of Christ, and indeed a member of the apostolic Church. Yet the same Judas was described by the Lord as a devil, and when he spoke about the elect and his true and lively members Judas was most plainly excluded, so that there is no reason to doubt that he was not a member of the inward and holy Church of God, even though he was a member of the outward Church, being reckoned as of the number of the saints. Therefore those who said that there is one visible and outward Church of God and another invisible and inward did not speak unadvisedly.(12) The visible and outward Church is that which is outwardly known by men to be a Church, by hearing God's Word, and partaking of his sacraments, and by public confession of their faith. The invisible and inward is so called, not because the men are invisible, but because it cannot be seen with the eye of man, but appears before the eyes of God, who are the true and unfeigned believers. For the true believers are the true and lively members of this inward Church, which I earlier called the Church militant in its stricter sense: but the other and visible Church comprises both good and bad, and has to be taken in a wider sense.

Now since we have said that the Church militant upon earth is marked by God with certain tokens and marks by which it

[44] Lat. *necdum deterso fuco.*
[45] E.V. "do well enough discern them."

may be known in this world, it follows that we must now speak of those outward marks of the Church of God. And there are two particular and principal marks, the sincere preaching of the Word of God, and the lawful partaking of the sacraments of Christ.(13) There are some who add to these the study of godliness and unity, patience in affliction, and the calling on the name of God by Christ, but we include these in the two already mentioned. St. Paul writing to the Ephesians says: "Christ gave himself for the congregation, that he might sanctify it, and cleanse it in the fountain of water through the word." In this testimony of the apostle you have the marks of the Church, that is, the Word and the sacrament by which Christ makes to himself a Church. For with his grace he calls, with the blood of Christ he purifies: and he proclaims this by his Word to be received with faith, and seals it with sacraments, in order that the faithful should have no doubts concerning their salvation obtained through Christ. Now these things properly belong to the faithful and holy members. If hypocrites are not purified, the fault is in themselves and not in God or his holy ministry: (14) they are certainly sanctified visibly, and for that reason they are counted holy amongst men; but these things do not properly belong to them. On this point St. Peter does not differ in the least from St. Paul, for when he preached the Word of God to the people of Jerusalem, and they demand what they should do, Peter answers: "Repent, and be ye every one baptized in the name of Jesus Christ for the remission of sins." Therefore St. Peter conjoined baptism with doctrine, the sacrament with the Word.(15) He had learned this from our Saviour himself in the Gospel written by St. Matthew, saying: "Teach ye all nations, baptizing them in the name of the Father, and of the Son, and of the Holy Ghost." So that in the Acts you do not read of any other tokens of the Church than those of the Word and sacraments as in the words: "They continued in the doctrine of the apostles, and in doing alms-deeds,[46] and in breaking of bread, and prayer": where you can see the Supper of the Lord, another sacrament, adjoined to the sacrament of baptism, and also the desire and study of unity and love, and calling upon the name of God.

These things are clear and firm enough, but I will add other testimonies out of the Holy Scriptures. Concerning the token of God's Word, or the preaching of the Gospel, the Lord himself speaks by Isaiah the prophet saying: "I will make this covenant

[46] Lat. *beneficentia.*

with them, My Spirit that is come upon thee (the Church), and my words which I have put in thy mouth, shall never go out of thy mouth, nor out of the mouth of thy seed,[47] nor out of the mouth of thy children's children, saith the Lord, from this time forth for evermore." For in the Gospel, too, the Lord Jesus says: "He that is of God doth hear the word of God," and again: "My sheep hear my voice, and I know them, and I give to them everlasting life; and they shall not perish for ever," and again: "He that loveth me will keep my commandments; he that loveth me not will not keep my commandments," and again: "Whoso is of the truth will hear my voice." Now concerning the marks and tokens of the sacraments St. Paul speaking of holy baptism says: "Through one Spirit we are all baptized in one body."[48] And speaking of the Lord's Supper he says: "Though we be many, yet are we one bread and one body; for we are all partakers of the same bread. Is not the cup of blessing which we bless partaking of the blood of Christ?" Therefore being approved [49] by testimonies of Holy Scriptures, it is most certain that the outward marks and tokens of the Church are the Word and sacraments. For these bring us into the society of one body ecclesiastical, and keep us there.

Now properly (as I said earlier) all these testimonies belong to the elect members of God, who are endued with faith and true obedience. They do not properly belong to hypocrites who are without faith and due obedience. Yet because these too hear the voice of the shepherd outwardly, and ensue virtue, and openly or outwardly are annexed to the elect and true believers in the partaking of the sacraments, indeed, to the true body of Christ, for the sake of the outward signs they are reckoned to be in the Church so long as they do not depart from it. On this point, for the sake of perspicuity, having treated of the marks of the Church, we must now add that it is as a common rule[50] that these marks declare and note the members of the Church. For there are certain special members who although they lack these marks are not excluded from the society and communion of the true Church of Christ. For it is most certain that there are many in the world who do not hear the ordinary preaching of God's Word, or come into the company of those that call upon God, or receive the sacraments: not because they despise them, or find pleasure in being absent from sermons and the preaching of God's Word,[51] but because

[47] E.V. omit this clause.   [48] Lat. *in unum corpus.*   [49] Lat. *traditum.*
[50] Lat. *lege communi.*   [51] Lat. omits "and . . . God's Word."

through necessity, such as imprisonment or sickness or the constraint of other evils, they cannot attain to that which they earnestly desire; and yet for all that they are true and lively members of Christ and of the catholic Church. In times past the Lord instituted or appointed to [52] the people of Israel a visible Church which he established by a certain law and set forth by visible signs. If any man despised this Church, or refused when he was able to hear the doctrine of the Church, or to enter in among the holy company and do sacrifice, or railed at it, or instead of the appointed order of worshipping God embraced some other kind, he was certainly not reckoned to be of the order and number of the people of God. And yet it is certain that there was an innumerable company of men dispersed throughout the whole world among the Gentiles who never did or could communicate with this visible company and congregation of God's people, and yet they were still holy members of this society and communion, and the friends of almighty God. There were a great many of the children of God with Joachim and Jechoniah taken prisoners by Nebuchadnezzar and brought captive to Babylon, to whom it was no prejudice or hurt that they were separated from the people of God, who still had the temple and visible worship at Jerusalem under Zedekiah: just as indeed it was of little value to a great many to be in the visible companies and congregations with the people of God in God's temple, when their minds and hearts were not sound and perfect. In these days we may find a great many of the faithful dispersed on the seas, condemned to the galleys for the profession of the true faith. We may find many held in captivity under antichrist, of whom we will speak in the next sermon. We may find also a great many in Greece, Natolia, Persia, Arabia or Africa, who are the servants of Jesus Christ and worthy members of the catholic Church of Christ, but excluded and debarred from the holy mysteries [53] of Christians through the impiety and cruelty of Mahomet. Yet we shall find them most closely joined together in one spirit and one faith with all the members of the Church who are also marked with the visible signs. Therefore the Word and sacraments are by common decree the marks of the Church, but they do not separate or mark off from the communion and society of the faithful those believers who by some necessity are shut out from the visible company of the faithful.(16)

[52] Lat. *in populo.*   [53] Lat. *a sacris.*

But to the perfect understanding of the marks of the Church there belongs this also, and principally: that it is not enough to brag about the Word of God or about Scripture unless we also embrace and retain and uphold the true sense and that which agrees with the articles of the faith. For if you corrupt the sense of Scripture and urge the same in the Church, then you do not bring forth genuine Scripture itself, but your own opinion and the fancies which you have devised in your own mind. The church of the Arians did not refuse the Word of the Lord, but rather laboured to adorn and defend their own blasphemous errors by the testimonies of Holy Scripture. That church denied our Lord Jesus Christ to be of one substance with God the Father, which the sense of Scripture and the orthodox faith both affirmed and urged as one of the principal points of our faith. Hence it did not allege the sincere and pure Word of God, however much it boasted of it, but an adulterated word, thrusting in and defending its own heretical opinion instead of the true and perfect meaning of Holy Scripture. Therefore it did not have the true mark of the Church and it was not the true Church of God. By this one unhappy example we may judge all other heretical churches, for although they may not seem to be without the testimony of God's Word, yet in fact they have no purity of God's Word in them.(17)

What we have said concerning the Word of God has necessarily to be understood of the use of the sacraments as well: for unless they are used orderly and lawfully, in the order in which the Lord himself instituted them, they are not marks or signs of the Church of God. Jeroboam sacrificed truly, indeed he sacrificed to God, but because he did not sacrifice lawfully he was reckoned a stranger and an apostate from the true Church of God. Indeed, David himself brought the ark of the Lord with great devotion and much joy and melody, but because he did not carry it lawfully on the shoulders of the priests, at once instead of great joy the great sorrow which followed declared that it is not enough to use the sacraments and ordinances of God unless you use them lawfully; and if you do, God will acknowledge you as his. Moreover those who formerly were baptized by heretics were not baptized again by the old catholics, because the heretics did not baptize into the name of any man, or into the society of their errors [54] or heresies, but baptized "in the name of the Father, and of the Son, and of the Holy Ghost," and they did not invocate

54 Lat. *ignorantiae*.

their own name or the name of arch-heretics, but of Jesus Christ. It was not the baptism of heretics which they did not refuse, but the baptism of the Church administered by heretics. Therefore they did not allow that the churches of heretics may be recognized as true by true signs, but they acknowledged that heretics use things which properly [55] belong to the true Church. And it does not in any way derogate or take from a good thing simply because a wicked or evil man administers it. (18) Today we do not acknowledge the upstart Romish church of the pope (we are not speaking now of the old apostolic Church) to be the true Church of Christ, but we do not rebaptize those who were baptized by priests imbrued with popish corruption, for we know that they are baptized with the baptism of Christ's Church and not of the pope, in the name of the Holy Trinity, to the articles of the catholic faith, not to errors and superstitions and papistical impieties. Finally we confess that today the unworthiness of the minister cannot derogate at all from the service of God. [56] Similarly we do not refuse the Lord's Prayer or the Apostles' Creed or finally the canonical Scriptures themselves simply because the Romish church also uses them, for that church does not have them of itself, but received them from the true Church of God. Hence we use them in common with it, not for the Romish church's sake, but we use them because they came from the true Church of Christ. (19)

Apart from these outward marks of the Church which true believers have in common with hypocrites, there are certain inward marks which belong specially to the godly alone: or if you prefer, call them rather bonds or peculiar gifts. It is these which make the outward marks to be fruitful and make men worthy and acceptable in the sight of God if for some necessary cause the outward marks are absent. For without them no man can please God. Therefore in them we have the true mark [57] of God's children. They are the fellowship of God's Spirit, a sincere faith, and twofold charity, for by these the faithful, as true and lively members of Christ, are united and knit together, first to their head Christ, and then to all members of the body ecclesiastical. And the consideration of this point belongs chiefly to the knowledge of the true Church of God, which although it tolerates rotten members is not defiled by them through their outward conjunction, for by continual study it labours by all means to keep itself undefiled to God. And

55 Lat. *peculiariter.*   56 Lat. *rei divinae.*   57 Lat. *typus.*

first of all the evangelical and apostolic doctrine teaches us that Christ is joined to us by his Spirit, and that we are tied to him in mind or spirit by faith, that he may live in us and we in him. For the Lord cries out in the Gospel saying: "If any man thirst, let him come to me and drink. He that believeth in me (as the scripture saith) shall have streams of living water flowing out of his body." To which saying the evangelist at once adds: "But this he spake concerning the Spirit, which they should receive that believed in him." Again, in his Gospel, promising his Spirit to his disciples and indeed to all his faithful, who was to abide with them for ever, he says: "In that day ye shall know that I am in my Father, and you in me, and I in you, that is, by the Holy Ghost": John the apostle expounding and saying: "By this we know that he dwelleth in us, by the Spirit that he gave unto us", and again; "By this we know that we dwell in him, and he in us, because he hath given of his Spirit unto us." St. Paúl, the vessel of election, does not differ from St. John, writing and saying to the Romans: "If any man hath not the Spirit of Christ, the same is none of his. And whosoever are led by the Spirit of God, they are the children of God." Now as touching true faith, which binds us to the Lord, St. Paul says: "I live now, yet not I, but Christ liveth in me. But the life which I now live in the flesh, I live yet through the faith of the Son of God, who loved me, and gave himself up for me." And again he says: "Christ dwelleth in our hearts through faith." In agreement again with these sayings, St. John the apostle says: "Whosover confesseth that Jesus Christ [58] is the Son of God, God dwelleth in him, and he in God." For earlier in the Gospel the Lord himself said: "He that eateth my flesh, and drinketh my blood, dwelleth in me, and I in him"; and it is he who believes who eats the flesh of Christ and drinks Christ's blood. Therefore Christ our Lord is joined unto us in spirit, and we are tied to him in mind and faith, as the body to the head. Therefore those who lack this knot and bond, that is, who have not the Spirit of Christ, nor true faith in Christ, are not the true and lively members of Christ, the Lord himself in the Gospel again witnessing and saying: "If a man abide not in me, he is cast forth as a branch, and withereth; and men gather them, and cast them into the fire, and they burn." In imitation of these words of our Saviour the apostle (as we have just quoted) says: "He that hath not the Spirit of Christ is none of his." But those who are not destitute of the Spirit

[58] Lat. omits "Christ".

of Christ are inflamed with the love of God. Nor do we separate love from faith,(20) for the same St. John teaches us the second time and says: "God is love; and he that dwelleth in love dwelleth in God, and God in him." For the Lord says in the Gospel: "If a man love me, he will keep my word; and my Father will love him, and we will come unto him, and will dwell with him."

But although, strictly, faith joins us to our head Christ, yet it also knits us to all Christ's members upon earth. For since there is amongst them only one faith, and therefore the same Spirit, there can only be the same mouth, the same mind and the same sentence, even though faith be understood not only as a confidence in the mercy of God through Christ, but also as an outward confession of faith. For as we all confess one faith and one and the same head, with one spirit and mouth we also profess together that we are all members of one and the same body. Nor is there anything in the world that more unappeasably dissevereth the minds of men than the diversity of faith or religion; and therefore there is nothing that can more closely join us together than unity of faith.(21)

We now come to speak of love, which, I said, joins together the members of the body ecclesiastical mutually among themselves. The Lord says in the Gospel: "A new commandment give I unto you, that ye love one another; as I have loved you, that ye also love one another. By this shall all men know that ye are my disciples, if ye have love one to another." There is therefore no doubt that after faith the only mark of the Church is love, a bond which most firmly knits together all the members. It grows from the communion of Christ and unity of the Spirit. For since Christ, the king, the head and high bishop of the catholic Church, enduing us all with one and the same Spirit, has made us all his members, the sons of God, brethren and fellow-heirs, whom without doubt he tenderly loves, the faithful man can only with fervent love embrace the members and fellow-heirs of their king, their head and their high bishop. For John the apostle says: "Every one that loveth him that begat, doth love him also that is born of him. If any man say, I love God, and hateth his brother, he is a liar: for how can he that loveth not his brother whom he hath seen, love God whom he hath not seen?" Paul, in order most properly to express for us and as it were to set before our eyes this unity and agreement of the members, uses a parable taken from the members of a man's body, saying: "For as we have many members in one body, and all members have not one office; so we being many are one body in Christ, and every one one another's members." In the twelfth chapter of the first epistle to the Corinthians he expounds more fully and plainly the conjunction of the heads and members, and that mainly by the same parable of the members of a man's body, expressing it very eloquently,[59] and witnessing that between the highest members of the Church and the lowest there is a great and fitting agreement, and also a diligent care, and assistance which is both continual and most faithful. From all this it appears that the marks of the true and lively Church of Christ are the communion of the Spirit of Christ, sincere faith, and Christian charity, without which no man is a partaker of this spiritual body. And by these things you may easily judge whether you are in the fellowship of the Church or not.

Moreover, from what we have already discussed concerning the marks of Christ's Church we gather what is the source of the Church and how it is planted, propagated and preserved. Its source is heavenly, for St. Paul speaking of the Church says: "Jerusalem which is above is free, which is the mother of us all." Therefore he calls the Church heavenly, not because it dwells completely in heaven, but because although it is on earth it has a heavenly beginning. For the children of God are not born of flesh and blood, but from heaven, by the renewing of the Holy Spirit, who through the preaching of God's Word plants faith in our hearts, by which faith we are made the true members of Christ and his Church. For Peter says: "Ye are born anew, not of mortal seed, but of immortal, by the word of God, which liveth and lasteth for ever." And Paul says: "I begat you in Christ Jesus through the gospel." And in another place the same apostle says: "Faith cometh by hearing, and hearing cometh by the word of God."

Therefore since faith comes by hearing, and hearing by the Word of God, and that distinctly, the Church cannot possibly spring up or be built up by the decrees and doctrines of men. Hence we affirm that only the Word of God is apt for the building up of the Church of God. The doctrines of men set up the churches of men, but Christ's Word builds up the Christian Church. For the doctrines of men proceed from flesh and blood. But Peter, confessing Christ with a true faith, and therefore grounded upon Christ who is the foundation of the Church, heard these words from Christ himself: "Flesh and blood hath

[59] Lat. *elegantissime expoliens.*

not revealed these things unto thee, but my Father which is in heaven." And therefore Paul says: "When it pleased God that I should preach his Son among the Gentiles, I conferred not of the matter with flesh and blood," etc. And obviously excluding all doctrines of men from the setting up and establishing of faith and the Church, and commending only the Word of God, he says to the Corinthians: "My word and preaching stood not in the enticing speech of man's wisdom, but in plain evidence of the Spirit, and of power; that your faith should not be in the wisdom of men, but in the power of God." The following testimonies of Christ are also relevant: "He that is of God heareth God's word." Again: "He that is of the truth will hear my voice." And again, more plainly, he says: "The sheep will follow the shepherd, because they know his voice. They will not follow a stranger, but will run away from him, because they know not the voice of strangers." But under the voice of strangers we include all the decrees of men which differ from the doctrine of Christ. To these the apostle Paul attributes the shape of wisdom, but he denies to them the truth, and calls them superstitious. For our Lord himself in the Gospel quotes from the prophet Isaiah that immutable [60] saying: "They worship me in vain, teaching for doctrines men's precepts." Therefore let us hold that the Church is not built by man's decrees, but founded, planted, assembled and built only by the Word of Christ.

We add that the Church of God is undoubtedly preserved by the same Word of God, lest at any time it should be seduced or should slip and perish, and that it can never be preserved by any other means. To this Paul again witnesses, saying: "Christ hath given some to be apostles, and some prophets, and some evangelists, some pastors and teachers, for the gathering together of the saints, for the work of the ministry (that is to say, to teach and preach the word), and for the edification of the body of Christ; till we all meet together in the unity of faith, and knowledge of the Son of God, unto a perfect man, and unto the measure of the age of the fulness of Christ; that we henceforth be no more children, wavering and carried about with every wind of doctrine, by the deceit of men (I ask you to note how the doctrines of men are again condemned with great and inviolable authority) and with craftiness, whereby they lay in wait to deceive. But let us follow the truth in love, and in all things grow up into him which is the head, that is,

[60] Lat. *irrefragabile.*

Christ; by whom all the body being coupled and joined together by every joint, for the furniture thereof (according to the effectual power which is in the measure of every part) receiveth increase of the body unto the edifying of itself in love." These words of the apostle are so plain that they do not need any better exposition than that which they have in themselves.

In this place, too, we ought properly to state the order and directing of the Church by the Word of God, that which many describe as the ministry of the Word or the Church: but we will speak of this (God willing) in the third sermon. In this place it will be sufficient to defend the truth that having given teachers to the Church our Lord God founds, builds, maintains and enlarges the Church by his Word and his Word alone.

Two things now call for consideration. The first is that by reason of the continual and constant study of the Word of God the Church of God is called prophetic and apostolic, and also orthodox. For it is called prophetic and apostolic because by the labour of the prophets and apostles it was first built, and by their doctrine it is preserved even to the present time and shall be propagated even to the end of the world. It is called orthodox because it is sound of judgment, opinion and faith. For without the Church there is no true faith, nor perfect doctrine concerning true virtue and felicity. The faith and doctrine of the Church was revealed from heaven by God himself through Adam and the patriarchs, through Moses and the prophets, through Christ and the apostles. For that reason the Church is also called a mother, of which we shall treat in the next sermon.(22)

Second, the succession of doctors or pastors of the Church does not prove anything of itself without the Word of God. The champions and defenders of the papistical church boast that they have a most certain mark of the apostolic Church, that is, in the continual succession of bishops which derives from Peter by Clement the First, and so to Clement the Seventh, and to Paul the Third who died recently, and so continuing to Julius the Third, who has only just been created pope.(23) Moreover they add that all those members are cut off which separate themselves from that church in which alone that apostolic succession is found. And we do not deny that the right succession of pastors was of great weight in the primitive Church. For those who were then called pastors were pastors indeed, and executed the office of pastors. But what kind of pastors those have been for some time who out of the rabble of cardinals, mitred bishops and sophisters have been called pastors of the church of Rome, only those are ignorant who are altogether without understanding. The prophet Zechariah heard these words spoken to him by the Lord: "Take to thee yet the instruments of a foolish shepherd; for lo, I will raise up a shepherd in the land, which shall not look for the thing that is lost, nor seek the tender lambs, nor heal that that is hurt, nor feed that that standeth up: but he shall eat the flesh of the fat, and tear their hoofs in pieces. Woe be to the idol [61] shepherd that forsaketh the flock," etc. Therefore by their continual succession of bishops who do not teach the Word of God sincerely or execute the office and duty of pastors, these men do not prove any more than if they were to set before the eyes of the world a company of idols. For who dare deny that many, indeed the majority of bishops of Rome since Gregory the Great were idols and wolves and devourers like those described by the prophet Zechariah? I ask then, what can the continual succession of such false pastors prove? Indeed, did not the later ones fill almost the whole Church with the traditions of men, and partly oppress the Church of God, and partly persecute it? In the ancient church of the Israelites there was a continual order of succession of bishops, without any interruption from Aaron to Urias, who lived under Ahaz, and to other wicked high-priests who also fell away from the Word of God to the traditions of men, and indeed to idolatry. But for all that, that succession did not prove the idolatrous high-priests, with the church which adhered to them, to be the true high-priests of God and the true Church of God. For the true prophets of God, the sound and catholic fathers,[62] who preached the Word of God alone apart from and indeed clean against all the traditions of men, were not able to reckon up any succession of priests to whom they themselves succeeded. Yet in spite of that, they were most excellent lights, and worthy members of the Church of God, and those who believed their doctrine were neither schismatics nor heretics, but even to this day are acknowledged to be the true Church of Christ. When Christ our Lord, the blessed Son of God, taught here on earth and gathered together his Church, the succession of high-priests ranged itself with his adversaries: but that did not mean that they were the rulers of the true Church of God, and Christ of the heretical church. The apostles of our Lord could not

[61] E.V. have "idle", an error which is no doubt due to sheer carelessness.
[62] Lat. *viri.*

allege for themselves and their doctrine an unbroken succession of high-priests: for they were ordained by the Lord, who was also himself created of God the High Priest for ever after the order of Melchisedek, outside the succession of the order of Levi. Yet the Church which was gathered by them is acknowledged by all to be the true and holy Church. The apostles themselves would not allow any to be counted their true followers [63] and successors but those who walked uprightly in the doctrine and way of Christ: for the saying of Paul is notable and manifest: "Be ye followers of me, even as I am of Christ." And though he speaks these words to all the faithful, and not only to the ministers of God's Word, yet he would have the latter his followers like all other Christians, that is to say, every man in his vocation and calling. The same apostle, speaking at Miletum to the bishops of Asia, says amongst other things: "I know this, that after my departing shall grievous wolves enter in among you, not sparing the flock. Moreover, of your own selves shall men arise speaking perverse things, to draw disciples after them." It is from the apostolic Church itself, indeed from the company or assembly of apostolic bishops and pastors, that Paul the apostle fetches out the wolves and devourers of the Church. But do you not think that these could have alleged the apostolic succession for themselves and their most corrupt cause, that is, that they were descended from apostolic pastors? But since forsaking the truth they have fallen from the faith and doctrine of the apostles, their derivation and apostolic succession does not in any way help them. Therefore we conclude that of itself the continual succession of bishops does not prove anything, but on the contrary that succession which lacks the purity of evangelical and apostolic doctrine is not valid.

And therefore Tertullian, although he greatly esteems (and rightly) the continual succession of pastors in the Church, yet he requires it to be approved by the sincerity of apostolic doctrine, indeed, he accepts as apostolic churches those churches which are instructed with pure doctrine and yet cannot make any reckoning of a succession of bishops. If any one wants the words of the author they are as follows: "But if there be any churches that dare presume to plant themselves in the very age of the apostles, that therefore they may seem to have been planted by the apostles, because they were under the apostles, we may say thus: Let them bring forth the first beginning of their

[63] Lat. *imitatoribus.*

churches, let them turn over the order of successsion of their
bishops, so that by successions going from the first beginning
that first bishop of theirs may be found to have for his author
and predecessor some one of the apostles and apostolical sort
of men, and yet such an one as continued with the apostles.
For by this means the apostolic churches give their judgment:
as the church of Smyrna testifieth that they had Polycarpus
placed there by St. John; and as the church of Rome sheweth
that Clemens was appointed by St. Peter; and as in like sort
also other do shew for themselves, who have their offspring
of apostolic seed, placed in their bishoprics by the apostles.
Let heretics feign some such matter (for after their blasphemies, what is unlawful for them?) but albeit they do feign,
they shall not prevail. For their own doctrine being compared
with the doctrine of the apostles, by the diversity and con-
trariety thereof shall shew that it had neither apostle nor
apostolical man for the author; because, as the apostles taught
nothing that was contrary among themselves, even so apostolical
men set forth nothing contrary to the apostles; but only such as
fell away from the apostles, and taught other doctrine."(24) In
this manner therefore may those churches appeal who although
they cannot bring for their author any apostle or apostolic man,
like those which are of a much later date and are even now
being daily erected, yet agreeing in one faith they are still
counted apostolic, for the likeness of the doctrine.

The same author, speaking of the ancient church of Rome,
and gathering the sum of what it either taught or learned, said:
"Happy is that church to which the apostles have uttered all
their doctrine with their blood: where Peter in suffering is
made like to the Lord: where Paul is crowned with the like
end that John had: where the apostle John, after that he was
plunged in hot scalding oil, felt no pain, and was banished into
the isle. Let us see what it learned, and what it taught, and how
it doth agree with the churches of Africa. It acknowledgeth
one God the maker of all things, and Jesus Christ, the Son of
God, the creator, born of the Virgin Mary; and the resurrection
of the flesh: it joineth the law and the prophets with the doctrine
of the evangelists and apostles, and from them drinketh that
faith; baptizeth with water, clotheth with the Holy Ghost,
feedeth with the Lord's supper, exhorteth with martyrdom;
and contrary to this institution receiveth no man. This is the
institution."(25) Thus far Tertullian in the book which he
entitled *Of the Prescription of Heretics*.

The last thing that is to be noted is this: that not only of old and up to the present time, but in these days too the Lord God gives doctors and pastors to the Church: doctors, I say, and not leaders [64] and captains of hosts, not princes, not soldiers, not crafty men using deceitful means which nowadays they call practices. For by no other means and manner, by no other instrument than by the doctrine of truth and sound and simple godliness, [65] is that holy and catholic Church of God built up, fenced and preserved, of which at the beginning simple men and Christ's apostles laid the foundation. Paul therefore sets aside all worldly wisdom and says: "I was among you, Corinthians, in weakness and in fear, and in much trembling; neither stood my word and my teaching in the enticing speech of man's wisdom, but in plain evidence of the Spirit and of power; that your faith should not be in the wisdom of men, but in the power of God." The same apostle also banishes all crafty counsel with all kinds of deceit when writing to the Thessalonians he says: "Our exhortation was not by deceit, nor by uncleanness, nor by guile. But as we were allowed of God that the gospel should be committed unto us, even so we speak; not as they that please men, but God, which trieth our hearts. Neither yet did we ever use flattering words, as ye know; nor coloured covetousness, God is record; neither sought we praise of men," etc. Therefore that man is greatly deceived and foolish who thinks that the Church can either be gathered together, or being gathered can be maintained and preserved, by practices, that is, by crafty counsels and the subtle deceits of men. The common people say truly that "that is overthrown by man's wisdom which was first built by man's wisdom." Besides this, the Lord himself removes force and arms from the building of the Church, since he forbids his disciples the use of the sword, and to Peter who was ready to fight he says: "Put up thy sword into the scabbard." Nor do we ever read that the Lord sent any as soldiers to bring the world into subjection with armed force, but rather Scripture witnesses that the great enemy of God, antichrist, shall be destroyed with the breath of his mouth. Hence there is no doubt that all those things which are read in different places in the prophets, and especially in the twelfth chapter of Zechariah, about wars to be made against all nations by the apostles and apostolic men, ought to be expounded figuratively.

[64] Lat. *doctores, quidem, non ductores.*
[65] Lat. *quam doctrina veritatis et pietatis sincera et simplici.*

For the apostles according to their manner fight as apostles, not with the spear and sword and bow of physical warfare, but of spiritual. The apostolic sword is the Word of God.(26) Meanwhile no one denies that the weapons of physical or corporal warfare have from time to time been of advantage to apostolic men and the Church, and do good even today.(27) No one denies that God does frequently use the help of soldiers and magistrates in defending the Church against the wicked and tyrants: on the contrary, everyone will confess that the good and godly magistrate has his duty [66] to the Church of God. For not without great cause does the worthy [67] prophet of God, Isaiah, call "kings nursing fathers and queens nursing mothers." Paul, when he is oppressed by the Jews in the temple at Jerusalem for preaching the Gospel among the Gentiles, is taken away and rescued by the army of Claudius Lysias, the tribune. And not long after the same tribune sent with the apostle no small company of soldiers, that is, a troop of horsemen and certain companies of footmen, by whom he was brought safely to Antipatris and Caesarea before Felix the proconsul of Judea: as Luke recalled, not hastily, but with much diligence and in great detail in the Acts of the Apostles. Ecclesiastical history recites many instances of holy princes who have defended and succoured the Church of God. But I have in some manner dealt with these things elsewhere, in the seventh and eighth sermons (as I remember) of the second decade. Thus far concerning the origin of the Church and its increase and preservation.

It seems to me that in this context we may not inappropriately handle or briefly expound the famous question, Whether the Church of God may err? In order that it may be better understood I will briefly discuss the parts of this question. I have taught that the catholic Church of God comprises, first the blessed spirits in heaven, then all faithful Christians here on earth: to whom I said that the wicked or hypocrites belong in that they feign faith for a time. Now, therefore, if we understand by the Church the blessed spirits in heaven the Church can never err. But if we understand the wicked or hypocrites joined and mingled with the good, and the wicked alone, they do not do anything else but err, but as they are joined unto the good and faithful and follow them, they either err or do not err. For the Church of the good and the faithful on earth both errs and does not err. This we will declare when we have

[66] Lat. *operam suam*.   [67] Lat. *clarissimus*.

weighed the diversities of errors and gathered them all together in a bundle. There are some errors in doctrine and faith, and some in life and conduct, and what they both are, everyone knows. Let us see then whether the Church of the faithful on earth does err or not, and if so, in what point and to what extent. As concerning the manners and life of the Church, it cannot wholly and clearly acquit itself of errors, that is to say, of sin.(28) For always, as long as it is living here on earth, it prays heartily: "And forgive us our trespasses, as we do forgive them that trespass against us." And God for his mercy's sake always purges in his saints all dregs and infirmities as long as they live in this world, the elect being continually renewed and defiled. I am not unaware of your difficulty, faithful reader. If the Church, you say, is not holy and pure, how does the apostle call it holy, without spot and wrinkle? I answer, If you will not acknowledge any Church upon earth but that which is completely without blemish, then you will not be able to acknowledge any. For there never will remain any such Church upon earth, where the most righteous God, as Scripture testifies, hath shut up all things under sin, that he might take mercy on all men. Therefore St. Paul calls the Church pure, without spot or wrinkle, on account of the benefit and sanctification of Christ. It is not that while it is in the flesh it is without spot in itself, but that those spots which might otherwise cleave to it, by the innocency of Christ are not imputed to those who embrace Christ by faith, and finally that in the world to come the same Church shall be without spot or wrinkle. For when it has put off the flesh and cast off all miseries, it will at length be in the position where it has no lack of anything. Moreover the Church is said to be without spot because of the continual study with which it labours and travails by all means to have as few spots as it possibly can. And by that means, and above all by the benefit of imputation, the Church does not err but is most pure and as it were without sin.(29)

Moreover, as touching doctrine and faith, the Church of Christ does not err. For it hears only the voice of the shepherd but does not know the voice of strangers: for it follows the one shepherd, Christ, who says: "I am the light of the world: he that followeth me shall not walk in darkness, but shall have the light of life." Paul also says to Timothy: "These things hitherto have I written unto thee, that thou mayest know how thou oughtest to behave thyself in the house of God, which is the church of the living God, the pillar and ground of truth." But the Church is the pillar and ground of truth because being established upon the foundation of the prophets and apostles, Christ himself, which is the everlasting truth of God and the Church's only strength, by the fellowship which it has with him it is granted to be with him the pillar and foundation of the truth. For the truth of God is in the Church, it is spread abroad by the ministry of the Church, and being assaulted and warred against by its enemies it abides fast and is not overcome, in so far as being made one body with Christ the Church perseveres in the fellowship of Christ, without whom it can do nothing. Again, the same Church does err in doctrine and faith whenever it turns from Christ and goes after men and the counsels and decrees of the flesh; for it forsakes the thing which has hitherto prevented it from erring, which is the Word of God and Christ. I do not think that any man will deny that the great congregation of the people of Israel in the desert was an excellent Church of God, with which the Lord made a covenant and bound himself to it by sacraments and ordinances. And yet we all know how shamefully it erred when it neglected God's Word, and because Aaron the high-priest of religion did not constantly and earnestly resist, it both made a golden calf and worshipped it as a god. For this reason it shall surely be necessary [68] more diligently to examine and mark the whole number of the Church, for when many in the Church err, it does not follow that none at all is free from error. For as in the church of Israel the Lord reserved to himself a remnant, I mean Moses, Joshua and undoubtedly many more, both in that congregation and elsewhere, so there is no doubt that although many do err in the Church the Lord by his mercy preserves to himself a certain number who both understand aright and by whose faith and diligence errors are destroyed and the wandering flock of the Lord are brought back again into the holy fold.

Therefore the Church is said to err when a part of it has lost the Word of God and errs. And it does not err wholly or altogether, for certain remnants (by the grace of God) are reserved, by whom the truth can flourish again and be spread abroad again in every place. St. Paul called the churches of the Corinthians and the Galatians the holy churches of God; yet these erred greatly in doctrine, in faith and in manners: but who doubts that among them there were many who were most sincere followers of the pure doctrine preached by St.

[68] Lat. *opportunum erit.*

Paul? Therefore that holy Church erred in so far as it did not continue steadfastly in true doctrine, and it did not err in so far as it did not depart from the truth delivered by the apostles.[69] Hence it may plainly appear to the whole world that those men are vain liars who commend to us churches which are not built on the foundation of the prophets and apostles, but on the decrees of men, and which they shamelessly commend as most true churches and such as cannot err. David cries out: "Only God is true, and every man a liar." And Jeremiah cries: "They have rejected the word of the Lord, and what wisdom is in them?" Therefore those churches do err and they are not the true churches of God. The true Church is grounded upon Jesus Christ and governed by his Word alone.

The discussion of the power of the Church of God on earth, and of its duties as directed according to the Word of God, amounts to much the same [70] as a treatise on the Word of God, which is the only rule by which everything is done in the Church. But before I give my own judgment, that is, the judgment delivered by the Scriptures, I will briefly rehearse the sum of those things which the papists have committed to writing in this matter and undoubtedly maintain as sound doctrine. John Gerson (who does not go far astray unless he has a bad interpreter) has defined ecclesiastical authority as a "power supernaturally and spiritually given of the Lord to his disciples and their lawful successors unto the end of the world, for the edification of the church militant according to the laws of the Gospel for the obtaining of eternal felicity."(30) But Peter de Aliaco, the cardinal, says that this authority is sixfold, covering consecration, the administration of the sacraments, the appointing of the Church's ministers, preaching, judicial correction, and the receiving of things necessary to this life.(31)

That which they call the authority of consecration is the power by which a rightly ordained priest can consecrate the body and blood of Christ on the altar. They say that this power was given to the disciples by the Lord when he said: "Do this in remembrance of me." But they think that in these days it is given to priests by the bishop when he gives them the bread and the chalice and says: "Receive ye power to offer up and consecrate Christ's body both for the quick and the dead." They also call this a power of orders, and a mark or character which cannot be wiped off. The power of administering the

[69] E.V. Lat. *apostolum*.   [70] Lat. *affinis est.*

sacraments and above all the sacrament of penance, is what they call the power of the keys. As they see it there are two kinds of keys: the keys of knowledge, that is to say, the authority of knowledge when a sinner makes his confession; and the keys of pronouncing sentence and judgment, or of opening or shutting up heaven, or forgiving or retaining sins. They say that this power was promised to Peter in Matthew when the Lord said: "Unto thee will I give the keys of the kingdom of heaven"; but also that it was given to all the disciples in John when Christ said: "Whose sins soever ye forgive, they are forgiven to them," and nowadays it is given to priests by the bishop when at their consecration he lays his hands on the heads of the priests who are to be ordained and says: "Receive ye the Holy Ghost; whose sins soever ye forgive, they are forgiven them." What they call ecclesiastical jurisdiction is the power of placing ministers in the Church, and it consists of prelacy: hence in the full sense it belongs only to the pope in respect of the whole Church. For it belongs to the pope alone to appoint rulers and prelates in the ecclesiastical hierarchy, because to him it was said: "Feed my sheep." Moreover, they say that all ecclesiastical jurisdiction comes from the pope to inferior rulers either directly or indirectly, the authority being limited according to the pleasure of him who has the fulness of authority, for a bishop has authority only in his own diocese, and a curate in his parish, etc. The power of apostleship or the preaching of the Word of God they call the authority of preaching, which the Lord gave to his disciples when he said: "Go ye into all the world, preaching the gospel to all creatures." But in these days doctors affirm that no one ought to be sent to preach except by Peter, that is, his successor, either directly or indirectly, etc. They say that the power of judicial correction was given to Peter by God, when he said: "If thy brother shall offend or trespass against thee," etc., for the words of the Lord are known well enough in Matthew, chapter 18. Therefore they say that God gave to the priests the power not only of excommunicating, but also of determining, judging and establishing commandments, laws and canons, because in that place it is said: "Whatsoever ye bind upon earth, it shall be bound in heaven." To conclude: they say that the power and authority to receive things necessary for this life, in reward of their spiritual labours, was given in the words of the Lord: "Eating and drinking such as they have."

Now these things are taught by them concerning ecclesiastical power not only foolishly but falsely. Of the power of consecration and sacrificing, we have often said before in other places how vain and foolish it is, and perhaps will say more (if God grant life) at the proper place and time. The power of the keys we will discuss (God willing) towards the end of the next sermon, and we have already contributed something in our discussion of penance and auricular confession. What they babble about ecclesiastical jurisdiction and the fulness of the plenary power (that is to say) of the bishop of Rome are only foolish and shameless trifles, which I have no doubt the whole world has known for some time, and later in these sermons we shall give some arguments in confutation. In so far as they usurp to themselves the office of teaching and cry out that no man can lawfully preach unless he is ordained by them, they try in that way to overthrow the Word of God and to defend and assert their own errors: which we shall also treat of in the proper place. The power of excommunicating they have abused so filthily and shamefully that by their negligence and wicked presumption the Church has not only lost true discipline but for the bishops of Rome excommunication itself has for a long time meant nothing but fire and sword, with which they have raged generally against the true professors of God's Word and persecuted the innocent worshippers of Christ. That there is no power given by God to the ministers of the Church to make new laws we shall also show in the right place. The authority and power to receive the means of life they have executed to the uttermost, but in recompense for their temporal harvest they have not sown spiritual things, but rather, being asleep, they have allowed him that is our enemy to sow cockle in the Lord's field, and that solely by their own means. For not being content with things necessary for this life, have they not under that pretext subtly invaded kingdoms and most shamefully and cruelly possessed them? Therefore if there are any who do not see that ecclesiastical authority as affirmed and practised by these men is simply a tyranny over simple souls, it is plain that they see nothing at all.

We will now append a true, simple, plain and evident doctrine of ecclesiastical jurisdiction. Power is defined as a right which men have to do things. The Greeks call it Ἐξουσία and Δύναμις, the first word signifying right and power, and the second ability to execute authority or power, for it often happens that a man has the authority to do a thing but has not the ability to perform it. But God

can do both, and he has given both to the apostles against those
that were possessed with devils, as Luke testifies, saying:
'ἔδωκεν αὐτοῖς δύναμιν καὶ ἐξουσίαν: "He gave them power
and authority over all devils," etc. And there is also one
kind of power which is free and absolute, and another which
is limited, which is also called ministerial. Absolute power
is that which is altogether free, and is neither governed
nor restrained by the law or will of any other. Of this
kind is the power of Christ as he himself speaks of it in the
Gospel, saying: "All power is given unto me in heaven and in
earth: go therefore and teach all nations, baptizing them" etc.
And speaking again of this power in the Revelation made to St.
John the apostle, he says: "Fear not; I am the first and the last;
and I am alive, but was dead; and behold, I am alive for evermore. And I have the keys of hell and of death." And again:
"These things saith he that is holy and true; which hath the
key of David, which openeth and no man shutteth, and shutteth
and no man openeth." The power which is limited is not free,
but subject to the absolute or greater power of others. It cannot
do all things of itself, but only those things which the absolute
or greater power allows to be done, and allows under certain
conditions: and of this kind surely is ecclesiastical jurisdiction,
which may rightly be called ministerial power, for the Church
of God uses the authority committed to it for this purpose by
its ministers. St. Augustine, acknowledging this distinction,
and referring to baptism in his fifth treatise on John, says:
"Paul baptized as a minister, and not as one that had power
of himself; but the Lord baptized as he that had power of
himself. Behold, if it had pleased him, he could have given this
power, but he would not; for if he should have given this power
unto his servants, that it should also have been theirs which
was the Lord's, then there should have been as many sundry
baptisms as servants" etc.(32) In the Church Christ reserves
that absolute power to himself, for he continues the head, king
and bishop of the Church for ever: and that head which gives
life is not separated from his body at any time: but it is the
limited power which he has given to the Church. And that
is what it ought to acknowledge, that is, an ecclesiastical jurisdiction which is hemmed in by definite laws and which proceeds from God. That is why it is effectual and in all things its
primary regard should be for God. And that ecclesiastical
jurisdiction is given to the Church in order that it might be
put into practice for the profit of the Church. For St. Paul says:

"The Lord hath given us power, to the intent we should edify, and not for the destruction of the church." And therefore the power which tends to the hindrance and destruction of the Church is a devilish tyranny, and not an ecclesiastical power which proceeds from God. And it is necessary that we should take note of this purpose of ecclesiastical power and keep to it.

But the limited power of the Church consists very closely in the following points: the ordaining of the ministers of the Church, doctrine and the discerning between doctrines, and finally, the ordering of ecclesiastical matters. We will now say something about all these points in order, showing what is the nature of the Church's authority and to what extent it is limited in every part.

The Lord himself appointed the first doctors of the Church, the apostles, in order that all men might understand that the ecclesiastical ministry is the divine institution of God himself, and not a tradition devised by men.(33) And for that reason when the Lord had ascended into heaven, St. Peter called the Church together and spoke from the Scriptures of appointing another apostle in the place of the traitor Judas, thus showing that power was given to the Church by God to elect ministers or teachers. The same Church shortly afterwards, being persuaded by Peter and the apostles under the undoubted inspiration of the Holy Ghost, chose seven deacons. The church of Antioch, being obviously instructed by the Holy Ghost, ordains and sends Paul and Barnabas, although they had already been assigned to the ministry for many years. We also read in the Acts of the Apostles that the churches by the commandment of the apostles ordained doctors for the sacred ministry whenever the need arose: yet in spite of that they did not ordain anyone without selection, but only those who were suitable for that office, that is to say, those whom they themselves later described in express rules, to wit, "If any man were faultless, the husband of one wife, watchful, sober" etc. The rule set down by the apostle is well enough known as it appears in I Timothy 3. But (God willing) we will speak of the ordaining of ministers in the third sermon of this decade. But if the Church has received power to appoint suitable ministers for the Church, I do not think that there are any who will deny that it has the authority to depose the unworthy and wicked deceivers, and also to correct and amend those things which if they are lacking may appear to be necessary for this purpose.

And since ministers are chosen chiefly to teach, it follows

necessarily that the Church has power to teach, to exhort, to comfort and such like by means of its lawful ministers: yet not the power to teach everything, but only that which it received as delivered from the Lord by the doctrine of the prophets and apostles. "Teach them (says the Lord) that which I commanded you." "Go ye, and preach the gospel to all creatures." And St. Paul says: "I am put apart to preach the gospel of God, which he promised before by his prophets in the holy scriptures." But this ministry and office of preaching is simply the power of keys received by the Church: the office (I say) of binding and loosing, of opening and shutting heaven. In another place, too, the apostles received power from the Lord over all; over all, I say, not absolutely, but over all devils, and not over all angels and men: and even the authority and power which they received over devils they did not receive absolutely, for it was added that they were to expel them and cast them out. Therefore they were not able to deal with devils according to their own fancy, but only as he would have them do who has absolute power over all devils, so that they could cast devils out of men but could not send them into men, however much they might have desired to do so. Similarly in the case of diseases they could not please themselves: otherwise Paul would not have left Trophimus sick at Miletum when he might have been very useful to him in the sacred ministry. If the two disciples had been able to do what they pleased they would have commanded fire from heaven to fall down upon Samaria, thus taking vengeance on the discourteous and barbarous people of Samaria because they refused to welcome the Lord. In the same way the same apostles received keys, that is to say, power to bind and loose, to open and shut heaven, to forgive and retain sins, but always with a clear limit, for they could not loose that which was bound in hell, nor bind those who were living in heaven. For he did not say, "Whatsoever ye bind in heaven," but, "Whatsoever ye bind upon earth"; nor did he say, "Whatsoever ye loose in hell," but, "Whatsoever ye loose upon earth." Again, they were not able to bind and loose those whom they themselves desired, not even upon earth. For they were not able to loose, that is, to pronounce a man free from sin, if he had no faith: again, they could not bind, that is, pronounce condemned, a man who was lightened with faith and truly penitent. And surely those who teach any other doctrine concerning the power of the keys deceive the whole world: a matter with which we shall deal more fully in the proper place. Similarly the Church has received from Christ the power to administer the sacraments by its ministers, but not according to its own will and pleasure, but according to the will of God and the form and manner set down by the Lord himself. The Church cannot institute sacraments, nor can it alter the ends and use of the sacraments.(34)

Furthermore, that the Church has power to give judgment on doctrines appears from the one sentence of the apostle Paul: "Let the prophets speak two or three, and the other judge." And in another place he says: "Prove all things, and keep that which is good." And St. John says: "Dearly beloved, believe not every spirit, but try the spirits, whether they are of God." But there is also a fixed order in this power to judge. For the Church does not judge according to its own pleasure, but according to the sentence of the Holy Spirit and the order and rule of the Holy Scriptures.(35) And here too order, moderation and charity must be observed. Therefore if at any time the Church of God, according to the authority which it has received of the Lord, calls together a council for some weighty matter, as we read that the apostles of the Lord did in the Acts of the Apostles, it does not incline there to its own carnal judgment, but surrenders itself to be guided by the Spirit, and examines all its doings by the rule of the Word of God and of twofold charity. Therefore the Church does not make any new laws, for the church of Jerusalem, or rather the apostolic Church, says "that it seemeth good both to the Holy Ghost and to the church, that no other burden should be laid upon" faithful Christians, but only a few and those very necessary things, and not either outside or contrary to the Holy Scriptures.(36) Now ecclesiastical matters of which the Church has power to dispose for the well-being of men are of many different kinds, as for instance those which concern the time and place of outward worship, or prophesying, or the interpretation of tongues, or schools. The Church also has power to judge in matrimonial causes: and above all it is charged with the correction of manners, admonitions, punishments, and also excommunicating or cutting off from the body of the Church: for the apostle also says that this power is given to him but in order that he may edify and not destroy. For all the things which we have remembered and others like them are limited by the rule of the Word and of charity, and also by holy examples and reasons deduced from the Holy Scriptures, of which we will perhaps speak more fully in the right context.

That is what I have to say about ecclesiastical power. And I have already shown how blatantly our adversaries declare the contrary. But they handle these matters so grossly that even children may see what it is that they really seek or try to defend, that is, not ecclesiastical power, but their own covetousness, lust and tyranny. Canonical truth teaches us that Christ himself holds and exercises absolute or full power in the Church, (37) and that he has given ministerial power to the Church, which executes it for the most part by ministers, and religiously executes it according to the rule of God's Word.

Having considered these things, we shall not have any great difficulty in knowing the duties of the holy Church of God. For (as I have just said) it executes the power which it has received of God most carefully and faithfully, in order that it may serve God, and be holy, and please him. And to reckon up the sum of its duties in particular: first, it worships, calls upon and serves one God in Trinity, and does not take anything in hand without having first consulted the Word of this true God. For it orders all its doings according to the rule of God's Word: it judges by the Word of God: and by the same Word it frames all its buildings, and when they are built maintains them, and when they have fallen down repairs or restores them. It fervently assists and loves the assemblies and congregations of saints upon earth. In these assemblies it listens diligently to the preaching of the Word of God, it partakes devoutly of the sacraments and with great joy and delight of heavenly things. It prays to God by the intercession of our only mediator Christ with a strong faith, fervently, continually and most attentively. It praises the goodness and majesty of God for ever, and with great joy it gives thanks for all his heavenly benefits. It highly esteems all the institutions of Christ, not neglecting any of them. But above all it acknowledges that it receives all the things which belong to its life, salvation, righteousness or felicity, from the only Son of God, our Lord Jesus Christ, as the one who alone chose it, and then by his Spirit and blood sanctified it and made it a Church, that is, a chosen people, who is its only king, redeemer, high priest and defender, and without whom there is no salvation. Therefore it rests alone in God by our Lord Jesus Christ; him alone it desires and loves; and for his sake it rejoices to lose all the things that belong to this world, and indeed to pour out its blood and its life. And therefore it cleaves inseparably to Christ by faith, nor does it hate anything more bitterly than apostasy from Christ and desperation, for without Christ nothing at all in life seems to be pleasant. With Satan it has an unappeasable enmity as with a deadly enemy. Against heresies and errors it strives both constantly and wisely. The simplicity of the Christian faith and the sincerity of the doctrine of the apostles it keeps most diligently. As far as possible it keeps itself unspotted from the world and the flesh, and from all carnal and spiritual infection. And therefore it flees from and in every way detests all unlawful congregations and profane religions, and all wicked men, and willingly and openly confesses Christ both in word and deed, even at the risk of its life. It is exercised with afflictions, but never overcome. It keeps unity and concord carefully. It loves all its members most tenderly. It does good to all men, as much as power and ability allow. It hurts no man. It forgives willingly. It bears with the weak as a brother until they are advanced to perfection. It is not puffed up with pride, but by humility is kept in obedience and moderation and all the duties of godliness. But I ask who can recite all the specific duties of the Church [71] even in a long discourse, much less in this short recital? And who would not desire to be a member of so divine and heavenly a congregation?

And now, lifting up our minds to heaven, let us give thanks to the Lord our God, who through his beloved Son has purified us and gathered us together, to be a chosen people to himself, and to be heirs of all his heavenly treasures. To him therefore be all praise and glory, world without end. Amen.

[71] Lat. *sanctae ecclesiae.*

NOTES

ZWINGLI

OF THE CLARITY AND CERTAINTY OR POWER OF THE WORD OF GOD

1. The title as given on the title page is: Of the Clarity and Certainty or Infallibility (*unbetroglische*) of the Word of God. In this context "infallibility" does not denote inerrancy in content but an absolute certainty of fulfilment. Gwalter omits altogether the second title, in which "power" (*kraft*) is substituted for "infallibility," and introduces a subsidiary heading: *De imagine Dei*, etc.

2. Zwingli seems to become aware of the danger of digression and returns to the theme of the divine image.

3. Melito of Sardis (active c. 150–170) was leader of the sect known as the Anthropomorphites, whose error was to ascribe to God a corporal existence. Melito's work on the subject is no longer extant, but it is attested by Origen (on Gen. 1:26) and Eusebius, *Hist. eccles.*, IV, 26.

4. Zwingli has to allow that God assumed bodily form at the incarnation, but he points out that this took place subsequent to the creation of man in the divine image.

5. Cf. Augustine, *De Trinitate*, IX, 11; X, 10, 18; XV, 7, etc.

6. The so-called Athanasian Creed, art. 35, *Nam sicut anima rationalis et caro unus est homo, ita Deus et homo unus est Christus.* Zwingli does not think that this defines the divine image: it is merely a useful comparison.

7. The argument now begins to lead up to the main theme.

8. Sardanapal was an Assyrian king noted for his luxurious mode of life. He committed suicide after the siege and capture of Nineveh in 883 B.C. Nero and Heliogabal were the dissolute Roman emperors of the 1st and 3rd centuries A.D.

9. Zwingli assumes that the author of the Epistle of Jude was Lebaeus, the apostle Judas, brother of James, son of Alphaeus.

10. The passage which follows is a typical example of Zwingli's detailed exegesis.

11. From this important statement we may see that Zwingli did not regard regeneration as a completely new creation but as a

327

reconstitution in the divine image. The divine image had not been destroyed by sin—otherwise there would be no universal desire for God. It had been obscured and weakened, but could still be renewed and restored.

12. This is a significant qualification: original sin is a proneness to sin, but is not guilty in itself. In this respect it resembles the scholastic (and Tridentine) concupiscence, which is not sin, but gives rise to sin and may become sin.

13. In spite of this sentence Zwingli proceeds to give several fresh illustrations: indeed these form the whole section.

14. A reference to the Greek myth. Zeus condemned the human race to destruction, but Deucaleon and Pyrrha were spared, and when they cast stones behind them a new race sprang up. See Ovid, *Metamorph.*, I, p. 253.

15. It may be noted that no power is ascribed to the external action.

16. Although this passage is incidental, explaining apparent delays in the fulfilment of the Word, it is of great importance for an understanding of Zwingli's theology. As Zwingli points out, the sovereignty of God involves independence of time, and it is in the light of this absolute transcendence that we must understand the divine operations in providence, election and effectual calling. It is of interest that in spite of the biblical basis the form in which Zwingli states the doctrine owes much to the philosophy which is later condemned. There is a similar passage in the didactic poem, *The Labyrinth*, C.R., I., p. 58.

17. This explanation of the parabolic method has a strangely modern ring. Zwingli makes it clear that the ultimate aim of the parable is positive, i.e., to teach, and it accomplishes this by making the path of learning attractive and interesting. But at the same time the parable makes a moral demand on the hearer, for only those who are fundamentally concerned will penetrate to the true meaning.

18. Zwingli cannot allow that parables conceal the truth—otherwise the Word would not be clear. The truth is obscured by the blindness or wickedness of those who hear without faith.

19. Cf. Hilary, *In Matthaeum comm. can.* XIII.

20. At this point Zwingli makes a first appeal to his hearers. Since he knew that many of the nuns were deeply opposed to evangelical teaching there is no doubt that the address is personal.

21. Zwingli cannot describe the Word itself as destructive, for if he did his opponents would at once argue that it ought not to be given to the people without careful explanation.

22. Cf. Josephus, *Antiquitatum Judaicarum, lib.* II.

23. The example of Micaiah is particularly valuable, since it illustrates the trustworthiness of inward conviction even in the face of majority decisions. The point is taken up again later.

24. We now come to the main theme, that the Word is to be understood from the Word itself and not from human commentaries upon it. On this grounds Zwingli demands an open Bible and rejects the Church's claim to be the interpreter of Scripture.

25. Zwingli now gives an example to show how easily the Word can be understood apart from official interpretation. It may be noted that in this case the understanding seems to be rational comprehension, and only the literal sense is in question. Many of the obscurities arose directly out of the complicated mediaeval scheme of exegesis.

26. The pretended interpreters of the New Law are here ranked with their counterparts under the Old, i.e., men like Annas and Caiaphas.

27. An even more pointed reference to those who were opposed to the message.

28. Zwingli is here alluding to the external splendours of church dignitaries, which he regards as obstacles to inward religion.

29. Zwingli now tackles the decisive question of authentication. He rejects all outward tests and relies upon the inward testimony of the Spirit.

30. The confusion resulting from reliance upon human opinions is contrasted with the certainty given by the Word itself when illuminated by the Spirit.

31. The Carthusian order was founded by Bruno in 1084, the first house being at La Chartreuse, in Grenoble. The Carthusians were noted for their extreme austerity.

32. The Benedictine order was founded by St. Benedict in 529. It was the oldest existing order in the West and a basis or norm for all the others.

33. Lit. *Predicant:* The Dominicans were an order of preaching friars founded by St. Dominic in 1215.

34. Lit. barefooted, probably in the sense of Franciscan (Gwalter has *Franciscanus*). There were many "barefooted" monks and friars in other orders (both calced and discalced), but Francis was the first founder of a barefooted order and the term was often used of the Franciscans at this period.

35. James the elder was traditionally supposed to have been martyred at St. Jago de Compostella in Spain, and his shrine was a famous place of pilgrimage. The knightly order of Compostella was founded by Pedro Fernandez in 1161 to protect the pilgrims.

36. A brief reminder in passing that free justification by faith is the essential evangelical message.

37. Zwingli takes it that the Magdalene is the same as Mary the sister of Martha, or Mary of Bethany.

38. A specific attack upon the monastic system and its inevitable misunderstanding of the Gospel.

39. Zwingli now attempts more fully to free Scripture from the over-riding interpretative authority of the Church.

40. The need for supernatural illumination does not mean that the Scriptures do not have a plain sense. Illumination is necessary because of our blindness rather than the obscurity of the text.

41. From this the opponents of Zwingli argue that tradition must supplement Scripture, and the way is opened up for all kinds of perversion. But Zwingli recognizes no authority apart from the Word given, and this is presumably enshrined only in Scripture.

42. Zwingli takes up again the defence of minority convictions, and he shows that exponents of the truth must often stand alone.

43. The past errors of church councils and leaders support his case. Anastasius II (496–498) attempted to resume communion with Acacius of Constantinople but was resisted by the Roman clergy. Gratian referred to him as a Pope rejected by the Church, and on that ground he was usually regarded as a heretic in the Middle Ages. Liberius (352–366) first supported Athanasius against the Arianizers and was banished (355), but in 358 he condemned Athanasius and was allowed to return to Rome.

44. The point is that we can understand Scripture only when we allow God to speak through it. Otherwise we read into it our own prior beliefs.

45. The example draws attention to two evils, the perversion of the office of bishop, and the false exegesis of Scripture.

46. Hilary, *De patris et filii essentia*. Zwingli hastens to add that the patristic support, although useful, is neither necessary nor decisive.

47. With this statement Zwingli boldly asserts a Protestant individualism in the apprehension of truth. An obvious weakness is that he does not allow sufficiently for the value of exposition by godly men in times past. And he does not answer the difficulty that humble and sincere scholars often reach mutually exclusive opinions, although this could be explained no doubt by the continuance of some prejudice or self-will in either the one or the other, or both.

48. In point of fact, Zwingli's repudiation of his debt to the past (as also to Luther) is probably exaggerated, but his main point is the valid one that a straightforward reading of Scripture had given him an insight into its essential message which the existing systems had hitherto obscured, and he felt that he could ascribe the experience only to the Holy Spirit illuminating the Word.

49. Zwingli's opponents accused him of ignoring the counsel of others, but they themselves were more blameworthy in that they disregarded the counsel of God himself.

50. The opportunity is taken to condemn yet another abuse of episcopal authority.

51. It may be noted that Zwingli endorses the traditional doctrine of the inspiration of Scripture, but he goes on to assert the need for divine enlightenment in the understanding of it.

52. Gwalter gives this closing section a separate heading: *Canones quidam et certae notae*, etc.

53. The somewhat fanciful application of Isaiah's words seems to indicate that Zwingli found it difficult to break away entirely from the mediaeval schema of exegesis.

OF THE UPBRINGING AND EDUCATION OF YOUTH IN GOOD MANNERS AND CHRISTIAN DISCIPLINE: AN ADMONITION BY ULRICH ZWINGLI

1. Gerold Meyer von Knonau (b. 1509) was the son of Hans and Anna Meyer. His father died in 1517, and Zwingli married the widow, probably in 1522, although the marriage was not celebrated publicly until 1524. Gerold was killed at the battle of Cappel (1531).

2. I.e., Baden-in-Aargau.

3. Glareanus (Heinrich Loriti of Glarus) was a noted Swiss humanist and musician and a friend of Zwingli until the latter's breach with Erasmus.

4. Hence the title of the first English translation of 1548.

5. An evident allusion to Horace: *Ars poetica* v. 386–388, *nonumque prematur in annum*.

6. Perhaps a proverbial saying which Zwingli remembered from the Toggenburg.

7. Zwingli introduces the prayer as a reminder that we cannot follow Christ simply in our own strength.

8. As always, Zwingli insists that true faith is the work of the Holy Spirit. He quotes his favourite verse from John 6.

9. Pericles was renowned in antiquity for his oratorical gifts.

10. It is worth noting that for Zwingli neither Word nor sacrament can accomplish anything apart from the inward work of the Spirit.

11. Zwingli does not reject the possibility of a natural theology. Through external phenomena we may learn the existence and providence of God, and upon this basis the doctrines of revelation may then be erected.

12. The picture is probably that of the ordered family life which Zwingli himself had known at Wildhaus. The providence and fatherhood of God exclude all possibility of Deism.

13. Zwingli now turns to the doctrines of grace, summarizing the main evangelical teachings.

14. The universality of original sin is strongly asserted by Zwingli, although elsewhere he repudiates any idea of original guilt.

15. Nero ordered his tutor Seneca to be put to death, although he allowed him to fulfil the order in his own way. There was a (probably unreliable) tradition that the poet Ennius and Scipio were buried in the same tomb.

16. An allusion to the supposed redemptive work of Jupiter.

17. Righteousness in the sense of innocence (*innocentia*).

18. Righteousness in the sense of justice (*justitia*).

19. There is an interesting thought here. Zwingli argues that the righteousness of Christ may be imputed to us by virtue of his self-identification with us in the incarnation.

20. Zwingli does not mean that the believer cannot commit sin, but as he goes on to explain, that the sin of the believer is not imputed.

21. This is the thought of Anselm in his *Cur Deus Homo?* Inasmuch as Christ is God, his merits are more than sufficient to make satisfaction for all the sins of men.

22. Zwingli now shows that justification by faith does not destroy the necessity of good works.

23. An "entelechy" is a complete and perfect being as opposed to mere possibility or potentiality. Both the word and the concept derive from Aristotle. Zwingli applies the notion of entelechy in a novel and interesting way. As the one who moves all things, God necessarily moves his people to service and good works.

24. Zwingli now considers the various aspects of the life of faith. It may be noted that he reverses the scholastic concept of faith formed by charity, speaking of virtue formed by faith.

25. It is still insisted that true virtue comes from within. The fact that Zwingli speaks of helping and counselling others seems to suggest that he has at the back of his mind the thought of the ministry.

26. Zwingli himself had undertaken to learn both these languages, and he was most anxious to introduce them at Zurich, as the reform of September, 1523, reveals. The purpose of this study was to arrive at an exact understanding of Scripture, the Bible being essential to the proper nourishment of spiritual life and therefore to right conduct.

27. Zwingli probably has in mind that the mediaeval corruptions were developments of faulty teachings of the Latin Fathers. Yet he learned a good deal from the Latins, as his early annotations show.

28. The reference is to the *Odyssey*, XII, 37–54, 154–200. Ulysses blocked his sailors' ears with wax lest they should hear the voices of the syrens.

29. A further reminder that for a true understanding of the Bible we are dependent upon God the Holy Spirit.

30. Zwingli is thinking of the supposed order of Pythagoreans, whose novices were reputed to have taken a vow of silence for periods varying between two and five years. Cf. the lives of Pythagoras by Diogenes, Laertius and Iamblichus.

31. It may be noted that Zwingli gave much time to the development of his powers as a preacher.

32. Probably a reference to Pliny, *Historia naturalis*, VIII, 1, 3 (6).

33. Zwingli does not advocate total abstinence, but he warns against the moral and physical dangers of intemperance.

34. The peasant days in the Toggenburg had taught him to value plain but wholesome food and to despise delicacies.

35. After Hippocrates, Galenus was the most famous physician of antiquity (second and third centuries A.D.).

36. Perhaps an allusion to the excessive fasting prescribed by monastic rule.

37. Milo of Croton was noted for his strength and was frequently a victor in the Olympic games. He belonged to the sixth century B.C.

38. A necessary warning in a century notorious for its extravagance.

39. E.g., Virgil, *Aeneid*, III, 57; Sallust, *Cat.*, X.

40. Zwingli was probably thinking of the dynastic and territorial ambitions which caused constant wars in his day.

41. It need hardly be recalled that Zwingli had considerable musical interests and talents.

42. This is not merely an abstract definition of the just war, but a practical warning against mercenary service, which Zwingli had come to regard as completely unjustifiable.

43. The city of Marseilles was founded c. 600 B.C. and was famous in antiquity for its culture, commercial enterprise and sound morality.

44. Seneca, *Epistola*, XCV, 52 f.

45. No doubt Zwingli recalled many many happy festivities in which he had taken part both in the Toggenburg and during his years at school and university.

46. Cf. Cicero, *De officiis* III, 29.

47. Perhaps Zwingli had at the back of his mind the occasion when his father and uncle prevented him from becoming a Dominican at Berne.

48. He is obviously thinking here of parents who refuse to accept the evangelical teaching.

49. By nature Zwingli inclined to prudence, and his reforming work was characterized by its caution and careful timing.

50. In the sixteenth century the Swiss were famous for their hardihood, which was demanded by their circumstances of life, both in war and peace.

51. A reference to Pontius Cominius, who swam the Tiber in order to give warning of impending attacks by the Gauls.

52. Chloelia also swam the Tiber, this time to escape from Porsena, who had taken her away as a hostage. She was handed over again, but later released, and other hostages with her.

53. As usual, Zwingli realizes that his work suffers from over haste, but he has neither the time nor the inclination to revise it.

54. Ovid, *ars amator*, III, 65 f.

55. The exact meaning of the phrase is not clear. Many commentators suggest that it is a reference to the impersonal tone, or the general nature of the treatment. In other words, Zwingli felt that he ought to have been more personal in writing to a step-son, but either because the marriage was still secret, or because he wrote with a view to publication he had to adopt a different course. Others suggest that he is merely excusing the inadequacy of the work. Strictly within the context, it may be that he is simply qualifying his previous statement: it is not a case of adding to the existing riches of birth, etc., but of attaining to the only true riches, which are spiritual.

OF BAPTISM

1. The full title is *Von dem Touff, vom Widertouff und vom Kindertouff*. The text is preceded by the dedicatory letter to St. Gall, which is dated May 27, 1525. Owing to limitations of space this letter is not included in the present translation.

2. The image of the mountain torrent was probably suggested by early experiences at Wildhaus.

3. Like Luther, Zwingli saw the importance of concentrating upon the essentials of scriptural truth. One of his main charges against the Anabaptists was their intolerant preoccupation with things indifferent. But of course the Anabaptists did not regard their doctrine of baptism as a non-essential.

4. This was a clear instance where the Reformer had to appeal to Scripture against all existing tradition. Where possible, all the Reformers appealed to the earlier Fathers, but the ultimate authority was always the Bible.

5. The remembrance was a name commonly used by Zwingli for the Holy Communion.

6. It is perhaps worth noting that Calvin took up this thought, that the sacraments were instituted as a concession to human frailty.

7. Zwingli means that in the everyday speech of the age the word sacrament had lost its original meaning, being coloured by the false sacramentalism of scholastic theology.

8. I.e., a supporter of the Confederation, which now numbered 13 cantons and had the white cross as its badge. In the German the word is *Eidgenosse* from which the French *Huguenot* is thought to derive.

9. The reference is to a famous victory in 1388 which the Swiss gained over the Austrians near Nähenfels in Glarus. On the first Thursday in April a memorial pilgrimage was made there every year, and there was a procession past the eleven cairns commemorating the men of Glarus who had fallen in the engagement.

10. It is of interest that the Anglican article (28) condemns transubstantiation on the ground that "it overthroweth the nature

of a sacrament," i.e., if the body of Christ is there, the bread is no longer a sign.

11. The doctrine that the New Testament sacraments succeeded and replaced the two Old Testament signs was to be an important one in Reformed teaching. The exclusion of any possibility of a repetition of Christ's sacrifice should be noted.

12. The thought of God's sovereignty over the means of grace is a crucial one in Zwingli's sacramental doctrine. It links up with his strong doctrine of predestination.

13. Zwingli pleads for a dynamic conception of the sacraments, but he pleads also for a dynamic conception of the Word. Neither Word nor sacrament can accomplish anything in itself, i.e., apart from the sovereign working of the Spirit.

14. This is an obvious dig at the existing hierarchy, which by and large was not distinguished for its activity in teaching.

15. The meaning is that others had baptized before John and therefore there was nothing unusual about the practice as such.

16. The discourse in John 6 played a great part in the development of Zwingli's doctrine, and he appeals to it constantly when dealing with the relationship between inward grace and the outward means of grace.

17. Augustine: *De haeresibus lib.* I *cap.* 1, *et asserebat se esse Christum.*

18. Zwingli was thinking of Jews who allowed themselves to be baptized for the sake of material advantage.

19. The description of Paul's work in Corinth as a form of baptism hardly seems to be warranted by the text.

20. The example of the dying thief was much used by the Reformers, partly to show the possibility of salvation without baptism, partly to prove that justification is by faith alone and not by faith and works.

21. Jerome: *Epistola,* LVIII, 1. Baptism in blood, i.e., martyrdom was a recognized equivalent for water-baptism, but as Zwingli points out there is no such baptism in this case.

22. The Anabaptists could not admit the accuracy of either term. As they saw it, infant baptism was not valid, therefore they neither denied baptism when they opposed it nor did they rebaptize when they baptized adults.

23. Zwingli thus denies the absolute necessity of external baptism. In making this point he was taking up the view of Augustine, that where water-baptism cannot be had, the lack of it may be supplied by internal conversion: a doctrine which is still the official teaching of the Church of Rome.

24. In this passage Zwingli goes rather far towards making baptism only an act of public testimony. This trend is in line with his almost complete separation between inward and outward baptism.

25. *Suasoria:* a word of counsel inclining in a certain direction.

26. It will be remembered that the later theologians of the Reformed school did not follow Zwingli in his rejection of this view, but thought it part of the office of the sacraments to confirm faith.

27. Zwingli seems to realize that he has proved too much, for if no material things can confirm faith this rule must apply to miraculous signs as well as covenant signs. He fails to draw any true line of demarcation between the two.

28. An obvious slip for Ahaz. Gwalter corrected the mistake in his Latin version. Zwingli was probably quoting from memory.

29. This is in direct contradiction to the view of Luther that infants not only can but do believe. There is no reason to suspect any conscious opposition.

30. An admission of earlier doubts in the matter of infant baptism. Cf. Grebel's *Protestation and Defence*, C.R., III.

31. Anabaptists variously attributed infant baptism to Pope Nicholas II and the devil. The falsity of the former legend was exposed by Zwingli in the third section, but it still persisted in Anabaptist circles.

32. It is difficult to prove that the majority of Anabaptists were perfectionists in the strict sense, but from this statement it certainly seems that they believed in the possibility of perfection.

33. This is the first of a number of illustrations taken from the disputations at Zurich. According to Bullinger the incident took place during the disputation which began on March 25, 1525.

34. Zwingli's meaning is that just as the monks and nuns regarded themselves as superior because they were under the monastic rule, so the Anabaptists regard themselves as superior because they are under the baptismal rule. In both cases the inevitable result is legalism and hypocrisy. The Anabaptists were perhaps building upon Luther's view that all monastic vows are superfluous because they are comprehended in the common Christian vow of baptism.

35. Zwingli preserved a proper sense of the fact that the true understanding of Scripture is a spiritual understanding of its message. The detailed study of the text is profitless unless it is directed to that ultimate goal. Therefore he disputes about words and order only to expose the hollowness of his opponents' claims.

36. *Theologi:* Zwingli is thinking especially of the schoolmen, but in this context the term could refer to the Fathers as well.

37. The meaning is that if only the Anabaptists will resist the spirit of contention they will quickly come to a true understanding of Scripture. As he sees it, the problem is primarily a spiritual one rather than an intellectual.

38. Only the children of Christians have a right to baptism: therefore children are always presented by those who have already received some instruction.

39. It was commonly held by the Church that in Matthew 28 Christ was laying down a form of words which must be used when

baptism is administered. Zwingli does not wish to vary the formula, but he disputes this interpretation, on the ground that Christ was really teaching the true meaning and significance of the sacrament.

40. Apart from that countered by Zwingli other explanations were that the name of one person of the Trinity includes the whole Trinity, or that the apostles baptized in the name of Jesus by special revelation.

41. *Kuntz hinderm Ofen:* the proverbial simpleton.

42. Zwingli repeats again that he has no wish to alter the form. He is obviously afraid that his exposition will be misunderstood.

43. This appears to be rather a precarious claim. The most that can be said is that there is no proof that John did not baptize infants.

44. Zwingli himself seems to realize that his earlier statement demands qualification—the matter is one which cannot be proved either way.

45. Attention is here drawn to the abnormal sensitiveness of the Anabaptists upon the point at issue: a characteristic which has persisted in many of their spiritual descendants.

46. Zwingli seizes upon an essential point, that rebaptism, or even adult baptism, involves a sectarian view of the Church. In combating this Zwingli was not merely defending an institutionalized church but the Reformed doctrine of the Church.

47. I.e., St. John the Baptist.

48. The stress is again placed upon the sovereignty of the inward work of the Spirit, and the consequent hiddenness of the true baptism to anyone but God and the individual believer.

49. The possibility of an inward work of the Spirit even in infancy cannot be ruled out, for God is sovereign in respect of the time of his work as well as its subjects.

50. The text in Romans 6 was much used by the Anabaptists, who claimed that only adult believers could know the experience described. Zwingli boldly claims the passage for his own view.

51. This was the antinomian deduction urged against the Reformers themselves.

52. This Pauline understanding of baptism had been powerfully brought out by Luther in his sermon *On Baptism*.

53. We see here the characteristic Reformed stress upon the signification of baptism rather than its effects.

54. The word "engrafting" is interesting, since it suggests a certain spiritual benefit. (Cf. the Anglican article 27.) Zwingli is thinking in terms of initiation or entry.

55. Zwingli allows that there is need of discipline even within the Church, but he attacks the legalistic use of the ban as found in the Anabaptist churches.

56. It seems that some of the Anabaptists had already begun to affect distinctive modes of speech and dress. Cf. the Hutterians.

57. The meaning is that the very severity of the rule defeats its object, since it causes a reaction in those who are subjected to it.

58. The Anabaptists despised the baptism which they had received in infancy, but their adult baptism was counted an important and indeed decisive experience.

59. Lit. *Linmag*, the old name for the river Limmat, on which Zurich stands.

60. The emphasis upon instruction in and with the sacrament is typical of the Reformed approach. All the baptismal services drawn up by the Reformers were designed to bring out the meaning of what is done.

61. Zwingli is adopting already the more radical attitude towards ceremonial which was to mark off the Reformed from the Lutheran churches. After modest beginnings, full-scale reforms were already being carried out in Zurich.

62. Two points may be noted here: first, that the New Testament is taken as an absolute standard even in matters of liturgical practice; and second, that the blessing of the infants is equated with baptism.

63. I.e., original sin. Zwingli admits a universal corruption of the nature of man, but he does not admit that any guilt attaches to it, at any rate in the case of Christians and their children.

64. The damnation of unbaptized infants had been asserted from the time of Augustine, although usually with some mitigation of the sufferings. Zwingli rejects the doctrine absolutely.

65. Augustine: *In Joann. evang. tract.* CXXIV, commenting on John 15: *Accedit verbum ad elementum, et fit sacramentum, etiam ipsum tanquam visibile verbum.*

66. Like all the leading Reformers Zwingli had a great regard for Augustine, and had learned a good deal from his writings, especially the work quoted.

67. It may be noted again that Zwingli will not ascribe any more power to the external word than he does to the external sacrament.

68. Cleverly he seizes on the metaphorical use of the word "water" in other Johannine discourses.

69. Zwingli apparently takes it that the cloven tongues were literally of fire.

70. Not John 3:5 but John 3:22–26.

71. It is not known how Zwingli knew of such a practice in the Indian church. One suggestion is that he was thinking of the σφραγις mentioned in the Gnostic Acts of Thomas and erroneously took it to mean a literal branding. More likely he had heard of an actual practice for which there are parallels elsewhere, e.g. the Copts who sometimes tattooed a cross on their hands, or the Carpocrates who according to Irenaeus branded the lobe of the right ear, *Adv. Haer.*, I c. 20, 4. If Zwingli had heard such a report it is impossible to judge whether it was correct or not.

72. Cf. the frequent quotation of John 3:5 as a proof-text for

infant baptism. The thought is that the external baptism of water is essential for spiritual cleansing and therefore it must not be withheld.

73. Oswald Myconius (1488–1552) was the schoolmaster at the Great Minster, and a friend and later biographer of Zwingli. It was largely through the good offices of Myconius that Zwingli was called to Zurich as people's priest.

74. The psychological acuteness of this analysis is typically humanist.

75. This is a characteristic Protestant assertion, that the good works of a Christian are the natural fruit of faith, not the result of a hard legal observance.

76. Zwingli now lays his finger upon the sectarian pride which was at the root of Anabaptism.

77. There is a reflection here, and perhaps a justification, of the sterner measures now being taken against the Anabaptists.

78. Note that Zwingli does not sanction an extravagant individualism in the interpretation of Scripture. The Church is bound by the Word of God, but the interpretation of the Word properly belongs to the Church.

79. This passage is very interesting in that it reflects Zwingli's own prudence in the carrying out of reform at Zurich. No reform was ever carried through until the people as a whole were ready.

80. For Zwingli Scripture itself is of course the final court of appeal.

81. Like Luther, Zwingli believed in the power of the Word as used by God. For that reason he thought that instruction must always precede action. Only when the ground has been prepared by faithful preaching can the work of reformation be carried through.

82. Zwingli means the outward calling by the congregation as a recognition of the inward calling by God. It may be noted that for Zwingli the minister was called to be a pastor. The words bishop and prophet were both applied by him to the pastor.

83. This was the disputation of March, 1525. Leo Jud had followed Zwingli at Einsiedeln and was now pastor of St. Peter's, Zurich.

84. These discussions took place in August, 1524.

85. The main point of this section is to show that the baptism of John was the same as that of Christ, a position peculiar to the Reformed school.

86. There is possibly a slight allusion to Luther, who had never had to face a combined attack by the papists and Anabaptists on any single issue.

87. Zwingli means that showing the true origin of baptism he will make plain the identity of John's baptism with that of Christ.

88. The papist view was that the baptism of John is only preparatory, and has no power to effect that which it signifies.

89. A play upon the word "shadow."

90. In the strictest sense even the papists would have to accept this, but they would reply that the Holy Ghost has guaranteed to work in Christian baptism, but there was no such work in the baptism of John.

91. Zwingli concedes that as the Son of God Christ could also baptize internally, but as far as the external form is concerned there is no difference between his baptism and that of John.

92. Although Christ was the supreme teacher, yet as man he did not teach anything different from others, nor with any greater effect.

93. Zwingli makes it clear that in these comparisons he is referring only to Christ after his human nature. The Christological teaching is fundamental to Zwingli's doctrine of both Word and sacrament.

94. Literally, this seems to be rather a far-fetched deduction. It is true only inasmuch as repentance unto life came through the Gospel, i.e., the two are bound up together.

95. Zwingli does not take into account Matthew 11:11.

96. These closing verses of John 3 are all taken to be part of John's discourse.

97. This distinction is perhaps over fine.

98. The question of the baptism of the disciples was always a thorny one for the Fathers and schoolmen, since there is no record that they were baptized either by Christ or each other.

99. Zwingli means that Christ is always the true author and giver of baptism, whether through John or the disciples.

100. It is pointed out that John's baptism of Christ was Trinitarian in the sense that it involved the participation of all three persons of the Trinity.

101. The Greek form was fully recognized by the schoolmen.

102. Note again that the meaning is emphasized rather than the correct form of words.

103. It must be noted that Zwingli deliberately interprets this passage in the light of a position already established.

104. The illustration reminds us of Zwingli's strong musical interests.

105. Timotheus was the famous musician who performed at the marriage of Alexander the Great. The story of the double fee is told in Quintilianus, *Institutiones oratoriae*, II, 3.

106. The reference is to Luther's New Testament of 1522, which has *Warauff seyt yhr den toufft*. This is followed by the Basle edition of 1524, and the English Authorised Version also has "Unto what," etc. The Zurich translation of 1524 has *Worinn sind ir den toufft*.

107. Zwingli means that there would have been nothing extraordinary in John's baptism simply as a baptism, for the Jews were already accustomed to ceremonial washings.

108. The text hardly seems to support the view that Apollos had only a defective knowledge of John's teaching, but Zwingli is forced to interpret it in this way because he will not allow that

John's preaching of the Gospel was in any way deficient. The obvious interpretation is that Apollos had no full knowledge of the Gospel because he did not know of the death and resurrection of Christ (even if he did perhaps know that the Christ had come).

109. Apparently there were many who were willing to profess Protestant views in order to advance their own interests, and it is to these that Zwingli is referring.

110. Zwingli means that as Christ died only once, so we can die only once in baptism.

111. It is interesting that although Calvin agrees with Zwingli that the twelve at Ephesus were not rebaptized, he explains the incident quite differently. According to Calvin the twelve had already received the water-baptism of John, but at the hands of Paul they received only the internal baptism of the Spirit accompanied by the laying on of hands.

ON THE LORD'S SUPPER

1. The Latin writings referred to were: 1. *Ad Matthaeum Alberum de coena domini, epistola*, Nov. 16, 1524, 2. *De vera et falsa religione commentarius*, Mar. 1525; 3. *Subsidium sive coronis de eucharistia*, Aug. 17, 1525; 4. *Ad. Joannis Bugenhagii Pomerani epistolam responsio*, Oct. 23, 1525.

2. In point of fact Zwingli had given a German statement of his doctrine in the exposition of the theses. What he means is that he has not written a particular work on the subject.

3. For example, the *Commentarius* was written in response to requests from outside Switzerland, being dedicated to Francis I.

4. Zwingli's books were now proscribed in Uri, and also in the city of Nuremberg (by an order of the Council dated July 14, 1525).

5. The appeal to antiquity ought not to pass unnoticed. The primary authority was Holy Scripture, but like all the Reformers Zwingli liked to think that the Protestant faith was also that of the early Church. The appeal also had good apologetic value.

6. This is a reference to the Lutherans.

7. This is the Roman Catholic view.

8. The reference here is to the views of Erasmus and his followers.

9. Zwingli means here the Lutherans.

10. I.e., the Romanist doctrine of transubstantiation.

11. I.e., the Lutherans, who insist upon a literal interpretation of the words of Christ.

12. I.e., the followers of Erasmus.

13. As in the treatise on baptism Zwingli thinks it necessary to begin with a definition of the word "sacrament". The reason is that the original signification of the word had been lost as a result of false doctrinal associations.

14. It may be noted that this is the doctrine of the Word which Zwingli himself had propounded in his sermon *On the clarity and certainty of the Word*.

15. This is the example which Zwingli himself uses in his sermon.

16. There can be little doubt that Zwingli knew that this argument was already being used against him in Zurich by his opponent Joachim am Grüt. Am Grüt developed the theme in his reply to Zwingli, *Christenlich Anzeygung*, using as his examples Genesis 1, Psalm 119, and the reply of Gabriel to Mary.

17. What Zwingli means is: (a) that it is not Christ who now says the words, but the pope or priest; and (b) that as spoken by the pope or priest the word "my" does not refer to the body of Christ. It follows, then, that we cannot ascribe power to the word of a mere man, and even if we could, the bread would become the body of the celebrant and not of Christ.

18. In other words, Christ accomplishes by the Word only what he himself means by the Word, and not what we think he ought to mean.

19. It will be noted that Zwingli will not allow a substantial presence which is not perceptible. Rather singularly, he does not try to destroy the usual distinction between "substance" and "accidents"—he takes it for granted that a substance cannot be present without its accidents.

20. This is the Lutheran doctrine of consubstantiation, that the bread remains, but in and with it is the substance of the body of Christ.

21. Cleverly Zwingli shows that the Lutherans themselves do not abide by the simple words of Christ literally understood. If they did they would have to accept the doctrine of transubstantiation, which is at least more self-consistent.

22. This is an allusion to Luther's work, *Wider die himmlischen Propheten, von den Bildern und Sakrament*. Quoting I Corinthians 10, Luther comments: "That is, I think, a judgment, yes, an axe of thunder, upon the head of Carlstadt and all his sects." Carlstadt replied with an exposition of the passage.

23. Already the Lutherans were claiming the plain statement of Scripture: a foreshadowing of the intransigent position of Luther at the Colloquy of Marburg.

24. Zwingli here states what was to be a classical Reformed doctrine, that Scripture must always be compared with Scripture.

25. The canons are useful, not because they have any ultimate authority, but because they contain the truth and they have authority for those whom Zwingli wishes to convince.

26. *Corpus juris canonici c.* 42, *Dist. II, de consecratione*.

27. Berengarius of Tours (1000–1088) was the great opponent of Lanfranc in the matter of transubstantiation. In 1079 he was forced to recant by Gregory VII.

28. Pope Nicholas II (1058–1061). It was this pope who was charged with initiating the baptism of infants.

29. The reference is to the Synod of 1059.

30. No reference to these supporters of Berengarius has been discovered.

31. In the Middle Ages the tabernacles were often built into the walls of churches and were therefore very damp.

32. This is perhaps a reference to the argument of Am Grüt, who denied a literal eating in the strictest sense.

33. Cf. *Ad Dec. Grat. P III, dist. 2, c. 1. Ego etc.*

34. Rabanus Maurus (d. 856) was one of the scholars who had resisted the doctrine of transubstantiation in its earlier stages in the ninth century. He was supported by Ratramnus and John Scotus Erigena.

35. *Ad Dec. Grat. P III, dist. 1, c. 1.*

36. Gratian belonged to the twelfth century. He was a monk of Bologna and was the first to teach Canon Law as a subject distinct from theology. Very little is known of his life.

37. Zwingli overlooks another possible interpretation, that it is dangerous to speak the truth concerning the sacraments because the truth can so easily be misunderstood.

38. Zwingli is thinking especially of Bugenhagen, who denied a literal eating with the teeth.

39. This is a reference to the book which developed out of Gratian's lectures and which formed the first volume of the *Corpus juris canonici*. It was originally known as the *Concordantia discordantium canonici*, but is now usually called the *Decretum*.

40. The canon consists of two quotations from Augustine: *Tract. XXV* and *Tract. XXVI, in Joannis evang.*

41. *Corpus juris canonici, c.* 59, *dist. II de consecratione.*

42. *De vera et falsa religione commentarius,* and *Subsidium sive coronis de eucharistia.*

43. The main foundation of Zwingli's sacramental teaching is to be found in this sixth chapter of St. John. Zwingli was helped to his understanding of the chapter by the reading of Augustine.

44. The reference is to the controversy with the Anabaptists concerning the state of the believer between death and the final resurrection. The Anabaptists claimed that there is no consciousness, i.e., the soul sleeps, but Zwingli argued that the spirit still enjoys conscious life in the divine presence.

45. Zwingli means that it is not the flesh itself which is the ransom for sin, but the flesh as it is crucified, i.e., the death of the flesh.

46. In this context the distinction between a carnal and a spiritual understanding is that between an understanding in terms of flesh, i.e., that the eating is literal, and an understanding in terms of the spirit, i.e., that the eating is believing in Christ.

47. *Corpus juris canonici, c.* 44, *Dist. II, de consecratione.*

48. The first part of the canon is from Augustine's *Enarratio in Psalmum* 54, the rest from his *Tractat. XXVII in Joannis evangel.*

49. The reference is to the Lutherans, and especially Bugenhagen.

50. At this point the question of the two natures of Christ is raised publicly by Zwingli for the first time. He had previously mentioned it only in a letter to Nuremburg.

51. The point may easily be overlooked that this fact does make possible a true presence of Christ in the Supper according to his divine nature—indeed this is almost taken for granted by Zwingli.

52. Zwingli maintains strongly the doctrine of the divine impassibility.

53. The reference is to the Romanists.

54. A reference to the party of Erasmus.

55. Zwingli means that the true omnipotence of God is not merely his power to do anything, but his power to do what he wills to do: it involves choice as well as capacity.

56. A reference to Genesis 41. Zwingli returns to the same example below, and cf. C.R., IV, p. 496.

57. This is another example of rather fanciful exegesis on Zwingli's part.

58. I.e., the followers of Erasmus.

59. *Theologi*, meaning especially the mediaeval schoolmen.

60. Marcion of Synope (85–160) was the famous heretic of the second century, who amongst other things maintained a strongly docetic view of Christ. He was excommunicated in A.D. 144 and founded his own churches.

61. Cf. Tertullian, *Adv. Marcionem*, lib. I, c. 14, lib. IV, c. 40.

62. The sequence of the argument is as follows: We eat the body which was given for us. If then we eat it miraculously, it follows that it was given for us miraculously.

63. A playful reference to the arguments with which the exponents of this theory supported their case.

64. *Corpus juris canonici*, c. 44: a quotation from Augustine.

65. Am Grüt disputed the rendering of *veritas* as *Treue* (faithfulness or fidelity). He did not agree that Zwingli had the right to go behind Augustine's Latin to the original Hebrew.

66. The passage is from Augustine's *Tractat. XXX in Joannis evangel.*

67. Zwingli has in mind the works of Billican (*De verbis coenae dominicae*) and Urban Rhegius, which he answered March 1, 1526. Billican (Theobald Gernolt or Gerlacher, of Billigheim in the Palatinate, was a supporter of Lutheranism in Weil and Nördlingen. After 1529 he inclined back to Romanism, but without definitely committing himself to either side. Rhegius was a pastor in Augsburg.)

68. The reply to Billican and Rhegius, which came out on March 1, 1526, only a few days after the present treatise.

69. Cf. C.R., IV, pp. 484 f.
70. A reference to the works of Billican, Rhegius, Bugenhagen and possibly Schwenckfeld and Konrad Ryss.
71. Origen: *In Leviticum Homilia* XIII, 3, and cf. *In Exodum homilia* VII, 4.
72. Zwingli is thinking especially of Schwenckfeld and Ryss. Cf. W. Köhler, *Zwingli und Luther*.
73. Cf. C.R. IV, pp. 500 f.
74. Zwingli will not allow that there is any guilt in respect of the body supposedly eaten in the sacrament, but only in respect of the body represented in the sacrament, the crucified body.
75. The book referred to is: *Joannis Oecolampadii de Genvina Verborum Domini, Hoc est corpus meum, juxta vetustissimos authores, expositione liber.* Basileae Anno 1525.
76. This translation was the work of Ludwig Hätzer and was published in Zurich early in 1526.
77. Jerome, *Commentar. in evangel. Matthaei, lib. IV.*
78. Ambrose, *Commentar. in epist. I ad Corinth.*
79. Cf. *Corpus juris canonici c.* 50 *dist. II, de consecrat.*
80. This latter rendering is obviously more favourable to Zwingli's view and he regards it as the correct one.
81. The word for "faith" is often used for "creed," but in the present context it seems to have the wider significance of "the faith" in general.
82. This interchangeability of the names of sign and thing signified was to play a prominent part in the later sacramental teaching of the Reformed school.
83. Cf. the exposition of the 18th thesis. Am Grüt in his reply seized upon a slight difference between the statement in this thesis and the later teaching of Zwingli in the *Commentarius*, the *Subsidium* and this present treatise.
84. *Corpus juris canonici, c.* 51, *Dist. II, de consecrat.*
85. Augustine, *In Psalmum XXI, enarratio II.*
86. Augustine, *enarratio in Psalmum III.*
87. The example of the marriage ring is taken from a letter of Cornelius Hoen. It was also used by Leo Jud in his book on the sacramental doctrine of Erasmus and Luther: *Des hochgelehrten Erasmi von Roterdam und Doctor Luthers maynung vom Nachtmahl.*
88. Augustine, *Epistola* XCVIII.
89. Zwingli is referring to the Reformed communion service then in use at Zurich.
90. The reference is to the attempted separation between Zwingli and Oecolampadius on purely grammatical grounds.
91. I.e., "communion," not as "partaking," but as "fellowship" or "community."
92. *Corpus juris canonici, c.* 36, *Dist. II, de consecrat.*
93. The words of these two canons have not been found in

Augustine, but have perhaps been collected from tractates XXVI and XXVII on St. John.

94. *Corpus juris canonici c. 62, Dist. II, de consecrat.*

95. The reference is to an anonymous work, probably by Konrad Ryss. The name Konrad Ryss is itself a pseudonym, but "Ryss" is thought to have been a disciple of Schwenckfeld.

96. Carlstadt (Andreas Bodenstein) was Luther's fellow-professor in Wittenberg. At this time he was under the influence of the Anabaptist extremists.

An Exposition of the Faith

1. A fuller version of the title is: *A Short and Clear Exposition of the Christian Faith.*

2. *ad cotem et palum exercerent*—the *palus* was a wooden stake which represented the enemy and was used for practice in close combat.

3. The reference is to false reports concerning the Swiss Reformation which were evidently in circulation at the French Court.

4. Either through ignorance or design Zwingli and his followers were being confused with the Anabaptists.

5. The reference is to the Apostles' Creed.

6. Zwingli's point is that a faith which derives from the one and true God is necessarily a reliable faith. He uses a philosophical argument to show that the God of Christianity is the one true God, but he then bases his certainty of faith upon the Word and revelation of that God.

7. The meaning is that although we may reverence holy things we must not allow them to usurp the place of God as in much mediaeval thought and practice.

8. This distinction between employing and enjoying derives from Augustine.

9. The text reads: λατρείᾳ *adorari.*

10. *pediculari morbo* or louse-disease. Cf. Virgil, *Georgica* 3,564 and Josephus, *Antiquities*, XIX, 8, 2.

11. *per essentiam.*

12. *eucharistia*—usually rendered by Zwingli either as thanksgiving or the Lord's Supper.

13. Lit. "like a reed"—a phrase which suggests rather a mechanical conception of inspiration.

14. *In symbolo.*

15. It is to be noted that although Zwingli clearly thinks of the atonement in terms of a reconciliation of the divine justice, he refers both justice and mercy to one and the same goodness in God, thus avoiding any suggestion of a division within the deity. And nowhere does he even hint that the justice is proper to the Father and the mercy to the Son.

16. Two points stand out in this paragraph: first, the obvious influence of the scholastic presentation; and second, the necessity of the incarnation and death of Christ for the purposes of reconciliation.

17. The separation of the divine and human aspects of Christ's being and works is essential to Zwingli's theology, and in spite of his stress upon the unity it inevitably suggests a fundamental Nestorian tendency.

18. This comparison derives from Augustine.

19. The reference is to the so-called Athanasian Creed.

20. *in unitatem hypostaseos: hypostasis* was the Greek term used to signify the individual person within the essence of the Trinity. Its Latin equivalent was *persona.*

21. Zwingli is perhaps hinting at the perpetual virginity of Mary, which he seems never to have denied.

22. ἀόρατος.

23. ἀνάλγητος.

24. Zwingli does not accept the view later propounded by Calvin that Christ tasted all the torments of hell, but he clearly links up the descent with the salvation of all who had died in faith or piety prior to the coming of the Redeemer.

25. A reference to Irenaeus, *Adv. Haer. IV*, 18, 5.

26. It is to be noted that the incarnation is vital to Zwingli's soteriology, since it makes possible the necessary identification both of Christ with the believer and of the believer with Christ.

27. The understanding of the incarnation is the key to a right understanding of the divine presence in the Supper.

28. παραλογίξῃ. Cf. Acts, 26:24.

29. The quotation is from *In Joannis evang. tract. XXX.*

30. I.e., the papists and Lutherans.

31. Zwingli here accepts the title which was officially accorded to the Virgin at the Council of Ephesus in 431.

32. This verse clearly indicates a creationist doctrine of the origin of the soul.

33. *sacramentaliter.*

34. For a full list of Zwingli's writings on the subject, see G. Finsler, *Zwingli-Bibliographie*, 1897; for those of Oecolampadius, E. Staehelin, *Oekolampad-Bibliographie*, 1918. On the relations between the two see E. Staehelin, *Das theologische Lebenswerk Johannes Oekolampad*, pp. 267 f., 598 f., 1939.

35. *improprie*, i.e., not properly, or strictly.

36. I.e., the Lutherans.

37. *fides historica*—an acceptance of the historical truth of the events proclaimed.

38. σεισάχθεια—the reference is to the act of Solon in 594 B.C. when he remitted all debts and prohibited slavery for debt.

39. Zwingli returns to the example of the ring which he had used in his *Treatise on the Lord's Supper.*

40. *analogia.*

41. By the body of Christ as redeemed from death he means the Church.

42. μετωνυμιχῶς.

43. *leberide sunt inaniores*—a Latin proverb used by Erasmus, *Adagia I*, 1, 26. *Leberide* is a transcription of the Greek λεϐηρίδη.

44. The reference is obviously to Revelation 21:2, but Zwingli is no doubt quoting from memory and erroneously ascribes the verse to Paul. He was perhaps thinking of Galatians 4:26.

45. As Zwingli sees it the true Church consists of the whole company of the elect, the visible of all external confessors. The two are united in that the elect are themselves confessors and therefore members of the visible Church.

46. Zwingli is probably thinking of the Smaller Council at Zurich.

47. A further reference to the charge of Anabaptism.

48. σύστρεμμα ἢ σύσασιν.

49. Strictly, the prophetic office, i.e., preaching.

50. Zwingli again uses the analogy of the twofold nature of man.

51. Cf. Jeremiah 29:7 and I Timothy, 2:2.

52. I.e., the apostle John.

53. It is to be noted that although Zwingli teaches a firm doctrine of assurance, the assurance is objectively based upon the grace and faithfulness of God inwardly attested by the Holy Spirit.

54. *intellectus omnis.*

55. The argument here used by Zwingli is a very acute one, that true good works are possible only where there is that radical change in disposition which takes place when a man has genuine faith. That is why faith must always precede works, and yet is always necessarily accompanied by them.

56. παραδόξως.

57. The reference is presumably to acts or payments which are alleged to reduce the period of purgatorial suffering.

58. Zwingli's dependence on Augustine is very marked. He appeals to him here as a witness against the merit of works.

59. The thought of the power and "busyness" of faith is one which is found frequently in Luther, but Zwingli here argues it on more philosophical lines.

60. The works of faith are done spontaneously, not in fulfilment of an external law. They are the works of that new law which is written upon the heart.

61. Zwingli perhaps finds it necessary to stress that the law is not cast off by the evangelical churches. He finds for it a true office in the guidance of Christians and the restraining or condemning of evil-doers.

62. Especially Aristotle.

63. ἐντελέχειαν. Both word and concept derive from Aristotle. An entelechy is real activity as opposed to potentiality.

64. This is the famous passage in which Zwingli claims the salvation of all the great and pious heathen. Luther attacked the idea as itself pagan (cf. his *Kurz Bekenntniss vom heiligen Sakrament* 1544), although he had hazarded a similar view in his sermon on Genesis 20 (W.A. XXIV, p. 364 f.).

65. Bullinger omitted the reference to Francis' ancestors.

66. The Valentinians were the disciples of the Egyptian Gnostic Valentinus. Cf. Irenaeus, *Adv. Haer. I,* 6, 3.

67. The Eunomians were Arians. Cf. Gregory of Naz. *Orat. XXVII,* 9.

68. This charge is probably based on more than idle rumour, for some of the wilder Anabaptist sects practised polygamy, as for example at Munster.

69. The Christian Civic Alliance had been inaugurated in 1527 by Zurich and Constance, and had been joined in 1528 by Berne and St. Gall, and in 1529 by Biel, Mühlhausen, Basel and Schaffhausen. It was on behalf of the Alliance that Zwingli was negotiating for a treaty with France.

70. Zwingli is here quoting a Latin proverb.

71. This is probably a reference to friends in Lyons and Paris who were well-disposed towards the reforming movement.

72. The kings of France bore the recognized title, Most Christian King, and it is on this that Zwingli bases his peroration.

73. It seems that Zwingli had hopes that if Francis could be won for the evangelical faith the whole of Europe might also be won. That is why he was ready to use every device of rhetoric and flattery in this concluding appeal. Future events were to reveal the extravagance of his expectations.

BULLINGER

OF THE HOLY CATHOLIC CHURCH

1. In this thought there seems to be some play upon the root "to call." The Church is the company of those who call upon God as well as of those who are called by him.

2. The reference is to the organized religions of heathendom, not to companies of believers outside Israel or Christendom.

3. Bullinger here accepts the traditional distinction, but he applies it in the Reformed way. The Church triumphant consists of all the elect now in heaven. The Church militant consists outwardly of all professing Christians, but inwardly of all the elect upon earth.

4. It is in relation to the Church militant that Bullinger develops the distinction between the external and the internal Church. In this respect he opposes the Romanist idea that there is one visible Church comprising both the good and the bad.

5. It is of interest that the words "the Communion of Saints" are regarded simply as an amplification or definition of the previous article. There is no real doctrine of the Communion of Saints as distinct from the holy catholic Church.

6. Cf. Bingham's *Antiquities*, I, 11, 1.

7. Cf. *Pacii Isagog. in Decretal.*, III, 29 *De paroeciis*.

8. Cf. Smith, *Dictionary of Antiquities*, p. 599.

9. This thought seems to be taken from Polydor. Verg., *De Rerum Inv.* IV, 9.

10. The distinction drawn here is between those who are hypocritical in the sense that they trust in their own righteousness and oppose the Gospel, like the Pharisees and Romanists, and those who are hypocritical in the sense that they adopt externally the forms and language of evangelical religion, but without an inward and personal faith.

11. The doctrine of election involves necessarily a doctrine of the final perseverance of the saints.

12. Bullinger is perhaps thinking of Zwingli, whose teaching on this matter he follows closely. Cf., too, the Helvetic Confession.

13. Here again Bullinger states the classical Reformed doctrine, that the two notes of the visible Church are the faithful preaching of the Word of God and the orderly administration of the two dominical sacraments.

14. The fact that the Word and sacraments have different effects in different persons does not mean that there is any change in the Word and sacraments themselves, i.e., the outward word of Scripture does not sometimes "become" the Word of God. The condition of effective reception is the operation of the Holy Spirit within the individual, not within the means of grace.

15. Hence the Reformed insistence that the sacrament must never be administered without the Word.

16. The meaning is that in certain circumstances it is possible to have true faith and yet not to be able to belong to an organized community of believers. It is only outside the invisible Church that there is no salvation. But in a true sense the visible Church is a "mother" of believers, and normally no true Christian will not be a member of it.

17. It is to be noted in this connection that Bullinger does not allow a right of private interpretation of Holy Scripture. The Church is bound by the Word of God rightly expounded. The mere possession of Scripture does not constitute a true Church.

18. Their firm grasp of the divine sovereignty enabled the Reformers to avoid what seemed to be the implication of Bullinger's argument, that since heretical churches have no purity of the Word and sacraments, they do not have the Word and sacraments at all. This deduction seems to have been drawn by Huss, but the sixteenth century reformers all accepted the traditional view that there is

a valid administration of the sacraments where the correct matter and form are preserved.

19. This was an argument which the Anglicans found most useful against the Puritans, who criticized many practices largely on the ground that they were used in the Romish church.

20. Bullinger maintains the vital interconnection of faith and love which underlies the whole Protestant understanding of the right and proper place of works.

21. In this as in other Reformed writings there is none of that unrestrained individualism which is supposed to characterize Protestant teaching. Even faith itself, which is the most personal thing, is regarded as a bond of fellowship.

22. The visible Church is highly esteemed, because it is through the visible Church that the revelation of God has been given to the world and is communicated to the individual believer.

23. Paul III died on Nov. 10, 1549. On Feb. 7, 1550, Jon Maria de Monte was elected to succeed him, and took the name of Julius III.

24. Tertull. *De Praescript. Haeret.*, 32. Bullinger's point is not actually made by Tertullian himself, and although it is no doubt a valid inference, it may be doubted whether Tertullian would ever have envisaged any such possibility.

25. *Ibid.* 36.

26. Bullinger is probably protesting against the use of diplomacy and military force which had produced the difficult situation following the Augsburg Interim. His criticisms are directed mainly against the Romanists, but he obviously repudiates also the policy of the Schmalkaldic League and even the later policies of Zwingli, against which he had openly protested at the time.

27. Bullinger refuses to draw the Anabaptist deduction that the use of force is always and necessarily wrong. He does not believe that force should deliberately be used to attain spiritual ends, but he does believe that God overrules the use of force as exercised by legitimate but not necessarily Christian rulers.

28. All foolish ideas of moral perfectionism are here set aside, probably in opposition to the Anabaptists.

29. A true understanding of justification and sanctification enables us to understand how a sinful Church can also be described as a holy and spotless Church. Without the doctrine of justification by faith the paradox is an absolute contradiction.

30. Gerson, *De Potest. eccles. Opp.* Tom. I, Col. 3, Par. 1606.

31. Petri de Alliaco, *Tract. de ecclesiae auctoritate Opp.* Tom. I, Col. 898, Par. 1606.

32. Augustine, *Tract. V in Joann.*

33. It is to be noted that with all the Reformers Bullinger accepts the divine institution and authority of the ministry.

34. It was on this ground that the Reformers would not accept as true sacraments the five observances of penance, etc.

35. This is a clear insistence upon the supremacy of Holy Scripture over the Church.

36. By this rule Bullinger excludes all practices, doctrines or regulations imposed by the Church simply on its own authority. He will not even grant to the Church the liberty (conceded by the Lutherans and Anglicans) to make laws in matters not covered by Scripture so long as nothing is done which is contrary to Scripture. He claims that the Church must never impose any rule which is either outside Scripture or in opposition to it. The only power of the Church is in matters of external order (e.g., the time of services) and the individual application of the laws of Scripture (e.g., in excommunication).

37. The lordship of Christ himself over the Church is here clearly safeguarded. To that lordship the power of the Church and its ministers is in all cases subject.

BIBLIOGRAPHY

ZWINGLI

A. Editions

Opera (Gwalter), Tiguri 1581 f. (4 vols).
Sämmtliche Schriften im Auszüge (Usteri & Vögelin), Zurich 1819–1820 (2 vols.).
Werke (M. Schuler & J. Schultess), Zurich 1828–1842 (8 vols.).
Zeitgemässige Auswahl aus Huldreich Zwinglis praktischen Schriften (R. Christoffel), 1843–1846.
Sämtliche Werke (Corpus Reformatorum), Berlin 1905 f.
Ulrich Zwingli: Eine Auswahl aus seinen Schriften. (G. Finsler, W. Köhler, A. Ruegg), Zurich 1918.
Zwingli-Hauptschriften (Volksausgabe), Zurich 1940 f.

B. Translations

Selected Works of Zwingli (S. M. Jackson), New York 1901.
The Latin Works of Zwingli (S. M. Jackson & others), New York 1912, and Philadelphia 1922 and 1929 (3 vols.).

C. Secondary Works

Allgemeine deutsche Biographie, Leipzig 1875 f.
Archiv für schweizerische Reformationsgeschichte, Freiburg-im-Br. 1869–1875 (3 vols.).
A. Baur: *Zwinglis Theologie: ihr Werden und ihr System*, Halle 1885 and 1889 (2 vols.).
J. Berchtold-Belart: *Das Zwingli-Bild und die schweizerischen Reformations-Chroniken*, 1929.
C. Bergmann: *Die Täuferbewegung im Kanton Zürich bis 1660*, 1916.
F. Blanke: *Zur Zwinglis Entwicklung* (Art. Kirchenblatt für die reformierte Schweiz), 1930. *Zwinglis Sakramentsanschauung* (Th. Bl. 10), 1931.
A. Bouvier: *Ulrich Zwingli d'après ses Oeuvres*, Revue de théol. et phil. 80, 1931.

P. Brockelmann: *Das Corpus Christianum bei Zwingli*, 1938.

H. Bullinger: *Reformationsgeschichte* (Ed. Hottinger & Vögelin), Frauenfeld 1838–1840 (3 vols.).

A. E. Burckhardt: *Das Geistproblem bei Zwingli*, 1932.

P. Burckhardt: *Huldreich Zwingli: eine Darstellung seiner Persönlichkeit und seines Lebenswerkes*, Zurich, 1918.

R. Christoffel: *Huldreich Zwingli: Leben und ausgewählte Schriften*, Elberfeld 1857. (Trans. J. Cochrane, Edinburgh 1858, but without the selected extracts.)

O. Clemen: *Zwingli und Calvin*, 1926.

D. Cunz: *Zwingli*, Aarau 1937.

Die Religion in Geschichte und Gegenwart, Art. Zwingli.

A. W. Dieckhoff: *Die evangelische Abendmahlslehre im Reformationszeitalter*, I, 1854.

E. Egli: *Actensammlung zur Geschichte der zürcher Reformation in den Jahren, 1519–1523*, Zurich 1879. *Analecta reformatoria* 1899 f. *Die Züricher Wiedertäufer zur Reformationszeit*, 1878. *Schweizerische Reformationsgeschichte*, 1910.

U. Ernst: *Geschichte des zürchen Schulwesens bis gegen das Ende des 16 Jahrhunderts*, 1879.

A. Farner: *Die Lehre von Kirche und Staat bei Zwingli*, 1930.

O. Farner: *Das Zwinglibild Luthers*, 1931. *Huldreich Zwingli*, Zurich 1917. *Huldrych Zwingli*, Zurich 1943 and 1946 (2 vols.). *Zwinglis Bedeutung für die Gegenwart*, Zurich 1919.

O. Farner and H. Hoffmann: *Die grosse Wende in Zürich*, Zurich 1941.

G. Finsler: *Zwinglibibliographie*, Zurich 1897.

B. Fleischlin: *Zwinglis Persönlichkeit, Bildungsgang und Werden*, Luzern 1903.

K. Guggisberg: *Das Zwinglibild des Protestantismus im Wandel der Zeiten*, 1934.

W. Hasties: *The Theology of the Reformed Church*, Edinburgh 1904.

Hastings Encyc. of Religion and Ethics, Art. Zwingli.

G. Heer: *Ulrich Zwingli als Pfarrer in Glarus*, 1884.

J. G. Hess: *Ulrich Zwingli*. (Trans. L. Aikin, London 1812.)

J. J. Hottinger: *Ulrich Zwingli*. (Trans. T. C. Porter, Hanisburg, 1856.)

H. Hug: *Ulrich Zwingli*, 1931.

F. Humbel: *Zwingli und seine Reformation im Spiegel der gleichzeitigen schweizerischen volkstümlichen Literatur*, Zurich 1912.

S. M. Jackson: *Huldreich Zwingli*, London 1901.

J. Kessler: *Sabbata*. (Ed. St. Gallen, 1902.)

B. J. Kidd: *Documents illustrative of the Continental Reformation*, Oxford 1911.

W. Köhler: *Das Buch der Reformation Huldrych Zwinglis*, Munich 1926. *Das Marburger Religionsgespräch, 1529.—Versuch einer Rekonstruktion*, Leipzig 1929.

Die Geisteswelt Ulrich Zwinglis, Gotha 1920.
Die neuere Zwingliforschung, Theol. Rund. N.F. IV, 1932.
Huldreich Zwingli, 1923.
Ulrich Zwingli und die Reformation in der Schweiz, Tübingen 1919.
Ulrich Zwingli: Zum Bedenken der Zürcher Reformation, 1519–1919.
Unsere religiösen Erzieher, II, Leipzig 1917.
Zwingli und Luther: Ihr Streit um das Abendmahl, Leipzig 1924.
J. Kreutzer: *Zwinglis Lehre von der Obrigkeit*, Stuttgart 1909.
C. von Kügelgen: *Die Ethik Zwinglis*, Leipzig 1902.
A. Lang: *Zwingli und Calvin*, Bielefeld and Leipzig 1913.
Lexicon für Theologie und Kirche, Art. Zwingli.
R. Ley: *Kirchenzucht bei Zwingli*, Zurich 1948.
G. W. Locher: *Die Theologie Huldrych Zwinglis im Lichte seiner Christologie*, I, Zurich 1952.
F. Loofs: *Dogmengeschichte*, IV, pp. 792 f.
A. Maurer: *Ulrich Zwingli*, 1931.
J. C. Mörikofer: *Ulrich Zwingli*, Leipzig 1867 and 1869 (2 vols.).
L. von Muralt: *Die Badener Disputation*, 1925.
Zwinglis geistesgeschichtliche Stellung, 1931.
O. Myconius: *Vita Huldrici Zwingli*. (Ed. *Vitae quatuor Reform.* Neander, Berlin 1841.)
E. Nagel: *Zwinglis Stellung zur Schrift*, Freiburg 1896.
L. I. Newman: *Jewish Aspects of the Zwingli Reformation*, New York 1925.
W. Oechsli: *Quellenbuch zur Schweizergeschichte*.
G. Oorthuys: *De Anthropologie van Zwingli*, 1905.
T. Pestalozzi: *Die Gegner Zwinglis am Grossmünsterstift in Zürich*, Zurich 1918.
Realencyklopädie für protestantische Theologie, Art. Zwingli.
A. Rich: *Die Anfänge der Theologie Huldrych Zwinglis*, Zurich 1949.
O. Rückert: *Ulrich Zwinglis Ideen zur Erziehung und Bildung im Zusammenhang mit seinen reformatorischen Tendenzen*, Gotha 1900.
J. M. Schuler: *Huldreich Zwingli*, Zurich 1819.
G. von Schultess-Rechberg: *Zwingli und Calvin in ihrer Ansichten über das Verhältnis von Staat und Kirche*, Aarau 1909.
A. Schweitzer: *Zwinglis Bedeutung neben Luther*, Zurich 1884.
E. Seeberg: *Der Gegensatz zwischen Zwingli, Schwenckfeld und Luther* (R. Seeberg Festschrift, 1929).
P. Sieber: *Bibliographie zur Zwinglis Gedenkfeier*, Zwingliana V.
S. Simpson: *Ulrich Zwingli*, London 1903.
B. V. Soós: *Zwingli und Calvin* Zwingliana, 1936, 2 pp. 306–326.
R. Stähelin: *Der Einfluss Zwinglis auf Schule und Unterricht* (in der Einladungsschrift z. Feier des 300 Jährigen Bestandes des Gymnasiums zu Basel, 1889, pp. 61–71).
Huldreich Zwingli, Basel 1895 and 1897 (2 vols.).
J. Strickler: *Aktensammlung zur schweizerischen Reformationsgeschichte in den Jahren*, 1521–1531, Zurich 1878–1884 (5 vols.).

J. Stumpf: *Chronica vom Leben und Wirken des Ulrich Zwingli*, Zurich 1932.
H. D. Türler: *Thomas Wyttenbach*, 1927.
J. M. Usteri: *Darstellung der Tauflehre Zwinglis*, 1882. *Zwingli und Erasmus*, 1885.
A. Waldburger: *Zwinglis Reise nach Marburg*, 1929.
P. Wernle: *Der evangelische Glaube nach den Hauptschriften der Reformatoren, II Zwingli*, Tübingen 1919.
Zeitschrift für Kirchengeschichte: Art. Zwingli and the Lord's Supper, 1927, 1.
Zwingliana, Beiträge für Geschichte Zwinglis, der Reformation und des Protestantismus in der Schweiz, 1897 f.

BULLINGER

A. Editions

The works of Bullinger have never been collected into one series, and are mostly available only in the early invidual editions. A comprehensive list may be found in the Parker Society edition of the *Decades*, Vol. III, Biographical Notice, pp. xv f.
Bullinger himself collected his principal writings into ten volumes (*Biblioth. Tigur*), but they have never been published in a complete form.
E. Egli prepared a modern edition of the important *Diarium* (Basel 1904).

B. Translations

Quite a number of Bullinger's treatises were translated into English in the sixteenth century, including the *Decades*.
The Parker Society republished the Elizabethan version of the *Decades* in their 4-volume edition of 1849–1852.

C. Secondary Works

F. Blanke: *Der junge Bullinger*, Zurich 1942.
A. Bouvier: *H. Bullinger, Réformateur et Conseiller oecumenique, le Successeur de Zwingli, d'après sa correspondance avec les Réformés et les Humanistes de Langue française*, Neuchatel 1940.
R. Christoffel: *H. Bullinger und seine Gattin*, 1875.
Die Religion in Geschichte und Gegenwart, Art. Bullinger.
E. Egli: *Heinrich Bullinger*, Zwingliana 1904, 2 p. 419.
Bullingers Beziehungen zu Zwingli, Ibid., p. 439.
N. Gooszen: *J. H. Bullinger*, Rotterdam, 1909.
S. Hess: *Lebensgeschichte Meister H. Bullinger*, Zurich 1823 and 1829 (2 vols.).

L. Lavater: *Vom läben und tod dess Eerwirdigen Herrn Heinrychen Bullingers, dieners des Kyrchen zuo Zürich*, Zurich 1576.

Lexicon für Theologie und Kirche, Art. Bullinger.

N. Paulus: *Hexenwahn und Hexenprozess im 16 Jahrhundert*, 1910.

K. Pestalozzi: *Leben und ausgewählte Schriften der Väter der reformierten Kirche*, V, 1858.

Realencyklopädie für protestantische Theologie, Art. Bullinger.

A. Ruegg: *Die Beziehungen Calvins zu Bullinger*, Zurich, 1909.

T. Schiess: *Der Briefwechsel H. Bullingers*, Zwingliana, 1933, 1 p. 369.

G. von Schultess-Rechberg: *H. Bullinger*, Halle 1904.

J. Simlerus: *Narratio de ortu, vita et obitu reverendi viri D. Henrici Bullingeri . . . Tiguri excudebat* Froschouerus, 1575.

J. Sutz: *H. Bullinger, der Retter der zürcherischen Reformation*, Zurich 1915.

J. M. Usteri: *Vertiefung der Zwinglischen Sakraments- und Tauflehre bei Bullinger*, Theol. Studien u. Krit. Gotha 1882–1883.

A. van t'Hooft: *De theologie van Heinrich Bullinger in Betreuking tot de Nederlandsche Reformatie*, 1880.

G. R. Zimmermann: *Die Zürcher Kirche und ihre Antistes*, 1877. *Heinrich Bullinger* (in *Grosse Schweizer*, Zurich, 1938, pp. 106–114).

INDEXES

GENERAL INDEX

(a) *Names*

Acacius, 330
Adlischweiler, 42
Adrian VI, 15
Alliaco, De, 317, 351
Ambrose, 41, 231–233, 345
Anabaptists, 28, 119 f., 241–242, 273 f.,
    334, 336–339, 346
Anastasius, 87, 330
Anselm, 332
Anthropomorphites, 60, 327
Arians, 87, 303, 349
Aristides, 242, 275
Aristotle, 242, 348
Athanasius, 61, 251, 330
Augustine, 41, 60–61, 124, 135, 154,
    197–198, 207–209, 212, 231, 233–
    234, 237, 255, 271, 320, 327, 335,
    338, 343, 344, 345, 347, 348, 351
Augustinians, 50

Baden-in-Aargau, 96, 102, 331
Basel, 13–14, 21, 42, 44, 97, 349
Beatus Rhenanus, 18n.
Benedictines, 83, 329
Berengarius, 193–197, 209, 342–343
Berne, 14, 23, 42–44, 120, 176n., 239
Billican, 344–345
Bremgarten, 40–42
Brentius, 43
Bucer, 177
Bugenhagen, 176n., 343–345
Bullinger, 40 f., 241, 283 f., 336, 349
Bünzli, 13

Calvin, 31, 37, 43–46, 184, 285, 334,
    341, 347
Camillus, 116, 275
Capito, 14, 177
Cappel, 22–3, 40–42, 44, 239, 240, 331
Carlstadt, 238, 342, 346

Carpocrates, 338
Carthusians, 83, 329
Ceporinus, 97, 100–101
Chloelia, 116, 333
Christoffel, 58, 128, 184
Chrysostom, 41
Cicero, 333
Civic Alliance, 21, 239–240, 277, 349,
Collin, 240
Cologne, 41
Cominius, 333
Compostella, 84, 329
Confederacy, 15, 18, 21, 31, 334
Copts, 338
Cyprian, 123

Deucaleon, 69, 328
Dominicans, 14, 49–50, 83, 329

Eck, 21
Edward VI, 101, 283
Einsiedeln, 17, 27, 97, 339
Emmerich-on-Rhine, 41
Erasmus, 16, 19, 177, 341, 344, 345
Eunomians, 276, 349
Eusebius, 327

Farel, 43
France, 23, 239, 240
Francis I, 24, 240, 349
Franciscans, 83, 329
Froschauer, 58, 184

Galenus, 111, 333
Geneva, 31, 44–45
Gerson, 317, 351
Glareanus, 19, 102, 331
Glarus, 14 f., 21, 97, 334
Gratian, 41, 196–197, 330, 343

359

Grebel, 120–121, 336
Gregory Nazianzus, 276, 349
Grüt, Am, 176–177, 342–345
Gwalter, 58, 128, 184, 327, 329, 331, 336

Hager, 128, 184
Hätzer, 345
Hercules, 242, 275
Hilary, 74, 89, 328, 330
Hippocrates, 333
Hoen, 179n., 345
Horace, 331
Hubmaier, 119–121
Hutten, 19

Indian Christians, 156, 338
Irenaeus, 276, 338, 347, 349

Jerome, 136, 231, 335, 345
Josephus, 76, 328, 346
Jud, 14, 18, 28, 42, 51, 122n., 160, 339

Köpfel, 184

Lambert, 25, 50
Lanfranc, 342
Leo X, 18
Liberius, 87, 330
Limmat, 152, 338
Lombard, 14, 41
Luther, 13, 18, 22, 28–29, 34, 37, 41, 126, 177, 238, 240, 242, 330, 334, 336, 337, 339, 340, 342, 345, 348, 349
Lutherans, 19, 177, 183, 239, 341, 342, 344, 347

Maigret, 240
Manz, 120
Marburg, 22, 239, 342
Marcion, 219, 344
Marseilles, 113, 333
Melanchthon, 41
Melitus, 60, 327
Meyer, Gerold, 19, 96, 102, 117, 331
Meyer, Hans, 19, 331
Milo, 111, 333
Myconius, 18, 157, 339

Nähenfels, 131, 334
Nicholas II, 124, 193, 336, 343
Nuremberg, 176, 341

Oecolampadius, 19, 21, 43, 177, 180, 231, 234, 258, 345

Oetenbach, 26, 42, 49 f.
Origen, 41, 227, 327, 345
Ovid, 328, 333

Pellican, 14
Pericles, 104, 331
Philip of Hesse, 22, 23
Pliny, 332
Pythagoras, 110, 332

Rabanus, 195, 343
Ratramnus, 343
Reinhard (Meyer), Anna, 19, 96n., 331
Ryss, 345, 346

St. Gall, 21, 120 f.
Sallust, 333
Samson, 18, 41
Schaffhausen, 21, 120, 349
Schwenckfeld, 345, 346
Scotus, 26, 50
Seneca, 106, 114, 331, 333
Socrates, 115, 275
Solon, 347
Speier, 22, 239

Tertullian, 311 f., 344, 351
Theseus, 242, 275
Thomas Aquinas, 26, 50
Timotheus 170, 340
Toggenburg, 13, 21, 331, 333
Tschudi, 18

Ulysses, 109, 332
Urban Rhegius, 344, 345
Uri, 176, 341

Vadian, 120–121, 177
Valentinians, 276, 349
Venice, 23, 239
Virgil, 333, 346

Waldshut, 119, 120
Weesen, 13
Westphalus, 43
Whitgift, 283–284
Widerkehr, 40
Wildhaus, 13, 15, 331
Wölflin, 14
Wyttenbach, 14

Zili, 121
Zurich, 17, 18 f., 40, 41 f., 43 f., 49–50 96 f., 119 f., 239 f.
Zwingli, Bartholomew, 13
Zwingli, Huldreich, 13 f., 24 f., 40, 42, 44–46, 49 f., 96 f., 119 f., 239 f.

(b) *Subjects*

Apostolic Succession, 285, 309 f.
Ascension, 178 f., 186, 206, 212 f., 232, 234, 257
Atonement, 39, 106, 250 f.
Authority, 317 f., 323

Baptism, 119 f., 132 f., 248
Baptism, Institution of, 123, 160 f.
Baptism, of Christ, 167
Baptism, of Fire, 156
Baptism, of Infants, 124–126, 149
Baptismal Ceremonies, 153
Baptismal Office, 26, 122

Cards, 99, 116
Christology, 36–39, 183, 212 f., 251 f.
Church, 35, 126, 158, 243, 265–266, 283 f., 288 f.
Church Calendar, 27
Circumcision, 131, 138
Civil Government, 241, 266–267
Classics, 28, 42, 97–98, 108–109
Clerical Marriage, 25–26
Communion of Saints, 292
Consubstantiation, 178, 188, 191 f.
Covenant, 122, 127
Creation, 59, 104

Debt, 92
Descent into Hell, 252
Dicing, 99, 116
Diet, 99, 111
Dress, 112

Ecclesiastical Government, 319 f.
Education, 28, 96 f.
Eternal Life, 273 f.
Eucharist, 36–37, 132, 176 f., 185 f., 254 f.
Evil, 33
Excommunication, 92, 152, 319

Faith, 34, 134 f., 138, 263, 269 f.
Fall, 32, 33, 52, 105
Forgiveness, 268–269

Glossalalia, 137–138
God, 31 f., 37 f., 104–107, 243, 246 f., 249 f., 274–275
Good Works, 34–35, 107, 269 f.
Gospel, 84 f., 98, 105 f., 164 f.

Heretical Baptism, 303
Holy Spirit, 34, 36, 55 f., 78 f., 82–83, 104, 127, 133, 136 f., 149, 183, 272
Hypocrisy, 286, 295 f.

Images, 26–27
Imago Dei, 51–52, 59 f.
Incarnation, 36, 39, 183, 212 f., 249 f.
Indulgences, 18
Inspiration, 57

Justification, 34, 243

Legalism, 35
Lent, 25
Lord's Supper, 36–37, 39, 176 f., 185 f., 241, 248, 254 f.

Marriage, 100, 112
Mass, 26–27
Mathematics, 98, 112
Mercenary Service, 15 f., 24, 239, 333
Ministry, 321

Notes of the Church, 286, 299 f., 304 f.

Original Sin, 52, 105, 126, 331

Papal Canons, 193 f., 207 f., 222, 232, 237
Parables, 72–73, 200, 328
Passover, 131, 138, 179, 225–227, 233, 234, 262
Perfectionism, 139 f., 314 f.
Preaching, 16–17, 24, 110–111
Predestination, 33 f., 242
Prophesyings, 27
Providence, 33, 104
Purgatory, 243, 253–254, 270

Real Presence, 22, 36–37, 177 f., 185 f. 254 f.
Reason, 32, 38, 242
Rebaptism, 123 f., 157–159
Recreations, 99, 115–116
Resurrection, 39, 202–203, 215, 234, 253, 255
Resurrection Body, 215, 217 f., 232
Return of Christ, 216–217
Rewards, 270–272

Sacraments, 131, 188, 247–248, 260, 262 f., 303
Sacramental Efficacy, 39, 153–154, 183–184, 260 f., 262 f.
Session, 178 f., 186 f., 212, 216, 254, 256
Sectarianism, 158

Signs, 138–139
Silence, 109–110
Scripture, 16–17, 24–25, 28–30, 31 f., 38, 41, 51 f., 59 f., 98, 104, 223, 243, 303 f.

Transubstantiation, 178 f., 186 f.
Trinity, 59 f., 243, 249

Tropes, 190, 223-224
Two Natures of Christ, 212 f., 255 f.

Virgin Birth, 106, 218–219, 256

War, 100, 113, 276, 313–314
Word of God, 36, 53 f., 68 f., 72 f., 189 f., 303, 307 f.

BIBLICAL REFERENCES

(a) OLD TESTAMENT AND APOCRYPHA

Genesis
1:3.............68, 189
1:24................64
1:26–27............59
2:7.............63–64
2:17................69
3:4–5..............194
3:16................68
3:17 f..............69
6:3................69
6:13 f..............76
7:4................69
15:6...............138
17:10.........138, 230
18:10..............69
19:13..............69
21:1...............69
21:12–13...........76
22:2...............76
28:12 f.............77
41:26.............224
47:7, 10..........236

Exodus
12:11.............225
12:24.............138
14:11–14...........77
24:8..............230

Deuteronomy
14:16–18...........60

I Kings
18:1 f.............78
19:10.............78
22:15 f............77

II Chronicles
36:15 f............74

Psalms
4:6................62
33:6...............64

Psalms—continued
36:9................78
49:3–4.............73
51:10–12..........298
77:2–3.............93
82:6...............62
85:8...............88
89:34............215
110:1........216, 218
116:11.......87, 317
119:130............75
132:13–14.........293
139:7..............72
144:1.............113
145:2.............236

Proverbs
18:3...............63

Ecclesiastes
1:6–7.............62

Song of Songs
3:4................84

Isaiah
6:9–10.........73, 164
19:25..............62
28:20..............67
29:13............308
40:3.............162
40:6.............209
42:2...............81
42:3.............131
49:23.............314
54:13..............79
55:1.............155
59:21.........300–301

Jeremiah
8:9...............317
26:1 f.............78
29:7.............267
31:33–34......81, 230

Ezekiel
12:21 f.............71
12:28..............72

Zechariah
11:15–17..........310
14:8.............155

Malachi
3:1..............161

Ecclesiasticus
39:3...............73

Wisdom
2:21–22...........74

(b) NEW TESTAMENT

Matthew
3:1.............146
3:1–2...........164
3:1–17..........123
3:5–6...........146
3:11...136, 146, 156, 163
3:17............269
4:4................68
5:8.............106
6:6................87
6:12............315
7:8................80
8:3..........70, 189
8:8........228, 261
8:13...............70
9:2 f..............71
9:9............70–71
10:18............104
10:29–30..........94
11:11............340
11:25.............80
11:28........84, 185
12:20............131
12:33............295
12:46 f............85

Matthew—*continued*

12:47–50	200
13:3 f.	73
13:8 f.	224
13:12	73–74
13:14–15	93, 164
13:24 f.	245, 296
13:25	206
13:47–48	297
14:29 f.	71
15:17	195
16:6 f.	200
16:17	308
16:18	192, 294
16:19	318
17:18	71
17:20	80
18:3	75
18:15–17	293
18:15–18	91, 318
18:20	212
21:22	90, 272
21:23 f.	83
21:24–25	134
21:44	223
22:21	267
22:37	67–68
24:26	221
24:27	217
24:50–51	294
25:31–32	216
26:8	147
26:11	214
26:26 f.	178 f., 187 f. 227–228, 248, 261, 264
26:29	227
26:64	216
27:46	213, 252
28:5–6	221
28:19	168, 171
28:19–20	123, 141 f., 160–161, 248, 300, 318–322
28:20	183, 212–214, 257, 294

Mark

1:4	147–148
1:5	156, 161
1:14 f.	164
6:12	165
7:34	70
9:23	108
9:41	271
10:16	153
11:23	90
12:30	68
14:22 f.	228 f.
16:16	124, 143, 165

Mark—*continued*

16:17	144
16:19	212–214

Luke

1:32	70
1:52	94
2:7	256
2:9 f.	75
2:29 f.	72
3:5	94
3:7–8	148
3:16	136, 149
3:17	297
5:8	227, 261
8:11	224
9:1	320
10:8	318
10:42	84
11:27–28	85
12:24, 27	104
13:12	71
16:16	162, 166
16:17	189
17:5	146
17:10	271
17:37	217
18:42	70
22:14 f.	228 f.
22:15	225
22:19	225, 317
22:32	298
23:34	252
24:39	232
24:47	164
24:51	232

John

1:9	78
1:14	237
1:18	60, 213
1:25	171
1:25–26	149
1:26	133
1:29	142, 165, 223
1:29–30	162
1:34	116
3:5	130, 154–155, 160, 322
3:6	154
3:13	212
3:16	252, 263, 328
3:22	134, 164
3:23	133
3:25 f.	165
3:26	134
3:27	54, 79
3:31	80
3:35–36	165–166
4:1	135

John—*continued*

4:2	134, 135
4:14	155
4:25	79
4:50	70
5:24	151, 274
5:37	60
5:42	89
6:26–69	200–207
6:27	155
6:29–30	139
6:35	81, 155
6:36	135
6:44	54, 79, 86, 137
6:45	79, 81, 89, 137
6:47	134, 155, 268, 274
6:51	223
6:53	155, 208
6:56	201
6:63	190, 205 f., 209 f.
6:64	80, 135
6:65–69	80
6:68	85, 298
6:70	135
7:37	82, 154
7:37–38	305
7:38	154
8:12	315
8:39	248
8:46	140
8:47	301, 308
10:4–5	308
10:27–28	301
10:30	212
12:26	221
12:32	155
13:34–35	306
14:3	106, 221, 275
14:6	155
14:12	272
14:16	294
14:20	305
14:23	306
14:23–24	301
15:5	190, 223
15:6	305
16:28	214, 257
17:3	275
17:11	257
17:24	222, 275
18:11	313
18:37	301, 308
20:23	318
21:11	71
21:16	318

Acts

1:5	133, 137, 149
1:9–11	217

Acts—*continued*
1:11...................217
2:31...................253
2:38...............169, 300
2:42...................300
7:22....................77
7:56...................212
8:13...................135
9:4-5...................82
9:15................71, 94
10:43..................165
10:44..................136
10:48..................144
11:18..................164
12:23..................247
15:28..................323
17:29...................62
18:6...................135
18:25..................172
19:1-6..123, 134, 169 f.,
   175
19:4...................166
19:5...................144
20:29-30...............311
26:24..................347
27:22...................71

Romans
1:1-2..................322
1:28....................63
4:20-21.................76
6:3 f...123, 150-152, 235
6:9...............195, 233
6:11....................67
7:18 f..................66
7:23....................61
8:9....................305
8:14...................305
8:32...............72, 250
9:6-7..................299
10:9..............142-143
10:17..................104
11:3....................78
12:4-5.................307
12:15..................114
14:13..................159
14:17..................152
14:23..................270

I Corinthians
1:11..............134-135
1:13...................167
1:23...................145
1:27....................89
1:30...................107
2:3-5..................313
2:4-5..................308
2:12....................54
2:12-13.............81-82

I Corinthians—*continued*
2:14....................63
2:14-15.................91
4:1.....................90
4:3-4...................92
4:15...................307
5:8....................227
5:11-13................297
10:1-4.................211
10:12...................94
10:16..153, 180, 236 f.,
   342
10:17..................162
11:1...................311
11:19...................93
11:23 f.............228 f.
11:25..............179-180
11:26..................217
11:28..............217, 261
12:12 f................307
12:13..................301
13:12...................61
14:23..................137
14:26 f.................93
14:29..................323
15:16..................255
15:20..................165
15:25..............216-218

II Corinthians
2:16....................75
4:16....................66
10:8...................321
12:10...................66

Galatians
1:15-16................308
2:20...................305
3:7....................212
3:28...................290
4:26..............307, 348
61:5...................156

Ephesians
3:17...................305
4:5-6..................167
4:11-16............308-309
4:22....................65
4:25...................116
5:25-26................300

Colossians
1:18...................237
2:10-12................124
2:12-13................235
3:9 f...................65

I Thessalonians
2:3-6..................313
5:21..............185, 323

I Timothy
1:20....................72
2:2...............268, 348
3:1 f..................321
3:14-15...........315-316

II Timothy
3:16....................93

Hebrews
8:1 f...................81
8:10....................81
9:9-10.................130
9:10...................171
9:14-15.................67
10:1 f..................81
10:16...................81
10:18-24...............291
11:1...................246

James
1:5-6...................90
1:8....................116
1:17...................162

I Peter
1:23...................307
2:9...............88, 230
2:20...................136
3:19-20................252
3:20-21...........153, 154
3:21...................134

II Peter
1:21....................92
2:15....................79

I John
1:8...............67, 139
1:9....................86
2:14..............297, 298
2:27...............82, 88
3:2.....................61
3:9....................107
4:1....................323
4:4....................152
4:13...................305
4:15...................305
4:16...................306
5:1....................306

Jude
:16....................63

Revelation
1:17-18................320
3:7....................320
7:9-10.................290
13:13-17...............290
21:2..............265, 348